PERSONALITY STRUCTURE AND HUMAN INTERACTION

PERSONALITY STRUCTURE AND HUMAN INTERACTION

The Developing Synthesis of Psycho-dynamic Theory

By

Harry Guntrip, Ph.D.

Fellow of the British Psychological Society
Psychotherapist, Leeds University
Department of Psychiatry

INTERNATIONAL UNIVERSITIES PRESS INC.
NEW YORK   NEW YORK

Library of Congress Catalog Card No. 61-12135
Second Printing 1964

ACKNOWLEDGEMENTS

I have to thank Dr. Fairbairn for reading through the parts of this book that concern his views, to check their accuracy; Dr. R. E. D. Markillie (Leeds Department of Psychiatry, Member of the British Psycho-Analytical Society) with whom I have had the opportunity to discuss the whole MS; Dr. J. D. Sutherland (Medical Director, Tavistock Clinic) for his criticism of chapter VII and his kindness in writing a Foreword; and above all Dr. M. Brierley for detailed and valuable criticisms and suggestions.

This book contains a certain amount of material that formed the first half of a thesis for the degree of Ph.D., presented to London University in 1953. The title of the thesis was 'The Implications of Recent Trends in Psycho-Analysis for Sociology'. By a happy coincidence one of the examiners appointed to judge the thesis was my early teacher, the late Professor J. C. Flügel, with whom subsequently I had the advantage of some discussion of its contents. The substance of chapters I, II, V, VIII and IX are taken from the thesis, with some expansion. Chapters III, IV, VI and VII are new, while the sections in the thesis on the views of Melanie Klein and Fairbairn have been entirely re-written. Chapters XVII and XVIII are also new. I have to thank London University for permission to reproduce the material indicated.

A book of this type, surveying in a detailed and historical way the developments of psychodynamic thought over a period of eighty years, must either make a large use of quotations or else risk subtle distortion by presenting the views of other minds in the present writer's own words. I have preferred the former course for the sake of scientific accuracy.

I am, therefore, all the more indebted to a long list of authors, Journal editors and publishers. Their permission to use their works thus has made it possible for me to employ this more accurate method. A full list of every book and article mentioned in the text will be found in the Bibliography, with full information as to author, Journal and publisher, both British and American. I take this opportunity of saying that in the case of all the books from which I have taken quotations, I have been able to do so because of the generous permission granted by the publishers named in this Bibliography. Quotation references in the text are given by author's name and date of book as listed in the Bibliography.

Finally my gratitude and thanks are due to my wife, not only for the typing of the whole MS, but also for her encouragement and her acceptance of much curtailment of our leisure together, without which the book could not have been written.

CONTENTS

FOREWORD

by

J. D. Sutherland

THIS is an important book because it grapples in a profound
and rigorous way with many of the basic theoretical questions
which confront psycho-analysts and all other students of personality and of human interaction. Many critical surveys have been
written of the growth of certain aspects of psycho-analytical theory,
but only a few comprehensive appraisals have been made of the
basic concepts of psycho-analytic thought as a whole. This lack
has been made more conspicuous by the fact that the fundamental
contributions of Mrs. Klein and other British psycho-analysts
have tended to be ignored by most psycho-analysts in the United
States. Marjorie Brierley's *Trends in Psycho-Analysis* (No. 39 in
this Series) in 1951 was a brilliant start in bridging this gap and
the present volume is a worthy successor.

Dr. Guntrip's qualifications for his task are exceptional. After
a training in philosophical, religious, literary and social studies he
became a full-time psychotherapist; and although not trained
formally as a psycho-analyst he had a long personal analysis with
Dr. W. R. D. Fairbairn. Ernest Jones in his Preface to Fairbairn's
book, *Psycho-analytic Studies of the Personality,* wrote that Fairbairn's geographical isolation as a psycho-analyst was conducive
to the indisputable originality of his ideas, ideas which would
'surely prove extremely stimulating to thought'. Jones was not
given to making such prophecies readily and on this occasion he
was certainly right. It does not require more than a look at the
chapter headings to see that Dr. Guntrip has been greatly influenced by Fairbairn's contributions to personality theory; and as
the author points out, Fairbairn's writings had made a great impression on him before his analysis.

Dr. Guntrip shares with Fairbairn a deep concern for the proper
status of psycho-analysis in relation to the natural sciences. There

are many signs to-day—e.g. the growth of interest in Existentialism amongst psychiatrists—of dissatisfaction with some of the basic
tenets in personality theory, especially those which Dr. Guntrip
summarizes as the loss of man as a person when science treats him
as an object of investigation. And this is his explicit theme, the
struggle to get psycho-analytic and personality theory towards a
position which does justice to the reality of the individual as a
person. As he stresses, this was a conflict which Freud experienced
with great intensity and which he was only partially successful in
overcoming, the unresolved residue being manifest in his theory of
instinct. In recent years many psycho-analysts have expressed their
dissatisfaction with the theory of the instincts as left by Freud. In
following Fairbairn's important concepts on the relation of structure and energy in psycho-analytic theory, Dr. Guntrip may seem
to go too far in his low estimate of the value of instinct-theory for
psychology. The work of the ethologists has not yet been assimilated by psycho-analysts, though its possible contribution to our
understanding of the development of the person is beginning, e.g.
in Bowlby's recent papers (*International Journal of Psycho-
Analysis*). This work, in fact, supports some of Dr. Guntrip's con-
tentions, e.g. that, despite innate *potential* response patterns, the
eventual behavioural repertoire is constituted or structured by the
individual's experience. Nevertheless, there is little doubt that the
degree of flexibility in innate human potentials introduces qualitatively different features, above all those described by the terms
'internal objects' and 'inner worlds'. Dr. Guntrip has much to say
of great interest on these concepts.

The value of precise theoretical formulation cannot be ques-
tioned. It is only as theory progresses that more pertinent questions
can be asked and problems approached in ways that permit new
developments. If I may follow my illustrious editorial predecessor
in the International Library, I predict that Dr. Guntrip's work to
this end will prove extremely stimulating. No serious student of
psycho-analysis will fail to get new ideas from the thoroughgoing
way in which he considers current concepts. The views he puts
forward on the nature of endopsychic structure, almost entirely
those of Fairbairn, have obvious theoretical interest and their
application to social relations can be readily appreciated. How far
they will affect clinical practice is difficult to assess. He ventures to
suggest that they will eventually influence therapeutic technique.
In this connection he quotes Winnicott and Balint, who have both
suggested modifications in technique as a result of theoretical considerations which have elements in common with those of Fairbairn. It is, however, in their conclusions regarding technique that

all of these psycho-analysts have met with least acceptance. In reaffirming Fairbairn's views, Guntrip stresses the role of the analyst as a good reliable person for the patient and the need for the latter to release his bad objects and his libidinal attachment to them. Here many analysts will feel they are dealing with statements which are as yet in too general a form to be useful. There is perhaps too much of an implication that the analyst's interpretations are given as something not central to his relationship with the patient. The manner of using the transference which the work of Mrs. Klein and her school has stimulated is certainly rooted in the understanding by the analyst of what is happening all the time in the relationship between the patient and himself. The analyst's interpretations are therefore his responses to what he thinks and feels the patient is wanting from him, consciously and unconsciously. In other words, it would be the view of many analysts, especially in Britain, that the most effective way to be a good reliable person for the patient and to release him from his ties to bad internal objects is by more accurate and more comprehensive interpretations; to play other roles—e.g. nearer that of the parent who does not withhold positive interest—may readily interfere with the exposure within the analytic relationship of some of the most dreaded primitive relationships.

New theoretical clarifications, however, do not always necessitate changes in the basic principles of technique. Such changes should follow only from long and patient work recorded as objectively as possible. Immediate practical effects may well be achieved by the views which Dr. Guntrip advances in this book without alteration of present technique. Most analysts will gain fresh insights into their patients' difficulties from the challenging consideration he gives to the nature of endopsychic activity and of human conflict. Their perceptions of the unconscious forces in the analytic relationship may be changed radically and they may thus be helped to interpret more accurately to their patients the nature of the forces at work within them.

AUTHOR'S PREFACE

THIS book is not intended to be a history of psycho-analytical theory. In any complete form that would be a far larger undertaking. Many important aspects of theory here omitted would have called for inclusion, particularly in the case of Freud and Melanie Klein. I have attempted something different, something that I believe needs to be done at about this time, something that arises as a problem out of the very nature of science as hitherto understood, as soon as it comes to be applied to human beings.

This involves making a historical survey, and I have sought to let the important writers speak for themselves. The justification for fairly frequent quotations and some lengthy ones must be found in this deliberate purpose.

But such a survey would be mere mechanical hackwork, more or less complete recording, unless the writer felt he could trace the emergence of deeper understanding along certain definite lines.

The close study of psycho-analysis over many years, against the background of philosophical, religious, literary and social studies, has bred in me the conviction that here at last, and here alone, scientific enquiry has come face to face with the intimate and fully 'personal' life of man. This constitutes as big a test for science as for man. Science has to discover whether and how it can deal with the 'person', the 'unique individual', we will dare to say the 'spiritual self' with all the motives, values, hopes, fears and purposes that constitute the real life of man, and make a purely 'organic' approach to man inadequate. On the other hand, man has to face the most penetrating searchlight focussed upon his essential nature, and must find out how to adjust to the stripping off of his psychic defences and self-deceptions, built up to hide failures in development towards maturity, while the struggle to cope with living in spite of immaturity is carried on.

This double challenge to both science and man, beginning some seventy-odd years ago, has begun to spread widely only in this present century. Its future effects are out of sight. But it is fraught with the most momentous issues for the final fate of mankind. If nuclear physics threatens us with the possibility of universal destruction, then genuine psychodynamic understanding, if only it be given time to work quietly, gives at least a realistic hope of new life. No one supposes that the mass problem of mental ill-health can be dealt with by individual psychotherapy, but we may hope that in time a profounder understanding of man, leavening all aspects of the life of the community and most of all those concerned with the treatment of children, may substitute prevention for cure.

Science is the emotionally detached study of the properties of 'Objects' which are held to be accounted for when they can be classified according to their species and genus. This remains true even at the most advanced positions of physics where 'objects' are resolved into 'events'. Either way, science seeks to establish what phenomena have in common so that the isolated individual object or event can be grouped with its fellows and 'understood' according to what science means by understanding. This scientific approach is as easily applicable to the human body as to any other body, and the medical sciences, beginning with anatomy, physiology and biochemistry, find no difficulty in adopting it. When science turned to the study of the 'mental life', as it was traditionally called, the same approach was automatically made. This seemed easy in the case of animal psychology, mainly because of unquestioned emotional assumptions. 'Animals have no souls'; 'Animals are different in kind from humans': traditional prejudices which are still very much alive. 'Animals don't feel as we do' and so their primitive kind of 'mental life' may be expected to yield to mechanistic scientific explanation. Physiological psychology grew up on the basis of neurological reflexes, simple and conditioned. Pavlov and J. B. Watson made the 'scientific approach'.

Psychology has moved far since those days. It is no longer so easy to regard the 'animal mind' in the above naïve way, still less the human. Nevertheless, in more subtle ways, the struggle to equate 'scientific explanation' with the 'elimination of individuality' goes on, aiming to produce theories which are still in principle materialistic and mechanistic, even though the earlier crude materialism and mechanism are outmoded. This has been the standard round which the modern battle rages for the capture and possession of the truth about man himself: for when science begins to treat man as an object of investigation, it somehow loses him as a person.

Nowhere is this more evident than in the fields of academic psychology, psychiatry and some aspects of earlier psycho-analytic theory. The traditional scientific approach tends always towards an impersonal type of theory, and this is not often honestly admitted to be an expression of a certain philosophical view of man, that the mind is the brain. A great deal of the drive in psychiatry for the discovery of physical treatments, and also the drive to work out a theory of therapy on the basis of 'reconditioning', is motivated as much by this underlying 'philosophy of man' as by the practical need to find methods of quick relief of symptoms. Such treatments also have the advantage of being less disturbing to the psychiatrist as an individual person than the attempt to treat the patient on a personal level, entering deeply and in a fully personal way into the heart of his disturbed personality.

Academic psychology has developed, in its modern methods of personality testing for diagnostic purposes, a skilfully impersonal way of dealing with personality, by means of which, once more, human beings can be classified and categorized without anyone ever coming into intimate personal human rapport with the patient as a meaningful individual in his own right. In the field of psycho-analysis, the conception of 'metapsychology' and the classic analytic technique in so far as it tended to impersonality belong to the same orientation. Meanwhile, theoretical trends and disguised philosophical prepossessions cannot alter *facts*, and reality forces itself on us. Thus it is noticeable that the central problem, how to understand and deal with human beings as 'individuals' and as 'persons', has been steadily pushing to the front. In psycho-analytical theory and practice this has, it seems to me, become increasingly obvious. The terrific, if not altogether successful, struggle of Freud to transcend physiology and neurology and arrive at a true psychology, the widespread criticism of his psycho-biology by thinkers influenced by sociology, the criticism of 'instinct-theory' in both academic psychology and psycho-analysis, the development of psycho-analysis towards the analysis of personality in more and more radically 'personal' terms, all add up to a challenging phenomenon in itself, a sign of the times.

I have taken this as my theme, to trace the way in which psycho-analysis has been in process of outgrowing its origins in a neurophysiological and psychobiological philosophy of man, using the instinct concept as the basis of theory, into a truly psychodynamic theory of the personality implying a philosophy of man that takes account of his reality as an individual person. At the same time this development forces us to question the traditional exclusion by science of the fact of individuality, the one fact that is ultimately inescapable in any realistic attempt to study and understand human beings. A human being can only be known as a living and highly individual, unique 'person'. Aspects of his total being can be reduced by analysis and abstraction to the level of classified phenomena, and that has its uses; but always what he really is, is then missed. Psycho-analysis is, or should be, the special custodian of this truth in the field of science. On its theoretical side, psycho-analysis is the attempt to find out in what terms science can deal with the person in his life as an individual with other persons, for that is the problem that has now become inescapable.

Thus I am consciously concerned to present a definite point of view. This leads me to observe that in psychology more than in any other study a writer's judgment is related to his own personal approach to the subject. This in turn arises out of the structure of his own personality and his experience of life. This fact is familiar to us in religious, philosophical and political thinking, where the objective and the subjective most plainly interact. In science it has always been the tradition that thinking is purely objective. This is now realized to be less true than used to be taken for granted, but it is least of all true in psychology. Often, in reading psycho-analytic and psychiatric literature, and trying to form a judgment on its conclusions about human beings, I have wished I knew what sort of person the writer was. Dr. Clara Thompson, in her Preface to *Psychoanalysis; Evolution and Development*, gives an all-too-brief statement of her personal approach and the influences that shaped it. It may not be out of place for me also to say how I came to the study of psycho-analysis.

The most usual, if not the only approach, to psycho-analysis is through medicine, though Freud did not regard it as desirable that psycho-analysis should be monopolized by medicine. In truth, since it has developed into an ambitious though justified attempt to provide a total theory of human nature so far as its psycho-dynamic constitution is concerned, it cannot very well be limited to any one discipline. It is bound to attract the serious notice of members of all the professions—medical, social, educational, religious—which are concerned with the problems of human beings in their personal and communal living. Only so can fully comprehensive research be maintained.

My own approach was from the religious starting-point. I became early impressed with the fact that, whatever people achieved in life, so long as they were at cross purposes within themselves they appeared to find little genuine satisfaction. My quest for an answer was directed into the only relevant interest I was then familiar with, that of religion. I found there no resting-place either in theory or practice. Intellectual and emotional problems turned me from 'theological fundamentalism' to left-wing 'liberal modernism', but answers to my questions were not forthcoming.

In the active Ministry I found that neither my theological and philosophical training, nor the devotional exercises of traditional worship, were sufficient to help those distressed individuals who brought their problems to me in private. I sensed hidden sources of trouble that I did not understand. I found no more help in this matter in the academic psychology of the type of McDougall and Spearman, which dominated my student days. But the lectures on psycho-analysis by J. C. Flügel at University College, London, pointed the way for me to a practical approach to human nature. In course of time I was drawn into psychotherapy through Dr. H. Crichton-Miller, Dr. W. MacAdam (Professor of Medicine, Leeds, 1938–46) and Dr. H. V. Dicks (Professor of Psychiatry, Leeds, 1946–8), in succession.

Nevertheless, I found my earlier studies in religion and philosophy were by no means irrelevant. I had been thoroughly trained in a 'personal relations' school of thought, not only in theology but in the philosophy of Professor J. Macmurray. Such books as J. Oman's *Grace and Personality*, Martin Buber's *I and Thou* and J. Macmurray's *Interpreting the Universe, The Boundaries of Science* and *Reason and Emotion* had left too deep a mark for me to be able to approach the study of man in any other way than as a 'Person'. I could never be content with the limitations of Freud's theory in that respect, and was constantly searching for a genuine synthesis, based on the handling of clinical evidence, of psycho-analysis and the philosophy of the 'Person'. This could come about, not by an artificial attempt to 'fit them together' but only by the natural emergence of a fully psychodyamic theory of personality within psycho-analysis. Psycho-analysis would then have far more to offer to all other 'human studies'. I found what I was seeking when my attention was directed by Professor Dicks and the late Professor MacCalman to the work of Dr. W. R. D. Fairbairn of Edinburgh. I take this opportunity of expressing my deep indebtedness to him, both for his writings and for the personal analysis I secured with him. I then had the experience which everyone must have had who first learned the theory and then had an analysis, namely of recognizing the difference between knowing something intellectually and knowing it in immediate experience and with that emotional insight that we refer to as 'getting the feel of it'.

It may be well to guard against one misunderstanding. I would not wish it to be thought that I ignore 'the body' and throw the baby out with the bath-water. In this case the baby is the organic basis of personality, and the bath-water is the attempt to explain the functioning of the 'person' in sub-personal terms. That leads to confused thinking, not to clear understanding. I believe that the best progress towards total understanding will be made by researching diligently on all the various levels of abstraction represented by the sciences that deal with man. Physiology, Biology, Neurology, Psychology, Sociology, with their sub-divisions, are all required but must each be pursued in their own appropriate terms. The physical is not illuminated by 'personal' terminology, nor the 'personal' by physical. The cobbler must stick to his last and it has only slowly become evident that the last of the psycho-analytical cobbler is 'the psychodynamics of man as a person'.

In criticizing chapter vii, Dr. J. D. Sutherland writes:

We all know how intractable the phenomena of the difficulties in personal relationships are and is it not this intractability that continually draws people to the properties of the organism, and, in particular, to its central nervous system as a means of changing? I am sure you are right that the kind of phenomena we deal with need psychological theories for their proper advancement. . . . On the other hand, by looking at behaviour from without, the kind of 'dynamic structures' that the ethologists are postulating . . . may well be extremely helpful to us. Thus, if it is true that the first sexual 'experience' is indelibly 'imprinted' into this dynamic structure because of the physical properties of this structure, we can then see why we are up against something virtually unchangeable. I do not mean that much of human behaviour can be explained in this simple way. . . . I think my criticism probably adds up to the impression that by posing the dilemma too sharply because of your proper reasons, namely, to get psycho-analytic theory into the right terms, you almost convey the feeling that psycho-analysts should not be concerned with other data about the organism. (Personal Communication.)

To this I would reply (1) that the psychotherapist, faced with the problem of both urgent symptom relief and long-term personality change, must accept help from every quarter; (2) he must not, however, simply 'hand over' his intractable problems to other disciplines, because his ultimate goal is the maturity of the personality, something that can be understood only in personal terms and promoted by personal experiences. While parallel lines of investigation are pursued, the psycho-analyst's special task is to study the psychodynamics of human intractability to personality change. This problem is nowhere near exhaustively understood on the psychological level. Not till we are sure we know all there is to know about 'motivated' resistance to change can we afford to turn to physiology for other explanations. Further, there is the problem of whether psychotherapeutic technique allows of emotional experiences sufficiently powerful to produce basic change; for the original experiences that produced the morbid patterns in the first place have often been of quite extreme intensity. What is important then is, not to ignore other lines of research, but to pursue 'psychodynamic science' to the uttermost. It is my hope that in the final section of this book I have been able to contribute something to this end.

Part I

PRELIMINARIES

Chapter I

INTRODUCTION: PRACTICAL AND THEORETICAL PURPOSES

'History shows that scientific effort tends to flow along channels leading to discoveries which contemporary society consciously needs and is ready to pay for. It is no coincidence that methods for working out the longitudinal position of any point were simultaneously discovered by two or more scientists at a time when geographical exploration appeared likely to pay a dividend.' (*The Social Sciences: A Case for their Greater Use.*) It has often been maintained that scientific enquiry is motivated by a pure disinterested love of knowledge for its own sake. This notion of simple inquisitiveness divorced from practical needs is now recognized as a substitution of thinking for living. The idea of the 'scholar' as a musty, eccentric bookworm who has lost all genuine contacts with real life must surely be restricted to very narrow circles to-day. Urgent needs light up the areas of our ignorance, and we must 'know' in order to 'live'. Schizoid detachment from the pressing emotional realities of human relationships may always play a part in the scientific attitude of mind, but is more likely to invalidate scientific thinking in psychology and sociology than it would do in mathematics and physics.

Science, having explored the field of physical and biological phenomena, has, in the last hundred years, arrived on the territory of the specifically human. Man has turned the scientific searchlight on himself, both on the individual and the community. The reason is one of dire practical necessity. To master our world without being able to manage ourselves creates the dangerous possibility of a massive orgy of self-destruction involving the whole human race. We have arrived at an age when we do not now have wars but world-wars. These are not occasional episodes disturbing the continuity of peace, but rather the acute phases of a chronic state of 'cold war'. This has its minor local exacerbations in Korea, Malaya, Indo-China, Formosa, Middle-East regions, Tibet and in the non-stop propaganda battles and subversive political and economic plottings which are so characteristic of this age of geographical unity and human disunity. There is no mistaking the profound anxiety which to-day motivates the creation of the Social Sciences. It is not now a search for 'discoveries which contemporary society consciously needs and is ready to pay for' because they are 'likely to pay a dividend'. It is rather a matter of whether we can make and utilize basic psychological and social discoveries fast enough for there to be anyone left to pay a dividend to, or indeed anything left to pay it with, after an atomic war.

How widely this is felt may be seen from two quotations. Ginsberg, writing as a sociologist in Britain, says :

Our control over inorganic nature infinitely surpasses our control over life, mind and society; and since the former type of control may be used for purposes of destruction, there is the danger that before mankind has acquired sufficient knowledge of the causes of social change, and sufficient moral wisdom to apply it aright, the whole social structure may be wrecked, and the work of organizing mankind have to be begun all over again. (1947, p. 33.)

Franz Alexander, writing as a psycho-analyst in America, says :

The discrepancy between man's technological mastery of nature and his ability to solve his social problems—both national and international—has become more pronounced, and the need for advancement in the field of social science and psychology appears more imperative than ever. . . . Men who are incapable of constructive social life utilize their scientific knowledge primarily to subjugate and exploit their fellow men. . . . There is a desperate necessity for understanding the fundamental principles of social life and of the economic structure, in order to adjust the individual to the new ways of living which natural and applied science have devised. (1952, pp. 13, 22, 27.)

This study of developments in psycho-analytic theory is, then, no mere academic exercise. It aims to clarify an understanding of the problem of living together in co-operative fellowship and the practical realization of love. The urgency of the problem of therapy is a sign of our pressing need to pool our resources obtained by the study of man from all angles. As Brierley says : 'The need for more adequate co-operation among all sciences bearing directly on human life problems is urgent; isolationism can only render them, individually and collectively, less effective than the older established so-called natural sciences that have so profoundly altered our environmental conditions.' (1951, pp. 117–18.)

Psychology with its primary orientation towards the individual, and Sociology with its primary orientation towards the group, are the centre and circumference of this scientific investigation of the problems of human living. They cannot fruitfully be pursued in isolation from each other. Thus we may not forget that psycho-analysis is at the heart of a very large field of enquiry. One of the best assured results of modern research is that individual and group mutually interpenetrate in such a way that any attempt to study either in complete separation from the other would be quite unreal. Family life, so intensively investigated by psycho-analysis, brings this home forcibly. We do not have first of all an individual, fully formed and neat and complete in himself, and then a group set up by the bringing together of a number of these self-contained individuals. Rather, the group goes into the making and structure of the individual while, *pari passu*, individuals in their personal relationships are constituting the group. Individuals and groups are mutually constitutive in highly complex ways as is shown by the psychodynamic study of human object-relationships.

Thus psychology and, in particular, psycho-analysis cannot be regarded simply as the intensive study of the isolated individual. While we shall not here be concerned primarily with the implications of psychology and psycho-analysis for sociology, we shall be concerned with the steadily increasing impact of a broadly sociological orientation on the developing theory of the mental life of the individual resulting ultimately in the analysis of the individual unconscious itself in terms of human object-relationships.

CHAPTER II

PSYCHOLOGY AND PSYCHO-ANALYSIS

THE development of psychology in general, and of psycho-analysis in particular, reveals an increasing degree of sociological orientation. Hartmann writes: 'Many schools of psychology have completely disregarded the individual's social relationships. They speak of laws governing thought processes without taking into account the world to which thought refers: they speak of laws of affectivity, neglecting the objects of the emotions and the situations which provoked them. In other words, they do not take into account the concrete objects in relation to which the behaviour occurred, nor the roots of the behaviour in concrete life situations. This is due to their studying the individual as if he were completely isolated from the world of social phenomena. The phenomena of group psychology are, therefore, completely inaccessible to this type of psychological approach. Such a separation of the individual from the world in which he lives is completely artificial.' (*Psycho-analysis and Sociology*, Lorand, 1948, pp. 326–7.)

The need for psychology to take account, not only of the individual and his 'mind', but also of his world, was responsible for the discarding of the old definition of psychology as 'the science of the mind' and the adoption of the definition of 'the science of behaviour'. A 'behaving' organism is an organism actively reacting to its environment, whereas a 'mind' could all too easily be regarded as a self-contained system.

This definition, however, is still not adequate to our purposes. 'Behaviour' can be regarded as the behaviour of an organism whose nature is biologically fixed as a pattern of innate instinctive drives prior to its having any dealings with its environmental objects. We then get a purely *reactive* psychology, and the world of objects is not recognized to be constitutive of the personality of the individual; object-relationships are not seen to enter deeply into the structure of the person. Objects become purely external entities in a psychological sense, to be simply 'reacted to' by an individual of fixed and fundamentally unmodifiable make-up. In spite of all variations, this 'instinct-theory' is the type of psychology we get when the orientation is more biological than personal, socio-logical and properly psychological.

Hartmann says:

Freud and psychoanalysis gave [psychology] a decisive change of direction. Surely, at the end of last century, few students would have anticipated that the basis for a psychology of relationships between human beings would have come from a study of the neuroses. As it actually occurred, through the new approach to the problem of neurosis, an approach completely foreign to the atmosphere of the psychological laboratory, the entire complexity of an individual's relations to his fellow men, as objects of love, hate, fear and rivalry, suddenly became the main focus of psychological interest, probably without Freud's having anticipated the direction which his work would take . . . the approach to this field was through pathology, and, beyond this, through the study of human instincts, their de-velopment, their transformations and their inhibitions. (Lorand, 1948, p. 327.)

This was a highly promising development, for social groups, both in their cohesion and disruption, must rest on 'the love, hate, fear and rivalry' of their component individuals. Neverthe-less, the classic Freudian theory, though it is the indispensable starting-point, does not prove, without modifications, to be as useful as we need for the understanding of cultural and sociological phenomena, or even of the deep inner life of the individual. While Freud hovered between a psychology of the organism and a psy-chology of the person, a theory of instincts and a theory of object-relations, his theory *in toto* remained fundamentally orientated to biology. Thus he makes character dependent on the organic maturing of the sexual instincts rather than dealing with sexual functioning as controlled by the extent to which character has matured in human relationships. Moreover, his radical subordina-tion of objects to the role of mere means to the gratification of instincts is unsatisfactory from a sociological and from a human point of view, since it treats of personal relationships on a sub-personal level. The same is true of his view that man is by nature narcissistic, non-altruistic and pleasure-seeking, not primarily object-seeking.

Freud's theory was primarily an instinct-theory . The basic innate drives, libidinal and aggressive, emerging out of their psychobiological matrix, the id, invade the ego and compel it to make use of objects as means to subjective instinctive gratification, the pleasure of organic, and therefore psychic, detensioning. The object has no intrinsic, but only utilitarian, value for the ego; and the impulses towards the object are not really the ego's own impulses, they are alien intruders from an impersonal id, on the surface of which the ego develops as a rather superficial phenomenon. We cannot deal constructively with human relationships with a biologically orientated theory of this type. *A truly psychological theory must be an ego-theory, not an instinct-theory, or, rather, it must not separate ego and instincts* in the way Freud did.

The fatal shortcoming of all instinct-theories, from the personal and sociological point of view, is that they are bound to be mainly *reactive* theories. The object is simply 'reacted to' with a pre-existing instinctive impulse which, so to speak, lay in wait for it to pounce upon it. In such theories the role of the object in determining the impulse is not allowed for. Ego and object do not mutually interpenetrate. This can give us only a psychology of *'adaptation to environment'* and *'exploitation of environment'* which is quite unable to deal with the complexity of interpersonal relationships. In *The Ego and the Id* Freud began to transcend this limited type of theory. For sociological as for psycho-analytical purposes, we need a psychodynamic theory which shows how the ego not merely *reacts to* and *adapts to* its objects, but is also *constituted* by its object-relationships. Culture is internalized by the personality, yet that can be accounted for in terms of affectively toned ideas. It is more important to see that the environment of objects is mentally internalized by the personality. A dynamic theory of object-relationships is now needed, as Erich Fromm and Karen Horney recognized; but their work is more a reaction away from instinct-theory than a full psychodynamic object-relations theory.

The idea that a personal object can be set up inside the ego and become part of its structure was propounded by Freud himself in his theory of the super-ego. Conscience is not a set of ideas, it is an ego in its own right, but it is a superior ego, a super-ego, imported from without; it is a psychic internalization of the authoritarian parent. Melanie Klein developed this idea of 'an internal psychic object' in revolutionary ways, and Fairbairn has utilized the results to work out a full psychodynamic theory on the basis, not of instincts, but of object-relationships.

We may quote him as saying that: 'In the earlier stages of psycho-analytical thought, the paramount importance of the object-relationship had not yet been sufficiently realized.' (1952, p. 33.)

As to the definition of psychology, Fairbairn writes : 'From the point of view which I have now come to adopt, psychology may be said to resolve itself into a study of the relationships of the individual to his objects, whilst, in similar terms, psychopathology may be said to resolve itself more specifically into a study of the relationships of the ego to its internalized objects.' (1952, p. 60.) It is impossible to over-emphasize the importance of this for the whole field of the human sciences. A theory basing human nature on immutable instincts will make one kind of contribution to sociology. The newly developed 'object-relations' theory will make quite another type of contribution. Instinct-theory can deal with social problems only at the 'super-ego' level of discipline and control, as is very apparent from the first three chapters of Freud's *The Future of an Illusion*. But, if human nature is determined by the early mental internalization of the environment and the reproduction in the unconscious of a psychic version of our early external object-relations, it emerges that we live in two worlds, an outer environment and an inner environment. *Our deeper emotions and impulses are then, not fixed instincts, but ego-reactions to personal objects in an inner world, surging up to complicate our reactions to our external objects in the outer world.*

Academic psychology has also moved steadily towards dealing, not with 'mind' or 'behaviour' simply, but with the human being viewed as a *whole person*. T. H. Pear writes : 'Psychologists, both here and in America, are often distinguished by the emphasis, theoretical and practical, which they place on one of two aims; the discovery of general laws of mind, or the description and understanding of the unique, undivided personality.' (1948, p. 160.) In 1937, G. W. Allport significantly chose as the title of his book, *Personality. A Psychological Interpretation*. In the Preface he wrote :

As a rule, science regards the individual as a mere bothersome accident. Psychology, too, ordinarily treats him as something to be brushed aside so the main business of accounting for the uniformity of events can get under way. The result is that on all sides we see psychologists enthusiastically at work upon a somewhat shadowy portrait entitled 'the generalized human mind'. Though serving well a certain purpose, this portrait is not altogether satisfying to those who compare it with the living individual models from which it is drawn. It seems unreal and esoteric, devoid of locus, self-consciousness, and organic unity—all essential characteristics of the minds we know.

With the intention of supplementing this abstract portrait by one that is more life-like, a new movement within psychological science has gradually grown up. It attempts to depict and account for the manifest individuality of mind. This new movement has come to be known . . . as the *psychology of personality*. Especially within the past fifteen years has its progress been notable. (1949, p. vii.)

This is a great advance on the attempt to reduce psychology to what is now called an impersonal 'process theory'. It does raise the fundamental issue of whether or not science can deal with the unique individual. If not, then there can be no real science of the 'person', who is always an unique individual. Sullivan therefore excludes the consideration of unique individuality from his psychiatric theory of interpersonal relations. This problem, as we shall see, proves crucial for psycho-analytical theory. (cf. ch. VII, 'Process Theory and Personal Theory'.) Macmurray maintains that the difficulty lies in the fact that philosophy has not yet solved the problem of 'the logical representation of the self', i.e. we have not yet evolved concepts and terms to represent personality with the same accuracy as for the 'thing' and the 'organism'. (1933, p. 122.) This he regards as the emerging central problem of philosophy to-day, to be solved co-operatively as psychology provides the data and philosophy refines the concepts with which science needs to work. The inadequacy of the description of personality apart from its object-relations is allowed for in Fairbairn's definition, already quoted, of psychology as the study of the relationships of the individual to his objects and psychopathology as the study of the relationships of the ego to its internal objects.

Thus we may summarize the changing ways in which the aim of psychological science has been understood. First it was the science of the *Mind* as a largely self-enclosed system. Then it became the science of *Behaviour* or the reactions of the instinctive organism to the environment. To-day it is developing into the science of *Personality and of Object-relationships*, which means basically *Human Relationships*, and which shows how impulse and object, ego and environment, mutually condition each other and interpenetrate in their development and structure. The personal object actually changes according to one's attitude to it. But in a human relationship each party is both ego and object, and each reacts to, and, because of the play of reaction, projection and introjection, enters into, the content of the other's personality. As Alexander says: 'The methods and principles of dynamic psychology created an entirely new field—*the science of human relationships*.' (1952, p. 234. Present writer's italics.)

The aim of psychodynamic theory is to explain the nature and functioning of the individual in the context of, and as he is himself fashioned by, his personal relationships. The aim of psychopathology is specifically to understand the disturbed, i.e. anti-social, functioning of human nature, man's aggression and in-ability to love and co-operate consistently, and his tendency to disrupt the socialized community life he so much needs. Criminal, delinquent, or generally unpleasant and aggressive behaviour, sexually compulsive or perverse behaviour, and psychoneurotic reactions, will, if examined in the light of an adequate psycho-dynamic theory, yield the most valuable data for the sociologist to apply to manifestations of group life as such. Psycho-analysis, beginning as a psychopathology pure and simple, has grown into a complete psychodynamic theory of human personality.

CHAPTER III

PSYCHIATRY AND PSYCHO-ANALYSIS

SINCE we are here studying psychodynamic theory with a practical aim in view, namely its ultimate bearing on the problems of psychotherapy, it is necessary to consider the relationship of psycho-analysis not only to general psychology on the one hand, but also to general psychiatry on the other. This raises in an acute form the *validity* of the psychodynamic, and therewith the psycho-analytical, approach to human problems, since psychiatry has always leaned heavily on neurology and physiology, the approach to the mind through the body. It is all the more necessary to consider this matter since Freud developed psycho-analysis out of his own prior physiological, neurological and biological standpoint : and psycho-analysis, in its inception, was deeply influenced by that standpoint.

The attitude of psychiatrists to psycho-analysis is anything but uniform. Some welcome the light it throws on mental illness. Thus O'Connor writes :

It must be conceded that, were it not for the stimulating and energizing work of Freud and of those who have come after him, we might still be blundering along among the psychiatric catacombs of last century. Much of what Freud first propounded has undergone modification, both by himself and by some of his brilliant successors and equally brilliant secessionists : in this respect we find him in the illustrious company of scientists of all ages. Much of his psychoanalytic therapy and speculation has become so much a part of psychiatric materia medica that the identity of the originator is liable to become lost in a wealth of long-accepted concepts and hypotheses. (1948, p. 136.)

Others are frankly hostile to it even when they have to accept many of its basic ideas. A recent textbook, *Clinical Psychiatry* by Mayer-Gross, Slater and Roth (1954), is a case in point. We make special reference to it here, since it forces on our attention the issue between the neurological and the psychodynamic approaches to psychiatric problems. It is characteristic of the peculiarly 'human' nature of the subject-matter in this field, that powerful emotional factors enter into the discussion of it. There is a clash of two opposite approaches to psychiatric problems, organic and personal. This is not a purely objective scientific matter of the weighing of evidence and disinterested discussion. If it were, there would be no clash but simply two parallel lines of research, one starting from the physiopathological and the other from the psychopathological side. They would each be happy to respect the other, go as far as they can, and find out if and where they meet. But because the subject-matter of psychiatry concerns the most disturbing things in human life, such objectivity is extremely hard to achieve. In fact, the two approaches often clash because they so often characterize individuals of two different kinds of experience, education, point of view, temperament and personality type, and even philosophy of life. It also arises in no small degree from the extent to which investigators are prepared to have psychological insight into themselves. A purely neurological approach dispenses with such insight and is less disturbing than a psycho-analytical one.

The emotional approach to psycho-analysis is all important. We have to distinguish between careful constructive criticism of the theory which is highly necessary, and rationalized emotional hostility which is suspect. Psycho-analysis is neither an universal panacea for all ills nor an irrational cult. It is a difficult, painstaking attempt to understand what is going on in the human mind, based on what individual human beings are able to tell us about their thoughts, feelings and impulses. It has as much or as little success as the difficulty of the undertaking allows, but there appears to be no other way of going about this properly psychological enquiry, except abreaction under hypnosis or drugs. Unfortunately, these methods simplify the problem by eliminating half of it, namely the socially oriented ego which is the source of resistances and defences. The extreme difficulty of recovering the earliest repressed material may justify this in practice. But if we want to investigate the total problem of psychodynamics in the human person we must resort to the slow and patient method of psycho-analysis, even though, when it comes to therapy, it is not seldom more practical and better to use shorter and even purely physical methods to secure symptom-relief. Psychiatry could not possibly limit itself to psycho-analysis, but neither need it be, as is not seldom the case, hostile to it.

If we turn to Mayer-Gross, Slater and Roth, we find that in fact they accept many of the basic concepts of Freud. In chapter 1 of *Clinical Psychiatry* there are five passages, on pages 16, 19, 21, 22 and 24, in which they accept the unconscious, repression, the influence exerted by repressed drives and unconscious motives on present-day experience and behaviour, the Oedipus complex, the fact that the 'repressed' consists essentially of the object-relation-ships of our childhood to parents, and the super-ego as an auto-matic unconscious controlling function operating unreasonably and derived from early parental training. They remark that 'these concepts represented a revolutionary advance and it is in them that Freud's more lasting contribution to psychology can be seen. As a result of his work no psychiatrist could now content himself with superficial or rational sounding explanations of conduct.' (*Op. cit.*, p. 19.) It is true they tone down their acceptances, for they present the super-ego mechanistically as 'a series of condi-tioned reflexes' (p. 22). Furthermore, although they write :

Until Freud's day the emotional attitudes of the infant and child were unexplored territory and in so far as they were thought of at all were submerged in sentiment. People were not prepared to see that the relations of parents and children could be governed by powerful emotions of a most primitive kind,

yet they add 'the significance for adult life of these relations has been grossly exaggerated' (p. 21). In their words, 'people were not prepared to see' the ramifications of that discovery lest we be dis-turbed in our adult illusions about our emotional maturity.

However, these authors speak finally of 'the magnitude of Freud's achievement', and say that 'where previous'/ there had been a complacent nescience and even humbug and wilful self-deception, Freud brought realism, clarity and a powerful tech-nique of investigating motivation' (p. 24). Yet on turning to their chapter on 'Neurotic Reactions', one finds that they do not them-selves make any effective use of what they accept. Their descrip-tions of Hysteria, Depression and Obsessional Neurosis are con-cerned solely with the conscious level, they leave the unconscious quite out of the picture, and little is added to the understanding of the psychic factors in the illnesses. Thus on Anorexia Nervosa they make the penetrating comment that 'anorexia is hardly so much a symptom as a guiding principle of life' (p. 139). The patient will not take food on principle. When they then say 'the patient has *no desire for food* [present writer's italics] of any kind, and foods are regarded with repulsion', that requires explanation in terms of the guiding principle in life. Such explanation could come only from unconscious motivation and they do not give it. An anorexia patient of mine dreamed of enormous meals going on endlessly, and said, 'I can't make moderate demands on people so I don't make any at all'. That explains why, having longed for her husband all day, as soon as he came home she at once lost interest in him but became ravenously hungry; she would then get herself a meal and as soon as she sat down at once lose interest in the food. No such psycho-analytical enlightenment, which is strictly in line with their own comment, do they attempt. The unconscious motivation is ignored. Must we conclude that, after all, they only accept what they do because they cannot at this late hour avoid it, and hasten to drop these disturbing lines of approach in practice lest they should open up the whole field of *the psychodynamics of personal living*? The conditioned reflex is a less disturbing concept.

When we turn to their criticisms of psycho-analysis their hostile bias is undisguised. They remark that 'In so far as Freud's ideas are well founded . . . they have been absorbed. There is very little sign that further new fundamental contributions are to be expected from members of this school' (p. 24). That is an old trick of depreciation and it is not accompanied by any evidence of awareness of the psycho-analytical developments we shall trace out in this book. In 1929 Professor Pillsbury, in his *History of Psychology*, wrote :

Freud's doctrine . . . is the center of a controversy between devout disciples and scoffing opponents. . . . Gradually its admitted practitioners are becoming fewer and fewer, and the ardour of those who were disciples is cooling. It stands as a strange episode in the history of psychology. (1929, pp. 267–8.)

These writers repeat that kind of attempt to prejudice the issue. The passage of time has not dealt kindly with Pillsbury's rash prophecy and will probably deal similarly with this renewal of it.

We need not deal specifically with their criticisms to the effect that Freud's theory is 'a crazy structure', 'a mythology' and 'a cult', and that 'it is popular with half-baked amateur psychologists, journalists, novelists and literary critics, but is in the main found antipathetic by neurologists, physicians and psychiatrists with any extensive experience' (p. 23). The tone of superiority in this statement does not commend it to scientific consideration, but it is important to note such so-called criticisms because they are evidence of the acute emotional ambivalence of these authors to psycho-analysis : When they say that 'Freud's superficially rational appeal, made under the cloak of science, is probably the most effective form of faith-healing to-day' (p. 17) and add that 'enthusiasts rather than sceptics submit themselves to analysis, which is why an uncritical enthusiasm is rife' (p. 24), it is clear that they have entirely failed to take account of *resistance* to analysis, a concept which is fundamental to psycho-analytical theory; and also of the anxiety and suffering involved in getting anywhere with analysis, which would soon weed out mere enthusiasts. Certainly every psycho-analyst found psycho-analysis 'antipathetic' to himself when he was undergoing his own personal training analysis. In *every* case psycho-analysis only makes slow and painful headway in practice, in the face of bitter resistance, and patients often break out in angry tirades against analysis when they are experiencing a negative transference. One of my own patients dreamed that she was passing my rooms on top of a tram and, looking down, saw herself at the same time on the pavement going into my rooms and she thought, 'Look at that silly creature going in there', and she went by on the tram; hardly an uncritical enthusiasm. If a hostile critic were tempted to agree with her dream, we would have to add that she also felt 'a silly creature' because, though possessed of marked ability, she had at the age of thirty given up a very worthwhile job to return home in an anxiety-state. She suffered a conflict between strong independent tendencies and equally strong though disowned dependent needs towards parents; this whole conflict was transferred into her relation to her therapist and caused her to experience an intense resistance against her own need to seek help. This marked ambivalence must be taken into account when we find the organic and the psychodynamic approaches to human problems being set in opposition. Yet we do not find hostile critics of psycho-analysis pausing to consider whether their antagonism may not be more an emotional resistance than a genuine scientific objection.

This problem is so important because there is abundant evidence that the conflict between the neurological and psychodynamic points of view which is active in psychiatry to-day existed in Freud himself, and though he transcended it in large measure there seems reason to think that he never fully resolved it. Freud, of course, must have had powerful resistances to his own discoveries. This conflict is the starting-point of the development of psycho-analysis and left deep marks on Freud's own theory. Neo-Freudian developments are very much concerned with the results.

We shall take up the position that every study of human beings, from any aspect whatsoever, should be kept well subordinated to the basic fact that, unlike all other organisms, it is man's potentiality to become what we mean by a 'person', and his true destiny (whether fulfilled or not) is to mature an individual personality in the medium of personal relationships. One may study men from the physiological, biological, psychological, or again from medical, social or religious angles. But all these studies get out of focus unless controlled by the over-all understanding of what a human being is in his total nature. The development in medical thinking towards the idea that what is to be treated is not a disease entity but a patient who is a human person, is itself an expression of that point of view which dominates modern culture. Freeman writes in a review of this book : 'Man is more than a compound of genetics, biochemistry and the accidental experiences of life which interact and leave an imprint of varying intensity.' (1955, p. 196.)

Freud's education and thinking for the first thirty-five years of his life placed him on the same fundamental ground as Mayer-Gross, Slater and Roth, the ground of an *organic* rather than a *personal* point of view. Intellectually he in large measure fought his way out and the pressure of his own discoveries pushed him into dealing with man as a 'person'. Yet was it to be expected that he could wholly emancipate himself from the intellectual stand-point of the first half of his life and of his cultural epoch ? There is much to show that he remained at heart a neurologist, a physio-logist, a biologist, even a mechanist. In chapter V and VII we shall look more closely into this conflict in Freud between neuro-logy and psychology. Freud was too early, in the cultural milieu of Vienna prior to 1900, to be deeply influenced by the 'personal' orientation of modern culture. Mayer-Gross, Slater and Roth seem to be out of touch with it.

The real underlying difficulty these authors have about Freud is that he *did* allow the pressure of clinical necessity to drive him beyond the neurology in which he had already achieved eminence, to a truly *psychodynamic* study of human beings, even though at bottom he could never completely emotionally reconcile himself to that. They, on the other hand, have not followed Freud's courageous example and while they cannot now (so great has been the impact of Freud's work) reject psychodynamic theory, they do not like it, and resent its being forced on them far more than Freud did.[1]

Competent observers who are outside medical, but not outside human, interests, watch keenly the drama of this struggle that goes on in psychiatry as much to-day as ever, between the organismic and the personal or psychodynamic orientations. Professor L. W. Grensted of Oxford has written as follows :

[1] This tendency to exaggerate the importance of heredity and under-value both the psychological and physical aspects of environment in the development of personality and mental illness is apparent throughout the work.' (T. Freeman, *op. cit.*, p. 195.)

'Modern psychiatrists are much more scientists and much better equipped scientifically than the pioneers of thirty and forty years ago, but their diagnosis and treatment are apt to be less personal, and in the deepest sense less humane. This lowering of personal values is the ground for the grave suspicions with which many people regard psychiatry to-day. They are rooted in a deep and justifiable resentment, perhaps only half conscious, at the suggestion that they are anything less than persons, of full and individual human worth. To depersonalize them at the very heart of their being is the final dishonour. It may be true that there are few psychiatrists who actually inflict this dishonour on their patients, but the fear and suspicion are there. It is perhaps the gravest issue that psychiatry has to face.' (Foreword to Guntrip, 1957, p. 7.)

The starting-point of these three psychiatrists is severely medical, and that orientation is adequate to many of the problems they have to deal with in the total field of psychiatry. But they make it quite plain that they would prefer to find a neurological explanation of every problem if possible and not have to be drawn out into the disturbing field of the psychological and the social. They dislike what they call 'the subjectivity and the lack of precision in psychological data' (p. 1). They state that: 'There is an immense body of evidence showing that in the major psychiatric disorders the specific factors in causation are those of a constitutional and physiopathological kind' (p. 4). They write: 'If psychiatry must concern itself principally with the study of mental illness, the patterns of behaviour studied in communities by sociology are not necessarily of immediate relevance. If a particular individual has a convulsion with loss of consciousness, which can be fully described and accounted for in terms of neurophysiology, then it is superfluous to attempt to describe and account for it in terms of the psychology of social relationships' (p. 3). But what if a problem arises that cannot be 'fully accounted for in terms of neurophysiology'. That seems to be an unwelcome fact for them. They reject the view of Lidz and Lidz that 'neurology is only one of several basic sciences for psychiatry', (p. 3) and they warn of the danger of 'psychiatry being divorced from medicine.' (p. 2). Certainly such a divorce would be a grave loss, but there is an equal if not greater danger in trying to reduce all human problems to neurophysiological ones.

The traditional psychiatric approach is one of primary emphasis on the organism; the psychodynamic approach is that of primary emphasis on the person who has an organic but also other aspects. Mayer-Gross, Slater and Roth state explicitly that they seek to base psychiatry on the ground of *the natural sciences*. Psychoneurosis, however, can arise in an individual with a normal brain and an otherwise healthy body, because he has had to cope with an abnormal traumatic environment. Since the incidence of neurotic personality disturbances is greater quantitatively than that of all other psychiatric disorders put together, it seems to be self-evident that *the human sciences and above all psychodynamic studies* have at least an equal claim with the natural sciences to be considered basic for psychiatry. In theory their 'multi-dimensional approach' implies that. In fact they show a marked one-sided bias in the matter, away from truly human studies. They write : 'the hypothesis of an active repressing force is a gratuitous assumption' (p. 18).

The fact is, however, that in a human being every psychic process is a *personal* activity, and that the neo-Freudian development of Freud's theory of the super-ego expresses the fact that the human environment does *not* remain a wholly *external* repressing force impinging on a unitary organism only from the outside : rather it comes to be psychically internalized in such a way as to form the endopsychic structure of a personality. Thus, in the long run, *the ultimate traumatic situations in which the individual suffers are no longer outside but are embedded in the personality itself.*

That is the problem that is fundamental for psychodynamic theory to-day and which the work of Freud alone has brought to light. It cannot be causally explained by neurology but only by a personal psychology of human relationships. We may summarize the psychodynamic point of view before we proceed to trace its full elaboration in the development of psycho-analytical theory. What is the fundamental fact that remains a constant, whether overt or disguised, in all abnormally developed types of personality? Is it not that so far as emotions are concerned such people live their outward life in terms of inner subjective factors. Their *emotional* relationships with their outer world are not objectively realistic. They may be *intellectually* objective in the matter of their correct appraisal of ways and means to their own ends, and in relation to matters that are of no private emotional significance to them. But the moment their personal needs and aims are involved they lose emotional objectivity and behave on the basis of inner mental situations. All patients live in an individual private mental world and to help them we have to discover its structure.

The bare existence of dreams and waking phantasies is sufficient to show the existence of an inner mental world separate from and divorced from outer reality. This inner mental world involves human beings in two main psychopathological dangers, projection and introversion; either projecting the inner scene into or forcing it on the outer one and then behaving in socially unrealistic ways; or else withdrawing all feeling and interest, all flow of energy and impulse which naturally goes outwards to real objects, and turning it inwards on to phantasied objects to become detached and schizoid.

How do these pathological states of mind arise? If this tendency to live one's effective emotional life much more inside oneself than in realistic touch with the world outside were only found in the constitutionally predisposed schizophrenic we would conclude that innate and organic factors were responsible. But that is not the case. It is found in varying degree in all types of case and in lesser degrees even in 'normal' people. In fact, *this introverted development, leading to internalized objects, splitting of the ego and loss of realistic contact with the outer world, is the basic psychopathological process.*

The child who finds his outer world frustrating turns inwards, and he turns his own mind into 'a place to live in' instead of using it as 'an active function to live with'. He starts doing his living in imagination, in phantasy, not in fact. He peoples his inner world with good and bad objects whom he hopes he can manipulate at will. He seeks what he wants inside in phantasied satisfactions. This is based on the capacity to hallucinate satisfactions so vividly (as in dreams) that emotionally they can substitute for a time for outer reality. Unfortunately, in this process, he sets up 'bad' as well as 'good' figures inside, and perpetuates disturbance. The inner world then becomes the enduring though repressed and unconscious structure of the dynamic personality, which is filled with conflict and self-frustration. Over the top of this at the level of consciousness, a superficial personality constructed mainly of social adjustments, and functioning without much real mature feeling, carries on the business of outer life in a way that is far more automatic than is usually recognized. Inside and unconsciously a hidden inner life is guarded against all intruders, and this is the source of resistance to analysis. Patients cling desperately to their secret inner world, even though it undermines them in their real outer life. This is the essence of all personality problems and it is in origin a psychodynamic and not a neurological problem. Various forms of it may be partially relieved in many ways as regards symptoms, by both physical and short-term pyschological treatments, but a *radical* solution cannot be arrived at except with the aid of psycho-analysis. We must hope that progress in psychoanalytical theory may be accompanied by fewer failures in therapy.

CHAPTER IV

THE DEVELOPMENT OF
PSYCHO-ANALYTICAL THEORY

PSYCHO-ANALYTICAL theory has been in a state of continuous development from the beginning. The genius of its creator, Sigmund Freud, so dominated this process that during his lifetime theoretical developments were almost if not quite wholly determined by himself. Here and there he adopts suggestions from some fellow-workers while their contributions were in the main elaborations and developments of new theories which he himself propounded. In sober truth all the fundamental new ideas *did* come from Freud himself.

Though we await the judgment of an impartial historian of psycho-analysis (if such there can be in matters so closely touching human emotions), it is probably not unfair to state that the works of men like Jung, Reich and Rank, each in different ways, exhibited ultimately a speculative bent rather than the predominantly scientific, analytical, clinical line of Freud, while Adler may be said to have raised the problem of ego-analysis prematurely and too superficially. It must be admitted that Freud's own speculative bent broke out in his theory of the death instinct. He himself regarded it as 'far-fetched speculation' and expected readers to accept or reject it according to their own point of view. (1920, p. 27.) Nevertheless, he thereafter refers to the conclusions of this book as if they were now established facts. His speculations in the realm of the application of psycho-analysis to sociology have less bearing on basic matters of theory than have those in the book just quoted.

It was, however, indisputably Freud's own work that established psycho-analysis as a coherent system. It is to be regretted that the unscientific atmosphere of 'orthodoxy versus heresy and deviation' came to invest too much of the theoretical controversy in this broad field of psychodynamic investigation. Schools formed and their representatives seemed more eager to refute than to learn from one another, though no one can have a monopoly of insight, and exclusiveness cannot be afforded in this field of enquiry. Few writers about psychodynamic theory quote (except to criticize) or seek to learn from workers outside their own school of thought. The result is a small group of psychodynamic theories differing in orientation among themselves, and developing in isolation from one another, with unorganized eclectics outside the schools picking and choosing theories at will. An open field of free and unfettered enquiry with rich and stimulating interchange of ideas on all sides would better suit a scientific discipline.

Yet, even so, it may well be that this was the inevitable character of the first phase of psychodynamic investigation. Each gifted pioneer had to follow his own insight in the early exploratory stage. Had it been otherwise, it is certain that the clear-cut, distinctive features of Freud's own work would have been obscured and lost, to the great disadvantage of future workers. We must here take note of one of the most difficult aspects of scientific enquiry in the realm of psychological and particularly psychodynamic phenomena. In studying all other areas of reality the enquiring mind is dealing with something other than itself. True, our perceptions of 'objective' phenomena are by no means free from contamination by subjective factors, as the theory of 'apperception' shows. There are even emotional factors at work determining the direction of interest of each individual investigator, and when a theory is evolved its creator cannot escape a personal attachment to the product of his own endeavour. Yet it is broadly true that the more impersonal the phenomena studied, as in mathematics, astronomy and physics, the more reliably 'objective' is the result. The nearer we approach to the scientific study of human living in general, as in sociology, the less is this true. But when the human mind turns back upon itself to probe the secrets of its own hidden emotional constitution—which is hidden because we have such good reasons for *not* knowing the truth about ourselves—then the influence of subjective factors in distorting objective investigation can be all but overwhelming.

Thus Brierley writes :

The psycho-analytic situation can be standardized only to a degree far short of uniformity. It is said, not without justice, that in psychoanalytic research intensity of examination replaces extensity of sampling (S. Isaacs. 'Criteria for Interpretation', *Int. J. Psycho-An.*, Vol. 20, p. 159, 1939), but intensity for examination is no safeguard against error due to subjective bias in the examiner. This may be corrected to some extent by comparing the results obtained by a number of different workers; pooling of clinical experience is an obvious and practicable, if incomplete, safeguard against errors due to individual bias. (1951, p. 91.)

Considering more specifically the problem of abstract thinking in general as well as in psychological enquiry, she says :

Abstract thinking is no less subjectively determined than perception and the risk that it will be dominated by unconscious preconceptions is, perhaps, even greater than in perceptual thinking. For this reason alone, constant reference to and checking of hypotheses by data is imperative. The form of any hypothesis is always influenced by unconscious determinants, since we can only apprehend things in ways permitted by the specific structure of our individual minds. The fact remains, however, that the objective truth of any hypothesis does not depend upon its subjective conditioning but upon its fitness to explain the facts it covers. Naturally, the more we become aware of the unconscious determinants of our own thinking the better chance we have of estimating how far our preferred conceptions are likely to correspond to the facts. We all have some coefficient of personal error which we cannot eliminate, and it is much safer to assume that one's own coefficient of error is high rather than low, and positively dangerous to forget that it exists. (*Op. cit.*, p. 96.)

These considerations are important in regard to the early history of psycho-analytic theory. This reads, at times, more like an account of the struggles in early Christian history of the orthodox to defend the true church against heretics and schismatics than an account of a scientific movement. Nor is this comparison irrelevant, for religion, like psycho-analysis, is a search for a psychotherapy for the emotional and personal ills of human beings even if the method of approach is different. Those who carry on the search by either path are as much in need of the cure, and as much influenced by their own wishes in that respect, as those to whom they may offer their findings.

The aims of psychotherapy and of scientific research are different. Emotion enters into the one but must be rigidly excluded, if that be possible, from the other; but there is no doubt that this has its bearing on theoretical divergences. Theologians have claimed too exclusively that their systems represent objective and indisputable truth, so that theological controversy early took the form of the establishment of an authentic revelation which was only correctly interpreted by the authoritative, orthodox and recognized leaders of the Church; who then sought to excommunicate heretics. The question as to how far theological differences were really expressions of different types of personality and of emotional stress and need among theologians, was not raised because thinkers felt that their own personal 'salvation' was involved in the truth of their views.

This question was raised by psycho-analysis, though, it seems, chiefly in reference to those who deviated from the basic psychoanalytical theory. Not only is it clear that direct clashes of personality caused some of the early schisms in the psycho-analytic movement, but also that the emergence of differing theoretical orientations was related to the differing personalities of the innovators. Since it is truer in psycho-analytical science than in other branches of science that a (psychodynamic) theory must be related to the psychodynamic constitution of its originator, two different questions must be always considered in seeking to judge of the theory; the question of motive and the question of truth. Though, by and large, Freud's contribution has stood the test of time and criticism far better than that of those who deviated from him, this holds good as much for Freud as for his rivals and for his frankly hostile opponents. With regard to the latter there is a difference between emotional hostility to psycho-analysis *per se* and *in toto*, and critical difference on particular points of theory. There is little purpose in discussing psycho-analysis with those who reject it root and branch, since their opposition is almost wholly of an emotional and non-scientific order. Those who seriously criticize details of the theory have a right to be met with equally serious scientific discussion and critical study of their alternative views. Not that this rules out subjective factors on both sides; and it seems to be involved in the nature of the case that this scientific discussion must include in the end an attempt to estimate the difficult matter of unconscious motivation of theory in *both* the orthodox view and any new view put forward. Probably this need would emerge most clearly where discussion came up against a fundamental difference of outlook. This is particularly important with regard to theories of psychotherapy, but even on more abstract 'metapsychological' points it arises. It cannot escape notice that the propounder of the theory of a death instinct was all his life preoccupied with thoughts about death (*vide* E. Jones's biography of Freud).

It would be absurd to maintain that neurotic factors in the analyst *ipso facto* invalidate his thinking and therapy. They may do and at times actually do, but they also provide the spur to psychodynamic discovery and the necessary basis of insight. If we can imagine a one hundred per cent mentally healthy person, he would be unlikely to feel any interest in such introverted directions and have nothing in his own experience to work on in achieving insight into the strange phenomena of the internally disturbed person. Freud once said that if he met with an emotion in a patient that seemed to have no echo in his own experience, it gave him an uncanny feeling. The subjective factor of personal experience of psychic conflict is essential to its understanding, though certainly that alone will not suffice. The question is always relevant as to how far the thinker's personal conflicts facilitate or distort the scientific objectivity of his conclusions, for we are here trying to be objective about the wholly subjective. The classic example is Freud's self-analysis of his own Oedipus conflict as the basis of psycho-analytic insight and theory. One must have a neurosis, but much more than a neurosis to do that.

Ernest Jones indicates some of the personal factors at work in the early schismatics, and just touches lightly on possible limitations in Freud's theories from the point of view of Freud's own personality. He courageously provides extensive information about Freud's neurosis, but is generally agreed to have played it down in estimating its persistence in his personality. A very difficult but necessary piece of work will need to be done some day, along the lines of Freud's own study of Leonardo da Vinci, in correlating Freud's theory with his own complex personality, as a contribution to the surer development of psycho-analytic theory. Of the early schismatics, the simplest case is that of Stekel. Though he had genuine gifts for understanding the unconscious and particularly symbolism, his personality was such that he did not have a scientific conscience and would invent data and evidence in a romantic and enthusiastic way. The scrupulously honest Freud could not work on that basis.

Adler's ambitious and aggressive personality certainly influenced his predilection for explaining ego-psychology in terms of a power-drive and ignoring the disconcerting deep unconscious. Jung's evident desire to play down the recognition of sexual phenomena (in part due to his Swiss culture and religion), and his flair for the speculative study of myth, legend and symbolism, look like the opposite aspects of a basic personality trait, and they correlate with his somewhat abstract, schematic and not directly clinical theory, and his moralistic and educative approach to therapy. There seems to be no likelihood that such personal factors can ever be negligible in either psycho-analytic theorists or their opponents, but they cannot be recognized in the case of critics only. The estimation of their influence is essential to the evaluation of all psychodynamic theories. In no other branch of science is it so important to know what sort of person the scientist is. This simply extends to the

psychodynamic theorist a criterion already applied to the psychotherapist.

There will, no doubt, be different schools of psychodynamic
theory for a long time, and they are more likely to learn from one
another and converge towards a more unified theory if they are
all frankly studied from the point of view, not only of logical con-
sistency and basis in clinical evidence, but also their emotional
foundations. Jones writes : 'Dissensions concerning psycho-analysis
are even harder to resolve than those in other fields of science
where it is not so easy to continue re-interpreting data in terms
of some personal prejudice.' (1955, p. 145.) Coming closer to the
root of the problem he states that : 'Investigation of the unconscious, which is a fair definition of psycho-analysis, can be carried
out only by overcoming the "resistances" which ample experience
has shown are displayed against such a procedure. . . . Only when
the manifold resistances have been thoroughly worked through is
the insight of a lasting nature.' (*Op. cit.*, p. 142.)

But no one would claim that all resistances ever are worked
through. Hence we are faced with fluctuations of insight, not only
in patients but also in analysts. Jones says : 'All this is equally true
for the analyst as for the patient. . . . When an analyst loses insight
he had previously had, the recurring wave of resistance that caused
the loss is apt to display itself in the form of pseudo-scientific explanations of the data before him, and is then dignified with the
name of a "new theory".' (*Op. cit.*, pp. 142–3.) That is undoubtedly true, but it is a truth that could be misapplied to stifle
all theoretical progress. Psycho-analysts have an exceptionally
severe discipline to impose on themselves. They must be prepared
to accept not only a psycho-analytical investigation of their personality as a preparation for psychotherapy, but also a psycho-
analytical investigation of their theories, both orthodox and in-
novatory, as a basis for objective scientific thinking. A similar
discipline is undoubtedly equally important for philosophers and
theologians.

One or two fixed points have already emerged. Any theory that
seeks to ignore the power and ramifications of the sexual factor, to
ignore the deep unconscious or to deny repression, is suspect as to
its motivation. In general, it cannot be denied, without loss of true
insight, that Freud did discover basic facts about our mental constitution and functioning, though many detailed aspects of his
theories are open to criticism. The scientific status of the psycho-
analytic method has been discussed by analysts themselves.
Psycho-analysis in the stricter sense could not maintain a policy
of self-containment without loss to itself, in spite of the fact that

the requirement of a training analysis (so necessary to the maintenance of a high standard) tends in that direction. There are signs that the pressure of events, especially since the war, is forcing a wider and more open interchange of ideas. The training analysis will be less than adequate if it does not make for increased objectivity and open-mindedness in thinking. As Brierley says : 'The inability to tolerate one or other aspect of subjective reality is one of the most important factors responsible for secessions and the formation of derivative movements. Persuasion by the structure of one's own mind can be a strong incentive to turn a personal solution into a new school.' (1951, p. 122.)

Development, however, has gone on within the psycho-analytic movement more narrowly defined, and it has been felt necessary to state that theoretical progress cannot be halted with the death of Freud. We quote Brierley once more.

Most scientific societies welcome deep and far-reaching differences of opinion among their members, because the occurrence of such differences is regarded as a sign of vitality and growth. . . . Psychoanalysts have two main reasons for attaching what may be unduly great importance to relative uniformity in theory. These reasons spring from the circumstance that we have three functions to perform : research, therapy, and the training of intending practitioners. It is in relation to the two latter functions that we hanker after uniformity and standardization. . . . It is, however, very necessary for us to recognize that uniformity easily conduces to stasis, and that a static science is dead. Scientific truth can never be absolute because hypotheses are formulated in the light of contemporary knowledge. In consequence, as knowledge grows, older hypotheses become inadequate and have to be revised, expanded or reformulated to contain newer facts. Freud did this himself, time after time, and if psychoanalysis is to continue to develop as a living science this process of recasting hypotheses and expanding theory must also continue. . . . To expect to conserve the letter of all Freud's statements, as a kind of 'Bible of Psycho-analysis' is to condemn psycho-analytic enquiry to stasis, and therefore psycho-analysis as a science to death. . . . But the main principles established by Freud will survive in so far as they do correspond with facts. The name of Freud will endure with the principles, but they will survive not because Freud established them, but because they are rooted in psychological facts. (1951, pp. 88–9.)

It is significant that these words were written in a review of the work of Melanie Klein which, in the present writer's judgment, forms the basis of the most far-reaching of recent developments.

In a broad sense an unconscious pattern of development as a process of a dialectical type can now be discerned. Recent developments have not been haphazard and purely individualistic contributions. They have rather been determined by, and have arisen out of, that larger and all-embracing milieu of cultural change within which psycho-analysts, like all other investigators, must do their thinking. For example, the influence of sociology (a science much less developed in Freud's creative period than now) on American psycho-analytic thought is recognized. Fairbairn has referred to the influence of a changing cultural orientation in calling for a revision of basic psycho-analytical theory at those points where it was determined by the atomistic scientific outlook of Helmholtz, a view that now no longer dominates physics or science in general. Furthermore, in Freud's day, the concept of the 'person' and of 'personality' had not assumed the importance in philosophical thinking that it came to do later, with far-reaching effects on all the human sciences. Culturally, to-day is the era of human personal relationships rather than of instincts; the problem is, given innate endowment, how is that shaped by what goes on between people.

In tracing out the broadly dialectical pattern of development in psycho-analytical theory we find some help (again, only in a broad way) in taking note of the differences between psycho-analytical thinking in different geographical areas. Balint, in 1937, wrote:

To-day we have to deal with several theories, often contradicting one another. . . . These differences somehow seem to depend on geography in a way that one is justified in speaking of regional opinions. Such 'regional' opinions have been formed during the last years in London, in Vienna and in Budapest. (1949, p. 265.)

This particular judgment referred to a specific theoretical issue. We can, however, recognize the same phenomenon over a larger area affecting total theoretical orientation. I shall suggest as a useful way of correlating recent developments in psycho-analytical theory the following dialectical scheme, which, however, is not intended to be pressed rigidly or regarded as a strictly chronological development, but used only as a guiding idea.

1. *Thesis.* The original *European psychobiology* of Freud and his early co-workers from 1890 onwards, an 'instinct-theory' which was not modified by the later development in the 1920s of his tremendously important and more purely psychological ego-analysis. This may be referred to as the classic psycho-analytical teaching.

2. *Antithesis.* The rise of a *psychosociology* in *America*, in the

'culture-pattern' and 'character-analysis' theories of writers like Karen Horney, Erich Fromm, and H. S. Sullivan, from the 1930s.

3. *Synthesis.* The elaboration in *Great Britain* of a different theoretical orientation which, while not indifferent to sociological and biological considerations, developed the concepts of *the 'internal object' and the 'inner psychic world' as parallel to external objects and the outer world*; and so comes to correlate the internal and the external object-relationships in which the personality is involved. This development arises out of the work of Melanie Klein and others and is worked out in a systematic and comprehensive way by Fairbairn. It, too, dates from the 1930s.

The recent book by Clara Thompson entitled *Psychoanalysis, Evolution and Development* (1952) unfortunately deals only with phases one and two and quite ignores the British contribution which is in truth an exceedingly radical and important one. The same apparent unawareness of British contributions characterizes P. Mullahy's *The Oedipus Myth*.

In the following chapters we shall make use of this scheme as a ground-plan to order our investigation. The results are summarized in chapter XVII, pp. 351 ff., and some readers may find it useful to refer to that before proceeding further at this point.

Part II

THE DEVELOPMENT OF
PSYCHO-ANALYTICAL THEORY

'Your surmise that after my departure my errors might be adored as holy relics amused me enormously, but I don't believe it. On the contrary, I think my followers will hasten to demolish as swiftly as possible everything that is not safe and sound in what I leave behind.' (Freud : letter to Jung, Dec. 19th, 1909, from *Sigmund Freud*, vol. II, E. Jones, p. 495.)

CHAPTER V

THE STARTING-POINT
CLASSIC FREUDIAN PSYCHOBIOLOGY

1. *Introduction*

To show clearly that developing trends in psycho-analysis have moved towards an increasing emphasis on human relations, and therefore towards a potentially sociological and personal rather than a basically biological orientation, we must deal with the main stages in chronological order. This does not mean attempting a history of psycho-analysis in detail, but rather a survey of those major theoretical positions which have a particular bearing on this orientation. After the first acts in the creation of psycho-analysis, namely Breuer's treatment of an hysteric patient in 1880–1, and Breuer and Freud's joint study, at Freud's instigation, from 1886 onwards culminating in their joint preliminary paper on Hysteria in 1893, Breuer fell away. Freud, having abandoned hypnosis, built up his technique of psycho-analysis and his theory of neurosis. Even at this early stage it emerged that this would ultimately overstep the borders of biological and purely medical concerns, since Freud discovered a social and moral factor at work in the creation of nervous illness. This was not so with Breuer. Freud writes that Breuer

supposed that the pathogenic ideas (in hysteria) produced traumatic effects because they arose during 'hypnoid states' in which mental functioning was subject to special limitations. The present writer rejected this explanation and inclined to the belief that an idea became pathogenic if its content was in opposition to the predominant trend of the subject's mental life so that it invoked a 'defence'. (1922, *C.P.*, V, p. 109.)

This 'predominant trend' which produced 'repression' and perpetuated a state of unconscious psychic conflict was, naturally, the result of parental and social education and influence in moral ideals and rules and community demands, i.e. all that Freud meant by 'culture'.

Nevertheless, for a long time Freud simply accepted without analysis this 'cultural factor' of conscience, and concentrated on the investigation of the instinctive or biological basis of human personality. (Cf. *The Interpretation of Dreams*, 1901.) Much later, about 1920, he turned his attention from 'the repressed' to 'the repressing factor', set about the analysis of the ego, and evolved his theory of psychic structure, the id, ego and super-ego. This analysis of the total personality, which is of such great sociological significance, he worked out in a series of monographs: *Beyond the Pleasure Principle*, 1920; *Group Psychology and the Analysis of the Ego*, 1921; *The Ego and the Id*, 1923; and *Inhibitions, Symptoms and Anxiety*, 1926. He had long before that come to consider the social bearing of his work in 1908 in the paper *Civilized Sexual Morality and Modern Nervousness*, and in 1913 in *Totem and Taboo*. But it is from 1920 onwards that we find psycho-analysis making major excursions into the field of social and cultural studies, and developing into a science of human relations. The small rivulet of the pre-1920 period broadened into a river. Premature attempts to widen the applications of psychoanalysis before its inner growth forced these issues to the forefront led to the breakaways of Adler and Jung in 1911 and 1913.

The two developments which have greater sociological importance than the work of Jung and Adler came after 1926 and derive from Freud's own later work. Karen Horney and Erich Fromm have, in a sense, taken up again the Adlerian 'deviation', viewing man largely from the social rather than from the deep psychogenetic viewpoint. Replacing 'instinct' by 'human relations', and the analysis of the deep unconscious by the analysis of character-trends in the contemporary social setting, they have lost touch with the Freudian psychological depths. However, they owe far more to Freud than did Jung and Adler. A much more important recent trend, which is a genuine development of, rather than a reaction against, Freud's work, is the 'object-relations' theories of Melanie Klein and W. R. D. Fairbairn.

To show how these recent trends develop psycho-analysis in a more sociological and personal direction, as a fully *psychodynamic* theory of personality and personal relations, we must examine first the classic Freudian orthodoxy. We shall not be concerned with Freud's entire theory, but only with those elements which have an explicit bearing on this theme. Before we proceed to problems and critical considerations, it will be as well to state concisely the incontrovertible hard core of psychic fact discovered by Freud, an achievement which will place him for all time among the immortals of scientific discovery. Freud himself stated, 'The doctrine of repression is the foundation-stone on which the whole structure of psycho-analysis rests.' (1914, *C.P.*, I, p. 297.) This is what fundamentally distinguishes psycho-analysis from the social psychologies of Adler and the more modern 'culture-pattern' school.

Repression carries with it the other basic phenomena which Freud lists in the same paper as *resistance, transference, infantile sexuality* and the significance of dreams as a revelation of *the unconscious*. It may be said briefly that *resistance* is the reverse side of *repression*, and accounts for the extreme difficulty of achieving self-knowledge and for the very slow and difficult progress made by all attempts at psychotherapy which aim not simply at conscious readjustment but at fundamental personality change. *Infantile sexuality* means more than Freud's assertion, a fact now proven beyond all doubt, that the sexual factor in the human constitution is active from earliest infancy and does not come into being for the first time at puberty. It means further, as later research shows, that emotional difficulties in human relationships in the infancy period become quite peculiarly focussed in and on sexuality and are repressed in that form to constitute the hard core of the dynamic unconscious which breaks through during sleep in dreams. *Transference* is the unconscious reliving of the repressed life of infancy in present-day relationships, both in treatment and in real life.

We must add to these essentials of Freud's discoveries, the *Oedipus Complex*. This is regarded as the hard core of all neurosis. Modern research has tended more and more to go back behind the Oedipal period of three to five years into the obscure problems of the first year. This involves also going back behind depressive to schizoid phenomena, and from the three-person Oedipal situation to the earliest two-person mother-infant situation, the extreme importance of which is now established beyond question. If, however, we look at the matter the other way round, it is apparent that the critical developmental problem in the earliest years is that of the transition from the potentially complete security of the two-person situation to the challenge and stimulus of the more fully 'social' three-person situation. All the problems of the earlier stage are carried forward into the later one, and the form in which the analyst comes upon neurosis in therapeutic investigation seems always at first to be the form in which it was finally shaped in 'the-child-in-the-family-constellation'.

Thus therapeutic analysis investigates the way in which the triangular jealousy situations of early life have become consolidated in the structure of a personality, to be automatically relived in the neurotic disturbance of personal relationships in adult life, and in psychotherapeutic treatment, i.e. transference phenomena.

For Freud then, neurosis had two aspects, symptom-formation and character-structure manifested in disturbed human relationships. Symptoms must be understood in the light of infantile sexuality; and character type with disturbed human relationships in the light of Oedipal problems. These two form one complex and indissoluble whole in the neurotic personality.

One other piece of later psycho-analytic theory can hardly be omitted as part of the 'fundamentals', namely, some form of *super-ego concept* as part of a threefold theory of psychic structure. Here, Freud's original concepts of id, ego and super-ego are due for revision but they represent actual facts of mental organization and development, the theoretical formulation of which must advance to greater accuracy. These facts in question are those of the loss of internal integrity of the psyche through ego-differentiation and ego-splitting. It was Freud's far-reaching discovery that this comes about through the infant becoming divided against himself by means of a part of his psychic life coming to function as an inner replica of external hostile powers, felt to be hostile because they oppose the gratification of his primary needs in his own way.

Thus the criterion of what is or is not psycho-analysis is the acceptance, as fundamental facts, as observable psychic phenomena rather than as theories, of repression, resistance, transference, dreams as a revelation of the unconscious, the centrality of the Oedipus problem in neurosis, and the 'super-ego'. It is inside this framework of facts that all questions of theoretical reformulation, and all problems of more extended research (as into the first year of life)—i.e. all questions of 'progress beyond Freud'—must be raised.

2. *Physiology and Psychology*

The great transition period in the development of psychoanalytical theory was 1920–6. A far-reaching reorientation began then, the full implications of which have only now come to be apparent. The change from a fundamentally biological to a primarily psychological and potentially sociological approach to the study of human beings may be more narrowly defined as a change from an 'organismic' to a 'personal' type of theory. Both are required, but it seems to be the special province of psychoanalysis to accept the findings of physiology and biology and proceed to a study of what goes on between human beings as developing 'persons' and how that determines the shaping and functioning of personality, i.e. to produce a psychodynamic theory.

At first the later orientation was simply superimposed on the earlier one. Much classical psycho-analytical theory betrays an uneasy tension between the two points of view. It is clear from Ernest Jones's *Sigmund Freud: Life and Work*, vol. 1, that this rests upon the never fully resolved conflict in Freud himself between physiology and psychology referred to in chapter 3, between 'science' in the narrower and in the broader sense, and also between the seeker after intellectual and theoretical understanding on the one hand and the doctor and therapist on the other. The publication of Freud's letters to Fliess, and Jones's authoritative and courageous study of Freud's early struggles and development, now put us in a position to understand far more of the way in which Freud's own personality conditioned his theory. Freud, evidently, was primarily a theoretician rather than a physician and therapist in his interests. Jones writes:

To medicine itself he felt no direct attraction. . . . I can recall as far back as in 1910 his expressing the wish with a sigh that he could retire from medical practice and devote himself to the unravelling of cultural and historical problems—ultimately the great problem of how man came to be what he is—and yet the world has rightly greeted him as, among other things, a great physician. (1954, p. 30.)

Jones quotes Freud as saying:

Neither at that time, nor indeed in my later life, did I feel any particular predilection for the career of a physician. I was moved rather by a sort of curiosity, which was, however, directed more towards human concerns than towards natural objects.

Here is another version:

After forty years of medical activity, my self-knowledge tells me that I have never really been a doctor in the proper sense. . . . I have no knowledge of having had in my early years any craving to help suffering humanity. . . . In my youth I felt an overpowering need to understand something of the riddles of the world in which we live. (1954, pp. 30–2.)

Jones comments that Freud's 'divine curiosity' focused on 'the riddles of human existence and origin' rather than on 'the nature of the whole universe' and was pursued with 'a remarkable capacity for abstract thought' and a powerful 'bent towards speculative abstractions' tempered by the rigorous discipline of 'scientific investigations'. (*Op cit.*, p. 32.)

Freud stated : 'I scarcely think, however, that my lack of genuine medical temperament has done much damage to my patients. For it is not greatly to the advantage of patients if their physician's therapeutic interest has too marked an emotional emphasis. They are best helped if he carries out his task coolly and so far as possible with precision.' (Jones, 1954, p. 32.) On the other hand, it may be equally true that Freud's lack of primary therapeutic interest was an unconsciously determined emotional attitude which influenced the development of his theory in the direction of an impersonal scientific orientation and thus obscured issues that are vital for psychotherapy because they are vital for a fully personal psychodynamic understanding.

We now know that Freud underwent a most disturbing conflict in his development from a physiological to a psychological point of view. That is not surprising considering that he faced this crisis in the 1880s and 1890s. What is surprising is that he did make the transition and was the only scientist of his time to do so effectively. Had he failed we might still have been groping in the dark for the all-important clues to the understanding of man. It is too much to expect that even with his genius and courage he could make the transition completely and that the struggle should leave no scars on his theory. His ninety-page *Project for a Scientific Psychology* and the Fliess letters show what a determined attempt he made to base psychology on physiology.

Jones writes :

It has often been assumed that Freud's psychological theories date from his contact with Charcot or Breuer or even later. On the contrary it can be shown that the principles on which he constructed his theories were those he had acquired as a medical student under Brücke's influence. [i.e. Helmholtzian physics and physiology.] *The emancipation from this influence consisted not in renouncing the principles, but in becoming able to apply them empirically to mental phenomena while dispensing with an anatomical basis.* [Present writer's italics.] This cost him a severe struggle. . . . He was later, in his famous wish theory, to bring back into science the ideas of 'purpose', 'intention' and 'aim' which had just been abolished from the universe. We know, however, that when Freud did bring them back he was able to reconcile them with the principles in which he had been brought up; he never abandoned determinism for teleology. (1954, p. 50.)

This is of such extreme importance for the critical appreciation of the eventual limitations of Freud's theory that we must pursue the matter further. Jones writes :

Freud had always been greatly puzzled by the old problem of the relation between body and mind, and to begin with had with his strongly held Helmholtzian principles cherished the hope of establishing a physiological basis for mental functioning. . . . During the years 1888–98 he passed through a severe struggle before he decided to relinquish the idea of correlating somatic and psychical activity. The dawn of the conflict in his mind in this matter may be perceived in his early theory of the anxiety neurosis . . . the bias of Freud's early training is evident. He was on the brink of deserting physiology and of enumerating the findings and theories of his clinical observations in purely psychological language. But with what he called the 'actual neuroses' he saw a chance of saving at least a section of psychopathology for a physiological explanation. . . . A remark he made to me years later dates from this attitude. It was a half-serious prediction that in time to come it should be possible to cure hysteria [sic] by administering a chemical drug without any psychological treatment. On the other hand, he used to insist that one should explore psychology to its limits, while waiting patiently for the suitable advance in biochemistry. (1954, pp. 283–5.)

If ever such a prediction came true it could amount to no more than a physical means of making a complete break with the patient's past history as enshrined in the character and structure of his personality. It would be a physical method of making repression and the splitting of the personality permanent, of destroying the continuous development of the patient's life as a person by the forcible suppression of (as distinct from emotional maturing beyond) the influence on him of the most significant personal relationships of his past. Since the real cure of neurosis is by a process of psychological maturing as a person, a process which can be achieved *only* by living through new experiences in the medium of personal relationships, it is clear that the hoped-for drug-cure would achieve a serious diminution of the integrity of the patient as a person. It would be the answer to the hysteric's prayer for the conversion of all personal problems into bodily ones, and would be the supreme escape from insight and true self-knowledge.

Freud's thinking, however, was not basically carried on in terms of personal categories, and this limited even his phenomenal insight, and exercised an important determining effect on the shaping and emphasis of his theories. Jones writes concerning sexual libido:

Is Libido a mental or physical concept in its origin? So here again might be found a clue to the riddle of the relation of body and mind, of *transforming psychology into a biological or even physiological discipline*. [Present writer's italics.] And it was this aspect of his discovery that really interested Freud. (1954, p. 299.)

Jones again comments:

It may be that Freud's dissatisfaction with the theoretical basis of the concept of 'repression' sprang from his old wish to unite physiological and psychological conceptions. (1954, p. 309.)

Finally Jones remarks:

It is plain that there was for Freud a security in knowledge of the anatomy and physiology of the nervous system. At the height of his anxious heart illness . . . he wrote (May 6, 1894), 'In the summer I hope to return to my old pursuit and do a little anatomy; after all, that is the only satisfying thing'. It was 'scientific', assured and a necessary check on 'speculation'. This was needed more than ever when he 'found himself studying mental processes', and for years he cherished the hope of amalgamating the two fields. Here surely Fliess could help him. For instance . . . 'Perhaps I shall find in you the foundation on which I can begin to build a physiological support and cease to explain things psychologically.' (June 30, 1896.) *It was a long time before Freud brought himself to dispense with the physiological principles of his youth. In a sense he never did entirely . . . a good deal of his later psychology was modelled on them.* [Present writer's italics.] (1954, pp. 329.)

When Freud did at last free himself from the effort to base psychology directly on physiology, he continued to base it on the characteristic pattern of physiological thinking, and never really grasped the fact that as compared with physical phenomena, personal phenomena require a completely new set of concepts for their description and understanding. Psychodynamic theory is an independent discipline whose subject-matter is the personal motivated life of human beings in their mutual relationships. Any attempt to construct such a psychological science on the pattern of physiological thinking involves a depersonalization and falsification of the subject-matter.

The problem of the nature of psycho-analytic terminology is discussed by Ernst Kris in his Introduction to the Fliess letters.

He quotes from a draft by Freud for the joint study in Hysteria with Breuer.

In this Freud put forward the proposition that 'the nervous system endeavours to keep constant something in its functional condition that may be described as the sum of "excitation".' . . . This theoretical assumption, borrowed from the world of physics . . . led eventually to theories about the regulating mechanism of the psyche which belong to the fundamental assumptions of psycho-analysis. . . . (1954, pp. 21–2.)

In those years the dominant idea in Freud's mind was to make physiological changes and the physically measurable the basis of all psychological discussion; in other words his aim was the strict application of ideas derived from Helmholtz and Brücke. (*Op. cit.*, p. 25.)

Not till after his self-analysis, when he was able completely to fuse the dynamic and genetic points of view, did Freud succeed in establishing the distance between the physiological and psychological approaches. (*Op. cit.*, p. 44.)

But in what sense did Freud establish a distance between physiology and psychology. Kris has already pointed out that the theory of the regulating mechanism of the psyche was based on the physiological concept of keeping constant the sum of excitation in the nervous system. Freud's metapsychology with its mental apparatus, defence 'mechanisms', and dynamic, topographic and economic modes of description, etc., is steeped in the impersonal physiological pattern of thinking. The assumption was that 'human science' must follow exactly the thought-forms of 'natural science'.

It is true that Kris states that :

Freud's self-analysis, which opened the way to understanding of the conflicts of early childhood, brought about a shift in his interests. Insights into the conditions in which individual conflict arose in the course of the interaction between the child and its environment—in other words the *intervention of the social aspect* [present writer's italics]—meant that the need to explain psychological processes by immediate physiological factors had lost its urgency. (*Op. cit.*, p. 35.)

But he goes on to say that :

Freud subsequently repeatedly spoke of the connection between psychological and biochemical processes as a field still awaiting exploration, and always emphasized that the terminology of psychoanalysis was provisional, valid only until it could be replaced by physiological terminology. . . . The result was that in studying the structure of the psychical apparatus . . . it was possible to preserve the connection between the physiological and psychological approaches without hampering psycho-analysis by the closeness of the connection. (1954, p. 45.)

The distance, evidently, between physiology and psychology is more apparent than real. It simply means that Freud no longer sought to correlate in detail psychic processes and the anatomy and physiology of the brain and nervous system. His psychology is tied, however, to impersonal physiological modes of conceptualization and no genuinely new type of psychological thinking was evolved adequate to psychodynamics as a new and independent discipline in its own right until Freud made his analysis of the ego. It was a psychology of the physiological organism and its symptoms, not of the 'person'; it discards 'physiological factors' but not 'physiological thought-forms'. It is this severe limitation that has made the development of 'object-relations theory' necessary.

Kris states that

some observers have gained the impression that the fundamental principles of psycho-analysis must be out-of-date because a good deal of its terminology derives from the scientific terminology of the eighties and nineties of last century. The fact is not in dispute. . . . But the terms thus taken over into psycho-analysis have acquired new meanings which have often little to do with their original meanings. . . . The question of the origin of the terminology and fundamental assumptions of psycho-analysis is therefore of only historical interest; it has nothing whatever to do with the question of the value of those assumptions and that terminology for psycho-analysis as a science. (1954, pp. 46–7.)

That, however, fails to grasp the serious nature of the fundamental issue at stake. It is plain that while Freud gave up the attempt to convert psychology into physiology, he never gave up the hope that one day that would be accomplished, and he never fully emancipated himself from the modes of thinking and conceptualization, and the general scientific orientation characteristic of his early physiological training. The result is that, while his clinical discoveries were pushing him in the direction of the study of personality and of personal relationships *per se*, he retained the modes of conceptualization with which he was familiar. Thus, though he initiated and provided most of the materials for a new science of *psycho*dynamics as a discipline in its own right, a 'study of personality', irreducible to any other discipline, his own conclusions and speculations tended to be couched in metapsychological rather than in personal terms. At this stage, he replaced physiology by psychobiology and retained the mode of thought characteristic of the natural sciences. His later concept of the super-ego and revised view of anxiety opened other possibilities.

3. *Psychobiology*

Freud gave us in the first place a psychobiology of man as an organism, not a psychosociology of man as a person. The outstanding fact in Freud's application of his theory to both the psychotherapy of the individual and to social problems is that he operated with an instinct-theory which has a heavy weighting in the direction of biology and physiology. In so far as this was due to his practical preoccupation with the medical problem of neurosis, it led him to the view that civilization was a menace to mental health, and that the problem of neurosis was that of the conflict between instincts and culture. This point of view is not so illuminating when we deal with human relations as it at first seemed in dealing with physical symptoms. It arose out of his attempt, studied in the last section, to cast psycho-analysis into a rigidly scientific theoretical form which led him to de-personalize man and treat the living human being as a 'psychic apparatus' which could be functionally analysed 'metapsychologically' into impersonal psychic processes and mechanisms concerned with the quantitative regulation of instinctive tensions. The 'person' is lost in his processes. As Freud saw the matter, man has a given instinctive constitution biochemically laid down, and the social problem is how to dispose of man's innate instinctive drives by means of release, repression or sublimation. From this he evolved a theory of the general nature of human relations, group psychology and culture.

(*a*) *Instincts.* Freud has permanently enriched our understanding of human nature and created *de novo* out of the study of psychoneurosis the scientific study of the intimate secret inner life of human beings. His discoveries relating to the psychosexuality of childhood, the emotional-cum-sexual conflicts arising for the child in the Oedipal or family-group situation, leading from conscious conflicts to repression and unconscious endopsychic conflict which not only involves the personality in states of acute unhappiness and frustration but also the body in states of tension, dysfunction and illness—all this is to-day accepted. It has revolutionized our approach to man and his problems, and initiated a new era not merely for the treatment of psychic illness, but for child care, the understanding of psychosocial tensions and the interpretation of the human needs and anxieties that motivate art and religion. It forces on us the reconsideration of all the traditional cultural answers to human problems, and is ultimately an indispensable pre-requisite for an adequate philosophy of human existence. To the present writer the work of Freud seems to be the most important of all the scientific developments of the last seventy years in its ultimate ramifications. All this, however, rested on a theory of human instincts.

The general development of Freud's instinct theory is well known. It passed through three stages. First, instincts of self-preservation and race preservation, of hunger and sex, were suggested, the former being regarded as ego-instincts and the latter as belonging to the primary unconscious. With the theory of narcissism, Freud recognized libidinal or sexual instincts in the ego ; and he finally determined on the dualism of libido and aggression in the form of Life instincts and Death instincts. These libidinal and destructive drives were both innate, operated prior to experience, and were at perpetual warfare in the organism. Aggression had nothing originally to do with frustration and operated primarily within the organism working towards its destruction. What we know practically and clinically as aggression was the extraversion of this original self-destructive innate drive, its turning outwards against objects in the interests of self-preservation. This theory means that the basic conflict within human nature is ultimately irreducible and its final outcome in the victory of the destructive drive is staved off for a time only by compromises in which the two opposite drives coalesce, as in sadism and masochism, or else are both turned upon objects as in ambivalence, a problem which is then practically solved for the time being through keeping the two drives apart by choosing different objects for love and hate.

The limitations of Freud's instinct-theory are most clearly revealed when it is examined in the setting of sociological investigation. By 1908 Freud was ready to go beyond individual psychotherapy, and with his paper on ' "Civilized" Sexual Morality and Modern Nervousness' (*C.P.*, II, pp. 76–99) he entered the sociological field. It illustrates a view of instinct from which he never really departed. The impulses of sex and aggression are dangerous innate forces which operate without regard to social necessities and moral values, and the ego must defend itself against them at all costs. Proceeding on the view of some physicians that nervous disorders were a result of the strains imposed on the individual by the pace, demands and overstimulation of modern civilized life, and accepting the view that neuroses were increasing, he singled out, as the chief etiological factor, the undue suppression of the sex instinct brought about by our sexual morality. The neuroses 'originate in the sexual needs of unsatisfied people. . . . We must regard all factors which operate injuriously upon the sexual life and suppress its activity or distort its aims as likewise pathological factors in the psychoneuroses.' (*Op. cit.*, p. 81.) The paper powerfully called attention to facts which needed to be faced. Moreover here Freud outlined plainly his conception of the psychology of civilized social life.

He writes :

Our civilization is, generally speaking, founded on the suppression of instincts. Each individual has contributed some renunciation of this sense of dominating power, and the aggressive and vindictive tendency of his personality.

But sex as well as aggression comes into this scheme.

The sexual instinct is probably more strongly developed in man that in most of the higher animals; it is certainly more constant, since, it has almost entirely overcome the periodicity belonging to it in animals. It places an extraordinary amount of energy at the disposal of 'cultural' activities

because of its

ability to displace its aim without materially losing in intensity. This ability to exchange the originally sexual aim for another which is no longer sexual but is psychically related, is called the capacity for sublimation. (*Ibid.*, p. 82.)

Thus civilization, culture and social life generally, arise from the suppression of the instincts of aggression and sex, and the diversion of their energy to non-sexual ends. (Aggression was regarded by Freud as a specific instinct from 1920.) Freud insisted on instinct as a fixed constitutional 'quantity of drive' always pressing for outlet. He says :

The original strength of the sexual instinct probably differs in each individual; certainly the capacity for sublimation is variable. We imagine that the original constitution pre-eminently decided how large a part of the sexual impulse of each individual can be sublimated and made use of.

The fate of those persons who differ constitutionally from their fellows depends on whether they are endowed with comparatively stronger or weaker sexual impulses in an absolute sense.

The task of mastering such a mighty inpulse as the sexual instinct is one which may well absorb all the energies of a human being. [Present writer's italics.] Mastery through sublimation, diverting the sexual energy away from its sexual goal to higher cultural aims, succeeds with a minority, and with them only intermittently . . . of the others, most become neurotic or otherwise come to grief. (*Ibid.*, pp. 83, 85, 88.)

Granting the correctness of this theory of biochemically determined instinctive drives possessing a fixed and absolute quantity of energy, Freud's conclusions no doubt follow quite logically. (1) 'The energies available for "cultural" development are thus in great part won through suppression . . . of sexual excitation.' (*Op. cit.*, p. 84.) (2) This process of sublimation, nevertheless, has its limitations. 'To extend this process of displacement illimitably is, however, certainly no more possible than with the transmutation of heat into mechanical power in the case of machines.' (*Op. cit.*, p. 83.) We see how Freud falls back on a purely mechanistic, quantitative, theory of motivation. 'Experience teaches that for most people there is a limit beyond which their constitution cannot comply with the demands of civilization. All who wish to reach a higher standard than their constitution will allow, fall victims to neurosis.' (*Op. cit.*, p. 86.) (3) The result of this demand, yet limited capacity, for sublimation, as uncompromisingly stated by Freud, is the production of either criminals or neurotics.

The man who in consequence of his unyielding nature cannot comply with the required suppression of his instincts, becomes a criminal, an outlaw, unless his social position or striking abilities enable him to hold his own as a great man, a 'hero'. Neurotics are that class of people, naturally rebellious, with whom the pressure of cultural demands succeeds only in an apparent suppression of instincts, one which becomes ever less and less effective.

Finally,

it is now easy to predict the result which will ensue if sexual freedom is still further circumscribed, and the standard demanded by civilization is raised to the level . . . which taboos every sexual activity other than that in legitimate matrimony. Under these conditions the number of strong natures who openly rebel will be immensely increased; and likewise the number of weaker natures who take refuge in neurosis owing to their conflict between the double pressure from the influences of civilization and from their own rebellious constitutions. (*Ibid.*, pp. 82, 86, 87.)

(4) Freud's practical conclusion is that we must sacrifice 'perfection' in order to maintain the 'possible', and must relax the stringency of our sexual morality : a view which he did not himself put into effect in his own exemplary marital life.

We have here a full scale social psychology, or rather a psychobiological theory of culture and civilization. It can be controverted only if the fundamental premise of instinct-theory is wrong. Those who see reason for believing that the diagnosis on the basis of this conception of instinct is erroneous will certainly feel that Freud is betrayed into some premature, rash and socially dangerous generalizations. His position differs little from that of Nietzsche for whom the possible alternatives were the superman who is above morality and simply gratifies his instincts because he is strong and no one can stop him, and the crucified Christian with his slave-morality of self-sacrifice and acceptance of suffering. The theory begs the whole question as to whether man is neurotic because he is instinctively anti-social, or whether he is anti-social because he is neurotic : or, to put it differently, whether criminality and neurosis are expressions of natural and vigorous instincts, or whether they are due to early emotional trauma and subsequent immaturity of development.

Freud is landed in the dilemma that the denial of instinct is necessary for culture and civilization, whilst the gratification of instinct and the relaxation of culture is necessary for health. This pessimistic conclusion should arouse our suspicions. Social life, on this view, can never be any other than unending warfare between instinct and morality, the needs of the individual and the demands of the group, or, in another form, the flesh and the spirit. Civilization, culture and social life would have no real roots in the inner nature of the individual who, apparently, is not formed for society in spite of the fact that on other grounds he needs it. They are simply matters of expediency imposed by external force and authority. One is reminded of St. Paul's view of the unending conflict between 'the law of the mind' and 'the law of the members', in which 'the law of the mind' is the external authority of God, just as with Freud the law of morality is the external authority of the social group. Naturally, if this instinct theory, which is the basis of the whole line of reasoning, were true, then Freud would be simply calling our attention to facts and we would have to make the best we could of the situation.

That this theory of the relation between human nature and society must be given careful and critical examination, is clear from the fact that it still forms the basis of much orthodox psychoanalytical social theory. In a book of essays written as a Festschrift in honour of Geza Roheim's sixtieth birthday, entitled *Psycho-analysis and Culture* (1951), we may find up-to-date psycho-analytical pronouncements on the subject. Weston la Barre speaks of the 'marked biologistic orientation (which is one of the great strengths of Freudian psycho-analysis)' (p. 157). Certainly this orientation towards biology, taking into account what La Barre calls 'the body as a place to live in', opened a pathway into the inner meaning of the psychoneuroses, but the question is whether it helps true insights into psychotherapeutic and sociological problems to have a psychodynamic theory which is so tied to biology.

Marie Bonaparte, in the same volume, writes :

In the various social structures man has elaborated he has had to reconcile his instinctual reproductive drives, his sex instincts, with the social exigencies of community living. This has not been accomplished without frustration and suffering. Not only has man had to restrain his sex instincts, but also his aggressive instincts. Social integration has meant renunciation of the right to kill or steal or even to harm his neighbour. Such renunciations also incur suffering, for every instinctual deprivation entails constraint and pain. . . . Man has imposed additional suffering on himself by his social organization which exacts repression of instincts. (*Op. cit.*, p. 145.)

It seems that as long as there are men on earth there will be rivalry between them—domestic rivalry, economic rivalry, sexual rivalry. No form of society appears able to establish paradise on earth, and all that we learn from pscho-analysis, anthropology and sociology shows human beings everywhere in conflict with one another. And although, as far as the sexual instincts are concerned, a healthier freedom prevails in our day, yet as far as the aggressions are concerned there seems little prospect of man's ever achieving equal happiness and goodness. For he is caught on the horns of a dilemma; either he must curb his aggressive instincts and suffer in the process himself, or he may give them free rein and cause suffering to others—his victims. (*Op. cit.*, pp. 148–9.)

Marie Bonaparte has given up as a bad job the possibility of the healthy socialization of man.

It would be idle, of course, to dispute that that is an accurate picture of the historical human situation, which continues to be the same to-day and appears likely to continue as such in any foreseeable future. Yet in fact these statements contain assumptions that cannot be called scientifically proven, or even, in the light of contemporary trends in psychology and psycho-analysis, reasonably substantiated. The whole position ignores the possibility that man's recalcitrant sexual and aggressive compulsions may not after all be due to instinct in the sense of innate and essentially unmodifiable drive, but may be due to a psychological factor not at that time appreciated. It is no argument to cite the fact that man has always been like this, for that need only imply that man has never hitherto understood enough of his own mental make-up to be in a position to bring about changes in himself in the direction of a more genuinely social capacity. The fact that only in our lifetime, for the first time in history, has a Freud laid bare to our understanding the existence of the dynamic unconscious, and that psycho-analysis itself has hardly had time to outgrow its own infancy, should lead us to hesitate before accepting such pronouncements as those cited above as final.

Where does the difficulty about Freud's position lie? It is not that his description of the actual sexual situation of civilized man in our time is inaccurate. He was far too acute an observer not to see the facts clearly, and he saw them far more clearly than most. His picture of the state of sexual frustration inside marriage, and its wider repercussions (1908, *C.P.*, II, pp. 89–99) is both true and challenging. Large numbers of human beings experience a strong and persistent pressure of sexual need either conscious or repressed, and the upsurge of sexual impulses, in a way that finds no gratification within the limits of monogamous marriage and civilized sexual morality. The result naturally is that many *rebel* against restriction, and many more *repress* their needs and fall ill of neurosis. The question concerns the *interpretation* to be put upon these strong sexual impulses. If they are indeed solely manifestations of an innate, constitutionally powerful instinct, then we have little option but to tolerate rebels or to endure the spread of neurosis. Freud, while advocating a relaxation of sexual morality (1908) (which has in fact occurred during this century, largely as a result of two world wars), does not draw a similarly detailed picture of what that can mean in practice, i.e. a weakening respect for marriage, the 'acting out' of neurosis in sexually indiscriminate behaviour which is rationalized as emancipation and enlightenment, and, in spite of contraception, an ever-increasing supply of unwanted children who are denied their rightful parental background and are likely to have to endure in themselves the neuroses their parents are supposed to escape by means of sexual freedom—a social problem of first rate importance. In fact, the relaxation of sexual morality since Freud wrote in 1908 has not led to a diminution of neurosis. Moreover, is the relaxation of morality in the interest of health to apply to the 'instinct' of aggression as well as sex?

But is the basic assumption, that disturbingly powerful sexual and aggressive needs are manifestations of fixed instincts, correct: or may it not be possible that 'instinctive' is here confused with 'neurotic'? Freud never relinquished his dualistic theory of instincts as innate, powerful, drives of a sexual and aggressive order, nor did he ever discard its corollary, that culture and civilization rest on renunciation of instincts. Again and again he takes up the theme. Thus in *Civilization and Its Discontents* he writes:

It is impossible to ignore the extent to which civilization is built up on renunciation of instinctual gratifications, the degree to which the existence of civilization pre-supposes the non-gratification (suppression, repression or something else?) of powerful instinctual urgencies. This cultural privation dominates the whole field of social relations between human beings.

Men are not gentle, friendly creatures wishing for love, who simply defend themselves if they are attacked . . . but a powerful measure of desire for aggression has to be reckoned as part of their instinctual endowment. Culture has to call up every possible reinforcement in order to erect barriers against the aggressive instincts of men and hold their manifestations in check by reaction-formations in men's minds. (1930, pp. 63, 85–7.)

That is an accurate description of our state of affairs, but is this state of affairs due to normal innate instincts or to their neurotic development?

On the face of it, it seems odd that our greatest achievements should arise out of the denial of our primary nature, and rest on our using for cultural purposes energies designed for different and anti-cultural uses. Such a theory calls for the most drastic scrutiny and testing. It implies that our fundamental drive to activity, our 'life-force', is simply the energy of physical appetite, and not a function of the 'total personality'.

In fact, the theory of the 'mighty instinct' is highly misleading and gravely falsifies the facts. Instinct-theory in general has come increasingly under the fire of criticism in both academic and psychotherapeutic circles.

The concept of instinct was borrowed by Freud as a working concept to start with. It was already current in the biological and general thought of his day and was much used by academic psychologists. Freud and W. McDougall made instinct the basis of their psychological theories. Broadly speaking, the concept has proved of more use in animal than in human psychology. Animal behaviour is largely based on *specific* instincts resting on a definite neurological structure. N. Tinbergen, in *A Study of Instinct* (1951), has carried this type of study of the problem of instinct to a remarkable degree of detail and refinement that leaves all earlier studies far behind. The nest-building instinct of birds, the web-spinning instinct of spiders, the pecking instinct of the newly hatched chick, are cases in point; though as one comes higher up in the scale of complexity of animal life, intelligence becomes an increasingly obvious factor in modifying pure instinctive reaction. McDougall's list of fourteen human instincts of a general kind did not establish itself and he ultimately replaced the concept of instinct by that of 'propensity', a more vague and general term, *in the case of human beings.*

The views of academic psychologists on the question may be found in *General and Social Psychology* (Thouless, ch. 3, 1935); and in *Personality* (G. W. Allport, ch. 4, 1949). Simple instinct theory is viewed with disfavour, though the existence of innate motivational factors is accepted. Thouless sums up his discussion as follows:

There seems to be no sufficient reason for saying that all motive forces behind human activity come from the inborn propensities, nor even for the more moderate statement that such motive forces as come from innate propensities are necessarily the strongest ones. To sum up there seems to be no reason for denying the existence of human instincts or propensities if these are defined as innate motive forces behind behaviour. It seems better to avoid the word 'instinct' in connection with human behaviour, since this word may lead to misunderstanding. On the other hand, it is doubtful whether the conception of human instincts or propensities is of much service in explaining differences between societies or between individuals, since it is not possible to determine how far these differences are innate and how far they are acquired. There seem to be strong reasons for rejecting the doctrine that the driving forces behind human behaviour are entirely derived from innate propensities. (*Ibid.*, p. 41.)

G. W. Allport writes:

Does the primordial stream of activity contain within itself directions which determine its own course of development. . . . The instinct theory asserts that there are . . . propensities operating 'prior to experience and independent of training'. . . . In recent years it has become common to reject this somewhat extravagant portrayal of human purposes. . . . The doctrine of drive is a rather crude biological conception. . . . The hypothesis herewith offered is that the doctrine, while inadequate to account for *adult* motivation, does none the less offer a suitable portrayal of the motives of young infants, and for that reason serves very well as the *starting-point* for a theory of motivation. After the level of infancy is passed primitive segmental drive rapidly recedes in importance, being supplanted by the more sophisticated type of motives characteristic of the mature personality. (*Op. cit.*, pp. 112–14.)

Only in its broader outline is the biological theory . . . acceptable . . . the personality itself supplies many of the forces to which it must adjust. (*Op. cit.*, p. 119.)

The psychology of personality must be a psychology of post-instinctive behaviour. . . . Whatever the original drives or 'irritabili-ties' of the infant are, they become completely transformed in the course of growth into contemporaneous systems of motives. (*Ibid.*)

In general the innate factors in human behaviour are now no longer regarded as suitable to be called instincts, a term that is more reserved for the innate specific behaviour patterns of the more primitive forms of life. G. W. Allport's arguments show why even the fascinating modern studies of animal instinct of N. Tin-bergen and the Ethologists do not provide a basis for human psychology any more than the older instinct-theories. Thus the sucking reflex in the new-born infant is instinctive, but the 'suck-ing need and the sucking attitude to life' of the adult neurotic is certainly no simple instinctive phenomenon. McDougall finally discarded the term 'instinct' with reference to man, and used instead the term 'propensity'. McDougall's successors in Britain (Myers, Thouless) adopted the view that instinct is not an actual hereditary impulse or drive, a reified psychic entity or force always pressing for an outlet, but rather an innate directional, determin-ing tendency, a potentiality for action, a latent capacity to react in a way which is appropriate to this or that given object or situa-tion. In particular, it is not held that *specific impulses* exist prior to experience. Rather an innate tendency is a precondition of a specific impulse arising in response to a specific environment. Thus we can react with aggression when there is something to be angry and aggressive about. An 'instinct' of aggression does not mean that we are permanently charged with a destructive drive which is always straining at the leash and seeking outlet whether there be good cause for anger and attack or not. Ginsberg writes :

I incline to the view that aggression is not a primary tendency to hurt or destroy, but rather an intensified form of self-assertion and self-expression, brought into play under conditions of obstruction, or of loss of independence. . . . If this be so, aggression and illwill generally may be a secondary result of thwarting and interference. (1934, p. 106.)

Fairbairn also takes this view that aggression is not a primary response of the infant in that it does not arise independently of frustration of the primary libidinal aims. The problem is not quite so simple when we turn to sex, for sexual impulses are related to a biochemical condition in the body, and the urgency of sexual feelings in adolescence is a result, in part, of physical sexual maturing. Yet if the biological factor of appetite were the only cause of sexual impulses, it is probable that the sex life of human beings would simply manifest the periodicity it has in animals. As Freud noted, 'the sexual instinct . . . is more strongly developed in man than in most of the higher animals, . . . is more constant . . . and has almost entirely overcome periodicity'. (1908, *C.P.*, II, p. 82.) This is because it is now no longer a function of a biological 'organism' merely, serving only the ends of procreation: it is a function of a 'person' whose dominant need is to achieve and maintain good personal relationships with other persons. Sex needs are most pressing and persistent in adult life when there has been a history of love-deprivation in childhood.

As the writer has expressed it elsewhere :

We cannot realise our nature as personal except in relationship with other persons. . . . A human being is an organism with a potentiality for becoming a person, but that potentiality for personality is his real and essential nature, which he does not always realise. Mostly we live more at the organismal level than at the personal level, but even when we behave more as an organism than as a person there is always either a blind or else a conscious striving for the personal life. . . . The appetitive compulsion symbolises our reaching out after personal relationship, as is conspicuously the case in sexual compulsions. It is the individual who is inwardly isolated from other people, who has no genuine flow of sympathetic, friendly feeling towards others, who cannot really love, who is driven in desperation to clutch at physical contact to make up for inability to achieve emotional rapport. If, on the other hand, such an individual has inhibited all emotional response and physical impulse with it, he may fall back on purely intellectual intercourse which is impersonal and concerned with ideas rather than with people. One can argue and discuss with people with whom one has nothing really in common, but if one has little capacity for having 'something in common' with other folk, then intellectual interests may give an illusory sense of still maintaining human contacts. Depersonalised physical and depersonalised intellectual intercourse should rank equally as betrayals of truly human living, as substitutes for genuine personal relationships. (Guntrip, 1949, pp. 159–62.)

Looked at in this way the so-called sex instinct appears in quite a different light. Relationship is achieved with both the mind and the body, and a sexual relationship is one among other pathways of escape from emotional and personal isolation into the security and fulfilment of sharing one's life intimately with another person. A human being whose basic human relationships in childhood and adult life were, and are, good, satisfying and permanent, does not experience a ceaseless upsurge of painfully imperious and demanding sexual impulses. Sexual desire arises rather as a realistic response to a really appreciated external love-object. There is no 'mighty impulse' the task of mastering which 'may well absorb all the energies of a human being'. (1908, *C.P.*, II, p. 88.) Actual sexual impulses, like aggressive impulses, when they possess this overmastering compulsive quality, are a response to a situation of frustration and deprivation. They are not 'innate' *qua* 'impulses', they are rather 'being aroused' all the time; and not simply by an externally frustrating present-day environment but by the way in which frustration in early development became embedded in the internal structure of the personality itself. It can happen that compulsive aggression and sexual need are experienced inside a good marriage where objective frustration is at a minimum. These upsurging emotions and impulses are, in truth, not primarily reactions to the objects and situations of the outer world of the present day even though they are directed to them. They are reactions to situations of frustration perpetuated from childhood in the inner, unconscious, psychic world which is played upon by the outer world. It is because these impulses surge up from within the psyche that they were for so long mistakenly misinterpreted as innate instinctive manifestations *qua* impulses. Academic psychology to-day no longer equates instinct and impulse, but regards instinct as the potentiality of impulse, while an actual impulse is the evoking of the potential reaction in response to an object. Thus Cohen finds occasion 'to cast doubt on the value of instinct theory altogether as an explanatory principle in human conduct'. (1946, p. 36.) The 'mighty impulses' of sex and aggression, which for Freud were instincts, are regarded by Karen Horney as 'neurotic trends', that is, not as the original data of psychic life but as developments needing explanation and correction.

A more accurate analysis of the nature of the unconscious

enables us to discard the older instinct theory with its pessimistic and fatalistic implications for social life. Sexual difficulties can now be seen as due not to the constitutional strength of the sex instinct, but to the developmental immaturity of the whole personality, and more specifically to the internal and unconscious perpetuation in the psyche of the frustrating object-relations of early life. Neurotic suffering is not due to the repression of strong and healthy constitutional sexuality, but to the struggle to master infantile and immature sexual needs which are kept alive by the situation in the unconscious inner world.

We are thus not tied down to Freud's conclusions that a relaxation of cultural and moral standards is the only escape from neurosis for the majority. The position is rather that cultural and moral standards, which, however, need to be subjected to rational and enlightened criticism and development, are, at their best, an expression of the way in which reasonably mature individuals behave, the way in which in fact Freud himself behaved in private life. The struggle to live up to them does not cause neurosis. That puts the cart before the horse. It is because neurosis is already there that reasonable moral standards cannot be lived up to. Relaxation of moral standards could be called for as a concession to the ubiquitous low level of mental health in all communities, but is not called for as a concession to the innate instincts of reasonably mature and healthy-minded persons. The notion that civilization rests on the renunciation of instincts is a misleading ideology that there is now urgent need to discard.

We must, however, pay tribute to Freud for his courageous and ruthless logic which, working with the best psychodynamic concepts available in 1908 (which were themselves the result of his own work) exposed faithfully a state of affairs which still urgently needs attention in our own day. The important issue at stake, theoretically, is that if his 'instinct-diagnosis' were true the problem could be solved only by repression or cultural regression. The diagnosis now available opens the prospect of solving the problem by promoting conditions that aid the emotional maturing of the individual, without necessitating the sacrifice of cultural aims.

(b) *Culture.* We must, however, look further into the general theory of culture, civilization and social life which Freud erected on the basis of his instinct-theory, for it involves many other matters of great importance besides sexual morality, such as the Freudian theories of science, art, morality in general, religion and the relationship between the material and psychic components of culture. Twenty years after the paper we have discussed, in *The*

Future of an Illusion (1927), Freud still held the same basic position. The book opens with a discussion of the nature of Culture. (*Op. cit.*, pp. 7–28.)

This we may summarize as follows :

(i) The ideal is a culture without coercion which gives free play to instinctive gratification.

(ii) This, however, is impossible because man's endowment includes destructive forces.

(iii) He defines culture as that which raises human life above animal conditions, and as consisting of two parts, material and psychical, i.e. knowledge and power to master nature and the arrangements for regulating human relations. He holds that coercion is the foundation of all actual culture.

The important part of culture is not the material part (mastery of nature) but the psychical part (mastery of human nature, of instinct). Freud regards every individual as naturally an enemy of culture, even though it is also a natural universal concern. He holds that although men cannot maintain their existence alone, they also cannot put up with the restrictions and sacrifices necessary to living together. Thus what is necessary for existence has to be defended against our very nature. Culture has to be forced on the resisting mass by a powerful few, and must, therefore, not only suppress man's destructive impulses but reconcile men to instinctual renunciation. The theoretical ideal of 'no coercion and full instinctual gratification' must be given up in favour of the practical ideal of producing superior people who have insight and can master their own wishes. Freud thinks that although it might seem that a social organization which did not coerce or suppress instincts ought to lead to satisfying enjoyment of living, it would not work out that way, for there are destructive and antisocial tendencies in everyone, and the majority of people are lazy, unintelligent and not prepared to be other than unruly. The main business of culture, then, is to compensate men for the sacrifices of natural impulse that must of necessity be enforced, while reducing these to a minimum, thus reconciling men to what is necessary for their very existence. (Cp. 1927, pp. 9–12.)

Freud shares his thoroughly pessimistic view of human nature with Hobbes, Machiavelli, Schopenhauer and Pareto (and also with Mussolini and Hitler who, as dictators are bound to be, were contemptuous of the masses they thought only fit to be controlled). He differs in his ultimate faith in the still small voice of scientific reason. He bases his view on the destructive tendencies actually existing in men, but in fact the matter goes deeper. *On his general theory, libido as well as aggression is basically antisocial.* Libido is, for Freud, fundamentally pleasure-seeking and narcissistic, which involves the prostitution of the object to the role, not of intrinsically valuable end, but merely of utilitarian means to the subjective gratification of the individual. On the theory that sensual gratification is the goal, it is, strictly speaking, an irrelevant matter what happens to the sexual object after she or he has been used. Freud has to resort to the theory of aim-inhibited instincts and sublimation to conjure altruistic—i.e. truly object-seeking—impulses out of non-altruistic human nature. This involves only a negative theory of culture as existing to enforce and reconcile man to the renunciation of antisocial instincts. Freud viewed culture as control of instinct to make human relations possible at all. He seems oblivious to the requirement of personality theory, that culture should be seen as the development and fulfilment of human beings as persons, not mere organisms. It is the meaning of human relations.

Freud's theory of culture rests ultimately on the view that aggressive and libidinal impulses are essentially non-altruistic and represent a basic biologically determined instinctive endowment, which lies behind even their frustrated form, and which cannot be changed.

Thus human nature is innately unfitted for, and hostile to, good personal relationships. It is only fitted for the exploitation of objects in the interests of biological appetitive needs. If good personal relations are preferred, it is for reasons of expediency and because mutuality heightens pleasure, not because they are an intrinsic good, the really needed experience, in themselves. Good personal relations must as far as possible be enforced, because, if they are not, even pleasure is ultimately impossible, a completely nihilistic theory. Freud outdoes Hobbes's 'state of nature' which is 'nasty, brutish and short'. He thinks that but for the coercion of culture any man would rape any woman he liked and kill anyone who tried to stop him, and rob without any hesitation, and life would be one long delight—but for the fact that others would do the same to him. There is no such thing as natural good feeling. Only fear can restrain human beings, for their nature is wholly antisocial.

It does not ease matters to say that coercion is a practical necessity because of the cultural embitterment of man. That is true, but *Freud's theory is that human nature is innately self-seeking, pleasure-seeking (not object-seeking), and is to be socialized only under very heavy pressure; and then only from non-altruistic motives, and under a never-relinquished repressed protest and revolt.* Recent developments more and more establish the opposite view that good personal relationship is not desired merely for the sake of pleasure but is in itself the basic need and aim of men, whose nature cannot be fulfilled without it, while aggression and pleasure-seeking only result from the frustration of this primary aim.

Karen Horney writes :

Freud had a pessimistic outlook on human nature and, on the ground of his premises, was bound to have it. As he saw it, man is doomed to dissatisfaction whichever way he turns. He cannot live out satisfactorily his primitive natural drives without wrecking himself and his civilization. He cannot be happy alone or with others. He has but the alternative of suffering himself or making others suffer. It is all to Freud's credit that, seeing things this way, he did not compromise with a glib solution. Actually within the framework of his thinking there is no escape from one of these two alternative evils. At best there may be a less unfavourable distribution of forces, better control, and 'sublimation'. (1951, p. 377.)

Freud did, in the sphere of psychodynamic theory, what Hume did in philosophy ; he pursued a possible negative theory with un-compromising logic to its final conclusions, and produced the same kind of effect, namely that of forcing enquiry into a new direction. If Freud's view of human nature, and hence of social organization, makes little positive contribution to sociology, it must be said that it clears the field for a constructive social psychology. Above all, he forces us to face the fact that the stability of any society depends on how far its structure and culture enable the individual to cope with his intrapsychic conflicts. Freud's problem, viewing man as he did, was to explain how social life could persist at all in face of man's antisocial nature. Here a curious fact emerges. Though we hold that man's nature is not primarily antisocial, and the antisocial factors at work in human behaviour are due, not to innate instinct, but to immaturity of development, the practical result, so far as immediate difficulties in socializing man are concerned, is much the same. Whether due to native instinct, or to the infantile condition of the emotional (as distinct from the intellectual) life of the majority of human beings, men do manifest socially destructive forms of both sexual and aggressive impulse. The basic theory makes a great difference to our view of the *final* possibilities of personal and social progress ; but, either way, the *immediate* cultural task is to devise ways and means of enforcing social organization. The question of control of (either innate or immature and neurotic) impulses, and of compensation for their renunciation arises, and with it what Freud calls 'the psychical inventory of culture', morality, art, religion and politics. Psychotherapy comes in here as an attempt not merely to relieve symptoms but to mature and socialize the individual. Before these special questions could be dealt with satisfactorily, we need a basic theory of human nature which will enable us to transcend Freud's pessimistic, psychobiological theory that (i) human instincts are intrinsically antisocial, and therefore (ii) culture must inevitably be basically disciplinary, coercive and negative, so that (iii) the possibilities of both individual therapy and social betterment are extremely limited. In fact, Freud's ego-analysis opened the way to this.

(c) *Psychotherapy*. The two halves of Freud's theory, the earlier psychobiology of instinct and the later psychological analysis of the structure of the ego, each involve a different approach to psychotherapy. This, it seems, was hardly realized, no doubt owing to the fact that it was not recognized that the later analysis of the ego called for a revision of the instinct-theory.

The view of psychotherapy necessitated by the instinct-theory remained the basis of Freud's views on the matter. This theory was the underlying cause of the pessimism Freud came to feel not only about social life but about the therapeutic value of psychoanalysis in contrast to its great value as a scientific method of research into the dynamic constitution of human nature. Dr. C. Thompson states that periodically the psycho-analytic movement experienced waves of disillusionment and pessimism about therapeutic results.

In face of powerful antisocial instincts, there are only three possibilities : one can *release* these drives and become criminal, or *repress* them and become neurotic, or (and this is a possibility only open to the favoured few to any extent) *sublimate* them into socially acceptable activities. Neurosis on this view arises out of the conflict of instinct and culture, the battle of a largely unmodifiable constitutional make-up in the individual against an unyielding environment. In so far as the environment won, neurosis was the result.

Freud's view of psychotherapy then was twofold, (i) to induce the environment to lower its standards and demands on the individual, and (ii) to support and strengthen the ego in its struggle against the overpowering strength of instincts. Psycho-analytic therapy would aim to ease off over-severe repression on these instincts, strengthen the ego to a greater capacity for rational control and for replacement of repression by sublimation, and thus induce the ego (and if possible society) to be more tolerant and permissive to them. Nothing could really be done about the instincts themselves which remain lord and master of all. Therapeutic possibilities on the basis of this doctrine are limited, and this is, in fact, the position with regard to all short-term therapeutic measures.

The hard core of neurosis was the Oedipus conflict, the imperious demands of the child's instincts for possession of one parent, with jealousy, hate and aggression against the other. This conflict developed from three to five years of age, which was the important period, and the conflict was basically a biological fact. The problems of earlier oral and anal phases were regarded as 'pre-genital' and dealt with in terms of their relationship to the genital and Oedipal phase. Human life was one long struggle with a recalcitrant organic make-up which does not fit us for social relationships. Psychotherapy was the problem of instinct-mastery and the possibilities of success were inherently very limited, confined to an amalgamation of repression, sublimation and control.

Naturally psychotherapeutic success was achieved in sufficient measure, or psycho-analysis would have broken down under the impact of clinical failure. The theory, however, did not adequately explain the success. Nevertheless, the permanent foundations of a true psychotherapy were laid in the aims of undoing repression by utilizing the transference. Furthermore, the psychobiological theory did open the way for the understanding of the physical symptoms of neurosis and the whole problem of the involvement of the body in the tensions and conflicts of the personality. The theory of 'hysterical conversion' was fairly established and the ground ultimately prepared for the present-day investigations into psychosomatic disease.

4. The Criticisms of Freud's Instinct-Theory by the 'Culture Pattern' School

These have recently been summarized by Clara Thompson in *Psychoanalysis: Evolution and Development* (1952). She says that her 'slant is towards the cultural interpersonal school' (p. xi), and she represents the critical approach to Freud characteristic of those in America who are influenced by Harry Stack Sullivan, Karen Horney and Erich Fromm. The general criticism is that Freud described 'man' as he saw him in Vienna at the end of last century, as shaped by the Western European culture-pattern, and uncritically took that to represent 'universal, biological man'. Man's typical impulses and emotions were assumed to come from innate instinctive drives. What he really described was the emotional condition which was typical of the majority of human beings developing under certain recognizable environmental conditions and social pressures at a given place and period. As the present writer would prefer to put it, *Freud equated average or general immaturity with innate constitutional make-up*. Therefore he saw the social problem as that of an unremitting battle to tame and control fixed antisocial instincts, instead of as the problem of how to develop mature individuals. Thompson writes:

The emphasis on constitution turned attention away from what we would now call the cultural orientation. . . . The impression grew on Freud that the patient fell ill primarily because of the strength of his own instinctual drives. . . . It tended to close his mind to the significance of environment and led him to pay too little attention to the role of the emotional problems of parents in contributing to the difficulties of their children.

Freud claimed that libidinal pleasure in body functions was important in the dynamics of neurosis, wheras many think to-day that the dynamics of neurosis are derived from other sources. Freud did not envision people in terms of developing powers and total personalities. He thought of them much more mechanistically—as victims of the search for the release of tension. (1952, pp. 9–10, 42–3.)

Thompson suggests that his essay on *Analysis, Terminable and Interminable* (1951, *C.P.*, V, p. 316) 'brought his biological thinking to its logical dead end' (p. 14).

Of Freud's two 'instinct-theories' the earlier placed the stress on libidinal drives, while the later brought aggression to the forefront.

(*a*) *Libido*. Referring to the fact that Freud 'often mistook cultural phenomena for biological-instinctual phenomena' (p. 34), Thompson says of the Libido theory, with its oral, anal, phallic and genital phases, that he observed accurately the 'general order of development in our society' (p. 35), but he failed to recognize how cultural factors determined and influenced the pattern. Thus customs with regard to feeding and cleanliness training of infants, and attitudes to infantile masturbation, vary enormously in different cultures, some of which are easy and permissive while others are rigid and repressive. Granted that the oral phase is biologically determined by the fact that the mouth is the baby's 'most adequate organ' (p. 35), difficulty arises, not out of an overstrong drive to oral pleasure but out of unsatisfactory and frustrating experiences with the feeding mother which would intensify needs and desire. One of my patients dreamed of having her favourite meal, and just as she came to the nicest bit her mother came in and snatched it away from under her nose; when she protested her mother said: 'Don't be a baby.' Moloney reports that among the Okinawans where nursing habits are free and the nursing period lengthy, the people grow up flexible, loving and anxiety-free. (J. C. Moloney, *The Magic Cloak*, 1949.)

Concerning Freud's anal stage Thompson holds that :

Cultural factors dominate the picture. . . . The emphasis at this stage belongs not on the pleasure the child gets from retaining and expelling faeces, but on the struggle with the parents. The child's wish to do what he wants whenever he wishes comes here for the first time into sharp conflict with the parent's plans. This is what puts its stamp on the character of the child. Parents who set a great store on regularity and neatness usually have in their whole attitude to life rigidities and rituals which are also forced on the child. (1952, pp. 36–7.)

How far parents can be tolerant or strict is in turn a reflection of the pattern of their culture. Even parents who, left to themselves, would be lenient, are afraid of what neighbours and friends will think of them and their child. Thompson observes that since 'The maturing of the nerve pathways of both anus and penis, in so far as they serve as organs of excretion, occurs at about the same time' (p. 37), the occurrence of an anal phase earlier than a phallic one must be culturally determined.

There is a biological factor determining interest in the genital at the phallic phase, but in our culture this is greatly frowned on by most parents and 'out of this cultural attitude comes the fear of castration which Freud considered one of the chief sources of anxiety in man' (p. 38). In fact, however, that is too superficial an explanation of castration-fear.

Thus, instead of a fixed, innate, biological process of the developing of the libidinal sexual drive through predetermined stages, the reality is a complex and by no means fixed but changing pattern of cultural attitudes and customs which shape the form and intensity of libidinal drives to the accompaniment of pleasure or anxiety in interpersonal relationships. The occurrence and form of the Oedipus complex and the latency period are also, for Thompson, largely culturally determined phenomena.

(*b*) *Aggression.* This was early stressed by Adler in opposition to Freud's emphasis on sex. It was more specifically accepted at a later period by Freud as an important factor in neurosis, and was provided for in his third instinct theory by the concept of a death instinct. This was a basic drive to eliminate, not merely the tensions of sex, but the tensions of life itself, by a return to the inorganic state. Clinically, Freud saw this as a *destructive* urge, aimed primarily against the self, and needing to be, either modified by mixture with libido to form masochism and sadism, or else turned outwards as aggression against others. We have to be aggressive to save ourselves from self-destruction. Now while this is true of neurotic aggression, which always operates destructively against the self within when damned up by anxiety and guilt and so blocked from outward expression, yet Freud's theory of the death instinct is an unnecessarily tortuous way of accounting for the primary capacity for aggression.

Few orthodox analysts have been able to accept the death instinct theory. Fenichel in particular has criticized it radically. Some of his objections are as follows :

There is no proof that (aggressive drives) always and necessarily came into being by a turning outwards of more primary self-destructive drives. . . . It seems rather as if aggressiveness were originally . . . a mode in which instinctual aims are sometimes striven for, in response to frustrations or even spontaneously. . . . A death instinct would not be compatible with the approved biological concept of instinct. . . . The facts on which Freud based his concept of a death instinct in no way necessitate the assumption of two basically opposite kinds of instincts, the aim of one being relaxation and death, the aim of the other being a binding into higher units. . . . The clinical facts of self-destruction likewise do not necessitate the assumption of a genuine self-destructive instinct. (1945, pp. 59–60.)

In his paper on *A Critique of the Death Instinct* (1954, pp. 370–1) Fenichel observes that when

the conception that in the neurotic conflict two kinds of instinct, i.e. ego and sex, struggle with each other was abandoned it was able to return in a more dangerous variant, namely, in the theory that neurosis rests upon a conflict of two kinds of instinctual qualities, a self-destructive one, the death instinct, and an 'erotic' ego which was afraid of its death instinct. Such an interpretation would mean a total elimination of the social factor from the etiology of neuroses, and would amount to a complete biologization of neurosis.

As Thompson points out, it is quite unproved that the processes leading to normal organic decay and death have any connection with the origin of destructive and aggressive drives. Freud

assumes that suicide and destructiveness towards others are products of the death instinct. More recent observation by others suggests, however, that they have much more to do with the feeling of being thwarted in living. . . . Freud did not give sufficient weight to the significance of the interplay of the personalities of parents and children. Therefore he attributed the frequent evidence of destructiveness in children to an inherent drive which began to assert itself at the anal stage. . . . The children who inflict pain with the intention of hurting are children who have been treated cruelly or oversternly. . . . Aggression normally appears in response to frustration. . . . Serious destructiveness seems to be developed by malevolent environments. . . . The tendency to grow, develop and reproduce seems to be a part of the human organism. When these drives are obstructed by neurotic parents or as a result of a destructive cultural pattern, then the individual develops resentment and hostility either consciously or unconsciously or both. In short, far from being a product of the death instinct, it is an expression of the organism's attempt to live. . . . [Freud] sees man predominantly as an instinct-ridden animal and does not give adequate weight to the overwhelming importance of social factors in moulding as well as distorting man's potentialities. (1952, pp. 52–5.)

Thus Freud's instinct-theory, carrying with it a social and therapeutic pessimism, is broken down by these critics into a theory of human nature as shaped during the course of its development by the pressures exerted on it by interpersonal relations in some given cultural pattern. The form and intensity of troublesome and anti-social sexual and aggressive impulses are not predetermined by the biological inheritance of fixed instincts; they are shaped in the course of individual developmental life-history, and are maintained by the culture patterns which determine the way interpersonal relationships are experienced.

CHAPTER VI

THE LATER FREUDIAN STRUCTURAL
THEORY AND ANALYSIS OF THE EGO

1. *Ego-Analysis and Endopsychic Conflict*

ANNA FREUD has stated that:

When the writings of Freud, beginning with *Group Psychology and the Analysis of the Ego* and *Beyond the Pleasure Principle*, took a fresh direction, the odium of analytical unorthodoxy no longer attached to the study of the ego and interest was definitely focussed on the ego-institutions. Since then the term 'depth-psychology' certainly does not cover the whole field of psycho-analytical research. (1936, p. 4.)

The publication of Freud's *The Ego and the Id* (1923) and *Inhibitions, Symptoms and Anxiety* (1926) may be taken as marking the maturing of the new development that came about in his writings from 1920 to 1926. Its practical importance appears with the publication of *Character Analysis* by Wilhelm Reich (1935) and *The Ego and the Mechanisms of Defence* by Anna Freud (1936), where it is clear that ego-analysis had taken a central place in psycho-analytical therapy. W. Reich realized that to analyse id-material (i.e. deep unconscious infantile material) direct, without analysing first the 'character-armour' of the ego with its defences and resistances against the deep unconscious, is to court failure or to arrive at intellectual insight only, unaccompanied by any dynamic emotional change in personality-structure.

Anna Freud wrote that the definition of psycho-analysis as

pre-eminently a psychology of the unconscious . . . of the id . . . immediately loses all claim to accuracy when we apply it to psycho-analytic therapy. From the beginning analysis, as a therapeutic method, was concerned with the ego and its aberrations : the investigation of the id and of its mode of operation was always only a means to an end. And the end was invariably the same : the correction of these abnormalities and the restoration of the ego to its integrity. (1936, p. 4.)

Nevertheless, on her own admission, 'the odium of analytical unorthodoxy' had, prior to 1920, attached to the direct study of the ego.

The development of the years 1920 to 1936 may be described in the words of the title of Franz Alexander's book of the same period, *The Psycho-Analysis of the Total Personality* (1930). A psychodynamic theory of the whole personality was what Freud aimed to provide in his theory of the id, ego and super-ego. Fairbairn maintains that in fact he imposed a new ego-psychology upon an earlier instinct- and impulse-psychology with which it was incompatible. It is clear from *The Future of an Illusion* (1927) and *Civilization and its Discontents* (1930), both written in this period, that Freud saw no need for modifying his earlier biological orientation in the light of this later more strictly psychological ego-analysis.

However, we must consider the immediate problem that confronted Freud. The objective of psychotherapy is the resolution of psychic conflicts which cripple the individual's capacity to live effectively in his outer world. Now psychic conflicts are broadly of two kinds; firstly, conflicts between the individual as a total self, a whole psyche, and his environment; and, secondly, conflicts within the individual as a divided psyche, in which he operates as a mentally self-frustrating entity. Conflict *originates* between the whole psyche and the environment, but comes to be reflected in the internal development of the psyche itself. Some external conflicts are primary, therefore, and due to an actually difficult or hostile environment. Others are secondary, and due to the projection back into the external situation of conflicts of internal origin. *It is the endopsychic conflict that constitutes the real problem for psychotherapy* for it may be activated by external difficulties, but it may also operate independently when the environmental situation causes no trouble. How often do we hear the complaint: 'I am worrying all the time and really I have nothing to worry about.'

Endopsychic conflicts, however, are structural phenomena. It was early realized that there is no such thing as isolated impulses or emotions, as entities *per se*, conflicting inside the psyche as in a kind of arena. Impulses and emotions are dynamic aspects or activities of psychic structures and *endopsychic conflict is a manifestation of structural differentiations of a contradictory kind*. That is what is meant by 'splits' in the originally unitary psyche. Freud regarded each differentiation as adding more difficulties for the functioning of the mind, thus causing greater instability and further breakdown-points for illness. (Cp. 1921, pp. 103–4.) It is important, therefore, for our understanding of psychic conflict and of our psychotherapeutic attempts to resolve it, that we should understand just how endopsychic structural differentiation develops; and whether, in spite of individual differences, it produces something like a common basic pattern of mental organization and inner conflict in all human beings. Freud's theory of the id, ego and super-ego boldly affirms that it does and we must trace the evolution of that theory.

2. The Development of Freud's Ego-Analysis

Beyond the Pleasure Principle (1920), in which Freud worked out his speculative theory of the death instinct, could, perhaps, be regarded as a neurological philosophy of human nature. At this stage we are concerned only with the account of the 'ego' it contains, as the starting-point of a new psycho-analytical development. Speaking of the ego of psychology Freud realized that psycho-analysis had first seen it only as an instrument of censorship and repression, and thought it better not to contrast the conscious and the unconscious, but the ego and what was repressed. This repressing ego is equivalent to the mental apparatus in its higher strata, which aims to bind any instinctual excitation that may reach the 'primary process' to prevent its causing a disturbance that would be like a traumatic neurosis. The previous growth of libido theory, he observes, had opposed 'sexual instincts' which aim at an object and 'ego instincts' such as those of self-preservation. But coming closer to the ego with the development of the theory of narcissism, he described it as the sole source of all libido. The ego becomes one of the child's 'sexual' objects, an object of 'narcissistic' libido; and this 'narcissistic' libido is both an expression of the sexual instinct and is identical with the instinct of self-preservation. The opposition between the sexual instinct and the ego instincts, therefore, no longer holds good. Libidinal instincts are not confined to the id but operate in the ego, and the distinction between id and ego begins to fade. Freud then went further and decided that there were other (non-libidinal) instincts in the ego besides the self-preservative instinct now newly recognized as libidinal, though he thought that ego-analysis was not sufficiently advanced to make it clear what they were.

The view that the ego contained libidinal instincts of a narcissistic nature and was the primary source even of object-libido (which is ego-libido turned outwards to objects, whence it may be introverted again in secondary narcissism) prompted Freud to closer ego-analysis. He decided that the ego contained also destructive instincts aiming at the reduction of all life-tensions, and restoration to the original status of inanimate matter, i.e. death instinct. Just as object-libido is the extraversion of narcissistic ego-libido, so aggression is the extraversion of self-destructive ego-trends. (Cp. 1920, pp. 68–72.)

At this point the position has become confused. Freud began with an unconscious which was the source of all energy, and from which libidinal drives surged up to be 'bound' and repressed by the ego or higher strata of the mental apparatus, in the interests of self-preservation. With the recognition of libidinal instincts in the ego, however, this distinction between the instinctive unconscious and a purely defensive ego broke down. Strictly speaking, what later came to be called the id was now no longer in its primary nature different from the ego or vice versa. The ego and the instinctual unconscious are both libidinally instinctive and the difference between them really disappears. The difference between the repressed instinctive sexual unconscious and the repressing conscious and preconscious ego has become unimportant by comparison with the much more fundamental opposition between libidinal and destructive, or life and death, instincts, all of which operate primarily in the ego itself, from which they are secondarily turned outwards on to objects. The ego has now become the primary reservoir of both libido and aggression. It would seem, then, that the instinctive unconscious and the ego are one and the same, while the unconscious in which psycho-analysis is interested —the repressed unconscious—is a secondary thing, originating in the splitting off from the primary ego of that portion of its libidinal and destructive energies which have become turned outwards away from itself on to objects, thereby encountering environmental dangers. This is not really a theory of an id and ego, but a theory of primary ego-splitting, and it is hardly possible to reconcile this with the later view of a primary instinctive id on the surface of which an ego develops by contact with the external world, and as a purely controlling agency. At least, in the two cases the term 'ego' is used in radically different senses.

In *Beyond the Pleasure Principle* the ego has swallowed up everything and has become in effect the basic unitary primary total psychic self. That is, in my opinion, the most satisfactory view of the ego to take, for then development takes place along the lines of the differentiation or splitting of this primary unitary psyche into opposing structures, as a result of difficulties encountered in external object-relations. The orthodox psycho-analytic ego is but a partial, secondary, controlling ego resulting from this splitting : for Freud did not hold to the view of the ego that he had here arrived at, evidently because his biological orientation forbade him after all to regard instincts as ego properties. Kris refers to the subsequent history of Freud's ego-analysis when he writes:

Freud's ideas were constantly developing, his writings represent a sequence of reformulations, and one might therefore well take the view that the systematic cohesion of psycho-analytic propositions is only, or at least best, accessible through their history. The clearest instance of such a reformulation was the gradual introduction of structural concepts. The introduction of these new concepts has never fully been integrated with the broad set of propositions developed earlier. (152, p. 304.)

In the next book, *Group Psychology and the Analysis of the Ego* (1921), Freud uses ego-analysis as a means of explaining the libidinal nature of group ties. His view was that what binds individuals together into an organized group is a complex process. He rejects the simple notion of a Herd Instinct, which in any case merely gives a name to group ties without attempting to understand them. Each individual identifies himself with the leader in that part of his ego which Freud calls the 'ego-ideal'. He then substitutes the leader for his ego-ideal, thus falling completely under the leader's direction, and he identifies himself in the remainder of his ego with all other group members as equal objects of the leader's love. This rests upon an analysis of the ego into two parts on what is clearly a different principle from the distinction between life and death instincts. There the starting-point is biology. Here the starting-point is psychology; i.e. not distinctions which are regarded as innate in the organism, but distinctions which arise in the ego after birth as a result of experiences in object-relationships.

He describes the historical development of 'mental differentiations' as taking place in three stages. First 'our mental existence' —i.e. the total primary psychic self as a unity—is separated by birth from the world of objects represented in the first place by the mother: the primary identification of subject and object is dissolved, or at least the condition of physical separateness of subject and object is established which makes possible its gradual dissolution. The second step is taken when after birth mental experience separates out into an organized ego and another part which is repressed and unconscious. This is further clarified by his note on Le Bon's unconscious which is largely a racial mind with which psycho-analysis is not concerned. Freud recognized a nucleus of the ego which he called an 'archaic heritage' which is unconscious, but distinguishes a 'repressed unconscious' from it.

So far we are on the same ground as in *Beyond the Pleasure Principle*. The ego is the primary reservoir of all instinctive energies, libidinal and aggressive, containing within itself an 'archaic heritage' of the human mind, and a split-off portion to form the *secondary* or 'repressed unconscious', i.e. the unconscious with which psycho-analysis is concerned. The implication is that what remains, as a repressing and controlling ego, is likewise secondary, and also that the 'repressed unconscious' has a basically ego-nature. It follows that the differentiation of the repressed unconscious and the repressing ego can be regarded as the first split in the primary fundamental ego. Nevertheless Freud did not recognize these implications or use them as the basis for his final scheme, for there the term 'ego' is used exclusively in a more restricted sense.

Freud now speaks of the 'coherent ego' (as if the unconscious had lost by repression, its coherent ego-quality and become something impersonal, later to be called an 'id'), and the third step is taken with its division into ego and ego-ideal. He had worked out this process in his earlier articles *On Narcissism: An Introduction* (1914, *C.P.*, IV, p. 30) and on *Mourning and Melancholia* (1917, *C.P.*, IV, p. 152) and now utilized the results. The ego-ideal is a differentiating grade in the ego which forms out of all the limitations imposed on the ego by the external world. His description of this division in the coherent ego, on the basis of his analysis of melancholia, shows that it is a purely psychological phenomenon arising out of experiences in object-relationships. The bitter self-criticism it carries on shows that it holds an identification of the ego with a hated object. The part which carries on the criticism is the 'ego-ideal' or conscience, in which the demands of the environment are enshrined. Thus the ego has become split into two mutually hostile parts, one of which remains fundamentally 'ego' and which has incorporated and is identified with a lost loved object, and the other of which has likewise incorporated and is identified with external, and especially parental, authorities. The first is libidinal in its direct aims, the second is plainly anti-libidinal since in its direct aims it persecutes and rages against both ego and object in their identificatory love-attachment. These two parts of the ego each function as an object to the other, with the same kind of relationship that the ego has to external objects.

Here is a clear enunciation of a new and profoundly important principle of psychological analysis, to be developed later by Melanie Klein and Fairbairn into the theories of the 'internal psychic object', the 'psychic inner world' and 'internal object-relationships'. At this point it would have been possible for Freud to have made a radical revision of his entire theory, and to have left instincts to biology while working out a purely clinically based theory of neurosis and personality-structure, as explained by post-natal developmental changes and differentiations within the total psyche as the primary, unitary ego, caused by that primary ego's involvements in object-relationships with the outer world whose chief and first representatives are parents. He has described (1) the emergence at birth of our 'mental existence' or primary psychic self, (2) its differentiation into and organized ego and a rejected portion or repressed unconscious, and (3) the differentiation of the organized ego into 'ego' and 'ego-ideal'. Taking instincts for granted as primary potentialities, this makes psychodynamics a pure ego-analysis.

In *The Ego and The Id* (1923a), however, Freud sought to marry his new ego-analysis to his earlier instinct-theory. It becomes clear in this book that his theory of the ego changed ground twice. Originally the ego was 'only a repressing and censoring agency'. (1920, p. 69.) Then, with the development of his theory of narcissism, the ego became equivalent to the basic, primary, psychic self with ' "the archaic inheritance" as its nucleus', and was the reservoir of all psychic energies, both libidinal and destructive. Now, in *The Ego and The Id*, Freud abandons that view and reverts to a more restricted theory of the ego as simply that part of the primary self (which is now called the 'id') which is moulded and shaped by the pressures and demands of the immediate (family, parental) environment into conformity to its requirements, while it still remains exposed, naturally, to the other and internal pressures of the repressed parts of the primary self. This use of the term 'ego' in conjunction with the correlated term 'id' is hardly satisfactory, since it implies a denial of 'ego-quality' to the repressed parts of the self which become an impersonal 'it', while at the same time it denudes the ego of any real energy of its own. It would be legitimate to employ two terms, 'self' and 'ego', and to use the term 'self' for the primary, total, 'mental existence', while 'ego' stands for the more restricted conscious 'I' that we are familiar with. We could then speak of the 'self' as split into an 'outer-reality ego' conforming to the pressures of the outer environment, and an 'inner-reality ego' owning the basic libidinal needs and drives that the child has had to repress (say in solving the Oedipus conflict problem, and/or conflicts over earlier anal and oral functioning). But where is the justification for depersonalizing the latter into an 'id', if the terms 'ego' or 'self' are adequate to cover all the phenomena as the concept of 'ego splitting' suggests. All psychic phenomena whatsoever are, and should be treated as, manifestations of the fundamental psychosomatic unity or basic self which loses its functional unity early by encountering mutually incompatible experiences of its object-world. Structural differentiation takes the form, as Freud showed, of ego-splitting. The basic self comes to be both for and against its own primary needs and the quest for their satisfaction. It develops out of its primary unity secondary selves which function antagonistically towards one another. But each of these structural differentiations retains the quality of a self or ego and unless the same term is used for the original unitary self and the secondary selves into which it comes to be differentiated, the personal quality of all the resulting phenomena is obscured, most of all by adopting such terms as 'id' and 'ego' set in opposition to each other. To depersonalize psychic phenomena is to alter the data we are studying.

That, however, is what Freud chose finally to do by restricting the term 'ego' to apply to the ordinary self of everyday life from which the 'repressed unconscious' is excluded. Repression was regarded as thrusting impulses which were operative in the conscious ego back into an instinctive unconscious regarded as prepersonal or impersonal. The ego is 'the part of the id that is modified by the influence of the perceptual system, the representative in the mind of the real external world'. (1923a, p. 34.) To make it clear that he now no longer regarded the ego as including or as identical with the primary nature of the individual, he stated explicitly : (a) 'Some earlier suggestions about a "nucleus of the ego", never very definitely formulated, require to be put right, since the system Pcpt-Cs alone can be regarded as the nucleus of the ego.' (1923a, pp. 34–5, footnote 2.) This rules out the 'archaic inheritance' of the mind as the nucleus of the ego, and restricts 'ego' to that part of the mind which is fashioned into conformity to the demands of the outer world. How unsatisfactory this is from a clinical point of view can be seen from the remark of one of my patients who said : 'I feel I have grown up to be an outer shell of conformities and I've lost touch with the real "me" inside.' Her 'outer shell of conformities' is Freud's 'ego' and she evidently felt that it had much less right to the title 'ego' than the dynamic, 'instinctive' part of herself which she had been forced to repress and had lost contact with. (b) 'Now that we have distinguished between the ego and the id, we must recognize the id as the great reservoir of libido mentioned in my introductory paper on narcissism.' (1923a, p. 38, footnote.) He thus explicity divorces the ego as a psychic structure from the sources of psychic energy which are relegated to the position of a non-ego, an impersonal 'id'.

In every individual there is a coherent organization of mental processes, which we call his *ego*. This ego includes consciousness and it controls the approaches to motility, i.e. to the discharge of excitations into the external world; it is this institution in the mind which regulates all its own constituent processes, and which goes to sleep at night, though even then it continues to exercise a censorship upon dreams. From this ego proceed the repressions, too, by means of which an attempt is made to cut off certain trends in the mind not merely from consciousness but also from their other forms of manifestation and activity. In analysis these trends which have been shut out stand in opposition to the ego and the analysis is faced with the task of removing the resistance which the ego displays against concerning itself with the repressed. (1923a, pp. 15–16.)

He replaces the antithesis between the conscious and the unconscious by 'the antithesis between the organized ego and what is repressed and dissociated from it'. (1923a, p. 17.) There can be no question as to the existence, and nature as Freud describes it, of that structural differentiation in the mind which he terms 'ego'. The only question, and it is one of fundamental importance for the theory of 'personality', is whether it has the exclusive right to the term 'ego' which Freud gives it.

Since, however, 'resistances emanate from the ego' (1923a, p. 16), and resistances work unconsciously, Freud was faced with the fact that part of the ego is unconscious though not repressed. To solve that problem he delved deeper into the question of mental structure. The way a problem is defined reveals the preconceptions of the investigator and influences his findings. Freud defined his problem as that of accounting for the fact that resistances are unconscious and yet also emanate from the ego. This was a problem to him because he assumed that the ego is not repressed. Indeed, the Freudian ego is by definition not repressed. Those aspects of the ego which are not in consciousness are preconscious but not repressed unconscious. But resistances are not preconscious, so the problem arises 'Can there be an unconscious that is not repressed?'

Clearly an alternative question can be asked. Does not the definition of 'ego' as 'not repressed' beg the important question as to whether part of the ego can after all be split off and repressed so as to become the source of unconscious resistances? The time, however, was not ripe for the asking of that question, which in the early 1920s would not have seemed psycho-analytically meaningful. Freud's own pioneer solution to the problem prepared the way for it to be restated later in that form. Freud's solution was determined by his view that the repressed unconscious was non-ego material, an impersonal id, raw impulse and emotion, and that the ego was constituted solely by what was non-repressed material. Thus the fact that resistances came from the ego so that they could not be regarded as repressed, and yet also operated unconsciously, compelled him to postulate a third aspect of endopsychic structure which was neither id nor ego. He decided that this must be 'a differentiating grade of the ego' (1923a, p. 34. Also 1921, p. 103), or a 'modification of the ego' which 'retains its special position' (p. 44) by virtue of its early origin and peculiar importance. He called it at first 'The Ego Ideal' and finally the 'Super-ego'.

This special differentiation of the ego comes about as a result of early identifications with parents, and predominantly, Freud believed, the father. He writes :

The character of the ego is a precipitate of abandoned object-cathexes and . . . contains a record of past object-choices.

The effects of the first identifications in earliest childhood will be profound and lasting. This leads us back to the origin of the ego-ideal; for behind [it] there lies hidden the first and more important identification of all, the identification with the father. (Footnote. Perhaps it would be safer to say 'with the parents'.) (1923, pp. 36 and 39.)

The mastering of the Oedipus complex is achieved by giving up the ambivalent object-relationship to parents under pressure from them, and turning object-cathexes of parents into identifications with them.

The broad general outcome of the sexual phase governed by the Oedipus Complex may, therefore, be taken to be the forming of a precipitate in the ego, consisting of these two identifications (i.e. the father-identification and the mother-identification) in some way combined together. This modification of the ego retains its special position : it stands in contrast with the other constituents of the ego in the form of an ego-ideal or super-ego. The super-ego is, however, not merely a deposit left by the earliest object-choices of the id; it also represents an energetic reaction-formation against those choices. (1923a, p. 44.)

The parents, and especially the father, were perceived as the obstacle to the realization of the Oedipus wishes; so the child's ego brought in a reinforcement to help in carrying out the repression by erecting this same obstacle within itself. The strength to do this was, so to speak, borrowed from the father. . . . The super-ego retains the character of the father, while the more intense the Oedipus complex was . . . the more exacting later on is the domination of the super-ego over the ego—in the form of conscience or perhaps of an unconscious sense of guilt. (1923a, p. 45.)

Thus the super-ego directs and reinforces the resistance of the ego against repressed Oedipal impulses seeking to re-emerge from the id, or the repressed unconscious. The fact that super-ego resistance is itself largely unconscious is explained as due to the fact that it is specially closely related to those repressed unconscious instinctive trends of the id.

The very free communication possible between the ideal and these unconscious instinctual trends explains how it is that the ideal itself can be to a great extent unconscious and inaccessible to the ego. The struggle which once raged in the deepest strata of the mind . . . is now carried on in a higher region [i.e. the super-ego]. (1923a, p. 53.)

The super-ego thus remains largely tied to these unconscious depths. This, however, is rather a statement of the *reason* than of the *mechanism* of the unconsciousness of part of the super-ego, and does not settle the question of whether part of the super-ego is unconscious by repression or by some other means. It is clear that this first theory of psychic structure leaves many problems unresolved. These may be summarized as (*a*) the impersonal, non-ego character attributed to the instinctive basis of psychic life, the id, (*b*) the limitation of the term 'ego' to the familiar ego of consciousness, and (*c*) a vague and unclarified dualism in the super-ego which has a more conscious aspect (the ego-ideal) and an unconscious part (the super-ego). Freud's penetrating analysis of structure must be seen as the pioneer effort opening the way to closer analysis. This could not be carried out until the concept of 'the internal psychic object' had been fully elaborated. Yet this was itself a development of Freud's concept of the super-ego as parents 'brought in' and 'erected within' the ego as a 'reinforcement' in the task of 'repression'. (1923a, p. 45.)

In *Inhibitions, Symptoms and Anxiety* (1926) the repercussions of Freud's ego-analysis on other aspects of theory begin to appear, first of all in a re-analysis of the problem of anxiety. He writes :

Formerly I regarded anxiety as a general reaction of the ego to conditions of unpleasure. . . . I assumed . . . that libido (sexual excitement) which was rejected or not utilized by the ego found direct discharge in the form of anxiety. It cannot be denied that these various assertions did not go very well together, or at any rate did not imply one another. (1926, p. 150.)

Anxiety was explained thus on biochemical and instinctive lines : sexual libido, when frustrated and dammed up in the organism with no discharge, turns into anxiety. When Freud brought the ego to the forefront he saw anxiety as the reaction of the ego to danger of either external or internal origin, and traced its evolution from birth-anxiety (as the anxiety prototype), through anxiety over the loss of the object (the breast, the mother) and loss of love, to its socialized form in super-ego anxiety, guilt and fear of social disapproval, rejection and punishment, especially in its internalized form.

The objection to (the earlier view) arose from our coming to regard the ego as the sole seat of anxiety. It was one of the results of the attempt to subdivide the mental apparatus which I made in *The Ego and The Id.* . . . . It is a question of id-anxiety (instinctual anxiety) versus ego anxiety. (1926, p. 151.)

It is also a question of a basically physiological explanation of anxiety versus a psychological one. These alternatives face us again with the question of whether it is a psychological fact that an instinctive and impersonal (depersonalized) part of the psyche can be distinguished from the ego. If we take, instead, the view that the total psyche is basically personal, that that is its essential nature which awaits development after birth, then the division Freud made will be seen not as a marking off of an impersonal id from an ego, but as a case of ego-splitting. He writes :

Since the energy which the ego employed is desexualized, the new view tended to weaken the close connection between anxiety and libido. (1926, p. 151.)

If, however, we regard Freud's division as representing a splitting of the ego into two egos, one of which remains sexual and libidinal and repressed, the other being desexualized and not repressed, then there is no need to give up the close connection between anxiety and libido. It is true, we shall not say that libido is transformed directly into anxiety. But we can say that the sexual ego in the unconscious experiences anxiety over the frustration of its libidinal aims, while a second development of anxiety would come about in the desexualized conscious ego over the threatened eruption of frustrated libido. It is still true, as Freud said, that anxiety is an ego-function, a reaction of the ego to danger. In the form in which he stated it, his new view implies that it is only a desexualized ego that experiences anxiety. The close connection between frustrated libido and anxiety is retained if, instead of saying that impersonal libido is transformed into anxiety we shall say that a libidinal, sexual ego experiences anxiety over the danger of the frustration of needs and aims. This also accounts for unconscious, repressed anxiety and ultimately for unconscious, repressed guilt. Freud's view that 'Anxiety is an affective state and as such can, of course, only be felt by the ego' (1926, p. 113) abides. But his further statement : 'The id cannot have anxiety as the ego can ; for it is not an organization and cannot make a judgment about a situation of danger' (1926, p. 113), ceases to be meaningful. Furthermore, a more intelligible meaning can be found in his statement that :

It is not so much a question of taking back our earlier findings as of bringing them into line with more recent discoveries. It is still an undeniable fact that in sexual abstinence, improper interference with the processes of sexual excitation or deflection of the latter from its psychological modification, anxiety arises directly out of libido. (1926, p. 114.)

We would, however, rather say that 'anxiety arises directly out of' the repressed sexual ego owing to the frustration of its libidinal aims.

Nevertheless, Freud's new theory of anxiety is much more illuminating for 'personality-theory', and it was an indication that his new development of an ego-psychology had started a process of liberating psycho-analysis from an excessive psychobiological bias, and of re-orientating it in the direction of a psychological theory of personality. However much the ego may be explained by Freud theoretically as formed on the surface of the id for the purposes of adaptation to external reality while all dynamic energy remains the property of id-impulses, in practice the ego is now seen to function as a definite powerful 'person'. Freud is aware of this and writes :

Just as the ego controls the path to action in regard to the outer world, so it controls access to consciousness. In repression it displays its powers in both directions. . . . At this point it is relevant to ask how I can reconcile this acknowledgment of the might of the ego with the description of its position which I gave in *The Ego and The Id*. In that book I drew a picture of its dependence on the id and upon the super-ego which revealed how powerless and apprehensive it was in regard to both and with what an effort it maintained its superiority over them. This view has been widely echoed in psychoanalytic literature. A great deal of stress has been laid on the weakness of the ego in relation to the id and of our rational elements in the face of the daemonic forces within us : and there is a strong tendency to make what I have said into a foundation-stone of a psycho-analytic Weltanschauung. Yet surely the psycho-analyst, with his knowledge of the way in which repression works, should, of all people, be restrained from adopting such extreme and one-sided views. (1926, pp. 28–9.)

Here, truly, is a reprieve for and a reinstatement of the ego of ordinary consciousness to a position of dignity from which Freud's earlier, biologically-orientated, instinct-theory threatened to dethrone it.

A further result is the renewed emphasis on character-analysis. In an appendix on *Resistance and Anti-Cathexis* under the heading of *Modifications of Earlier Views* Freud deals with the character-structure of the ego in its aspect of *defence* against the repressed and *resistance* to therapeutic analysis and change. He gathers up previous psycho-analytic observations on these matters and paves the way for the later systematic investigations of Anna Freud and W. Reich (1935–6). The study of the ego as a dynamic source of resistance again makes towards a less impersonal orientation of theory.

One extremely interesting passage contains a clear prophecy of the developments of 'internal objects' theory that were to come. Freud writes :

There can be no doubt or mistake about this resistance on the part of the ego. But we have to ask ourselves whether it covers the whole state of affairs in analysis. For we find that even after the ego has decided to relinquish its resistance it still has difficulty in undoing the repressions; and we have called the period of strenuous effort which follows after its praiseworthy decision, the phase of 'working through'. The dynamic factor which makes a working through of this kind necessary and comprehensible is not far to seek. *It must be that after the ego-resistance has been removed the power of the repetition-compulsion—the attracion exerted by the unconscious prototypes upon the repressed instinctual process—has yet to be overcome.* [Present writer's italics.] This factor might well be described as the *resistance of the unconscious*. There is no need to be discouraged by these emendations in our theory. They are to be welcomed if they do something towards furthering our knowledge, and they are no disgrace to us so long as they enrich rather than invalidate our earlier views. (1926, p. 148.)

More radical emendations than Freud realized have proved essential on some fundamental matters, yet it was Freud himself who pointed the way, and certainly it is true that they have enriched and not invalidated his basic psycho-analytical approach to human nature. The 'unconscious prototypes' which attract the 'repressed instinctual process', so creating a 'resistance of the unconscious', are surely an adumbration of the theory of 'internal objects' and of repressed ego-object relations in the unconscious inner world. Likewise the 'resistance of the super-ego' to which Freud refers is also a resistance coming not primarily from the ego but from an internal object (with which, it is true, the ego comes to identify itself). That points the same way. The implication of Freud's view that id and super-ego as well as ego resist the psychotherapeutic process, necessitates an ultimate theoretical reformulation of the theory of the unconscious in terms no longer of id-instincts solely, but in terms of repressed ego-object relationships. Freud did not take this step, but his own work made it necessary and inevitable that it should be taken.

3. *Later Orthodox Development of Freud's Structural Theory*

Space forbids a detailed study of later developments of Freud's ego-psychology, but we may refer to four contributions: Franz Alexander's treatment of the id and super-ego (1925), Anna Freud's and W. Reich's development of character-analysis (1935–6), a paper on 'Comments on the Formation of Psychic Structure' by Hartmann, Kris and Loewenstein (1946), and the bearing of Winnicott's recent views.

(*a*) *The Super-ego and the Id. Alexander* made Freud's new theory of endopsychic structure the basis of an important paper entitled 'A Metapsychological Description of the Process of Cure' (1925). He recognized the direct bearing of the new theory on psychotherapy, though we are not here concerned with that aspect of the paper. He described the super-ego as 'an introjected legal code of former days' (p. 22), 'an anachronism' (p. 25), 'a boundary-formation' separating the two systems of the ego and the id (p. 22) and dividing the mental system into two parts, an ego in excellent touch with reality and an id quite out of touch with it (p. 23). Therapeutic endeavour must be directed against the super-ego whose prohibitions function blindly and automatically. Only the ego can remember. The super-ego can only repeat. The dissolution of the super-ego is and will continue to be the task of all future psycho-analytical therapy. (1925, p. 32.)

This, however, turns out to be somewhat ambiguous, for he adds a very important footnote, which brings out the ambiguity and vague dualism of the super-ego concept. He writes:

The foregoing concept of the super-ego has been somewhat schematic and therefore more narrowly defined than in Freud's descriptions. *I limit the super-ego to the unconscious alone. Hence it became identical with the unconscious sense of guilt, with the dream censorship. The transition to conscious demands, to a conscious ego-ideal, is nevertheless in reality a fluid one.* [Present writer's italics.] We might regard those parts of the super-ego which project into consciousness as the most recent and final imprints in the structure of it. . . . They are not so fixed as the categorical unconscious constituents of the conscience, and are more accessible to conscious judgment. . . . Freud's conception and description, which takes into account the complete 'super-ego' system, is nevertheless the more correct psychologically. (1925, pp. 32–3.)

In 1930 in his book *The Psycho-Analysis of the Total Personality* he made a definite distinction between the entirely unconscious super-ego and the conscious ego-ideal. The latter comprised the consciously held values acquired in later life by which conduct is guided in outer contemporary reality. The former is primitive, created in the infancy period, and is likened by him to a set of automatic conditioned reflexes which inhibit primary anti-social impulses of cannibalism, incest and murder. He held to that view still in a paper, 'Development of the Ego-Psychology', in the volume *Psycho-Analysis To-day*. (Lorand, 1948.) In *Fundamentals of Psycho-Analysis* (1949), however, he writes :

I question to-day whether such a rigid structural distinction is possible. In the normal individual most of the early regulations are slowly modified by later influences. . . . It appears more convenient to distinguish different functions of the mind than to divide it into air-tight compartments. . . . The notion of the id, as originally defined, is problematical. Strictly speaking, a completely unorganized, inherited mass of instinctual urges is not found even at birth. Learning . . . starts immediately with birth, and it is therefore difficult to see at what period the sharp distinction between an unorganized id and an organized ego obtains. (1949, p. 83.)

This is a realistic approach and shows how the need to modify Freud's original conceptions of structure have arisen. However, repression does in fact create something like 'airtight compartments', and while it is a move in the right direction to drop the distinction between an *inherited* id and a *psychologically developed* ego as separate structures, or rather as energy and structure in separation, it is not similarly valuable to drop the distinction between an unconscious super-ego and a conscious ego-ideal.

There is a problem here for which Alexander did not find a solution. He had recognized the unsatisfactory complexity of the 'super-ego' concept. He wrote in 1944 :

It seems to me questionable whether we should consider the ego-ideal more closely connected with the super-ego, as its continuation in consciousness, or more allied to the actual ego. (Lorand, 1948, p. 145.)

Undoubtedly the latter alternative is the correct one, but his orthodox theory of psychic structure confused the issue. At that date he described the id as 'the inherited reservoir of chaotic instinctual demands which are not yet in harmony with each other [and] called, on account of its impersonal nature, the id (p. 146). He thus related and opposed the super-ego (representing the parents of infancy) to an impersonal congeries of isolated instinctive drives, while on the other hand he relates the ego-ideal hesitantly (representing later social reality) to the Freudian ego. He makes no use of Melanie Klein's distinction between persecutory and depressive anxiety and her concept of the early sadistic super-ego. This would make it possible to present a view of an internal unconscious (repressed) object-relation between infantile parental imagos and an infantile sexual ego on a primitive emotional level, as distinct from a non-repressed object-relation between the post-Oedipal ego of everyday conscious life and outer reality on a developed moral level. The problem is not solved in the orthodox theory and the super-ego remains an ambiguous concept.

One difficulty for Alexander arises from the fact that he regards the super-ego as basically and all through a moral phenomenon. It is conscience, in the fear of which our childhood fear of our parents is embodied ; and its function is to adjust us to society and to the rights of others, and enforce the social code. However, the properly moral motive is not fear but an understanding and sympathetic regard for other people. Alexander says that but for the super-ego every citizen would need a policeman at his side all the time (Lorand, 1948, p. 144), but those who do right only through fear of punishment are not regarded as moral people and it does not make any difference in principle when the punitive retaliator and the fear of him are wholly internal phenomena. When he writes :

The super-ego, in a fully developed personality, has lost its connection with external reality. It is more or less rigid and has sunk to

the depths of the personality. It is consequently to a high degree unconscious. (Lorand, 1948, p. 145),

he makes it clear that this bottom layer of the total 'super-ego' is
not a moral function, but a survival of the primitive fear of the
infant who has not reached the moral level of development. This
coincides with the discovery of Melanie Klein, namely, that the
farther back we trace the 'super-ego', the more cruel, sadistic and
persecutory it is. That the super-ego is not necessarily basically
moral should be clear from the fact that it is possible for it to arise
in the first place from the introjection of absolutely immoral or
non-moral parents who are merely regarded with terror because
they are overwhelmingly powerful. A suicidal patient of mine had
a self-hating and self-destructive 'super-ego' based on the internalization of a mother who not only beat her throughout her whole
childhood but on one or two occasions burned and scalded her
deliberately to break her will and reduce her to abject submission.
Even apart from such real bad objects, the baby's perception of
his objects is so coloured by his own violent emotions through
projection that he builds up phantasied monsters who never had
any existence as such in real life, yet who form the hard core of his
primitive sadistic super-ego. The deepest strata of the super-ego
have this non-moral or pre-moral character of being merely persecutory.

Yet the more usual and obvious manifestation of the super-ego
is taken to be guilt, albeit it is a guilt that masks primitive terror.
Alexander might have cut the Gordian knot of the problem had
he realized that he was differentiating the pre-moral and the moral
levels of development.   Freud gives warrant for this since he regards the 'moral super-ego' as a post-Oedipal phenomenon. This,
however, must really be the ego-ideal, beneath which an earlier,
non-moral and sadistic super-ego lies hidden, a very primitive
structure which *has* lost contact with outer reality in a way that
the ego-ideal has not. The term 'super-ego' evidently covers at
least two different sets of facts and is applied indiscriminately
to two distinguishable psychic structures. It is not possible to treat
the super-ego as a moral conscience, then to separate off the only
really moral part of it as the ego-ideal, and elect to treat the
primitive remainder as the super-ego proper while still treating it
as a moral function creating unconscious guilt. As we shall see,
Melanie Klein does the same thing when she treats her early
sadistic internal bad objects as a super-ego, and carries the
Freudian Oedipus situation back, by means of it, into the first
year of life, a view that many analysts have not agreed with. The

dilemma can be avoided only by distinguishing a pre-moral from a moral level of development (a pre-Oedipal from an Oedipal level). We have been somewhat forced to anticipate later chapters in order to complete to some extent the discussion of this question, but it is important at this stage to indicate the unsolved problems that Freud's scheme of psychic structure left to the future.

(b) *Ego-Analysis. W. Reich and Anna Freud.* Freud's scheme of psychic structure had the effect of directing attention not only to the new theory of the super-ego, but also to the detailed study of the now more closely defined ego. In fact, we can now see that a far-reaching reorientation of the entire theoretical approach had slowly and almost invisibly begun to take place. The psychotherapeutic interest very much dominated this steadily increasing concern with the analysis of the ego. This is particularly apparent from the two important books of the middle 1930s, *Character Analysis* (1935) by Wilhelm Reich and *The Ego and the Mechanisms of Defence* (1936) by Anna Freud. Reich's book was more especially concerned with the technique of psychotherapeutic analysis, and he emphasized the uselessness of attempting to by-pass ego-defences and go straight to the deep infantile unconscious. It had come to be understood that the tendency of inexperienced analysts, and still more of those who tried to practise analysis without specific training and on the basis of book knowledge only, to rush into premature 'interpretations in depth' before the patient was ready to assimilate these, led to no therapeutic result. Instead it led to what Freud called the co-existence in the mind of two versions of the neurosis at the same time without their meeting or in any way mutually influencing each other, an intellectual version in the conscious mind, and a repressed emotional version which was the real neurosis in the unconscious.

Thus Wilhelm Reich dealt with neurotic character traits as forming a compact defence mechanism against both the outer world and the pressure of internal libidinal needs. This 'character armor' as he called it binds anxiety and it blocks every effort to bring about psychotherapeutic changes. Thus it becomes imperative, in order to open the way for therapeutic analysis into the deep unconscious, to analyse the character-structure of the ego which Freud held to be the source of repression and therefore of resistances to treatment. Reich stressed the importance of those resistances which had become congealed in the patient's habitual manners and posture, so that the peculiar and individual way in which a patient says and does things is as important and revealing as the actual content of what he says and does. He also made a special study of certain general 'character forms', such as the hysterical, compulsive, phallic-narcissistic, and the masochistic characters. The formation and structure of the neurotic characters is quite different from that of healthy-minded persons who are capable of normal activities and human relationships. He compares the mature character, which he calls the 'genital character', with the neurotic character as ideal types, and points out that all real characters are mixtures of the two.

He did not critically examine but rather expounded Freud's id-ego-super ego scheme of psychic structure from the above point of view. The id of the neurotic character appears largely in the form of unresolved Oedipal impulses of the incest wish for the parent of the opposite sex and aggression against the parent of the same sex; the super-ego of the neurotic he holds to be simply 'sex-negative' and sadistic, enforcing impotence and turning social achievement into little more than an attempt to over-compensate and find some proof of potency. The ego of the neurotic is doubly paralysed by impotence and inferiority feelings. In the mature, or as he calls it the genital, character, the ego does not have to defend itself against the id and the super-ego. This absence of internal division means that the ego has at its disposal all the energies it needs for genuine love and work, resulting in a capacity for true satisfaction.

By contrast, in the neurotic character the ego is severely limited and subject to serious inhibitions. It is guilt-ridden, subject to infantile impulses which naturally are inappropriate in real life, and it is therefore much more liable to feel 'unpleasure' than 'pleasure'. In short the neurotic character is quite unable to experience life fully and freely and naturally. Thus Reich gives general characterizations of the ego in its defensive operations.

We may make two comments on Reich's exposition. Firstly, he brings out clearly the double purpose of the character-structure of the Freudian conscious ego. It faces two ways, outwards and inwards. Its external function is that of adaptation to environmental material reality. The individual has, when all is said and done, got to live in the real world outside himself. Its internal function is that of defence against the eruption of disturbed internal psychic reality. But Reich, true to the dominant psycho-analytical trend, only saw the ego's external function as the negative one of defence against the impact of stimuli, not as a positive quest for meaningful relationships. Secondly, he reaffirms the classic psycho-analytic theory that the sole source of trouble is libidinal and sadistic drives, so that all forms of fear are secondary phenomena. This view we shall ultimately see reason to reject, though it is still maintained, even by writers in other respects so divergent as Anna Freud and Melanie Klein, as the unquestioned basic psycho-analytic theory.

Anna Freud makes a more specific analysis of the particular major defensive operations or so-called 'mechanisms' of the ego. Her book is more oriented to theoretical considerations. In *The Ego and The Mechanisms of Defence* she states that:

> Analytical theory has ceased to hold that the concept of the ego is identical with that of the system of perceptual consciousness; that is to say, we have realized that large portions of the ego-institutions are themselves unconscious and require the help of analysis in order to become conscious. The result is that analysis of the ego has assumed a much greater importance in our eyes. Anything which comes into the analysis from the side of the ego is just as good material as an id-derivative. . . . But of course anything which comes from the ego is also a resistance in every sense of the word : a force directed against the emerging of the unconscious and so against the working of the analysis. (1936, p. 26.)

Thus the ego has two facets, one is that of the perceptual system of knowledge of the outer world as the basis of adjustment to outer reality, the other is that of the system of ego-defences against the inner world of the unconscious. The defences are themselves unconscious.

All the defensive measures of the ego against the id are carried out silently and invisibly. The most that we can ever do is to reconstruct them in retrospect : we can never really witness them in operation. This statement applies, for instance, to successful repression. The ego knows nothing of it; we are aware of it only subsequently when it becomes apparent that something is missing (p. 10).

It is the analyst's business first of all to recognize the defence-mechanism. When he has done this, he has accomplished a piece of ego-analysis (p. 15).

While id-derivatives can be observed directly as actual emotions and impulses emerging into consciousness, the ego's defensive activities can be inferred only from results or when a conflict between the id and the ego has become conscious.

Whenever the interpretation touches on the unknown elements of the ego, its activities in the past, that ego is wholly opposed to the work of analysis. Here evidently we have the situation which we commonly describe by the not very felicitous term 'character-analysis' (p. 22).

Anna Freud regards the analysis of the ego as technically more difficult than that of the id, since, according to the classic theory, it is the source of resistance to the unconscious and to all attempts to make it conscious. To use W. Reich's term, character is the ego's defensive armour against the repressed and is constituted by the system of ego-defences. Freud, however, opened up a wider problem of resistance when, in *Inhibitions, Symptoms and Anxiety* (1926, p. 148), he spoke of 'the *resistance of the unconscious*'. This, we have seen reason to think, should also be regarded as an ego-resistance, though not in Anna Freud's sense of either 'ego' or 'resistance'. Freud explained it as due to the 'power of the repetition-compulsion—the attraction exerted by the unconscious proto-types upon the instinctual process', a fact which Fairbairn re-interprets as a case of the libidinal cathexis of an internal bad object on the part of a repressed portion of the ego. (1952, pp. 72 ff.) The earliest resistances to be discovered reflected the ego's rejection of 'the repressed'. Here is a deeper resistance reflecting an attachment to 'the repressed', what Freud called an 'adhesive-ness of the libido'. (1937, *C.P.*, V, p. 344.) This serves again to remind us of unsolved problems in the classic id-ego-super ego scheme.

Anna Freud lists the ten stock methods of defence known to analysts, as regression, repression, reaction-formation, isolation, undoing, projection, introjection, turning against the self, reversal, and sublimation or displacement of instinctive aims. These defences

meet our eyes in a state of petrifaction when we analyse the permanent 'armour-plating of character'. [i.e. rigidities of posture, mannerism, etc.] We come across them, on a larger scale and again in a state of fixation, when we study the formation of neurotic symptoms (p. 36).

Thus different neuroses have their respective characteristic defences, such as repression in hysteria, and isolation and undoing in obsessional neurosis. Anxiety is the motive of the ego's defence against the dangers of instinct; in adult neurosis this takes the form of super-ego anxiety or fear of guilt and condemnation by the super-ego, in infantile neurosis it is objective anxiety or fear of punishment by parents and other actual outer real figures, while in times of critical and rapid internal change, as in infancy, adolescence and the climacteric, instinctive anxiety or fear of the strength of instincts arises. Ultimately all fear of instincts, however, is due to fear of the outside world and its hostile reactions to their active quest for gratification.

Under the heading of 'Preliminary Stages of Defence' by avoidance of panic and danger, Anna Freud discusses the denial of intolerable realities by phantasy, word, or act, and restriction of the ego. 'Identification with the aggressor' is a 'preliminary phase of super-ego development, and an intermediate stage in the development of paranoia' (p. 129). It is a combination of introjection or internalizing the external criticism and threat of punishment, and projection or externalizing the offence and the guilt, so turning the tables. (This is usually followed, at the instance of anxiety, by 'identification with the object of one's own aggression'.) An important defence against super-ego anxiety is to develop a form of altruism in which one's own wishes are made over to other people and one becomes devoted to getting gratifications for others instead of oneself. Finally, asceticism and intellectualization are discussed as ego-defences in adolescence against the increased strength of instincts.

In this valuable development of ego-analysis, one thing stands out as a striking result of founding clinical theory upon a theory of instincts, namely the underlying assumption that the cause of trouble is to be found in instincts *per se*. It is implied that it is the natural, healthy, normal functioning of instincts that calls out from the ego such elaborate systems of defences. Anna Freud treats the antagonism of the id and the ego as inevitable, and does not raise the question of the possible harmonious development of the individual's basic nature; in fact she seems distinctly pessimistic about any such possibility (cf. pp. 60–4), since the ultimate source of trouble is held to be fear of the strength of instincts rather than of opposition to their gratification by the outer world. Why should the ego fear the strength of instincts even when that is increased at puberty? This is a natural development in the growth of 'the whole man' and it is not proved that the disturbances that so frequently accompany adolescence are an innate inevitability. There are relatively undisturbed adolescents and cultural differences in this respect are marked. Disturbance seems to be more due to a revival of infancy troubles than to inherent necessity for adolescence to be a period of 'sturm und drang'. The real problem as to whether trouble is due to healthy or unhealthy and neurotic instinctive drives is passed over.

Thus, about the same time as Anna Freud's book, Freud himself wrote in 1937, in the paper on *Analysis, Terminable and Interminable. (CP., V, p. 331–2.)*

The quantitative factor of instinctual strength in the past opposed the efforts of the patient's ego to defend itself, and now that analysis has been called in to help, that same factor sets a limit to the efficacy of this new attempt. If the instincts are excessively strong the ego fails in its task. . . . We shall achieve our therapeutic purpose only when we can give a greater measure of analytic help to the patient's ego.

Here Freud states that what is to be feared is the innate strength of instinctive drives as a fixed factor. It is not discussed whether this dangerous quantitative strength of instincts may be due rather to that internalization of frustration and over-stimulation which constitutes the neurosis. Anna Freud writes :

On their way to gratification the id-impulses must pass through the territory of the ego and here they are in an alien atmosphere . . . the instinctual impulses can no longer seek gratification without more ado—they are required to respect the demands of reality and, more than that, to conform to ethical and moral laws by which the super-ego seeks to control the behaviour of the ego. Hence these impulses run the risk of incurring the displeasure of institutions essentially alien to them. They are exposed to criticism and rejection and have to submit to every kind of modification. Peaceful relations between the neighbouring powers are at an end. The instinctual impulses continue to pursue their aims with their own peculiar tenacity and energy, and they make hostile incursions into the ego, in the hope of overthrowing it by a surprise-attack. The ego on its side becomes suspicious; it proceeds to counter-attack and to invade the territory of the id. Its purpose is to put the instincts permanently out of action by means of appropriate defensive measures, designed to secure its own boundaries (pp. 7–8).

Evidently these 'undistorted id-impulses, which become subject to a censorship on the part of the adult ego' (p. 20), are regarded as representing an instinctive endowment in the human being which is essentially both ego-alien and opposed by the super-ego, since the Freudian ego is an institution formed on the basis of adaptation and conformation to outer reality. If, however, the id is the primary nature of the human being, it would be healthy in itself prior to any disturbed functioning forced on it by the environment. In that case instinctive drives would become dangerous and to be feared only in so far as the child's nature is not understood or tolerated by the environment. The fear of the innate strength of instincts and the hostility of the id and the ego are thus not inevitable, even though in fact to some extent unavoidable. They are artifacts arising out of early development in the setting of bad-object relationships. This is really implied in the quotation Anna

Freud makes from her father's book, *Inhibitions, Symptoms and Anxiety*.

It may well be that before its sharp cleavage into an ego and an id, and before the formation of a super-ego, the mental apparatus makes use of different methods of defence from those which it employs after it has attained these levels of organization. (A. Freud, p. 55; S. Freud, pp. 157–8.)

Before structural differentiation has set in, conflict, in fact, can only be with the environment, and it is unsatisfying object-relationships that lead to internal structural differentiation. Fear of instincts is secondary to fear of objects and comes about through instinctive reactions becoming disturbed by frustration. If it were possible to have an ideal environment which steered the child through the early developmental stages with maximum satisfaction of healthy needs and a minimum of frustration, there should be no inevitable warfare of ego and super-ego against id. The emphasis is shifted from innate instincts to post-natal object-relationships. The great danger of the classic instinct-theory lies in the fact that it obscures this. It is all too reminiscent of St. Paul's theology of a natural and inevitable warfare between the law of the mind and the law of the members. Hartmann, Kris and Loewenstein say that :

It seems reasonable to assume that the infant's apparatus of control and adjustment are given their best training chances at a distance considerably closer to the maximum of indulgence than to that of deprivation. (1946, p. 21.)

Their view confirms that the difficulty about the antagonism of the ego to the so-called id is not that of the innate strength of instincts but of the practical problem of securing the best conditions in which the child's nature can develop in a healthy and undisturbed way. It seems probable that (1) in infancy natural and healthy libidinal needs are felt towards the object and if accepted and satisfied cause no trouble, but (2) if they meet with denial and frustration the libidinal needs become over-intense and greedy through lack of satisfaction, and furthermore they fuse with anger at the frustrations. As Freud explains, at this stage, 'Under the influence of its upbringing, the child's ego accustoms itself to shift the scene of the battle from outsde to inside and to master the *inner* danger before it becomes external.' (1937, *C.P.*, V., p. 338.) Thus instinctive reactions remain in a disturbed state because they are now always confronted with internal frustration, and (3) this entire situation, being repressed, sets up the neurotic state in which needs can no longer be felt in normal, natural and healthy ways. All libidinal needs have become basically greedy and angry and therefore antisocial, and they must thenceforth be opposed by the ego and the super-ego. All our actual experience of human beings both in ourselves and in others is not experience of healthy nature but of nature disturbed in varying degrees. Thus the analysis of the ego and the question of psychic structure shows again the need to reconsider instinct-theory, particularly as it is implied in the conceptions of the id, ego and super-ego.

(c) *'Comments on the Formation of Psychic Structure'. Hartmann, Kris and Loewenstein.* (1946, pp. 12ff.) These three writers gather up and survey critically from the orthodox standpoint the Freudian theory of psychic structure some twenty years after it had been propounded. They write :

Psycho-analytic hypotheses have undergone far-reaching modification in Freud's own work and in that of his earlier collaborators. The importance of some of these reformulations was in many instances underrated at the time of their publication; and we believe that the importance of the most radical and far-sighted ones, suggested by Freud in *Inhibitions, Symptoms and Anxiety*, has not yet been fully appreciated. Briefly, *since a structural viewpoint was introduced into psycho-analytic thinking, hypotheses previously established must be reintegrated.* [Present writer's italics.] The task of synchronization is larger than it might seem at first (p. 12).

They point out that 'the concept of a psychic conflict is integral to many religious systems and many philosophical doctrines (p. 13). Clinical phenomena suggested to Freud 'that the forces opposing each other in typical conflict situations were not grouped at random : rather that the groups of opposing forces possessed an inner cohesion or organization' (p. 13). The concepts emerged which, in the 1920s, Freud introduced under the names of id, ego and super-ego.

These three psychic substructures or systems are not conceived of as independent parts of personality that invariably oppose each other, but as three centres of psychic functioning that can be characterized according to their developmental level, to the amount of energy invested in them, and to their demarcation and interdependence at a given time (p. 14).

That is certainly true in intention but we have seen how even Freud and Anna Freud slipped insensibly into describing the id and ego as independent and invariably opposed. These three writers define the three structures as follows :

The functions of the id center around the basic needs of man and their striving for gratification. These needs are rooted in instinctual drives and their vicissitudes. . . . The functions of the ego center around the relation to reality. In this sense, we speak of the ego as of a specific organ of adjustment. . . . The functions of the super-ego center around moral demands. Self-criticism . . . self-punishment, and the formation of ideals, are essential manifestations of the super-ego (p. 15).

Like Alexander they are critical of the id concept and also remark that 'Freud's use of the term [ego] is ambiguous. He uses ego in reference to a psychical organization and to the whole person' (p. 16). Where Freud writes: 'The ego presents itself to the super-ego as love-object' they would replace the term 'ego' here by the wider term 'self' which covers 'the whole person'. By implication since 'self' includes the id as well as the ego the id is to be recognized as personal in quality just as much as the ego. This is further implied in their statement:

Freud speaks of a gradual differentiation of the ego from the id; as an end result of this process of differentiation the ego, as a highly structured organization, is opposed to the id. Freud's formulation has obvious disadvantages. It implies that the infant's equipment at birth is part of the id. It seems, however, that the innate apparatus and reflexes cannot all be part of the id, in the sense generally accepted in psycho-analysis. We suggest a different assumption; namely, that of an undifferentiated phase during which both the id and the ego are formed. . . . To the degree to which differentiation takes place man is equipped with a special organ of adaptation, i.e. with the ego . . . the differentiation accounts for the nature of the instinctual drives of man, sharply distinguished as they are from animal instincts. . . . Many manifestations of the id are farther removed from reality than any comparable behaviour of animals (p. 19).

This is strictly in line with Anna Freud's quotation from Freud cited on page 111. Thus we have the id and the ego as parallel differentiations within the primary and at first undifferentiated total psychic self, while the id is no longer simple instinct such as is found in animals. The id, just as much as the ego, is a product of differentiation and development. They further describe the differentiation of ego and id as brought about by the infant's mixed experience of part deprivation and part gratification. The ego is evidently the primary self in so far as it adjusts itself to reality by reconciling itself to deprivation or postponement of satisfaction, while the id is that same primary self in so far as it goes on demanding gratification. *All justification for the continued use of the impersonal term id seems to have gone.* It is in no sense a mere impersonal biological energy. In Freud's sense and scheme, the id is not a structure properly speaking, and what it represents can only be included in a structural scheme if its proper 'ego' or 'personal self' quality is recognized. It is a libidinal ego, as distinct from the Freudian ego which is that part of the primary self which is modified to *conform* to the demands of the environment, becoming an 'organ of adaptation'.

The concept of the *super-ego* is held by these writers to be complex, but in a somewhat different way from that suggested by Alexander. They adhere rigidly to Freud's view of the super-ego as a specific creation of the Oedipal problem, whose solution it marks. It is a rigid structure, highly, if not entirely, resistant to later modification. It is a castrator *par excellence*, the internalization of the hated, feared yet loved father-rival who will allow the boy no sexual access to his mother. It is a phallic-phase phenomenon.

On the other hand they regard morality as having its origins in the earlier pre-Oedipal period. The super-ego functions have 'precursors' (p. 33) which, like the super-ego, develop on the basis of identification with parents, compliance with their demands, guilt over failure and the turning of aggression against the self (p. 32). Thus the super-ego appears now to be, not the origin of morality, but only one, even a very special one, of its later developments at the particularly critical Oedipal phase. This complexity is not unravelled in detail. Their position seems to be the opposite of that taken up by Melanie Klein and Alexander, for whom the origins of the moral 'ego-ideal' are later than the formation of a cruel, sadistic, castrating super-ego. It is clear that of these three Freudian terms, the super-ego is the most unsatisfactory by reason of its confusing complexity which stands urgently in need of closer analysis on the basis of clinical material.

We may summarize the problems that have emerged from the critical study of the terms id, ego and super-ego from the point of view of orthodox writers.

(i) The term 'id' is impersonal and stands for psychobiological energies without organization, while the terms 'ego' and 'super-ego' are personal and represent psychic organizations which have to borrow their energy from elsewhere. This is not a criticism but a statement of the orthodox concepts, yet it is clear that the scheme rests on mixed principles of classification.

(ii) The id cannot be accepted as psychologically primary, according to Alexander, and to Hartmann, Kris and Loewenstein.

It is as much the result of differentiation as the ego. They appear, rather, as two different aspects of the primary total self, the id characterized by libidinal needs (and therefore surely having an 'ego' or 'self' quality), the ego being characterized by adaptation or conformity to outer reality.

(iii) The super-ego has two recognizably distinct parts or aspects, one sadistic and cruelly persecuting and the other moral; though writers differ as to which of the two parts is primary and which secondary.

(d) *Winnicott's Views on Mind, The Psyche-Soma and Regression.*

Two articles by Winnicott in 1954-5, though not ostensibly a reconsideration of the classical theory of psychic structure, in fact amount to that. We have already observed that Freud's scheme is clearly linked to the traditional tripartite division of man into body, mind and spirit—i.e. id, ego and super-ego—or instincts, the socially functioning person, and conscience. The way in which the equating of body and id, mind and ego comes about, is set forth in Winnicott's paper on *Mind and Its Relation to the Psyche-Soma.* (1958, p. 243.) He writes :

The mind of an individual . . . specializes out from the psyche-soma. The mind does not exist as an entity in the individual's scheme of things provided the individual psyche-soma or body scheme has come satisfactorily through the very early developmental stages; mind is then no more than a special case of the functioning of the psyche-soma. In the study of a developing individual the mind will often be found to be developing a *false entity*, and a false localization (p. 201).

Certain kinds of failure on the part of the mother, especially erratic behaviour, produce over-anxiety of the mental functioning. Here, in the over-growth of the mental function reactive to erratic mothering, we see that there can develop an opposition between the mind and the psyche-soma. . . . Clinically this can go along with . . . a false personal growth on a compliance basis. . . . The psyche of the individual gets 'seduced' away into this mind from the intimate relationship which the psyche originally had with the soma. The result is a mind psyche, which is pathological (p. 244).

The original unitary psyche-soma, the primary total self, has become differentiated or 'split' into a mind-psyche which is then located in the head, and a soma-psyche which is left to reside in the body. This is, in fact, a clinical rather than a theoretical description of Freud's view of the differentiation of the ego, as an adaptive, conforming function, from the id which it is supposed to control. Still more closely does it agree with the view of Hartmann, Kris and Loewenstein, of a primary undifferentiated phase (psyche-soma) out of which the id and the ego are differentiated (soma-psyche and mind-psyche). But like Horney, Winnicott recognizes that this ego is a pathological false growth, 'a false personal growth on a compliance basis'. The same is really implied in the view of Hartmann, Kris and Loewenstein of the ego as 'an organ of adaptation', for while it cannot be said that adaptation to outer reality is in itself pathological, being a necessity, the way in which the adapation is in fact made is usually highly pathological, amounting to a denial and suppression of the infant's own proper nature. Thus Winnicott also clearly implies that the id is much closer to the primary psyche-soma, and is in fact much more the real stuff of the original, natural self than is this 'mind' or conforming ego. In that case the id can no longer be regarded as impersonal. The infant comes to be differentiated into a false self or ego of a conforming kind and a natural self or ego which is no longer accepted and consciously lived, but left in an undeveloped, repressed state.

In his later paper on 'Metapsychological and Clinical Aspects of Regression Within the Psycho-Analytical Set-up' (1958, p. 278), the psyche-soma becomes the 'true self' and the 'mind' becomes the 'false self'. The patient may have a genuine need for a therapeutic regression in order to recover contact with his 'true self', while the 'false self', with its conforming and adapting, acts meanwhile as a 'caretaker self' to deal with the outer world, until such time as the 'true self' has developed in an increasingly realistic relationship to the outer world and the 'false self' can be surrendered to the analyst. We are very far here from the Freudian concepts of the id and ego, but we are much closer to psychological realities. Winnicott has not suggested that his views imply a revision of the orthodox scheme of psychic structure. Yet clearly the psyche-soma is not an impersonal id but the primary, natural self, the libidinal psyche, and it is the 'true self' with which the patient must recover contact; while the 'mind' or conforming ego cannot really be called a reality-ego in the Freudian sense if it is a pathological false self. Moreover, there is no place in Freud's scheme for the concept of a 'true self', for it is certainly neither id nor ego in his sense. An impersonal id is not the concept of a 'true self', and Freud's concept of the ego does not provide for the recognition of the pathological aspect of the 'mind' or 'false self' as an ego-growth 'seduced away' from the soma and opposed to the psyche-soma, id or true primary self (unless this be held to be implied in the idea that the ego develops on the surface of the id by contact with outer reality). Freud's concepts conceal the probability, supported by much clinical evidence, of splitting of the original unitary psychic self which is the basis of all psychosis and psychoneurosis.

We may observe that Winnicott's terms 'true self' and 'false self' are not, strictly speaking, scientific but rather descriptive and evaluatory terms. A new terminology is needed to replace the id and ego of Freud's scheme, a terminology that does justice to the clinical facts set forth by Winnicott. This question of terminology, however, takes us into even more fundamental problems. The whole question of the nature of psychological enquiry is in fact prejudged by the kind of terminology that is regarded as properly scientific in this field of study. It is apparent that mixed types of terminology are in use in psycho-analysis; according as the interest of the writer is primarily theoretical and 'metapsychological' on the one hand or clinical on the other, the terminology tends to be more impersonal or more personal. Difficulty arises, however, because the two different types of terms are so often mixed up in illegitimate and confusing ways. The whole question of the nature and status of psycho-analysis as science is involved, and we must go into the question thoroughly before proceeding to post-Freudian developments.

CHAPTER VII

PROCESS THEORY AND PERSONAL THEORY

1. *Freud's Early Terminology*

CHAPTERS III and V have raised a problem so fundamental to the development of psycho-analytical theory that we must now give it particular attention. The work of Marjorie Brierley (*Trends in Psycho-Analysis*, 1951) has introduced specifically into psycho-analysis the question of whether its theory should be cast into the form of an impersonal theory of mental functioning or a personal theory of the active, purposive whole self in its living human relationships. Brierley has worked out psycho-analytical theory along both lines, as, first, a 'Process Theory', and, secondly, a 'Personology'. This is at bottom the problem of whether psycho-dynamics is a 'natural science' or whether it calls for a new type of theory which can take account of that 'individuality' of the human 'person' which is lost in any presentation of 'general laws of mental functioning'. Metapsychology is an attempt to present psycho-analysis as a natural science. Brierley writes:

The word 'personology' is borrowed from Smuts as a convenient term to distinguish the science of personality from metapsychology. Referring to academic psychology, Smuts writes: '... The procedure of psychology is largely and necessarily analytical and cannot therefore do justice to Personality in its unique wholeness. For this a new discipline is required, which we have called Personology, and whose task it would be to study Personality as a whole and to trace the laws and phases of its development in the individual life. ... Personology would study the Personality not as an abstraction or bundle of psychological abstractions, but rather as a vital organism, as the organic whole which *par excellence* it is; and such a study should lead to the formulation of the laws of growth of this unique whole, which would not only be of profound theoretical importance, but also of the greatest practical value.' (Smuts, *Holism and Evolution*, 1926, p. 293.) (1951, p. 124.)

Brierley comments: 'It is advisable for psycho-analysts to emphasize that they study people not as abstract problems but as more or less well integrated living persons. . . . Psycho-analytic personology is a psychology, not an anatomy or physiology, of personality; it is concerned with subjective experience and the motivation of behaviour.' (*Op. cit.*, pp. 124–5.) We have traced Freud's never quite completed struggle to make the transition from the natural science of neurophysiology to his own new psychological studies. The problem of the choice between process theory and personal theory as the form requisite for psycho-dynamic science emerged, even if it was not recognized as such, with his analysis of the ego in the 1920s. It was this ego-psychology which opened up the field of the dynamic psychology of man as a *person*. The creator of psycho-analysis was at first convinced that what E. Jones calls the discovery of 'scientific law and order . . . in the apparent chaos of mental processes' (1954, i. 416) could be achieved only by approaching the mind through the body. His later concept of the super-ego was a departure from this principle, since it looked to the human environment rather than the organic basis of mental life for the origin of a mental function or structural differentiation.

Jones writes:

The language of physics and cerebral physiology in the Project was Freud's natural one, to which he in great part adhered even later when he was dealing with purely psychological problems. It is true that he then gave the terms he used psychological meanings which take them away from their original context, but even so they are often terms that no pure psychologist would have used to start with. . . . In the realm of the visual, of definite neural activities that could be seen under the microscope, he had for many years felt entirely at home; he was as safe there as at the family hearth. To wander away from it and embark on the perilous seas of the world of emotions, where all was unknown and where what was invisible was of far greater consequence than the little that was visible, must have cost him dear . . . we may regard the feverish writing of the Project as a last desperate effort to cling to the safety of cerebral anatomy. If only the mind could be described in terms of neurones, their processes and synapses! How fond the thought must have been to him. (*Ibid.*, pp. 420–1.)

But Freud gave up that attempt. Jones quotes from

a letter of September 22, 1898, when he wrote: 'I have no inclination at all to keep the domain of the psychological floating, as it were, in the air, without any organic foundation. But I have no knowledge, neither theoretically nor therapeutically, beyond that conviction, so that I have to conduct myself as if I had only the psychological before me'. He never moved from that position. (*Ibid.*, p. 433.)

The problem, however, is not whether psychic life has an organic foundation. It has, and no one seeks to dispute that. The question is whether psychic development and functioning, particularly in the human person, can be understood solely from the organic end, and explained in neurophysiological terms, or whether it needs a new terminology appropriate to itself and belonging to a new science that does not, and cannot, operate on the same lines as the so-called natural sciences. Freud did later make a new start from the personality-end of the psychosomatic whole of the human person, and in his ego-psychology he actually initiated a fully *psycho*dynamic analysis of the development of the personality in and through the medium of personal relationships. In 1898, however, he effected a compromise which arose naturally out of his medical work and his involvement with the bodily symptoms of neurosis. He replaced 'neurones' by 'instincts' and the physiology of the brain and nervous system by the biochemistry and the phasic development and maturation of the sexual component instincts. This, however, did not enable him to achieve a true psychodynamic theory of the personality as distinct from a dynamic metapsychology, and he made another new development of theory in the 1920s.

Freud approached the 'human being in his personal life' with the training and mentality of the natural scientist. Writing of the theory of the mind that Freud expounded in the seventh chapter of *The Interpretation of Dreams,* Jones says:

Freud still uses the word 'Apparatus' and the model he provides is constructed on lines very similar to those of the physiological model. (*Ibid.*, p. 437.)

He probably never recognized the extent to which his later ego-psychology was a new departure. It is easier for us to see this now that his work has had its effect.

2. *The Philosophy of Science*

The question 'Process theory or Personal theory' involves some deeper problems that belong in the end to philosophy, the philosophy of science. Freud frequently expressed a hostile attitude to philosophy and religion, both of which he regarded as 'nothing but' purely speculative attempts to evolve a set of beliefs primarily designed to serve as a basis for personal security, and representing nothing but wishful thinking. Philosophy and theology were to him intellectualized forms of the phantasy life, aiming at the creation of a *Weltanschauung*, a comprehensive view of the universe by the aid of which the thinker can feel defended against uncertainty and insecurity. It is true that philosophers from Plato to Hegel and the Subjective Idealists devoted much energy to the construction of such theories of the entire universe, but they did much else besides that, such as defining the major problems for thought, refining and clarifying the definition of terms, and seeking a synoptic point of view arising out of a synthesis of the knowledge available at the time without any claim to finality. Freud's approach to philosophy was hindered by an emotional prejudice as is shown by the language and tone of his reference to it in *Inhibitions, Symptoms and Anxiety*. He wrote :

I must confess that I am not at all partial to the fabrication of *Weltanschauungen*. Such activities may be left to the philosophers, who avowedly find it impossible to make their journey through life without a Baedeker of that kind to tell them all about everything. Let us humbly accept the contempt with which they look down on us from the vantage-ground of their superior needs. (1926, p. 29.)

It seems rather that Freud was looking with contempt on the philosopher.

Philosophy cannot be dismissed so easily and one of the penalties Freud paid for doing so was that he was not able to criticize the philosophic assumptions underlying his own theorizing. With the rise of modern science, philosophy has been little concerned with the construction of a *Weltanschauung*. To-day, for example, Existentialism is mainly an attempt to relate human existence to the basic fact of anxiety, while Logical Positivism concerns itself with determining the exact meaning of words and terms. All scientific thinking is compelled to use, as intellectual tools, certain terms and concepts which are not created by the science in question though they are influenced by its development, but are philosophically defined assumptions in constant need of testing and criticism. Freud embarked on his psychological investigations with certain assumptions taken over from the natural science of his day, and learned from Helmholtz via Brücke and Meynert. These assumptions belong to the general outlook that is commonly called Scientific Materialism, and was the philosophy, or perhaps we ought to say pseudo-philosophy, of most scientists at the turn of the century. Professor John Macmurray writes :

There is in our own day a widespread attitude of mind which is itself a kind of immanent philosophy and which is often referred to as the scientific view of the world, or more simply as scientific materialism. It should be recognized that this 'philosophy of science' is neither scientific nor philosophical. It is rather in the nature of a popular ideology or of a reaction to the impact and prestige of scientific achievement upon the minds of intelligent people who are neither scientists nor philosophers. It is not scientific for two reasons. The first is that it is in no sense the result of any scientific investigation carried out by scientific methods. . . . The second is that it is not necessarily the view taken by scientists. Eminent scientists may explicitly repudiate it without any damage to their effectiveness as scientists. On the other hand it is not a view which is the result of any philosophical discussion of science nor a view which is held by trained philosophers. . . . It is the product of an uncritical response to the success of science in its own field, a response which is rather emotional than intellectual, and which substitutes Science, vaguely personified, as an object of faith and worship for the God of religion. This scientific materialism is rather a theology of science than a philosophy. (1939, pp. 18–19.)

There are, however, scientists who do hold this pseudo-philosophy of science, regard it as basic to the scientific outlook, and do not realize that they are not scientists by virtue of holding this ideology but only by virtue of their accurate and painstaking investigation of matters of fact. More especially in Freud's day this ideology constituted a kind of religion of science, especially with those who, like Freud, substituted science for religion in all other senses. That scientific explanation consists in the analytical reduction of all phenomena to material terms whereby they become amenable to being subsumed under the laws of physics in the end, was an uncriticized axiom of thinking, for Brücke, Meynert and Freud. For Freud it was clearly as much a 'faith' as any religious faith, which explains the tremendous emotional struggle he had to transcend the categories of neurophysiology in his psychological investigation. The results are written large over his theorizing as a whole, though it throws into all the more striking relief the power of his genius that in spite of this he should have been able to make the astonishing new discoveries in the realm of 'mind' that he did.

It is unfortunate that, owing to Freud's overpowering influence, psycho-analytical thinking should have become so deeply impregnated with this type of philosophical assumption which is opposed to the essential nature of psycho-analytic theory. It is reassuring to find a more realistic attitude to philosophy in the work of Brierley, which shows the extent to which psycho-analysis comes under the influence of intellectual changes going on beyond its own borders. Brierley writes :

The remarkable thing about Freud's work is not that it should have been influenced by the intellectual climate of his time or should occasionally express personal preferences, but that its principles and implications should have been so far in advance of his time. (1951, p. 155.)

Concerning Freud's own position she says :

Since Freud stated his opinion [*New Introductory Lectures*, p. 232] that the young science of psycho-analysis was in no state to formulate *Weltanschauungen* but must share the common *Weltenschauung* of science, which he thought hardly merited such a high-sounding name, two things have become more evident than they were even ten years ago. Firstly, the *Weltanschauung* of science is not static; in recent years it has undergone quite revolutionary changes. . . . Secondly, though Freud himself was abundantly influenced by the mechanistic *Anschauung* dominant in his earlier years, he had ample evidence that his work was revolutionary. He himself admitted this, but he does not appear to have fully realized quite what a challenge his work as a whole was to the older *Weltanschauung*. But clearly, his conceptions of psychological reality and mental dynamism are absolutely incompatible with any of the older conceptions of mechanistic materialism. (1951, pp. 153–4.)

As to the present position regarding the philosophy of science and its bearing on psycho-analysis, Brierley sums up as follows :

The essence of science is its realistic mode of approach to the object of study. Any subject can therefore be studied scientifically and any technique can claim to be regarded as scientific which devises adequate checks and standards of probability suited to its individual field. The realism with which science is equated is no longer mechanistic materialism. . . . There is as yet little tolerance of psychological reality among many psychologists and sociologists, and, for that matter, still too little among psycho-analysts themselves. But it is a fact that mechanistic materialism is now outmoded . . . the *Weltanschauung* of Western science is in a state of flux; it is a welter of different viewpoints rather than an integrated outlook. . . . Professional philosophy appears to aim at the elaboration and synthesis of defined intellectual conceptions. . . . Some philosophic wholes savour of wish-fulfilment pure and simple, of a personal rebuilding of the universe nearer to the heart's desire. . . . However, all thinking has subjective determinants and some philosophers are less intent on the formation of closed 'systems' than on the synthesis and evaluation of trends of thought and advance in knowledge. (1951, pp. 155-7).

Broadly speaking, reality confronts us with phenomena on three different levels, which we refer to as matter, life and mind; and science needs a different set of basic concepts and terms for the investigation of each of them. Some types of scientific thinker assume that biological and psychological phenomena are only truly scientifically explained when reduced to terms of chemistry and physics. This was a very general assumption at the end of last century and was the view of the teachers under whom Freud grew to intellectual maturity. Other thinkers, as for example A. N. Whitehead, do not regard reductive analysis as adequate to the understanding and explanation of 'higher' phenomena. The mathematical concept of a 'unit' and the physical concept of a 'thing' are not adequate to explain the biological organism, nor is the biological concept of 'organism' adequate to explain mental phenomena, particularly at the level where what we call the 'person' emerges. Macmurray writes:

The unity-patterns of mathematical and of organic thought have already been worked out in the history of philosophy. The unity-pattern through which personality could be represented has not. The problem of the logical representation of the self has, indeed, been the central problem of all modern philosophy. (1933, p. 122.)

In view of the present-day development of what is called 'object-relations' theory in psycho-analysis, two of Macmurray's further comments are clearly of great significance. He says:

The self only exists in the communion of selves. . . . My own existence as a person is constituted by my *knowledge* of other persons, by my objective consciousness of them as persons, not by the mere fact of my relation to them. The main fact that has to be represented is not that I am because you are, but that I am I because I know you, and that you are you because you know me. My consciousness is rational or objective because it is a consciousness of someone who is in personal relation to me and, therefore, knows me and knows that I am I. I have my being in that mutual self-knowledge (pp. 137-8).

To put it in the familiar terms of modern controversy, mathematical relations are external to the terms they relate. Organic relations are internal to their terms. But personal relations are at once internal and external (p. 140).

We here face the crucial issue for psychological thinking. Are the results of the psychological study of human beings as 'persons' capable of being adequately formulated in the impersonal terminology characteristic of the natural sciences of mathematics, physiology and biology, or by evolving a new terminology capable of representing 'personal phenomena'? Freud faced this problem in making the transition from physiology to psychology, but he did not solve it largely because the means to do so did not exist at that time. Perhaps even now we have only just got so far as to see the problem more clearly, and Freud's own work was one of the major factors in forcing that much progress.

Is psychology a discipline in its own right, or only a subordinate sub-division of physiology in the end? For psychology the issue may now be said to present itself in terms of the choice between 'process theory' and 'personal theory'. In this form it has been explicitly dealt with by Brierley, who expounds psycho-analysis in both ways, while distinguishing clearly between them. Not all analytical writers are as careful, and there is great harm in mixing and confusing the two types of theory, presenting what purports to be a theory of personal relationships in what is actually a process theory which reduces the personal to the impersonal.

3. Freud's Metapsychology; the Pleasure Principle

We must indicate in some detail how the two types of theory clashed in Freud's own work even while he held predominantly to the 'process theory' thinking which he had learned from the natural sciences. We have to distinguish between the clinical facts which Freud discovered and the theory he evolved to explain them. The theory is built on certain assumptions which Freud elaborated in a number of his writings, among others in *Beyond the Pleasure Principle* (1920). His hypotheses of the pleasure principle and the Death Instinct express the ideology and mode of thought he acquired in his earlier physiological and neurological studies, and which he *brought to* the study of clinical psychological data rather than *inferred from* them. They represent the philosophical orientation underlying Freud's theorizing as his neurologist's philosophy.

Freud states, in the above monograph, that psycho-analysis takes for granted that unpleasant tension 'automatically' sets going mental events which then aim at decrease of unpleasant tension. It is arbitrarily assumed that increase of excitation is the meaning of 'unpleasure' and decrease means 'pleasure'. This quantity theory is held to explain the operation of the mental apparatus to reduce excitation to a low level and keep it there : this is the pleasure principle, for the increase of excitation above a *constant* low level means 'unpleasure'. The constancy principle and the pleasure principle are the same. This principle of keeping cerebral excitation constant goes back to the Breuer period. (Cp. pp. 7–9.)

Thus the pleasure principle is, strictly speaking, a physiological, not a psychological, concept. Though it is put forward to explain *mental* events and related to the quantity of excitation that is held to be present in the *mind*, this 'mind' is in fact regarded as a mechanical model, an apparatus (as E. Jones emphasized) in which events are automatically regulated—not for the fulfilment of *meaningful aims*, which would be a psychological conception, but for the reduction of *quantity of excitation* to a constant level. This is simply the psychology for neurologists which Freud was supposed to have abandoned in 1895.

As late as 1920 the concepts and thought-forms of the physiologist are transferred unaltered in essence to psychology and applied to mental phenomena, thereby reducing them to the status of a mere parallel though psychic version of physiological events. This attempt both to separate and to combine neurophysiology and psychology at one and the same time throws no extra light on either of them. It is the description of a physiological process to which a psychological label—i.e. 'pleasure and unpleasure'—has been attached. This mixing of disciplines leads to serious error when it is applied to 'personal' phenomena.

We must either set out to explain neurological events in the appropriate physiological, biochemical and electrical terms, or else set out to explain a different set of facts—the psychological events of the mental and personal life of man—and discover what are the appropriate terms for that. We can then include and correlate both in a synoptic view of a human being as a whole, but to seek to explain the latter in terms only appropriate to the former darkens all issues. We can have a physiological 'process theory' or a psychological 'personal theory'. So-called 'metapsychology' purports to be psychology while in fact it is physiology with a psychological label. Pleasure and unpleasure are psychological experiences and cannot be simply related to diminution and increase of excitation respectively. Sometimes the reverse is the case. Furthermore these are qualitative terms and a physiologist would not find them useful for the explanation of his quantitative phenomena; neither are the physiologist's quantitative terms really useful to the psychologist to explain his qualitative phenomena. This way of thinking is, in reality, an expression of the ultimate wish of the natural scientist to reduce the mental to the material, or, failing that, to treat it as T. H. Huxley did, as an irrelevant epiphenomenon having no more importance than the steam whistle has for the driving of the train. (Huxley died in 1895, the year in which Freud wrote his Project for a 'Psychology for Neurologists'.)

Freud himself speaks of the hypothesis of the Pleasure Principle as a speculative assumption which he justifies in the statement that no philosopher or psychologist has shown the meaning of feelings of pleasure and unpleasure, and he thinks his hypothesis is the best because he regards it as the least rigid one. But firstly, on the properly psychological level of personal aims and object relationships, the meaning of pleasure and unpleasure is not so obscure after all. Secondly, Freud's 'quantity of excitation' hypothesis and his 'constancy principle' appear to form the *most*, rather than the *least*, rigid hypothesis, since it allows of no properly psychological explanation of what are actually psychological facts.

Concerning Freud's terms we must ask whether this pleasure- or constancy-principle is a *pleasure* principle or an *energy-tension* principle? Is mental or psychic activity the characteristic of a *person* dealing with an environment that has significant meanings for his personal needs and aims, and who therefore feels pleased when he is satisfied and pained when he is thwarted; or is it the characteristic of a *mental apparatus* for the equalization of energy-pressures? In the latter case it need not have any 'meaning', nor is there any reason why tension should give unpleasure and discharge should give pleasure. This 'apparatus' is pictured on the model of the pressure of a weight of water piling up behind a dam, which it then bursts through so that it flows out and finds a common level where pressure is equally distributed and tension is for the time being non-existent. We cannot suppose that the water has any 'aim' in this nor that it finds any part of the process either pleasant or unpleasant. The accumulation and discharge of the pressure of dammed-up excitation may be thought of neurologically as occurring in the brain and nervous system, or 'psychologically' as occurring in a 'mental apparatus' for the regulation of psychic tensions. But in fact these are only two parallel ways of saying the same thing, and no genuine psychological thinking has yet taken place. We are talking in terms of impersonal 'processes'. So-called *psychological process theory* is not in principle different from *neurological process theory*. There is not really any place here for the use of the psychological term 'pleasure', for this is a qualitative term expressing the fact that an experience has a satisfying significance for a personal experiencing subject. Neither a nervous system nor a mental apparatus can feel pleasure. Only an experiencing subject can feel pleasure according as his needs and aims are fulfilled or frustrated. Freud would find in Drever something 'offered to our purpose', a 'psychological theory which was able to inform us of the meaning of the feelings of pleasure and unpleasure'. In Drever's view, pleasure is experienced when an activity is progressing optimally towards the achievement of an aim, and unpleasure when the activity progresses either too slowly or too quickly towards such achievement. (Drever, 1917.)

It is not even true that increase of excitation (tension) is necessarily unpleasant and diminution pleasant. In a sexual relationship both increase and diminution of tension and excitation are pleasurable if and when they are phases of a total satisfying relationship. Excitation becomes unpleasant only when the relationship is interfered with and left incomplete. If we use the terms 'pleasure' and 'unpleasure', then we are dealing with mental or psychic activity as a characteristic of a personal subject achieving or being frustrated in achieving experiences in object-relationships which are meaningful for the satisfaction of his needs and aims. We are then thinking in terms of 'personal theory', not of 'process theory'.

Freud's pleasure principle is thus not a properly psychological hypothesis. The psychological problem is confessedly given up as 'obscure and inaccessible'. (1920, p. 2.) 'Pleasure principle psychology' is but a pseudo-psychology in which the mental life of man is represented as an apparatus concerned with the regulation of quantities of excitation, energy and tension, which must be kept as far as possible at a low and constant level. A clinical example shows the pitfalls in the path of this type of theory in practice. A patient of mine had a mother of exceptionally strong personality, of extremely rigid and 'high' moral and religious principles, who had brought him up with excessive emphasis on routine, orderliness and strict discipline. In his late teens he developed insomnia and restless 'nerviness' for which he was taken to a neurologist. This consultant said that his brain was overactive and he must be kept from all exciting and stimulating experiences, go to bed at 8 p.m. every night and rest as much as possible. This managing mother was to see that this was done. The unpleasure of excitation must be reduced to a low level. The patient, however, got worse rapidly, and soon refused point-blank to go to bed at 8 p.m. Even his mother's powerful hold over him could not prevent his going out in the evenings with his friends, though she did her best. The 'nerviness' continued, but the patient discovered that when, a year or two later, his job took him away from home (and from his mother) he felt much less tense than he had done for a long time. His life did not, in the ordinary sense of the term, contain anything unusually or grossly exciting or over-stimulating. His mother had all too successfully enforced on him a distinctly quiet, orderly and somewhat uneventful life. The explanation lay rather in the psychological and qualitative sphere of the peculiarly frustrating nature of his relationship with his mother which had *meanings* for him of the most unpleasant kind in the denial of his right to become a self-directing and purposive person on his own initiative. Pleasure and unpleasure in this connection are not intelligible in terms of quantity of excitation, but only in terms of the significance of personal fulfilment and personal relationships. But for the pseudo-philosophy of scientific materialism, Freud would surely not have attempted to explain clinical data of the above kind by means of 'process theory' of an impersonal and, at bottom, physiological type. A properly psychological theory must be a 'personal theory', and any type of non-personal theory is not genuine psychology but disguised physiology.

4. *Freud's Metapsychology: The Death Instinct*

For psycho-analysis, psychology is the study of the personal human mind. If the human mind is depersonalized it ceases to be human, but it is not possible to create a science by the falsification of the data. That is the peculiar problem that faces science in dealing with 'personality', unless Brierley's broader definition of science is borne in mind. On this question of depersonalization, she writes:

The natural trend of science . . . is towards objectivity and abstract thinking. Since the real existents are particulars, whereas universals are ideal existents, this trend is also towards de-personalization. . . . The trend of scientific thinking towards objectivity and de-personalization is represented in psycho-analysis by the development of metapsychology. Metapsychology is the 'pure science' aspect of psycho-analysis and the metapsychologist's approach to the study of mental organization is essentially the same as the physicist's approach to the study of the atom. (1951, pp. 127–8.)

Personology is individual psychology, whereas metapsychology is a general theory of mental processes and their organization. In its concentration on endopsychic events, metapsychology isolates mental life more artificially than does personology which studies the mental and motor behaviour of persons accepted as living in an actual world among other people (p. 130).

Whether an approach to the study of the 'person' which is 'essentially the same as the physicist's approach to the study of the atom' is a correct scientific approach in this particular case, clearly raises the whole question of what is meant by science. A person and an atom are not the same kind of object, and it seems clear that metapsychology springs from the assumption that the only type of study that is truly scientific is one that reduces all phenomena to their lowest, physical terms. It is the normal procedure for science to abstract some particular aspect of total reality for study, but the abstraction must be relevant to what we seek to understand. Mental processes in a human being are 'personal processes' and it does not appear relevant to abstract them in such a way that they are treated as impersonal processes. Would such a procedure give any valid knowledge of a kind relevant for psycho-analysis? Moreover, is it really *psychological* knowledge for, by admission, it is an attempt to treat mental processes not simply as impersonal but on the model of physical processes, a thinly disguised attempt to 'reduce mind to matter' as the earlier materialists did? Materialism as an emotional prejudice still underlies this type of so-called science.

In chapter II (pp. 31–2) a passage from G. W. Allport was quoted to the effect that science regards the individual as a 'bothersome accident', so that psychology has worked at 'the generalized human mind'. This, he says, is devoid of all the 'essential characteristics of the minds we know'. Hence a new development has arisen, 'the psychology of personality'. Psycho-analytic metapsychology is the equivalent of the study of 'the generalized human mind' and it is not clear what truly psychological purpose is served by it. The fact is that the problem of 'the individual', which science has always hitherto been pretty safe in ignoring, cannot be ignored when it is the human person that is studied, for here 'individuality' is far more of the very essence of what is being studied. There is a grave danger of so-called metapsychological or 'pure science' habits of thought secretly infecting the study of personality in ways that distort and invalidate the study. This seems to have been the case with Freud, in his more speculative thinking, and it is nowhere more clearly shown than in his development of theory beyond the pleasure principle to the concept of a death instinct.

It is clear that if the 'constancy principle' could fully prevail, it would turn out to be a 'stagnancy principle', which would ultimately prove to be equivalent to Freud's death instinct. He decides that increase of excitation must hinder the smooth working of the apparatus and therefore be unpleasurable. In other words the function of our mental life as human beings is to reduce as quickly as possible any tendency to respond to, and deal actively with, our environment, and reduce us to a state of quiescent equilibrium or eternal sleep in which nothing happens. Life is the negation of living, and passivity is the true aim of existence while activity is an adverse nuisance. To such straits are we reduced by this neurophysiological psychology. Such a theory would admirably express unconscious anti-libidinal processes that enforce passivity and sabotage the active enjoyment of living. Brierley writes :

The average standard of modern Western normality has been an average of psychological impoverishment. This average not seldom corresponds to a viable degree of ego-stability dearly purchased at the cost of a host of major and minor impairments of zest for living. . . . These conditions may never result in illness or prevent the subject from making a reasonable success in life, judged by average standards, but the impairments of function may, nevertheless, be appreciable in a host of major and minor psychological impediments to vigorous and joyful living. (1951, pp. 187, 193.)

It is in a culture so characterized that the scientific study of human personality has begun and it would be strange if unconscious determinants of theoretical thinking did not betray their presence in the type of theory favoured. Freud's metapsychological views, from the pleasure or constancy principle to the death instinct seem to be a case in point. At best a human person seems to have become something like a boiler with an electrical immersion heater thermostatically controlled so that as soon as the temperature rises beyond a very low level, the 'apparatus' at once begins to turn itself off.

Freud really had no need for what he calls his 'far-fetched speculation' (1920, p. 27) in the rest of this book which led him to the concept of the death instinct, for that is not 'beyond the pleasure principle' in the long run; it is already contained in essence in the pleasure or constancy principle. This turns out to be a drastic inhibitor of living which, carried to its logical extreme, is in fact a 'death principle'. The pleasure or constancy principle really suffices in itself to take us the whole way to the final goal of the reduction of all organic and psychological tensions to an original inert state in which it appears that death is the aim of life. We can summarize the whole trend of thought as follows :

The pleasure principle, which the mental apparatus is said to operate, aims to regulate excitation (tension) in a definite direction by :

(*a*) *keeping it constant,* i.e. arresting any tendency to increase, which is declared to be unpleasant, by securing discharge or tension-relieving;

(*b*) *keeping it low,* i.e. reducing tension to as low a level as possible, and presumably avoiding stimuli which would increase it, for increase is adverse to the functioning of the mental apparatus;

(*c*) so leading in the direction where we come upon the hypothetical death instinct which calls for *the elimination of excitations and tensions altogether.* This appears to be a psychophysiology of the inhibition of the active process, which defines the aim of living as a steady progress towards the achievement of its own decease. The aim is not given as the satisfaction of positive needs but the prevention, reduction and ultimate cessation of activity.

5. *Freud's Metapsychology: The Reality Principle*

At this point a complication arises, for Freud regarded the pleasure principle as opposed by a reality principle. The pleasure principle characterizes the primary process and the sexual libido, and, after repression, operates in the unconscious. The reality principle characterizes the secondary process of the reality-ego in consciousness. It is true that, as Freud wrote to Ernest Jones: 'The reality principle is only continuing the work of the pleasure principle in a more effectual way, gratification being the aim of both and their opposition only a secondary fact.' (Jones, 1955, p. 502.) The self-preservative interests of the ego enforce delay, when immediate gratification would be dangerous. It is, however, difficult to see why, on Freud's view, the concept of a reality principle should be needed, or why there should be any self-preservative interests in the ego for it to serve. The theory, of course, is supposed not to give sole sway to the death instinct, but to picture living as an opposition of life and death instincts, libido and destructiveness. However, in developing his theory piecemeal Freud did not always recognize when early and later views were incompatible. This was the case with the pleasure principle theory and the life and death instincts theory, for the pleasure principle, which is held to characterize the libidinal process, is only a milder version of the death instinct or the destructive process. For pleasure is not held to characterize the total active libidinal process but only the discharge and dissipation of its tensions. If reduction of tension and ultimately death is the real aim of life, then the sooner it is achieved the better. The most successful operation of the death instinct—suicide—would indeed be the virtue and the source of pleasure and satisfaction (at least in contemplation and in prospect) that the Roman Stoics held it to be. It seems pointless to say that the pleasure principle, in face of external difficulties, is not efficient and is dangerous, because it may lead too rapidly to the goal of death which in the last resort is aimed at. In any case the so-called reality principle is only a matter of 'delaying tactics' in the search for pleasure. Since pleasure or satisfaction is the reduction of excitations which had better never have arisen, and the termination of unpleasure and of adverse tendencies towards greater activity in the apparatus (which is in conformity with the final aim of death), this delaying tendency of the reality principle must be a nuisance to be classed with everything that disturbs the smooth working of the apparatus unpleasurably. The reality principle is merely the postponement of satisfaction in a quick death. It gives up chances of obtaining this satisfaction by tolerating unpleasure for the time being on the long winding road to the goal. This reality principle is a radical inconsistency in the whole theory if the constancy (or pleasure) principle and the death instinct are true. If the clinical facts call for a reality principle, which is really an 'object-relations principle', then the constancy principle and death instinct need drastic reconsideration.

Yet the pleasure principle, which on the one hand reduces to the negative constancy principle, is on the other hand regarded as the principle of operation of the primary process, the positive libidinal urge for satisfaction. Here, then, is a curious contradiction. The reality principle, as Freud conceived it, in its immediate operation is an anti-libidinal principle with an ultimately libidinal aim, and the pleasure principle is a libidinal principle with an ultimately anti-libidinal aim. Such are the anomalies to which this neurophysiological quantity theory leads us. It is, of course, strange that, if the goal of life is death, life should have arisen at all. It can only be an irrelevance and a passing disturbance. It seems doubtful, however, if the significance of life can be understood for those who live it by the observation that life is merely a running round in a circle to come back to the starting-point.

Freud arbitrarily equated unpleasure with increase, and pleasure with diminution, of excitation, without taking into account the *total situation* of the satisfaction of a need in and for object-relationship. Pleasure is supposed not to be felt in the rising of desire and the increase of tension, but only in the activity that leads to energy discharge, relief of tension and subsequent quiescence or equilibrium. The theory is based on the neurophysiology of the sexual process. It implies that pleasure is not a characteristic of activity *per se*, for activity can be aimed at the increase of excitation. When Freud says that increase of tension is equivalent to unpleasure, he is meaning that the mounting up of tension without as yet any discharge is unpleasant. In actual fact it may be characterized by either pleasure or unpleasure, for excitement itself can be pleasure-toned, otherwise it would not be capable of serving at all as a substitute for the satisfaction of real good-object relations of which the deteriorated pleasure-seeker is incapable. Tension without discharge is only purely unpleasurable when the prospect of satisfaction of the psychological aim is hopeless. To have to go on wanting what one cannot get is painful. Resort is then had to *ad hoc* tension-relieving devices, which, far from bringing pure pleasure in their train, are usually experienced as disappointingly unsatisfying, because mere decrease of excitation is not what is wanted and in itself gives nothing that can produce a sense of deep satisfaction.

On the other hand, the mounting of the tension of desire is itself pleasurable when satisfaction is possible and expected. It can hardly be maintained that the physical tension differs in the two cases. What differs is the psychological and personal setting. The reality principle is primarily the object-seeking principle, and secondly the adjustment of desire to the possibilities of satisfaction. If tension *qua* tension were unpleasant in itself and the aim were simply its reduction, then any method of relieving excitation would be as good as any other, i.e. autoeroticism would be as satisfactory as object-love and much more easily come by. In reality the reverse is the case. If, however, the aim is not mere reduction of tension *per se* but the achievement of a goal in personal relationship concerning which there is both prospective and retrospective pleasure, then the reality principle is not a mere principle of delayed pleasure. Prospective pleasure, pleasure in possession, and retrospective pleasure in satisfaction obtained are different phases of the total personal relationship.

The pleasure principle, in so far as it leads on to the Death Instinct, is really an 'elimination-of-pleasure principle', for the more tension is reduced the less capacity there is for feeling anything at all. At best it is an 'absence-of-unpleasure principle'. So long as it is viewed as simply a matter of quantities of increase or decrease of tension or excitation, no other view is possible. Only when we view psychic activity as a matter of achievement or frustration of personal aims can an intelligible meaning be given to the terms 'pleasure' and 'unpleasure'. Satisfaction, however, is not something confined simply to the point and process of energy discharge.

It characterizes the entire process of desire, working for the end in view, reaching the goal and retrospective enjoyment of the result. Temporary obstacles may enhance pleasure in working. It is only hopeless frustration that is personally experienced as unpleasure. Otherwise, the entire active process can be experienced as pleasure-giving.

Enjoyment is the enjoyment of reality, of a satisfying relationship to reality, so that the pleasure principle is itself, properly speaking, a reality principle. Only when pleasure is sought as substitute for real relationships can any distinction be made, and that is the description of a psychopathological condition. Fairbairn holds that *there is only one principle in nature, a reality principle governed by an object-relationships aim.*

6. Freud's Metapsychology and Ego-Analysis

In taking up the analysis of the ego, Freud confronted himself with the issue of process theory versus personal theory, and took the important step of introducing the terminology of personal theory at this point. His analysis of the ego came about through observing that a personal object who is lost or given up so far as external relationship is concerned, is usually introjected or installed in the ego itself by means of a psychic identification of part of the ego with the object. The ego in part takes on the task of representing the object in the inner mental life so that relationship can be kept up. This sets going a differentiation of structure in the ego, in view of the fact that what was an external object-relationship has now become represented internally by a relationship between one part of the ego which still remains itself, and another part which now represents the object. Thus, Freud held, the super-ego is formed by the psychic internalization of parents. This is a theory of psychic development by means of experience in personal object-relationships, not by means of impersonal 'processes' of instinct-maturation, impulse-discharge or else repression and tension-relieving.

Hartmann, Kris and Loewenstein distinguish between impersonal metapsychology and 'metaphorical language', which really amounts to what Brierley calls 'personology', in relation to Freud's structural concepts. They write:

The structural concepts of psycho-analysis have met with much criticism. It has been said that through their use clinical description has been obscured, since the terms were dramatic in an anthropomorphic sense. Clearly, whenever dramatization is encountered, metaphorical language has crept into scientific discourse. . . . The

danger obviously begins if and when metaphor infringes upon meaning, in the case in point, when the structural concepts are anthropo-
morphized. Then the functional connotation may be lost, and one of
the psychic systems may be substituted for the total personality.
(1946, p. 16.)

They remark that in Alexander's *Psycho-Analysis of the Total
Personality* the id, ego and super-ego have become exalted actors
on the psychic stage. To test the issue they select a statement by
Freud in metaphorical language to the effect that 'The ego
presents itself to the super-ego as love-object', and turn it into
process-theory language. They state that :

The metaphor expresses the relation of two psychic organizations
by comparing it to a love relation between two individuals in which
one is the lover and the other the beloved. However, the sentence
expresses an important clinical finding : self-love can easily and does,
under certain conditions, substitute for love of another person. Self-
love in this formulation indicates that approval of the self by the
super-ego concerns the self in lieu of another person. (*Ibid.*, p. 16.)

Turning this into process-theory terms, they replace 'ego' by 'self'
since 'ego' by Freudian definition stands for only a part of the
personality; and they reject 'love' or 'approval and disapproval'
by the super-ego in favour of 'different kinds and degrees of
tension between the two psychic organizations, according to the
presence or absence of conflict between their functions. Approval
would be characterized by diminution of tensions; disapproval by
its increase.' (1946, p. 16.) Conflict, however, is also a dramatic
and anthropomorphic term and should be omitted. The statement
'The ego presents itself to the super-ego as love-object' has now
become, presumably, 'The self is related to the super-ego by increase or diminution of tensions'. Concerning this process-theory
terminology they say :

There can be little doubt that a reformulation of this kind that tries
to restrict the use of metaphor, considerably impoverishes the plas-
ticity of language as compared with Freud's mode of expression.
Man frequently experiences self-satisfaction as if an inner voice expressed approval, and self-reproaches as if an inner voice expressed
disapprobation. Thus the metaphorical expression comes closer to
our immediate understanding, since the anthropomorphism it introduces corresponds to human experience. Our reformulation shows
that not the concepts which Freud introduced are anthropomorphic,
but that the clinical facts he studied and described led us to under-

stand what part anthropomorphism plays in introspective thinking.
(1946, p. 17.)

Evidently, as compared with pure process-theory terminology, which casts psychology into a 'natural science' form by the use of thought-forms characteristic of physiology, Freud's structural terms are indisputably a personal terminology. For that reason they have been accused of being dramatic, anthropomorphic and metaphorical. But these writers distinguish between the strict and the metaphorical usage of these terms. The strict usage seeks to reduce them by the restriction of metaphor to the impersonal form of process-theory language which, though more 'scientific', is admitted to be considerably impoverished in its ability to represent clinical findings, i.e. the actual psychological data. They agree that 'the metaphorical expression comes closer to our immediate understanding, since the anthropomorphism it introduces corresponds to human experience', and they comment that it is not Freud's terms but the clinical facts that are 'anthropomorphic'. Yet they also fear that metaphor may reduce the scientific accuracy of terminology. Like Freud himself they are relentlessly driven by the facts away from impersonal process terminology towards personal theory terms, to the accompaniment of anxiety lest this should be less scientific. Is the criticism valid that personal terminology is dramatic, anthropomorphic and metaphorical?

The Student's English Dictionary (Ogilvie and Annandale) states that *anthropomorphism* is 'the representation or conception of (the non-human) under a human form or with human attributes'. *Metaphor* is 'A figure of speech founded on resemblance, by which a word is transferred from an object to which it properly belongs to another, so that a comparison is implied. Thus "that man is a fox" is a metaphor.' (*Student's English Dictionary.*) Hence to criticize the description of the psychic phenomena of the human person in personal terms as anthropomorphic and metaphorical is incorrect. If it is metaphorical to say 'That man is a fox', it is simply a statement of fact to say 'That man is a man'. It would be odd if the psychical processes of *man* were not *anthropomorphic*. What else can they be? Anthropomorphism in this case is not metaphor, or personification of the impersonal, but an objective and scientific statement of the fact that, since man is a person, all his psychic functions are personal activities. When structural differentiations develop within the totality of the psychic life, each differentiated aspect of the self is still *a person functioning*, not an impersonal process going on inside a personal psyche which would be a meaningless idea. Even depersonalized states of mind are

really only pseudo-impersonal states due to the defensive withdrawal of a person from too disturbing contact with his outer
world. The scheme of Freud cannot therefore be criticized for
using personal concepts like 'ego' and 'super-ego' to denote two
of the functional differentiations of the total self. It can more justly
be criticized for using the non-personal term 'id' for the third
differentiation.

These writers choose the excellent example of ego-super-ego
relations in terms of self-approval or self-disapproval as a test case.
They write :

> Man frequently experiences self-satisfaction *as if* [present writer's
> italics] an inner voice expressed approval, and self-reproaches *as if*
> [ditto] an inner voice expressed disapprobation. Thus the meta-
> phorical expression comes closer to our immediate understanding.
> (1946, p. 17.)

But the expression is not metaphorical but a literal statement of
fact. The inner voice is a voice, it is my own voice, it is me speaking
to myself, and it is me speaking as mother or father because I feel
that in that part of myself I am one with mother or father. The
psychic fact of 'identification' is being represented. One of my
patients used repeatedly to fall into periods of compulsive shouting
at herself. On one occasion, after a trivial mistake, she spent the
best part of two hours going about her household duties and all
the time shouting at herself aloud : 'You silly thing', 'You ought
to have known better', 'Why don't you think before you speak?',
'You ought to be ashamed of yourself' and so on. Presently she
began to feel worn out under this barrage of criticism, and suddenly she realized that these were the very words that her mother
used when heaping abuse on her and that she was feeling exactly
as she used to feel when her mother would go on and on at her.
Auditory hallucinations and split-personality phenomena show
how literally functional differentiations within the total psyche
retain personality in themselves, for the simple reason that they
are the person acting in that way.

Freud's discovery of the super-ego, and the development of
'internal object-relations' theory accurately represents the human
psyche as the kind of entity that carries on its own internal development by differentiating itself into a number of *dramatis personae*. Thus it maintains its own inner life in the personal form of
a mental reproduction of its outer life as it feels and experiences
it. The one person functions actually as a group of persons and
that is the psychologically objective fact that theory has to represent. Only a personal terminology is adequate to this.

This problem of 'process theory versus personal theory' was discussed in a B.B.C. Third Programme broadcast by Nigel Walker. (*The Listener*, Oct. 6, 1955.) He regards personal theory as more adequate for the purpose of psychotherapy than process theory but is not clear as to the use of the term metaphor. His position seems to be that process-theory terminology is ultimately just as metaphorical as personal-theory terminology, and that it is a case of choosing the most useful metaphor. That is a defensible position, but he also suggests that process theory is closer to the literal truth, while personal theory, though metaphorical, is more useful for psychotherapy. My own position would be that either both are (within the limits of possibility) literal truth within their respective spheres, the one physical and the other psychological, or else both are metaphorical since the ultimate 'thing-in-itself' is unknowable; but not that the one is literal and the other metaphorical.

He says :

Unless you believe that the human mind is a thing separate from the nervous systems of the body and brain, it is likely that the only literal account of the changes wrought by psycho-analysis—the only account that is not to some extent metaphorical—has got to be in terms of such things as neurons and electrochemical impulses that run through them. . . . But it would not be of any use to a psychotherapist who has to think in terms of desires, emotions and memories, if only for the very good reason that this is the language he has to talk to his patients. I am not suggesting that these terms themselves are metaphors; a memory or a fit of rage is as real an event as a change in axon potential. . . . My point is that psychotherapy is a field in which a good metaphor is worth more to the technician than the literal truth.

Walker, however, is not easy about this conception of the literal truth. He states that in the 1930s the first steps were taken

in the formulation of a new terminology, so that it is now possible to distinguish in psycho-analytic literature two different languages, the 'process' language and the 'object-relation' language. . . . Most [analysts] are bilingual and even use both terminologies in the same breath without realizing that they are mixing their metaphors. The 'process' language talks of all mental events, emotions, desires, decisions, memories, phantasies, as processes which can be classified. . . . The process theory is a direct descendant of Freud's own attempts to describe mental phenomena in terms that would link them with nervous processes . . . a long time he had hopes (as cerebral anatomists still have) of describing the emotions, memories and desires of our mental life in terms of the electric potentials and neuronal circuits that can be studied in the neurological laboratory. He called this language his 'metapsychology'. The process theory developed out of it. I said . . . that the literal explanation of the effect of psycho-analysis is probably something that can be worded only in terms of neurology. The process theory looks very like an attempt to do this—to substitute the literal truth for metaphors. But in fact it is not based on any objective study of the changes that take place in the central nervous system during psycho-analysis. This kind of observation is not yet possible. Attempts have been made to use the electro-encephalograph . . . for this purpose, but without impressive results. . . . Thus the process theory is an attempt to explain the workings of psycho-analysis in language that is supposed to be as close as possible to that of neurology, but—and here is the trouble—without any means of knowing whether it is anything like the truth. It is a metaphor masquerading as the real thing. To my mind this is far more dangerous than a metaphor that cannot be mistaken for a literal, neurological explanation.

Thus it appears that Walker still regards neurological explanation of mental events as the literal truth and rejects process theory because it is not based on objective neurological study, and is itself only metaphor. We have, then, literal neurological truth, process-theory metaphor and personal-theory metaphor, and in the psychological realm he regards personal-theory metaphor as better than process-theory metaphor. I cannot feel satisfied with that position, since it implies that literal truth can be stated only in materialistic terms, and that to hold that there is a literal psychological truth must imply that 'you believe that the human mind is a thing separate from the nervous systems of the body and brain'. This conclusion does not appear to me necessary. It is better to take up the position that literal truth in an ultimate sense is impossible since we cannot know 'the-thing-in-itself'. In that sense all terms are metaphors. In the realm, however, of phenomenal truth, we have no choice but to be dualists in practice even if we are monists in theory. We have to take body and mind as twin aspects of one reality and study each of them in their own terms, since neither of them throw any light on the nature of the other. The neurologist would like to reduce mind to matter and usually makes the simple assumption that it is so reducible. The psychologist does not usually want to reduce matter to mind as the idealist philosophers did, though for anything we can prove the one position is as defensible as the other, but in practice neither is tenable. We have to deal with two qualitatively different aspects of reality and should frankly study them as such without making unwarrantable assumptions such as that the only literal truth is neurological truth while psychological explanation is metaphor. The study of the organism is one thing, the study of the person is a different thing, even though in the realm of ultimate reality organism and person are, we suppose, the same thing. Neurological and psychological truth are accepted as relatively literal in their own respective spheres. In my opinion, process theory is an attempt to find a middle position based on the illegitimate assumption that the only scientific truth is that which is stated in impersonal terms, after the pattern of thought appropriate to the study of material phenomena in the so-called 'natural sciences'. However, psychological phenomena are as 'natural' as physical phenomena, and have as good a right to be studied in whatever terms lead to understanding. The position taken here is that psychology is a distinct discipline in its own right, the attempt to reduce it to physiology and make it a 'natural science' in the traditional sense of that term fails to enlighten us about the very phenomena we seek to understand, that all psychological phenomena in human beings are, properly speaking, personal phenomena and must be studied by means of a personal and not an impersonal terminology, and that in its own sphere psychological truth stated in personal terms, as in the recently developed 'object-relations terminology', is to be accepted as just as much literal truth as is neurological truth in its own sphere, and is not to be dismissed as metaphor.

Walker states of the 'object-relations' terminology that:

This is very largely the creation of two people, Melanie Klein and Fairbairn . . . the important thing is the patient's 'object-relations', by which they mean, roughly speaking, his attitudes to people. The first people with whom the infant comes into contact are his parents, and he carries the effect of his relationship with them to the grave. This is described in metaphorical terms by saying that in addition to the adult relations with the people with whom he is really associating, he has also got to cope with an inner world of relations to the important figures of his infancy as he saw them.

But in the realm of psychic phenomena this is a literal fact, not a metaphorical statement. The confusion arises out of a failure to grasp the significance of Freud's conceptions of 'psychological reality and mental dynamism' which, as Brierley points out, 'are absolutely incompatible with any of the older conceptions of mechanistic materialism. . . . There is as yet little tolerance of psychological reality among psychologists and sociologists, and, for that matter, still too little among psycho-analysts themselves. But it is a fact that mechanistic materialism is now outmoded.' (1951, pp. 154-7.) It is only from the external and material point of view, and from the point of view of philosophical materialism, that statements about psychological reality in its own appropriate terms appear to be metaphorical.

7. Brierley's Process Theory and Personal Theory

Brierley has discussed this problem extensively and has expounded psycho-analysis in both process-theory and personal-theory terms. She relates the two in the following way. Therapy and research both aim at understanding the patient, but understanding a patient is more than intellectual apprehension; it is empathy, thinking and feeling *en rapport* with the patient. *Empathic understanding* is akin to identification and produces personology, which she regards as 'subjective theory'. On the other hand, *Intellectual Understanding* is more akin to object-relationship and produces metapsychological process theory, which is to be regarded as 'objective theory', i.e. thinking about, rather than thinking with, the patient. She writes:

Subjective theory deals with the data from the standpoint of the living person and should, therefore, express itself in terms belonging to experience . . . objective theory deals with the same data from the standpoint of a temporarily detached observer. Since its approach is essentially impersonal, it should express itself in impersonal language. (1951, pp. 93-4.)

This, however, is a questionable mode of representing the antithesis. To begin with there is an objective mode of emotional relationship as well as an empathic and identificatory one. It is essential both to feel with and to feel about a person, in order to know him as a person. Neither of these are at the level of scientific thinking or theory making. They yield the data about which the detached observer must think. In physical science the question of empathic understanding of the object does not arise. The electron does not feel and the scientific observer cannot feel with it. It is doubtful whether he feels much about it either, other than scientific interest. Neither feeling with nor feeling about the non-personal object is essential to 'knowing' it. It can only be known intellectually. A person, however, is not 'known' if he is only known intellectually; he must be known emotionally as well, for that arises out of what is meant by his being a person. The problem of emphatic understanding arises only when we deal with the living object, and only fully when we deal with the human person. Impersonal and purely intellectually detached observation is not now adequate to the full apprehension of the object. But we are here still at the level of direct experience.

Empathic understanding and emotional object-relationship are not scientific theory; they constitute, practically, the effecting of personal relationship without which a person cannot be known as a person at all. They may be regarded scientifically as the means of collecting data about persons as persons and thus they correspond to the scientific experiment with the impersonal object. Science can deal with persons only through the medium of experiments in personal relationship, which is what the psychotherapeutic relationship is. H. S. Sullivan calls the psychotherapist a 'participant observer'. This point has been put by Ezriel and Fairbairn in considering the scientific status of the psycho-analytical session as a basis for scientific theory. This approach to the object of study is not required in dealing with 'things'—atoms, rocks and non-personal objects in general.

The stage of thinking, of scientific theory-making, is one of standing back to examine the data collected from the experiment; even though in practice this thinking may be going on at the same time as the experiment, it is logically distinguishable. Both the physical scientist and the psycho-analyst can conduct his experiment, and observe and think about what he observes at the same time. In both cases the gathering of the data is by subjective experience of the experiment which is in the one case an impersonal relationship to a non-personal object, and in the other a personal relationship with a personal object. In the first case the emerging theory will be couched in impersonal terms because the object is impersonal. In psychology, however, the theory should be couched in terms appropriate to the personal nature of the phenomena studied. In both cases, the collection of the data is by subjective experience, the making of the theory is by objective intellectual thinking by a temporarily detached observer, with this difference that in one case the subjective experience was impersonal and in the other personal. We can hardly, therefore, with Brierley distinguish between subjective and objective theory, for all theory is objective.

The position may be set out thus :

(1) Experimental Collection of Data

    (a) Physics. Personal subjective experience of objectively observing and experimenting with the non-personal object.

(*b*) Psychology. Personal subjective experience of objectively observing and dealing with the personal object, plus subjectively thinking and feeling with the personal object, both in the situation of a personal relationship.

(2) Theory-making by Abstract Thinking

(*a*) Physics. Explanatory theory about the non-personal object in terms of non-personal processes, couched in impersonal terms.

(*b*) Psychology. Explanatory theory about the personal object in terms of personal—i.e. motivated—activities (personal processes), couched in personal terms—that is to say in terms appropriate to the personal nature of the object.

'Metapsychology' falls between two stools. It is neither physics nor psychology. A generalized or abstract statement about a person and his personal processes or motivated activities is not necessarily a statement in an impersonal form, as seems to be assumed in metapsychology. Brierley's Personology seeks to create a science of psychology in terms appropriate to the personal nature of what psychology deals with, and is as much 'objective theory' as exposition of impersonal process theory. The contrast should not be between objective process theory and subjective personology, but between impersonal process theory and personal process theory, of which both are objective theory but only the latter is psychology.

The real issue at stake is the nature of psycho-analysis as psychological science. Foulkes writes: 'Psycho-analysis does not belong exclusively to the natural sciences but to the social sciences as well. . . . Dynamic psychology or psycho-analysis needs new criteria . . . distinct from those of physics. . . . The concept of *science* might have to be changed so as to do justice to a dynamic psychology which is based on the social nature of man, on the interpersonal nature of the data.' (1957, pp. 327-9.)

I would rather say that all sciences are natural sciences, that the limited meaning of the term in its traditional usage is not in accord with facts, but if that traditional meaning is adhered to, then we may say that psycho-analysis, or dynamic psychology, does not belong at all to the natural sciences. Natural science terminology throws no light on psychological phenomena, i.e. on the nature and motivated activities or personal processes of persons. Brierley writes: 'Psycho-analytic personology is a psychology, not an anatomy or physiology, of personality; it is concerned with subjective experience and the motivation of behaviour.' (1951, p. 125.) By contrast process theory or meta-psychology is an attempt to create a psychophysiology, or rather a psychology in physiological thought forms and is neither psychology nor physiology. It would be better to abandon it as a relic of the scientific outlook of Freud's day and generation. Freud's theory of psychic structure was an attempt to create a true *psychodynamic* theory, a psychology of man as a person, after the false start of instinct and process theory. In analysing ego-structure Freud was dealing with man as a person whose psyche became internally differentiated and organized as a result of his experience in personal object-relations. He was formulating a new type of theory, different in kind from his early theory. If our argument is valid, it is to be accepted not as 'metaphorical thinking' but as the properly scientific form for a theory of personality.

All concepts are symbols, but symbol and metaphor are not the same thing. At each level of scientific investigation and abstraction, symbol-concepts are needed which are appropriate to the subject-matter, whether it be nuclear physics, biochemical processes or psychological (i.e. personal and motivated) activities. Metapsychology tends to reify the 'process' as a thing-in-itself in much the same way as instincts have been reified. There is nothing specially explanatory about the term 'process'; it is simply a label for 'activity' of some kind, and activity can be activity of either an impersonal or a personal object. Freud's metapsychological process theory of organic instinctive tensions, mind as an apparatus of control working by the unpleasure and pleasure principles (or rather the tension and discharge principles) tending ultimately to elimination of all tensions in quiescence and death, is a model of mechanical energy displacement and throws no light on man as a person whose psychological fate depends on his self-realization in good personal relations or his frustration in unsatisfying ones. Here the important concepts are needs, purposive activities, meanings and significances. Metapsychology abstracts from the personal whole and chooses to express what it abstracts in impersonal ways. Thus it automatically debars itself from giving any account of the personal, which, in human psychology is the very thing we are trying to understand. The term 'metapsychology' itself is questionable. It is formed as a parallel to metaphysics which goes beyond physics to philosophy, and it ought to mean going beyond psychological science to its philosophical implications; but metapsychology is an attempt to go back to physics from the properly psychological point of view. Brierley writes:

Processes are initiated by inner and outer stimuli. Analysts, however, regard instinct as the prime mover, the continuous stimulus to psychic activity. (1951, p. 105.)

Instinct, therefore, is not regarded as itself psychic activity, not as the impulse of a whole psychosomatic self towards an object; it is a stimulus operating upon the psychic apparatus from outside that apparatus (even though from inside the organism), just as external stimuli operate upon the psychic apparatus from outside. Here metapsychology lands us in an ultimate body-psyche, or matter-mind dualism. Instead of being presented with a personal subject owning his own impulses which express his own vital forms of activity, we have the internal motive forces of psychic activity presented as something external to that activity. We have here the basic reason why Freud's ego-psychology was incompatible with his instinct theory, for it was in principle a personal theory while his instinct theory was a depersonalized process theory.

Brierley advocates 'metapsychology as process theory' partly on the ground that it will appeal to the natural scientist and reconcile him to psychology. She writes :

Process thinking is a kind of thinking familiar to modern biologists, physiologists, and experimental psychologists, and the language of our general theory is therefore better known to other scientists than the more private clinical jargon that serves us very well but is often abhorrent and meaningless to them. (1951, p. 120.)

In fact, however, it can only go on encouraging them to believe that psychology can be reduced to a natural science, and help them to avoid the challenge of the necessity to think about 'persons' in terms of a 'personal theory' which does not have to be 'a private clinical jargon'. The alternative is not between impersonal process theory and clinical jargon, but between impersonal process theory and a theory of man in terms appropriate to his personal nature. To advocate a depersonalized theory on the ground that it will appeal to non-psychologists is dangerously reminiscent of the compromise which Freud charged against Jung, namely that of advocating a desexualized theory on the ground that it would appeal more to those who were outside psycho-analysis.

8. *Recent Discussions in 1955–6*

Chapter III, chapter V, section 2, and this chapter have raised what must be regarded as the fundamental question for psychoanalytical theory, namely its nature as science. This arises out of the fact that since Freud's time radical changes have taken place in basic scientific concepts, above all in physics where change was least of all expected to take place in Freud's day.

Freud belonged to the era of Helmholtzian physics and physiology. Behind the work of Helmholtz lies that of Newton one hundred and fifty years earlier. Newton gave his complete demonstration of his theory of gravitation in 1687. Helmholtz died in 1894. By 1905 Einstein propounded his theory of Relativity initiating a radical revision of all basic physical concepts. Freud's scientific orientation belonged to the pre-Einstein era. Fairbairn regards the most important effect of that as his divorce of energy from structure as seen finally in his concepts of the id on the one hand and the ego and super-ego on the other. It reflects a scientific ideology which had held sway some two hundred years when Freud began to explore the psyche. The Newtonian scheme was a dualism of matter, time and space on the one hand and force on the other. A natural law was a statement of how absolute matter moved in absolute time and in absolute space. These three entities were fixed and unchangeable. Yet matter was held to be dead, inert, unable to move of itself if at rest or to stop of itself if moving. Newton hypothesized a 'force'—the force of gravitation—to account for change. This gravitational force of attraction between any two bodies could be calculated, and it became the scientific ideal to account for every variation of movement by a single law, that of the force of attraction or gravitation which was proportional to the product of the masses of two bodies divided by the square of the distance between them which changed as the force pulled them towards each other. Other origins of 'force' such as electricity, magnetism, radiation, came to be regarded as operating in the same way as Newton's gravitational force. Physics aimed at one all-embracing law which should explain all things as reducible to matter in motion under the influence of force (energy). This was the basis of so-called scientific materialism and was carried over into Helmholtzian physiology which was the basis of Freud's thinking.

The theory of relativity gave the death-blow to this rigid materialism. Matter, space and time ceased to be absolute and were found to be themselves changeable or relative to the velocity or else absence of movement of the observer. As the velocity of motion of a body increases relative to the observer, time and space diminish and mass grows greater. Matter, space and time have been turned into relations between 'events' so far as our perception is concerned. Perception itself takes time, and this is treated as a fourth dimension. Objects, so far as their perceived existence is concerned, are 'events', and 'events' make up the physical world. The old dualism of matter (structure) and force (energy) is resolved away into 'events'. There is no 'matter' or 'structure' separate from energy, and there is no 'energy' separate from matter or structure. These are two aspects of one and the same thing, the event. Had Freud been trained in the post-Einstein physics of the present day, even if he still took the thought-forms of physical science as the basis of his psychological theory, he could not have evolved a theory in which psychic energy was conceived as an id separate and distinct from psychic structure conceived as an ego and super-ego, or, as in his original scheme, psychic energy conceived as a dynamic unorganized instinctual unconscious, and psychic structure represented by the psychic apparatus developed to control instinctive tensions. This kind of dualism in basic concepts has become untenable. Fairbairn writes:

> Freud's divorce of energy and structure represents a limitation imposed upon his thought by the general scientific atmosphere of his day. (*Op. cit.*, p. 150.)

E. Jones's biography of Freud enables us to understand why Freud's properly psychodynamic analysis made such difficult headway against his deep-rooted metapsychological tendency, to transfer into the psychological sphere the thought-forms characteristic of physical science. It is that which makes necessary the radical rethinking of the theories he developed to explain his discoveries concerning mental functioning.

The line of argument followed in this chapter has received recently much support, in Britain in articles in the Freud Centenary number of *The British Journal for the Philosophy of Science*, May 1956, and in America by Dr. K. M. Colby in a book entitled *Energy and Structure in Psychoanalysis* and in an article by Dr. T. Szasz on the concept of Entropy. Three of the contributions in *The British Journal for the Philosophy of Science*, by independent students of psycho-analysis, are of especial interest, since the philosophical implications of psycho-analysis as a science is a subject on which the analyst *qua* analyst may rightly be expected to pay heed to the expert on the philosophy of science who has a competent knowledge of psycho-analysis.

The first two writers deal specificially with the pleasure-pain principle, constancy principle or reduction of tension principle as the basic concept of Freud's theoretical structure. This concept is now known as the principle of *Homeostasis* and accepted into psycho-analysis, as by Franz Alexander who wrote in 1949:

Life consists in a continuous cycle of supply and output of energy
... the primary function of the cerebrospinal and autonomic nervous
system is to maintain this dynamic equilibrium, which is upset both
by external stimuli and by the process of living itself. Disturbances of
equilibrium appear psychologically in the form of needs and wishes
which seek gratification and serve as the motive of voluntary behaviour. A basic tendency of the organism is to keep these psychological tensions at a constant level. Freud borrowed this principle
from Fechner and called it the 'principle of stability'. Its physiological counterpart was first recognized by Claude Bernard and
formulated by Cannon in his principle of 'homeostasis,' the tendency
of living organisms to preserve internal conditions like temperature
and the concentration of body fluids at a constant level. The principles of stability and homeostasis are identical, one describing it in
psychological, the other in physiological terms. The psycho-analytic
theory of the ego is that its function is to implement the principle of
stability. (1949, pp. 35–6.)

Concerning this foundation principle of Freud's theoretical thinking, *R. S. Peters* (of the Department of Philosophy and Psychology, Birkbeck College, University of London), in an article entitled *Freud's Theory*, writes:

Human beings, like other organisms, tend to preserve a state of
equilibrium. They are enabled to do this by their nervous system
which is an apparatus having the function of abolishing stimuli, or
of reducing excitation to the lowest possible level, an apparatus which
would even, if this were feasible, maintain itself in an altogether un-
stimulated condition. Our mental life is a function of this apparatus
and our experience of pleasure and pain reflects the manner in
which this mastering of stimuli takes place. (1956, p. 4.)

Nigel Walker (Chairman, Davidson Clinic, Edinburgh), in a paper
on *Freud and Homeostasis* (1956, pp. 61–72), embarks on a
specific study of this question. He writes:

Freud's use of the concept of homeostasis, in the hypothesis that
'the nervous system is an apparatus having the function of abolishing
stimuli' (Freud, 1915, *C.P.* IV, p. 60) is of great interest, not only
because it represents the pessimistic core of his materialism but also
because it appears to anticipate by a quarter of a century the
notions of cybernetics. Although it is usually overlooked in psycho-
analysts' expositions of psycho-analysis it is the unifying concept that
links together the wish-fulfilment explanation of dreams, the defence
mechanisms of the ego and the repetition compulsion. (1956, p. 61.)

Dreaming reduces the tension of unsatisfied wishes by hallucinated gratifications and defends sleep against the disturbing demands of instincts, just as the defence mechanisms of the ego represent the efforts of the central nervous system to escape the impact of those same instinctive demands as internal stimuli. Thus the psychic apparatus returns to quiescence or stable equilibrium. Walker comments : 'This was twenty years before W. B. Cannon invented the word "homeostasis" : but the notion is clearly developed in Freud's mind' (p. 61).

After the first world war Freud brought forward the idea of a 'repetition-compulsion', impelling

the organism to repeat earlier experiences, whether pleasant or not. . . . Freud was on the point of observing that the central nervous system, in addition to the innately homeostatic operations of the sleep and defence mechanisms, could actually be 'set', deliberately or accidentally, to return homeostatically to states acquired during its lifetime. Had he done so, he would have been within one step of a most fruitful explanation of memory. But his pessimism sidetracked him into the notion of the death instinct. He asked himself : 'What is the state which the organism is always trying to restore?'; and answered : 'The earliest state of all—non-existence, death. (1956, p. 62.)

Walker here supports the argument of this chapter that the death-instinct idea is implicit in Freud's pleasure or constancy principle and is its logical development. Two problems arise : (*a*) the suitability of the biological or physiological principle of homeostasis to be carried over into the realm of psychological phenomena, and (*b*) the relation between Freud's choice of this basis for his psychological theory, and his pessimism of emotional outlook.

Freud's pessimism, written large in his estimates of human nature in *The Future of an Illusion* and in his views of the immutability of instincts, especially sadistic instincts, is clearly related to his neurological philosophy and general scientific outlook. Either may be regarded as leading logically to the other. Walker says :

Even without the death instinct, Freud's conclusions are pessimistic enough. Even if the goal of the central nervous system is not death, but merely 'the abolition of stimuli', this is something which, by the values at least of Western European civilization, is not much better. We are not offended when we are told how the rest of the body operates homeostatically to maintain its temperature, salinity and so forth, for it is possible to regard this as an excellent arrangement for allowing us to get on with the work that really matters, whether it is the creation of art, the spreading of a gospel, the betterment of human life, or some less common but equally highbrow task. But when we are told that our central nervous system is doing all this simply because its slogan is 'anything for a quiet life', we are outraged and discouraged. Can this be so? Is this the verdict of modern science? (*Ibid.*, p. 63.)

Freud carried over the principle of homeostasis, which is so relevant and illuminating for the study of the biological organism, into the realm of psychic life, instead of approaching the latter without presuppositions and letting the facts speak for themselves. This so dominated his thought that, while he discovered all the data essential for the formulation of a properly psychological theory of personality, he never produced such a theory. The world's greatest psychologist and most intrepid explorer of the psychic life remained in his basic outlook a neurologist tied to 'homeostasis' to the end.

The effects of this on his theory are brought out plainly by Peters.

The external world, with its reservoir of stimuli, presents itself as alien and hostile to the developing ego. But the ego also has to defend itself against danger from instinctual wishes whose satisfaction would bring about disaster in the face of the physical or social environment. (1956, p. 6.)

Thus, because of the rule of the homeostatic principle, both the external world which stimulates and the internal needs it plays upon, have to be seen not positively as the means to full and satisfying life, but negatively as resented disturbers of the 'homeostatic peace' of equilibrium. Peters says further that for Freud:

The relationship of hate to objects is older than that of love. It is derived from the primal repudiation by the narcissistic ego of the external world whence flows the stream of stimuli. As an expression of the pain reaction induced by objects, it remains in constant, intimate relation with the instinct of self-preservation, so that the sexual and ego instincts readily develop an antithesis which repeats that of love and hate. (*Op. cit.*, p. 9.)

The innate pessimism of Freud's total theory springs from the fact that his neurological homeostatic principle involved logically the ideas that (*a*) the basic relation between the person and his environment is hostile, (*b*) that hate is more fundamental than love, and (c) that the aim of life is the reduction of activity even to the point of death.

Walker defines a 'homeostatic system' as 'one which through the operation of a mechanism restores a certain end-state unless and until the point of breakdown is reached'. (1956, p. 63.) With regard to Freud's assumption that in fact the central nervous system does operate as a homeostatic system he writes : 'When we turn to science for confirmation or disproof, we are struck by the lack of conclusive observations.' (Ibid., p. 66.) After briefly reviewing what psychology and neurology have to contribute, he concludes that 'the most we can say is that it is possible to conceive of Freud's hypothesis being expressed in the language of neurology'. (Op. cit., p. 68.)

Freud's hypothesis makes sense in the language of psychology, neurology and cybernetics, but it is curiously hard to extract confirmation of it from any of these sciences. (Ibid., p. 70.)

And finally :

It is clear how much more Freud's general hypothesis depends on his definition of stimulus than on observation. What made this sort of reasoning so dangerously attractive to him was his hankering for simplicity—for a unifying equation. (Ibid., p. 71.)

Unhappily, this simplicity, dubiously achieved on a neurological basis, hamstrung his psychological theory, and made it incapable of dealing satisfactorily with psychic life qua personal. Homeostasis is not a principle that makes sense of personal phenomena.

The third writer in the Journal referred to is E. H. Hutten (Professor of Physics, University of London), in a paper entitled 'On Explanation in Psychology and Physics', which goes into the deeper problem behind the question of whether a physiological principle such as homeostasis is adequate when carried over into the realm of psychic phenomena. He points out that in psychoanalysis we are dealing with phenomena that are said to be 'overdetermined', i.e. they are not to be traced to one and only one single and simple 'cause' but

there exists more than one set of antecedent conditions, or causes, and each set alone is capable of explaining how it [the effect] occurs. . . . This disagrees with the ordinary causal explanation as we know it from physics. (1956, p. 73.)

This kind of problem arises, for example, when the same act can be produced from any one of several different motives, and this is, for psycho-analysis, the typical psychic problem owing to the complexity of conscious and unconscious levels of motivation, and of conflict on both levels.

Professor Hutten points out that : 'before we can explain anything we must specify the concepts used for this purpose, and, in general, provide a model.' (*Ibid.*, p. 73.) 'Psycho-analysis provides a *genetic-dynamical model* of human personality. The main assumptions are about the genesis of mental processes and the forces involved in them.' (*Ibid.*, p. 75.) As a minimum outline of 'the model' he cites three assumptions, that most mental activity is *unconscious*, that it is concerned with basic *conflicts* concerning the ambivalent love-hate of infantile sexuality, and that it can be investigated by means of *free associations* in transference situations. 'The model itself functions, in a way, as a non-formalized theory.' (*Ibid.*, p. 74.) 'We can discuss and criticize psycho-analytical explanations only against the background of the genetic-dynamical or some similar model.' (*Ibid.*, p. 76.) He points out that in this context we speak not

about causal laws but about the *aetiology* of a symptom or illness. Similarly, instead of description and prediction, we have *diagnosis* and *prognosis*. . . . Unlike mass points human beings have a history, and we cannot possibly hope to predict their future from the present alone. (*Ibid.*, p. 76.)

He makes it clear that the 'single cause' picture of reality in natural science depends on

replacing the actual real process by a simplified, ideal schema. . . . We prescribe a closed universe of moving mass-points and fixed forces, and this enables us to specify simply boundary conditions and initial conditions so that the differential equation describing the motion has a unique solution. The behaviour of human beings cannot be simplified in this manner; indeed we should not accept an explanation that presupposes such a picture. Many stimuli act on us and our future does not lie along a single path. (*Ibid.*, pp. 76–7.)

He regards an aetiological explanation as involving a reference to biological, predisposing, precipitating and social conditions and it

introduces immediately the so-called plurality of causes—in contrast to the causal scheme of physics. . . . We are able to retrodict in a unique manner from the present symptoms to the 'underlying causes', at least in principle; and it is this characteristic of uniqueness that we customarily demand of a valid explanation. (*Ibid.*, pp. 77–8.)

Professor Hutten regards Freud's 'determinism' as having nothing to do with 'necessity' and writes :

Neither psychological nor physical causality implies a metaphysical belief in 'the iron rule of law'. The import of psychoanalytic determinism lies elsewhere : what is strict about it is, so to speak, not the rule of law but the rule for collecting evidence. . . . Everything a human being may feel, say or do—or not do, though the occasion calls for action—provides legitimate data for the theory. . . . Freud's determinism merely implies that anything connected with human behaviour can, and *must*, be used in support of a psycho-analytic hypothesis. (*Ibid.*, pp. 78–9.)

Furthermore, the body-mind problem is obviated for when we have collected the evidence comprising the whole of human behaviour :

We must always express whatever we observe by means of the concepts of the theory we wish to apply. It is exactly one function of the model to allow us to do so; we describe all happenings in terms of psychical reality and so can dispense with the frame-work of physical space-time which does not apply to mental phenomena. (*Ibid.*, p. 80.)

Professor Hutten here uses Freud's work in a much more radical way than did Freud himself to establish psychology, and specifically psycho-analysis and psychodynamic theory, as a science and a discipline in its own right for which the concepts of physical science are irrelevant. He accepts the multiplicity of causes and over-determination as essential to psychological theory, and in no way militating against its scientific status.

Human actions are affected by cultural, social, economic, physical and other factors. . . . Classical physics is taken as a standard when it is said that a scientific theory must explain a given phenomenon in one way only; but this is not really true even there, and certainly not in modern physics. Underneath this ideal is, I think, the metaphysical belief in the mechanical determinism of past centuries, according to which everything in the world is connected by the iron chain of necessity. Multiple explanations are acceptable and valid as long as each of them is open to observation and experiment. (*Ibid.*, pp. 80–82.)

In psychology the situation is not as simple as in physics, where we have a single set of fixed *static* (initial and boundary) conditions and *constant* forces. (*Ibid.*, p. 83.)

In psychology it often happens that because of the conflict between conscious and unconscious levels of motivation and intention 'opposite hypotheses about the future behaviour of a person' (*Ibid.*, p. 82) can both be true, and also that

the same set of data leads to two exactly opposite results . . . [which] shows that the processes underlying human behaviour are *dynamical* in the sense that they represent a conflict or a tension between two poles. (*Ibid.*, p. 82.)

Hutten concludes, therefore, that 'it is justified to say that over-determination is accessible—at least in principle—to observation and experiment'. (*Ibid.*, p. 83.) In psycho-analysis :

A model of human personality is presupposed that includes various psychic levels and structures and especially the idea of unconscious conflict. The diagnosis and prognosis must be put in terms of a *process* rather than of opposing constant forces and things. (*Ibid.*, pp. 83–4.)

He uses the term 'process' in opposition to that of 'entity' (such as 'an instinct'), and is stressing the fact that in psycho-analysis we always deal with a 'process'—that is, a 'conflict', i.e. a personal process. We cannot resolve this conflict

into the two polarities and treat each of them as an independent static entity. . . . The usual cause-and-effect language breaks down when we want to treat of processes in which we cannot recognize immediately some constant element. It works only if the process is no more than the displacement of a permanent thing in space-time under the influence of a constant force. This is largely true for physics but even there exist examples when this no longer holds. . . . A psycho-analytic explanation is about a conflict or a process. We may express the hypothesis in terms of the relative strength of the two opposites. (*Ibid.*, p. 84.)

The upshot is that the terms of physical science and the physical cause-and-effect type of explanation are not relevant or suitable to psychic phenomena. Psycho-analysis provides a new type of model for personality as a complex of various psychic levels and structures that enables the phenomena of personal living—i.e. those of conscious and unconscious conflict—to be explained on the basis of over-determination and plurality of causes, 'cause' being no longer understood in the physical sense. Thus, though Freud both created a new model for psychic phenomena and at the same time sought to conceive of it in the old terminology of physical science, he really paved the way for the thorough emancipation of dynamic psychology as a science of personality with a right to its own appropriate terminology.

Dr. K. M. Colby in *Energy and Structure in Psychoanalysis* (1955) gives systematic consideration to the problems raised in this chapter. He regards metapsychology as an attempt to give an account of psycho-analysis in terms of pure science, and he selects psychic energy and psychic structure as its basic postulates. The dynamic-genetic, topographic and economic approaches to psychic events form three basic viewpoints in conceptualization, showing that Freud saw that one set of concepts could not give a complete account of such complex and diverse data. The dynamic-genetic and economic viewpoints deal with the energy aspect, and the topographic viewpoint deals with the structural aspect of psychic phenomena. Dealing with the relationship between psychological and neurophysiological aspects of the human organism, with its central governing agency, the central nervous system, he says that some of its functions such as thought and consciousness are not satisfactorily dealt with in biochemical and neurological terms. Psycho-analysis must use a different language and deal with such data on a different level of abstraction, which lies between the neurological and social levels.

What we theorize about is in one sense the brain, but in another sense neurones are not meaningful on the properly psychological level. This question of the level of conceptual abstraction proper to psychological study is the primary theoretical question that psycho-analysis has to settle. Colby points out that at each level of abstraction new characteristics appear, requiring new terms for their study. This question is discussed by T. S. Szasz.

Psychology ... [is] an area of enquiry concerned with experiences in their process of transition from affect and imagery to verbal and other symbolic representation. By agreeing to such a conception of psychology—and psychiatry—one thereby puts a limit on the degree of abstraction to which one can subject human experience and still consider the treatment to be 'psychological'. In other words mathematics can function as a tool in physics and in astronomy without the identity of those sciences suffering thereby. Psychology cannot so use mathematics without altering its own identity. It appears that in psychology the very process of expressing experiences in highly abstract symbols—even if they pertain to phenomena which are ordinarily thought of as psychological—alters one's conception of the nature of the problem. (Szasz, 1956, p. 199.)

Attempts to make psychology more 'objective' ... run the risk that in so doing the subject-matter becomes altered and can no longer be considered to be psychology. (Szasz, 1956, p. 200.)

This would appear to be Colby's position, and therefore it is somewhat disappointing to find him merely adopting the terms of the earlier Freudian metapsychology with a view to improving their meaning. He works still with the idea of a Psychic Apparatus, not a Person. He does not recognize that Freud's mechanistic and materialistic term 'apparatus' with all its neurological and physiological implications, is of such a degree of abstraction, and reduction of psychic phenomena to lower levels of integration, that in using it what we are dealing with ceases to be psychology. This is apparent when Colby has to deal with perception as an active function. It is not an apparatus passively receiving stimuli and operating defences to ward them off. The 'person' psycho-analysis studies goes out to meet the external world and we have to conceptualize what Colby calls his 'proceedances'.

For this, the psychological level, the concept of an 'apparatus' is inadequate. We need, not an impersonal term, but a new type of term that can do justice to personal phenomena. Colby works out what he feels to be an improved model of the psychic apparatus. One feels, however, that the chief value of his work lies in the first half of the book where he arrives at the same conclusions as Fairbairn had already done as regards the rejection of any separation of energy and structure. He criticizes the orthodox psycho-analytical theory which works with the idea of 'instinctual energies' flowing into the ego or psychic apparatus like water into pipe-lines. He does not, however, see any inconsistency in attributing such personal functions as the active organizing of experience to an 'apparatus'. Such an entity is not any longer suitably called an 'apparatus' and, if we use such terms, as Szasz puts it, 'one alters one's conception of the nature of the problem'. We are making personal data fit an impersonal theory, not developing a theory suitable to the data. When Colby recognizes that many thinkers do not seem able to grasp what is meant by explanation on the psychic level and that we cannot afford to be limited by their limitations in theory, we would expect something different from another model of a psychic apparatus, his cyclic-circular model.

Colby's contribution deals with two main points, first the insistence that structure and energy cannot be separated, and second the attempt to provide a new scientific model for human personality to remedy the defects in Freud's id-ego-super-ego model. On the first point he holds that psycho-analysis must work with a theory of dynamic structure in which energy and structure are never considered in separation from one another as is the case with Freud's energetic if chaotic id, and organized, structuralized but energyless ego and super-ego. Adopting the term 'cathexis-energy' to denominate psychic energy, Colby points out that energy and structure can be separated as concepts but in reality cannot exist apart. Energy of any kind performs work only by operating in a structure, and a structure is impotent without energy. That is exactly Fairbairn's position, called by him 'dynamic structure'.

The question of instinct illustrates the problem. Colby surveys various instinct-theories and shows that Freud treated instincts as drives having a direction or aim in themselves, and flowing into the psychic apparatus from outside, whereas in fact energy purely by itself can have no specific aim and could only be dissipated. Thus he holds that instinct or drive is always structured energy, and that only a theory of dynamic structure can deal with *psychic* phenomena. Pure energy is an abstraction, a concept only. Colby regards drives as structured parts of the psychic apparatus with their own energy, not, as Freud did, separate psychic entities invading it from outside. For these structural components he uses the term 'schemas' as units in a whole organizational pattern. This is the opposite of Freud's view of the id as chaotic and unorganized energy outside the ego. He does not regard aggression as an instinct or primary drive, but rather as a means, not an end, to be used in the service of any aim at need. He limits the term 'instinct' or 'drive' to stand for the psychic representations of inherited bodily requirements which call for bodily activity in the outer world. He classifies these, as four Maintenance Drive schemas to breathe, sleep, ingest and excrete, and two Reproduction Drive schemas to mate and rear. He regards pleasure, not with Freud, as the end aimed at, but with Fairbairn, and indeed all non-hedonists among the philosophers, as the accompaniment of the fulfilment of all drive-aims. Therefore, he points out, since not all drives are sexual, not all pleasure can be treated as by definition sexual. Colby's theory and classification of instincts seems to me the most useful so far proposed.

Thus, it seems, that *criticism of the inadequacy of Freud's pioneer concepts, converging from various quarters orthodox and neo-Freudian, is leading to views that supersede Freud's metapsychological instinct-theory, and his separation of energy and structure, or drives and controls, in terms of the id on the one hand and the ego and super-ego on the other, in favour of a unitary view of the psyche as a dynamic structure. What is still at issue is whether this dynamic structure in its development and functioning is to be described by means of an impersonal process theory which uses some such mechanical notion as that of a psychic apparatus as a scientific model, or whether 'psychological' and 'personal' will come to be recognized as equivalent in meaning, and a personal model of the psyche be achieved.* Colby regards Freud's earlier models, the first neurological model of *The Project for a Scientific Psychology* (1895), and the second and apparently more psychological model set forth in *The Interpretation of Dreams*, Chapter 7 (1900), which Colby calls The Picket Model, as superseded by Freud's third model, the endopsychic structural scheme of id-ego-super-ego. The first model was frankly neurological but he thinks that Freud did not really abandon it as much as he appeared to do in the second model. This is a model of the flow of mental processes, initiated by external stimuli, from the perceptual to the motor end of the psychic apparatus, the mid regions of the apparatus comprising memory traces, the unconscious, the preconscious and the conscious, with the censor standing guard on the threshold of the unconscious to control what emerges.

There is an approach here to psychic structure which, however, is specifically developed only as the basis of the third model. This in turn Colby regards as inadequate, and calls for new structural concepts to save our theory from fossilization, as indeed did Freud himself (1938). Having mentioned the theoretical impossibility of a completely chaotic and unorganized id as part of a structural scheme, he also suggests that the id-ego-super-ego model is too simple to represent the complexity of psychic reality and activity. What then is the next step? What kind of model is now needed to do justice to the study of human personality in its dynamic aspects of feeling and striving? Colby proposes a new 'cyclic-circular model' which aims to represent, as did Freud's second model, the movement of psychic processes along a psychic apparatus or system from the sensory to the motor end. Is such a model what is needed for specifically psycho-analytical purposes, i.e. the understanding of the motivational life and the dynamic structure of the human person? R. F. J. Withers, reviewing Colby's book in *The British Journal for the Philosophy of Science* (1956, pp. 110–13), regards his discussion on the concepts of energy, structure, instincts and drives as of great importance, but criticizes Colby's model as involving 'the confusion of aims between model-building and statement-forming'. Colby should be talking about 'types of statement and not about types of cogs in a sort of psychic engine'. Colby himself describes his model as reducing the structural organization of the psyche to fixed parts and moving parts. This is so conceived that he can draw a diagram of it of a wholly mechanical kind. This may be useful for some purposes but it is not a model of the 'personal' type adumbrated by Freud when he represented by means of the super-ego concept a psychic development through the structural internalization of external ego-object relationships. Colby's model is a regression from Freud's tripartite model back to the earlier impersonal psychic apparatus model. *Freud's third model moved towards representing the human psyche as a functioning person developing an endopsychic structure under the impact of object-relations experience. Surely, the course of development of the theoretical problem points rather to a further development beyond, though of the same type as, Freud's tripartite model which is essentially personal.* Colby has not grasped the fact that this is the specific psycho-analytical line of progress. He falls into the trap of regarding Freud's personal terminology in the id-ego-super-ego scheme as personification and anthropomorphism. This is a repetition of objections already discussed. He has not recognized that the real issue at stake is that which is the subject of this chapter, the question whether psycho-analytical theory should be cast in personal or impersonal terms. He complains that since Freud put forward his id-ego-super-ego scheme, further work has only aimed at clarifying and reformulating this model and no new model has been suggested. This, however, is what is still most required and not a new model, for, in principle, it is a model of the psyche functioning as a person. It is a misfortune that Colby was not aware of the prior work of Fairbairn ten years earlier, especially as in other respects he is so close to Fairbairn in his basic approach to these problems. Fairbairn's scheme of endopsychic structure (see chapter XV) is in essence exactly a clarification and reformulation of Freud's tripartite model, which represents the activities of the psyche as carried on at a completely personal level in terms of object-relationships in both the internal and external affairs of the psyche. Yet, in my opinion, it is a revision strictly in line with Freud's own new departure and provides an example of what a genuinely *personal* model of the structural organization of the psyche is like.

CHAPTER VIII

THE 'CULTURE PATTERN' THEORY
AND CHARACTER ANALYSIS
(ADLER, KAREN HORNEY, ERICH FROMM)

W E shall group together four writers in this section: Adler, Karen Horney, Erich Fromm and Harry Stack Sullivan. Though the last three would hardly regard Adler as their spiritual father, they do, nevertheless, pursue his general type of approach and the orientation of all four has a sociological trend in common. They do not deny unconscious motivation, yet they sit so loosely to Freud's discoveries in 'depth-psychology' that they do not really make use of 'the unconscious' in the all-important Freudian sense of the term. They analyse conscious and pre-conscious motivations, and particularly analyse the more deeply unrealized character-traits manifested by an individual in his human relationships in the present day. Valuable as this is, we feel that their contribution is condemned to an ultimate superficiality from the point of view of psychodynamic theory. Whatever inadequacies may be discovered in Freud's theories, his was the true pioneering work, and the most fruitful developments have come by building on his foundations, as Melanie Klein, Fairbairn and others are to-day doing, in this matter of 'depth-psychology', rather than abandoning them as did Adler, Horney, Fromm and Sullivan.

In her first book Karen Horney raised the question 'whether my interpretation is somewhat Adlerian?' Her answer was:

There are some similarities with certain points that Adler stressed, but fundamentally my interpretation rests on Freudian ground. Adler is in fact a good example of how even a productive insight into psychological processes can become sterile if pursued onesidedly and without foundation in the discoveries of Freud. (1937, pp. ix–x.)

In her last book, *Neurosis and Human Growth* (1951), she presented an analysis of the adult neurotic character in its present-day human relationships which goes far beyond anything Adler attempted or could have achieved at that date in its subtlety and complexity. Yet she had moved much farther from the basic Freudian position than she perhaps foresaw in 1937.

These four writers provide a dynamic psychology of the conscious and pre-conscious ego in its human relationships. They supply a fund of acute analytical observation as to the character-structure and motivations of man as a social being living in 'interpersonal relationships' with his fellows in the external 'here and now'. From the point of view of theory, however, they illustrate the influence of sociology on psychopathology rather than the reverse.

Adler did more than substitute the power-drive for the Freudian sex-drive. He raised the whole question of the relationships of a 'person' as a social unit interacting with other 'persons' in the world of to-day, when he stressed the importance of feelings of inferiority and the urgent need to overcome or compensate for them. This could be done by achieving a sense of power in some way which would be significant for the individual, either by overcoming his particular inferiority or by giving him value in the eyes of others in some alternative direction. Adler raised the question of 'ego-psychology' as against the 'psychology of the unconscious'. In fact, feelings of inferiority have far deeper causes than Adler ever suspected.

Erich Fromm, and Karen Horney who began as an orthodox Freudian and was influenced by Fromm's sociological approach, formally discarded Freud's instinct-theory but found no true substitute for it by means of which they might give an account of the deep unconscious. Instead, they put forward a theory of neurosis based on the analysis of compulsive (i.e. neurotic) character-trends developed and operated in the individual's relationships with other people, originally in childhood, but now in the present day, and in his particular social setting. We may therefore call them, along with Sullivan who in a different way followed a similar path, the 'Culture-Pattern' Group of Character Analysts. Horney and Fromm must have been influenced by Freud's developing ego-psychology, but made more use of sociological findings than did Freud. This has come to be characteristic of a large group of broadly psycho-analytical therapists in America. Possibly Adler himself, who settled in America later in life, did something to prepare the soil for this development by his general influence. American psycho-analysts seem to be divided into two large groups: the orthodox, reinforced by European analysts who escaped from the Nazis and who remain remarkably true to the theories of Freud himself, offering only small critical improvements of classical psycho-analytic teaching; and those who have devel-

oped away from the 'depth-psychology' of Freud and substituted
a psychology of ego-development under the weight of cultural
pressures. Dr. Thompson's *Psychoanalysis; Evolution and Development* is a valuable summary of their views. Much of what
they say by way of criticism of Freudian psychobiology is important, and we have already taken account of it in earlier
chapters. Their theory, however, does not provide a satisfactory
alternative theory for the problems that Freud's depth-psychology
sought to solve.

Horney regards the tracing out of childhood history as important for finding the starting-point of given character-trends,
but she does not appear to appreciate the perpetuation of the
'childhood situation' *per se* into the present day in the deep unconscious. For her, the character formed in childhood, as a result
of problems in relationships with parents and others at that time,
is brought forward into adult life, developed and consolidated, and
it becomes the character with which we react to other people in
the present day. She rightly regards adult motivations as what
G. W. Allport would call 'a post-instinctive phenomenon' but,
using his terms, we may say that Horney's is a theory of the 'functional autonomy' of character trends formed in early life. The
unconscious is no longer the deep unconscious of fixation to childhood love-objects in Freud's sense; it is rather the unrealized and
unrecognized aspects of contemporary character-structure, an
inability to see in oneself what may be visible to other people.

There is an important implication here for sociology. Horney
corrects the somewhat one-sided 'depth' emphasis of orthodox
Freudianism with regard to both biological determination and
infantile conflicts.

The disputable aspects of [Freud's] findings concern mainly three
assumptions : that an inherited set of reactions is more important
than the influence of the environment; that the influential experiences are sexual in nature; that later experiences to a large extent
represent a repetition of those had in childhood. Even if these debat-
able issues are discarded the essence of Freud's findings still remains :
that character and neuroses are moulded by early experiences to an
extent hitherto unthought of. (1939, pp. 32–3.)

On the first of these three points we shall agree with Karen Horney
but must part company with her on the rest.

Concerning 'biological determination' Horney writes :

The reverse side of (Freud's) biological orientation is a lack of
sociological orientation, and thus he tends to attribute social

phenomena primarily to psychic factors and these primarily to biological (libido theory). This tendency has led psycho-analytical writers to believe, for example, that wars are caused by the working of the death instinct, that our present economic system is rooted in anal-erotic drives, that the reason the machine age did not start two thousand years ago is to be found in the narcissism of that period. Freud sees a culture not as the result of a complex social process but primarily as the result of biological drives which are repressed or sublimated, with the result that reaction formations are built up against them. The more complete the suppression of these drives, the higher the cultural development. Since the capacity for sublimation is limited, and since the intensive suppression of primitive drives without sublimation may lead to neurosis, the growth of civilization must inevitably imply a growth of neurosis. Neuroses are the price humanity has to pay for cultural development. The implicit theoretical pre-supposition underlying this train of thought is a belief in the existence of biologically determined human nature, or, more precisely, a belief that oral, anal, genital and aggressive drives exist in all human beings in approximately equal quantities. Variations in character formation from individual to individual, as from culture to culture, are due, then, to the varying intensity of the suppression required, with the additional qualification that this suppression affects the kinds of drives in varying degrees. Historical and anthropological findings do not confirm such a direct relation between height of culture and the suppression of sexual or aggressive drives. (1937, pp. 282–3.)

We have to take a definite step beyond Freud . . . in his over-emphasis on the biological origin of mental characteristics. . . . He has assumed that the instinctual drives or object-relationships that are frequent in our culture are biologically determined 'human nature'. . . . Freud's disregard of cultural factors not only leads to false generalizations, but to a large extent blocks an understanding of the real forces which motivate our attitudes and actions. (1937, pp. 20–1.)

We agree with Horney on this point. MacIver, the sociologist, writes : 'It remains gravely doubtful whether a study of physiological structures and processes can help us to interpret or understand the processes of consciousness.' (1937, p. 20.)

With regard to the influence of childhood Horney says :

The relation between childhood experiences and later conflicts is much more intricate than is assumed by those psycho-analysts who proclaim a simple cause and effect relationship. Though experiences in childhood provide determining conditions for neuroses they are nevertheless not the only cause of later difficulties. When we focus our attention on the actual neurotic difficulties we recognize that neuroses are generated not only by incidental individual experiences, but also by the specific cultural conditions under which we live. In fact the cultural conditions not only lend weight and colour to the individual experiences but in the last analysis determine their particular form. It is an individual fate, for example, to have a domineering or 'self-sacrificing' mother, but it is only under definite cultural conditions that we find domineering or self-sacrificing mothers. (1937, pp. vii–viii.)

Though I hold that a complete understanding of a neurosis is not possible without tracing it back to its infantile conditions, I believe that the genetic approach, if used one-sidedly, confuses rather than clarifies the issue, because it leads then to a neglect of the actually existing unconscious tendencies. . . . Genetic understanding is useful only as long as it helps the functional understanding. (1937, p. 33.)

As a general statement this is certainly true. A one-sided genetic approach is too limited to cover all the relevent factors, because any form of one-sided approach is too limited. Human relationship situations in childhood and also in the present day have both got to be taken into account together if we are to understand the outbreak of a neurosis. But when Horney writes : 'Though experiences in childhood provide determining conditions for neuroses, they are nevertheless not the only cause of later difficulties', that statement is ambiguous. The *other causes* Horney would include are the pressures of the cultural environment on the adult, but those pressures do not make *all* adults neurotic. A mature and stable adult may well experience anxieties and frustrations in the cultural environment in which he lives, but he copes with these without developing a clinical neurosis. The adult who reacts to his cultural milieu by developing a neurosis is the adult in whom the essence of the neurosis was created or laid down in the emotional constitution of his personality in childhood. The frustrations of adult life *occasion the outbreak* of neurosis rather than *cause* the neurosis itself. The neurosis has been at best latent, repressed and over-compensated ever since childhood and is *reactivated* by stress in adult life.

This does not mean that cultural conditions are excluded as *causes* of neurosis in a more ultimate sense, but their pressure on the individual is causal for neurosis in a fundamental way more in childhood than in adult life. Moreover, the most important aspect of this disturbing cultural pressure is its *indirect* impact on the child through the parents, long before the child comes under direct pressure from the larger community with its mores and public opinion as he grows older. Culture patterns are mediated first by mothering. Long before the infant has any awareness of neighbours or of the larger outer world, the mother's handling of the child is being determined by her anxiety as to what others will think of the way she 'trains' her baby, and by the extent to which the accepted cultural norms of behaviour have become stamped on the mother's personality. The frustrating aspects of the mother-child relationship become incorporated in the growing structure of the child's personality, in the form of repressed emotional ties to parents which have specific relationship patterns.

The Oedipus complex is a case in point. Here a child develops an intense frustrated need for the parent of the opposite sex, accompanied by a hostile, rivalrous relationship to the parent of the same sex, and this is perpetuated by repression in the adult unconscious. It constitutes a latent neurosis which is the real cause of the adult overt neurosis which will break out if and when environmental conditions in later life play upon it and reactivate it. But the unfortunate owner of a repressed Oedipus complex may not wait for any extraordinary difficulties in real life to intervene. When early bad-object relationships have become encapsulated in the unconscious, the potential neurotic will unwittingly mould later situations and experiences to fit the pattern of the internally preserved early ones. An Oedipus complex significance is forced upon relationships and situations in adult life which do not of themselves necessarily carry that meaning. Horney casts doubt on the view that 'later experiences to a large extent represent a repetition of those had in childhood', but the clinical evidence of deep analysis confirms that this is a fact. The neurotic person, as it were, will have it so without realizing it. There may be any number of differences in detail between the early situations and the later ones, but the point is that the basic emotional pattern, the dynamic hard core, turns out to be the same, and often with startling and uncanny exactness. This reliving of the past in the present can be ignored only by losing touch with the deep unconscious as Horney does. We must recognize the great importance of this point for sociology, for its ramifications in social phenomena are endless.

Karen Horney is able to allow sociology to influence her psychopathology, but because she discards the deep unconscious she is unable to produce a psychopathology which can have a profound influence on sociology. The net result is a too exclusively environmental and cultural conception of neurosis and patterns of relationships, and an inability to judge clearly as to whether a culture itself may be neurotic. Since neurosis is itself a social problem of the first magnitude, we must, however, look carefully at what Horney has to say about the relationships between culture and neurosis. She writes :

A great frequency of neuroses and psychoses in a given culture is one of the indicators showing that something is seriously wrong with the conditions under which people live. It shows that the psychic difficulties engendered by the cultural conditions are greater than the average capacity of people to cope with them. (1939, pp. 178–9.)

Her theory of neurosis, however, hardly gives an adequate conceptual tool with which to work on this problem, for it is concerned almost wholly with the influence of cultural factors on the shaping of neurosis, and says little about psychopathological factors shaping cultures. She writes :

Three main sets of factors are to be taken into account; those which represent the matrix out of which a neurosis may grow; those which constitute the basic neurotic conflicts and the attempts at their solution; and those entailed in the façade which the neurotic shows to himself and others. A neurotic development in the individual arises ultimately from feelings of alienation, hostility, fear and diminished self-confidence. These attitudes do not themselves constitute a neurosis, but they are the soil out of which a neurosis may grow, since it is their combination which creates a basic feeling of helplessness towards a world conceived as potentially dangerous. It is basic anxiety or basic insecurity which necessitates the rigid pursuit of certain strivings for safety and satisfaction, the contradictory nature of which constitutes the core of neuroses. Consequently the first group of factors bearing on neuroses which is to be looked for in a culture is the circumstances which create emotional isolation, potential hostile tension between people, insecurity and fears, and a feeling of individual powerlessness. (1939, pp. 172–3.)

That is undoubtedly true, and Horney fastens on the essentially competitive nature of Western civilization at this point as the main cause. Competitiveness pervades political, economic, social and sexual relationships, along with gross inequalities both as to possessions and opportunities, and the possibilities of exploitation. In such an atmosphere individuals react with hostility, insecurity and impaired self-confidence, which last is increased by the 'ideology that success is dependent only on personal efficiency' and the 'contradiction between factually existing hostile tensions and the gospel of brotherly love.' (1939, pp. 173–5.) Furthermore :

The most obvious influence of cultural factors on neuroses is to be seen in the image the neurotic is anxious to present to himself and others. This image is determined mainly by his fear of disapproval and his craving for distinction. Consequently it consists of those qualities which in our culture are rewarded with approval and distinction, such as unselfishness, love for others, generosity, honesty, self-control, moderation, rationality, good judgment. Without the cultural ideology of unselfishness, for instance, the neurotic would not feel compelled to keep up an appearance of not wanting anything for himself, not only hiding his egocentricity but also suppressing his natural desires for happiness. Thus the problem of the influence of cultural conditions in creating neurotic conflicts is far more complex than Freud sees it. It involves no less than a thorough analysis of a given culture from such points of view as these : In what ways and to what extent are interpersonal hostilities created in a given culture? How great is the personal insecurity of the individual and what factors contribute towards making him insecure? What factors impair the individual's inherent self-confidence? What social prohibitions and tabus exist and what is their influence in bringing about inhibitions and fears? What ideologies are effective and what goals or rationalizations do they provide? What needs and strivings are created, encouraged or discouraged by the given conditions? (1939, pp. 176–7.)

This is a highly important emphasis and it is unlikely that psychoanalysis will be able henceforth to ignore this line of approach. It is quite properly complementary to the genetic line of investigation. But beyond this point we begin to feel difficulties. The problem is also far more complex than Horney sees it. Her theory seems to resolve itself into the view that culture moulds the character which in turn is incapable of dealing with the culture, and that this explains neurosis. Undoubtedly Horney steered investigation into the right direction when she stated that neurosis arose out of disturbances in human relationships. In *Our Inner Conflicts* (1946) she worked out the view that the basic neurotic conflict is between *aggressive* and *compliant* reactions. Caught in a perpetual disturbing oscillation between these two equally unsatisfactory ways of dealing with other people, the neurotic may then retreat into *detachment*—i.e. give up human relationships as far as possible and deal with life in an impersonal way—so as to escape anxiety and conflict. In her last book, *Neurosis and Human Growth* (1951), she developed this along a line that somewhat pushes the primacy of human relations into the background. The neurotic, caught in such distressing conflicts with other people, ceases to accept his own real feelings and impulses, ceases to know himself, and builds up an idealized image of himself as he thinks he ought to be, instead of discovering his own proper nature and potentialities. He thus becomes a more and more frantically unreal person as time goes on, hates his 'real' self in the name of his 'idealized' self. Self-realization of the 'real' self has now become the goal of therapy, in contrast to a compulsive conformity with the culturally imposed patterns and ideologies found in the neurosis. Self-realization of the 'real' self—i.e. of the individual's actual 'nature'—is certainly of the greatest importance, and is an emphasis now coming more and more to the forefront in psychoanalysis, as for example in the work of Winnicott, but it is also imperative to recognize that it can happen only *in* the medium of personal relationships. The two problems of achievement of self-realization and achievement of good personal relationships cannot be separated, for they are two sides of the same process.

At this point Horney seems to be involved in a contradiction. In *The Neurotic Personality of Our Time* (1937), she wrote: 'Feelings and attitudes are to an amazingly high degree moulded by the conditions under which we live, both cultural and individual . . . neuroses are deviations from the normal pattern of behaviour.' (*Ibid.*, p. 19.) 'Neurotic persons are different from the average individuals in their reactions', so that, concerning people with inhibitions on ambition or on the desire to earn more money, she says: 'The reason that we should call such persons neurotic is that most of us are familiar, and exclusively familiar, with a behaviour pattern that implies wanting to get ahead in the world, to get ahead of others, to earn more money than the bare minimum for existence.' (*Ibid.*, pp. 13–14.) But now, in her last book, it appears that neurotics are those who *accepted* the prevailing patterns and idealogy of their culture instead of developing their own personality. No doubt Horney would answer that our culture is in conflict with itself at this point and that it is that conflict which divides the individual against himself and drives him into neurosis.

There is certainly much truth in all this, and Karen Horney's analysis of the neurotic ego as it operates in the social setting of the present day is valuable. Particularly must we be grateful for her emphatic way of bringing 'human relationship' to the forefront, even though in her last work 'self-realization' seems to become the primary emphasis, too one-sidedly isolated from its matrix in interpersonal relationships. It was very necessary that the genetic approach of Freud, dealing with the past and childhood, as it lay hidden by repression in the deep unconscious, should be balanced by this more sociological approach to the individual as a person who lives in the 'here and now' of present-day human relationships. Yet her work is too much a pendulum swing from one extreme to the opposite. In being seized of the importance of actual external human relationships in the social and cultural setting of the present day, she has lost touch with the deep Freudian unconscious which is still there, enormously influencing present-day behaviour, and constituting an inner world in which the past is perpetuated into the present. Having thrown over instinct theory, Horney has no means of giving an account of the deep 'structural' unconscious as a region of psychic life outside the socially adapted ego. She has only a 'functional' view of the unconscious in terms of the ordinary social self. It consists of those of our reactions, to people in the present day, of which we are not aware. This is not adequate to the facts, and is not a view that can contribute much to sociology or to psychopathology. It amounts to little more than the superficial idea of the unconscious put forward in the 1920s by the philosophers, Bertrand Russell and C. D. Broad, to the effect that the unconscious was merely the unrecognized emotions of which we were conscious but did not wish to see them for what they really were. That is not at all what Freud meant by the unconscious, even though this phenomenon is related to it.

Therapy for Horney is helping the patient to see himself as he really is so that he can correct his antisocial feelings and impulses. But can he, if the deep unconscious is left out of account? There is much to show that this type of therapy develops a distinct moralistic tendency which is even more marked in Erich Fromm, and increases a patient's guilt about his 'bad' impulses. Analysts lay bare unsuspected antisocial drives and it matters little whether they are due to Freud's instincts or to Horney's neurotic character-trends; the patient feels them as his own bad characteristics, feels guilty because of them, and all the while the vital question remains unanswered: what is it that has kept these antisocial drives in being for years from childhood onwards, why was it not possible to grow out of them, and why are they so active to-day, often when there is not really enough external provocation to arouse them at the time when they are so urgent? If Horney is unsatisfied with Freud's attempt to explain *impulses* in terms of biological instincts, her own theory of ego-character-structure carries us not much farther. They arise out of a character-formation the persistence of which is assumed rather than explained. Since she makes no use of the all-important clue of reactions to internalized objects, she is thrown back on a too exclusively cultural explanation, which lacks psychological depth. We need a theory which has both a genetic and a contemporary social and cultural orientation.

Horney does not clear up the problem constituted by the fact that while culture-patterns and culture-conflicts determine the outbreak and the form of neuroses, they do not account for their deep unconscious etiology; for she fails to give an account of why or how her 'basic neurotic conflict' persists structurally in the psyche. She is betrayed into a superficial antithesis between a situation-neurosis and a character-neurosis, for a character-neurosis is a neurosis in terms of an inner situation persisting in the unconscious. The distinction should be drawn between an internal and an external situation-neurosis, and the interaction between the inner and the outer worlds. Horney shows how cultural tensions in adult life can evoke a neurosis, but she seems to assume culture-patterns as primary data studied by the sociologist and does not venture on a psychopathology of cultures. After all, the culture of a given society is maintained by the individuals who compose it. Why? Culture in a society is like character in an individual; it is partly a rational relationship to external objects, but partly also a defence against intrapsychic tensions. Thus culture and character more often than not very largely coincide. The culture patterns and institutions support the individual against his internal conflicts. But the whole structure of culture-cum-character needs a psychodynamic explanation. Different cultures, like different character-types, are, in addition to being ways of dealing with external reality, different lines of defence against basic internal conflicts which are formed, from the infant's point of view, at a pre-cultural phase of its existence. Culture has its influence, through the personality of the parents, in creating the external stresses with which the infant has to deal, but the infant's own reactions are 'raw' and primitive and not yet fashioned by the direct impact of cultural influences on its own mind. That comes later with the development of the 'super-ego', a level of 'civilized' development which is, in the first place, a defence against pre-existing problems. Neuroses have their roots in the pre-moral, pre-cultural depths of the individual psyche; they are reactivated in later life by stresses in outer object-relationships of the present day.

Thompson considers that Karen Horney made four important contributions. Horney was 'among the first to develop in detail a description of some of the effects of cultural pressures in producing neurosis'. (1952, p. 200.) Secondly, she modified the repetition-compulsion by showing that in transference there is no exact literal repeating of early attitudes to parents, but rather an end-result of a whole series of influences brought to bear on the original attitude by subsequent experiences with substitute parent-figures. Thirdly, she pointed out the development of psychological vicious circles whereby ego-defences set up against primary anxieties created in turn fresh anxieties which necessitated more defences and so on, till the personality becomes a complex structure of anxieties and defences which, as Wilhelm Reich held, must be removed in layers. Horney's fourth contribution was to recognize that these ego-defences further conflict among themselves, driving a person into incompatible strivings and creating secondary anxieties. Dr. Thompson writes:

Her approach has much in common with Adler, although her out-look is not as limited as Adler's. In place of Freud's sexual etiology Adler substituted the will to power as the basic problem in human beings, and there is no very definite recognition of it as primarily a neurotic force. Horney definitely sees the will to power as a neurotic mechanism and only one of several possible neurotic mechanisms. Thus in her first book she accords the neurotic need of love a com-parable significance. I believe the latter idea was presented for the first time by Horney. That the craving for love itself could have neurotic aspects seems to have escaped the notice of previous analysts. (1952, pp. 197–8.)

Thompson's final estimate of Karen Horney's views is as follows:

Her emphasis is almost entirely on how the current neurotic trends work and produce difficulties; and she shows little interest in how such trends developed in the first place. (*Ibid.*, p. 201.)

But it seems even more important that she displays little interest in the problem of what endopsychic factors are responsible for keeping these neurotic trends going in the personality through so many years of environmental changes. Thompson remarks:

The great emphasis on the present, in therapy, to the relative ex-clusion of the past has its unfortunate aspect too. It really gives a one-sided picture, a kind of structure without a foundation (p. 201).

This is even more true when we remember that the past is, psycho-logically, not merely the historical past; it is a psychological present, a dynamic, if unconscious, inner world, structurally underlying the persistence of Horney's neurotic trends in external object-relationships. It is very valuable to have it shown clearly by Karen Horney that the troublesome sex drives and power drives met with in disturbed people are themselves neurotic phenomena, anxiety-motivated compulsions, and not normal and natural manifestations of healthy innate instincts. But these 'neurotic character trends' still remain inexplicable solely in terms of culture-patterns and external social pressures. A theory of the structural unconscious is required to account for their stubborn persistence. Horney lost touch with Freud's basic discovery that they persist because they are rooted in the individual's continuing inner unconscious world in which the traumatic past is perpetuated.

Erich Fromm's work bears mainly on politics, morality and religion. Here we may say briefly that he expounds the 'culture-pattern and social pressure' theory chiefly as a social psychologist. He regards human problems as arising, not out of the need to satisfy instincts, which in human beings are not at all specific, but out of 'the specific kind of relatedness of the individual towards the world and to himself'. (P. Mullahy, *Oedipus Myth and Complex*, p. 241. Quoted by Dr. C. Thompson.) Our specific ways of dealing with our human environment are cultural, not instinctive, phenomena.

> The most beautiful as well as the most ugly inclinations of man are not a part of a fixed and biologically given human nature but result from the social process which creates man. (*The Fear of Freedom*, p. 12.)

Fromm's main emphasis in tracing the development of man, both in European history and as an individual, is on the escape from primary dependence on and security with parents and the parental community. Man achieves individuality at the price of isolation and insecurity, and then is driven to set up ego-defences such as sado-masochism (dependence in terms of aggression and suffering), destructiveness or automaton conformity. (Cf. Jung's 'persona'.) The aim of therapy is to release the individual from his anxieties and defences so that he can realize his own genuine potentialities and become his true self.

This is a valuable line of approach offsetting the biological pessimism of Freud. But as with Horney, so with Fromm, no contribution is made to the understanding of the problems of endopsychic structure and the unconscious determinants of ego-defences. Still more clearly do we feel this lack when we turn to the last important figure in this group, Dr. Harry Stack Sullivan.

CHAPTER IX

H. S. SULLIVAN'S INTERPERSONAL
THEORY OF PSYCHIATRY

FROMM and Horney went to America from Europe where they both began as classic Freudians. Harry Stack Sullivan was an American psychiatrist of the school of William Alanson White and Adolf Meyer, and it was round him that the Washington Group formed. He is the least influenced of the three by psycho-analytical orthodoxy in the sense that while Fromm and Horney revolted from it, Sullivan never belonged to it. He cannot, how-ever, be omitted from this survey because of his importance for the 'culture-pattern' school of thought and his links with psycho-analysis. He brackets Freud with Meyer and White as making the the modern psychiatric outlook possible, but he says: 'My psycho-analytic reading began with Hart: *The Psychology of Insanity*.' He mentions two books of Jung, one of Ferenczi, three of Freud (*Three Contributions to the Theory of Sex, Traumdeutung* and *Psychopathology of Everyday Life*), along with Freud's discussion of the Schreber case, Kempf and Groddeck, and says that, aside from these, his 'subsequent reading of the more purely psycho-analytic contributions has fallen under the law of diminishing returns'. (1955a, p. 178.)

Sullivan, therefore, cannot properly be called a psycho-analyst. At most he has taken suggestions from psycho-analysis and pur-sued his own independent psychiatric way. His position is closely related to that of Horney and Fromm, whose work represents a development of (the orthodox would say a deviation from) psycho-analysis. Dr. Clara Thompson, herself a member of the American Psycho-analytic Association, brackets Ferenczi, Sullivan and Fromm in their influence on her thinking, and includes Sullivan in her book *Psychoanalysis: Evolution and Development*.

His views bring out clearly both the strength and weakness, the value and the limitations, of the 'culture-pattern' type of theory which has become so influential in America despite the criticism it draws from more orthodox analysts such as Franz Alexander.

Thompson writes :

Sullivan calls his the theory of interpersonal relations. He holds that, given a biological substrate, the human is the product of inter-action with other human beings, that it is out of the personal and social forces acting upon one from the day of birth that the person-ality emerges. The human being is concerned with the pursuit of two inclusive goals, the pursuit of satisfaction and the pursuit of security. (1952, p. 211.)

His theory, in brief, is that the social pressures of the 'culture-pat-tern', mediated by parents and teachers, mould the character of the developing 'self-dynamism'. This 'self-system' or 'self-dynam-ism' grows in such a way as to admit what avoids, and to exclude what does not avoid, the anxiety resulting from parental disap-proval. In *Conceptions of Modern Psychiatry* he writes : 'Man is not a creature of instinct' (1955a, p. 30), and he regrets that

The mesalliance of neurology and psychiatry has by no means been dissolved. The emergency of the World War brought us *neuro-psychiatrists*; and a cultural factor, the aversion to mental disorder which is the linear descendant of belief in demoniacal possession and witchcraft, still makes it more certainly respectable to be treated by a neurologist for a 'nervous breakdown' than to consult a psychia-trist about one's difficulties in living. The euphemism covers super-stition and protects conceit : both are powerful checks on the progress not alone of psychiatry, but of civilization as a whole. (1955a, p. 7.)

The inborn potentialities which . . . mature over a term of years are remarkably labile, subject to relatively durable change by experi-ence, and antithetic to the comparatively stable patterns to which the biological concept of *instinct* applies. The idea of 'human in-stincts' in anything like the proper rigid meaning of maturing pat-terns of behaviour which are not labile is completely preposterous. Therefore, all discussions of 'human instincts' are apt to be very mis-leading and very much a block to correct thinking, unless the term *instinct*, modified by the adjective *human*, is so broadened in its meaning that there is no particular sense in using the term at all. (1955, p. 21.)

Biological and neurophysiological terms are utterly inadequate for studying everything in life. . . . I hope that you will not try to build up in your thinking correlations (i.e. 'of "somatic" organization with psychiatrically important phenomena') that are either purely imaginary or relatively unproven, which may give you the idea that you are in a solid, reliable field in contrast to one which is curiously intangible; such a feeling of reliability is, I think, an illusion born out of the failure to recognize that what we know comes to us through our *experiencing* events, and is therefore always separated from anything really formed or transcendentally real by the limited channels through which we contact what we presume to be the per-during, unknown universe. So if a person really thinks that his thoughts about nerves and synapses and the rest have a higher order of merit than his thoughts about signs and symbols, all I can say is, Heaven help him. (1955b, pp. 82–3.)

In this uncompromising statement he makes it clear that he regards any attempt to understand human beings by reducing their psychology to biology and neurology, physiology and anatomy, as foredoomed to failure. Referring to neuroanatomy, he says: 'What we have to learn [is] in a quite different universe of discourse—namely psychology, so-called psychobiology and psychiatry.' (1955b, p. 82.) This is a welcome assertion of the right of the psychological study of man as a person to be accepted as an independent discipline in its own right which may be correlated with, but cannot be reduced to, any other supposedly more basic study. He defines the psychiatric field as 'coeval with man as a social being'. (1955a, p. 5.)

Psychiatry is the study of processes that involve or go on between people. The field of psychiatry is the field of interpersonal relations, under any and all circumstances in which these relations exist. . . A *personality* can never be isolated from the complex of interpersonal relations in which the person lives and has his being. . . . The unique individuality of the other fellow need never concern us as scientists. It is a great thing in our wives and our children. They have, however, aesthetic and other values that are outside of science; when it comes to science, let us confine ourselves to something at which we have a chance of success. We can study the phenomena that go on between the observer and the observed in the situation created by the observer participating with the observed. I hold that this is the subject-matter of psychiatry. (1955a, pp. 10–12.)

He classifies 'interpersonal phenomena' therefore, not in terms of 'instincts' but in terms of 'sought end states', i.e. 'needs'. These fall into two groups, 'satisfactions' and 'security'. The needs for satisfactions are the basic biological or appetitive needs, hunger, thirst, sex, sleep, etc. The needs for security are what, by contrast, we would call personality needs, though Sullivan prefers to speak of 'cultural needs'.

The pursuit of security pertains rather more closely to man's cultural equipment than to his bodily organization. By 'cultural' I mean what the anthropologist means—all that which is man-made, which survives as monument to pre-existent man, that is the cultural. And as I say, all those movements, actions, speech, thoughts, reveries and so on which pertain more to the culture which has been embedded in a particular individual than to the organization of his tissues and glands, is apt to belong to this classification of the pursuit of security. (1955a, p. 13.)

Sullivan regards these security-needs as summed up in the need for 'prestige', or, with Lasswell, for 'security, income and deference'.

All these pertain to the culture, to the social institutions, traditions, customs and the like, under which we live, to our social order rather than to the peculiar properties of our body or somatic organizations. This second class, the pursuit of security, may be regarded as education of the impulses or drives which underlie the first class. In other words, given our biological equipment—we are bound to need food and water and so on—certain conditioning influences can be brought to bear on the needs for satisfaction. And the cultural conditioning gives rise to the second group, the second great class of interpersonal phenomena, the pursuit of security. (1955a, pp. 13–14.)

It follows naturally from this analysis that Sullivan regards the need for 'the feeling of ability or power' as the most important factor leading to the conditioning process. 'We seem to be born with something of this power motive in us', and it is its frustration, as when the baby cries for the moon and cannot get it, that dominates early development.

The full development of personality along the lines of security is chiefly founded on the infant's discovery of his powerlessness to achieve certain desired end states, with the tools, the instrumentalities, which are at his disposal. From the disappointments in the very early stages of life outside the womb . . . comes the beginning of this vast development of actions, thoughts, foresights and so on, which are calculated to protect one from a feeling of insecurity and helplessness in the situation which confronts one. (1955a, p. 14.)

Sullivan's position is set forth by Patrick Mullahy in his article 'A Theory of Interpersonal Relations and the Evolution of Personality', included as an expository appendix to Sullivan's own lectures in *Conceptions of Modern Psychiatry*. He points out that Sullivan distinguished between the power motive and the power drive. A power drive is a neurotic over-compensation for a repressed feeling of helplessness. The power motive is the primary, natural and healthy need to experience the feeling of power, ability, effectiveness or capacity to *do* things, to carry out one's purposes. The power motive is the expression of our basically *active* nature. Concerning this Mullahy writes:

The power motive, although given originally in the human organism, is not a fixed entity. It is manifested in activity, usually, although not always, in an interpersonal situation. . . . The energy of the infant, or rather its manifestations in the power motive, become quickly modified or transformed. But to modify or to transform is not to destroy. Sullivan's theories of interpersonal behaviour are, therefore, rooted in biology. . . . The energy of a human being, however transformed as to its expression by acculturation, is still, obviously, biological. There is continuity between the biological and the cultural. A human being is an acculturated biological organism. (1955a, pp. 244–5.)

This recognition by Sullivan of the biological foundation of psychic life, even though made more specific by recognition of a group of energetic pursuits of bodily 'satisfactions', is not the same thing as Freud's theory of instincts. Sullivan expressly repudiates any such psychosomatic entities. Mullahy says that 'one must invent a new terminology in order to convey the new reference frame of study' (1955a, p. 245), in psychiatry, for here we deal not with isolated and self-contained biological organisms but 'situations'.

According to Sullivan, to speak about impulses, drives, striving towards goals, is to use a figure of speech necessitated by the structure of the language. One never observes such impulses and drives. What one does observe is a situation 'integrated' by two or more people, and manifesting certain recurring kinds of action and behaviour. How is one to explain what occurs? In common everyday language, it said that 'A is striving towards so-and-so from B'. This mode of speech seems to imply that there are certain ready-made, isolated impulses or needs in A which B can satisfy but which existed completely independent of any influence from B. The traditional psychology postulated and termed these apparently pre-existing and independent drives as 'instincts'. . . . The goals of human behaviour were thought to be rather rigidly fixed by the nature of such self-contained, independent, predetermined, instincts. Whatever reciprocal interplay, interaction, occurred between A and B was thought to be more mechanical than transformative. But, according to Sullivan . . . two people acting in a certain way together, reciprocally, make the situation. Their mode of reciprocal action-interaction, defines the situation. That is what an interpersonal situation is, a mode of interaction of two or more people. . . . Pre-existing, fixed drives do not explain an interpersonal situation because they are not observed. . . . [Human behaviour] is malleable, fluid, changeable to an almost incalculable degree . . . interpersonal behaviour does not occur, obviously, in a mechanical, rigidly stereotyped manner. . . . It is, then, a person-integrated-in-a-situation-with-another-person-or-persons, an interpersonal situation, which one studies. . . . It is inaccurate, unscientific to speak of a person-in-isolation-manifesting-this-or-that-tendency-or-drive. (1955a, pp. 245–7.)

This is a highly important formulation of a truth Freud apparently never saw, namely that the actual emotions and 'impulses' we deal with in psychology are not innate and pre-existing biological drives but reactions of individuals to one another in the interpersonal situation that comes about between them. *'Impulses' are functions of object-relationship situations.* I accept Sullivan's view unreservedly on this point. In a further comment Mullahy arrives almost at the point of presenting Sullivan's views in terms of what we shall presently study as Melanie Klein's internal objects, and of Fairbairn's theory of dynamic structure, but he misses the implications of his own statement.

What one observes is a situation, integrated by two or more people. . . . Because all but one of the people may be 'illusory' personifications, or inhabitants of dreamland or the imagination, the problem is more complicated. . . . To have an impulse or drive is to have or manifest a tendency to action in some kind of interpersonal situation. *Impulses and drives cohere in 'dynamisms', relatively enduring configurations of energy, which manifest themselves in numerous ways in human situations.* [Present writer's italics.] The traits which characterize interpersonal situations in which one is integrated describe what one is. . . . Generally speaking, personality is . . . a function of the kinds of interpersonal situations a person integrates with others, whether real persons or fantastic personifications. (1955a, 247–8.)

We are almost on the verge of object-relations theory here. If Sullivan's 'fantastic personifications' were recognized more fundamentally as Melanie Klein's 'internal psychic objects'; and if the theory of impulses as cohering in 'dynamisms' or 'relatively enduring configurations of energy' were seen to imply Fairbairn's theory of impulses as reactions of dynamic ego-structures to objects, internal as well as external; then Sullivan would have transcended the purely 'culture-pattern' type of theory. He does not, however, take that step, but proceeds to outline only the process of acculturation of the conscious and pre-conscious ego in relationships with external objects.

The description of all motivations as reducible to the pursuit of biological satisfactions and cultural security is hardly satisfactory. The biological needs or organic appetites are concerned primarily with the preservation of mere bodily existence, and on that level are themselves a pursuit of security. They acquire the significance of personal satisfactions in very different ways and degrees for different individuals and that is very highly culturally determined. The term 'satisfaction' is also quite as applicable to purely culturally created aims. On the other hand, to limit the significance of culturally conditioned strivings to the pursuit of security is too negative. This view is determined by Sullivan's conception of the ego as purely and solely an anxiety-product. But it leaves out of account the fundamental fact that the chief aim of the human being is to achieve good-object relationships, not for utilitarian, but for intrinsic reasons, not for protection and security merely but for the very positive fulfilment of the nature of personality in itself. As Professor Macmurray puts it, we can only be persons at all in a personal relationship. It is secondary that good relationships are the best of all defences against anxiety. Here, again, Sullivan's views fall short of a true 'object-relations' theory. To make physical needs positive and personality needs merely negative is far from satisfactory.

However, beginning with the infant's cry, he regards the development of language-behaviour as largely a tool for the achievement of security. As the infant becomes a child it is *trained* in 'select excerpts from the cultural heritage, from that surviving of past people, incorporated in the personality of the parents'. (1955a, p. 18.) This includes 'toilet habits, eating habits and the learning of the language as a tool for communication'. (1955a, p. 18.)

Sullivan's theory of the development of what Freud calls the ego and what he calls the *'self-system'* or *'self-dynamism'* is a process of acculturation involving restraints, and

from these restraints there comes the evolution of the self-system— an extremely important part of the personality—with a brand-new tool . . . anxiety. With the appearance of the self-system or the self-dynamism, the child picks up a new piece of equipment which we technically call anxiety. Of the very unpleasant experiences which the infant can have we may say that there are generically two, pain and fear. Now comes the third. It is necessary in the modification of activity in the interest of power in interpersonal relations . . . that one focus one's interest into certain fields that work. It is in learning this process that the self is evolved and the instrumentality of anxiety comes into being. . . . Disapproval . . . becomes more and more the instrument of the signficant adult in educating the infant in the folkways, the tradition, the culture in which he is expected to live. (1955a, pp. 19–20.)

Thus parental disapproval, prohibitions and the privations suffered in the course of education gives his experiences

a peculiar colouring of discomfort, neither pain nor fear but discomfort of another kind. Along with these experiences there go in all well-regulated homes and schools a group of rewards and approbations for successes. These, needless to say, are not accompanied by this particular type of discomfort, and when that discomfort is present and something is done which leads to approbation, then this peculiar discomfort is assuaged and disappears. The peculiar discomfort is the basis of what we ultimately refer to as anxiety. (1955a, p. 20.)

Here Sullivan either confuses together, or fails to distinguish between, anxiety and guilt. What he is evolving is a theory of the social self, the conscious and externally operative ego as built up by the instrumentality of an anxious need for approval and acceptance. At this civilized, moral level of organization, anxiety takes the more specific and developed form of guilt. Thereafter both anxiety and guilt continue to operate as parallel but distinguished reactions, while guilt acquires an importance of its own and gives rise to a new set of problems. Sullivan does not make this clear. In his book *The Interpersonal Theory of Psychiatry* (1955b), anxiety is dealt with exhaustively, but there are only three incidental and passing references to guilt as 'a complex anxiety derivative' (p. 344). One would never suspect from this book the tremendous and devastating part played by repressed guilt in seriously depressed conditions. The fact that Sullivan's interest was far more in schizoid and schizophrenic than in depressive phenomena perhaps accounts for his confusing and fusing anxiety and guilt so easily. The fact that it is specifically *guilt* that Sullivan has in mind is clear. He says :

The self-dynamism is built up out of this experience of approbation and disapproval, of reward and punishment. The peculiarity of the self-dynamism is that as it grows it functions, in accordance with its state of development, right from the start. As it develops it becomes more and more related to a microscope in its function. Since the approbation of the important person is very valuable, since disapprobation denies satisfaction and gives anxiety, the self becomes extremely important. It permits a minute focus on those performances of the child which are the cause of approbation or disapprobation, but, very much like a microscope, it interferes with noticing the rest of the world. . . . It has a tendency to focus attention on performances with the significant other person which get approbation or disfavour. And that peculiarity, closely connected with anxiety, persists thenceforth throughout life. It comes about that the self, that to which we refer when we say 'I', is the only thing which has alertness, which notices what goes on, and, needless to say, notices what goes on in its own field, *The rest of the personality gets along outside of awareness. Its impulses, its performances are not noted. Not only does the self become the custodian of awareness, but when anything spectacular happens that is not welcome to the self, not sympathetic to the self-dynamism, anxiety appears, almost as if anxiety finally became the instrument by which the self maintained its isolation within the personality. . . . Not only does anxiety function to discipline attention, but it gradually restricts personal awareness. The facilitations and deprivations by the parents and significant others are the source of the material which is built into the self-dynamism.* [Present writer's italics.] Out of all that happens to the infant and child, only this 'marked' experience is incorporated into the self, because through the control of personal awareness the self itself from the beginning facilitates and restricts its further growth. In other words, it is self-perpetuating . . . it tends very strongly to maintain the direction and characteristics which it was given in infancy and childhood. For the expression of all things in the personality other than those which were approved and disapproved by the parent and other significant persons, the self refuses awareness . . . those impulses, desires and needs come to exist disassociated from the self, or *dissociated*. When they are expressed, their expression is not noticed by the person. Our awareness of our performances, and our awareness of the performances of others, are permanently restricted to a part of all that goes on and the structure and character of that part is determined by our early training; its limitation is maintained year after year by our experiencing anxiety whenever we tend to overstep the margin. . . . *The self may be said to be made up of reflected appraisals.* [Present writer's italics.] (1955b, pp. 20–22.)

This long quotation is of extreme importance for the critical assessment of the whole 'culture-pattern' type of theory. Karen Horney criticized the Freudian ego as a neurotic phenomenon, but Sullivan's 'self-system' or 'self-dynamism', being totally motivated in its development by anxiety, is also a neurotic phenomenon. This cannot be the whole truth about the nature and development of the self, the ego or 'I' with which we are familiar. That does not prevent there being a very large amount of truth in what Sullivan says. Even a cursory survey of human beings is enough to reveal the chronic state of limitation, inhibition and under-development of potentialities that is prevalent.

Thompson points out that while for Fromm the true self consists of all a man's potentialities, Sullivan's 'self-system' or 'self-dynamism' (i.e. the social self) consists only of those potentialities which were acceptable to the cultural milieu of his childhood. She writes :

The self is eventually formed out of the mass of potentialities in the effort to meet with approval and avoid disapproval. The avoidance of anxiety which is at first evoked by disapproval is the most potent force in its formation. Since anxiety is directly the result of the loss of the sense of well-being as determined by the significant people, it is apparent that the trends of the culture determine to a great extent whether the self includes many of the positive potentialities of a person, or he becomes an 'inferior caricature of what he might have been' (Sullivan). . . . Sullivan's self-system is a part of the personality which can be observed. One must conclude that Sullivan thinks that transcending the culture is, at the very least, difficult. Man is moulded by his culture, and all attempts to break with it produce anxiety. What can be accomplished are modifications within the general framework brought about by the impact of different personalties. (1952, pp. 214–15.)

Questions of far-reaching importance are raised here. It is apparent that this type of research into the nature of the socially adapted self, the Freudian 'reality-ego', is of great value, and we have here a more thorough-going attack on the problem than biologically orientated classic Freudianism produced. Freud's picture of the ego struggling to reconcile the claims of the id and the external world points in this direction ; and Jung's doctrine of the Persona was a first rough approximation to a description of the result. Sullivan's theory of the 'self-system', Horney's 'idealized image of the self' and Fromm's theory of 'automaton conformity' all in different ways constitute a detailed study of the results of social and cultural pressure on ego-development.

Having, however, conceded this much, we must look to the weakness and limitations of this theory, in the form in which Sullivan presents it, as a comprehensive theory of personality development. In the first place the persistence of the rigidities of the self-dynamism is not adequately explained by the view that it is self-perpetuating. The self-dynamism is primarily a reaction to the 'culture-pattern' of the parents. It would be natural to suppose that, since it is essentially an adaptation to the immediate human environment through an anxious desire to please, it would change readily in response to a changing environment. In fact, within restricted limits it does. What is not approved is never so completely excluded from 'awareness' as Sullivan held. The only hope of a development beyond the narrow parental pattern lies in the child being able later on to react to the influence of different types of people. But the crucial fact is that the self-system actually proves highly resistant to change in face of a changing environment as the child goes away from parents and out into the wider world beyond the home. When a dramatic revolt from the parental pattern is suddenly staged on the threshold of adult life, that pattern can always be rediscovered still persisting under repression in the unconscious. In fact, what gives such persistence to the self-system (or the defensive character-structure in Wilhelm Reich's sense) is the fact that the original parental environment, as we shall see presently, still persists under repression as a hidden inner world. The internal causes of the persistence and rigidity of the self-system are unconscious, and as such are beyond reach of being influenced by the changing environment. The most unconscious and rigid portion of Sullivan's 'self-system' must really correspond to the primitive Freudian super-ego. However much the growing child encounters a changing world without, it remains tied to an unconscious and unchanging environment within itself. It is this fact that enforces the persistence of the original developmental pattern of the ego. We need what Sullivan quite fails to supply, a theory of the unconscious in terms of internalized object-relationships. Without that, this whole 'culture-pattern' theory is 'a structure without a foundation', as Thompson says of Horney's teaching.

Such 'theory of the unconscious' as Sullivan has, fails to account for many facts met with in clinical practice. The unconscious for him is 'the rest of the personality (which) gets along outside of awareness. Its impulses, its performances, are not noted.' The unconscious is 'the ignored', and is built up by 'selective inattention' and by 'dissociation'. Such ideas are powerless to explain the aggressively rejective attitude of the main self towards the highly personal, dynamic, frightening figures which appear in dreams as devils, ghosts, sinister men, burglars, wild animals and so on, and which cause dreamers to start up out of nightmares with pounding heart and bathed in sweat. The unconscious is not simply the 'selectively inattended', it is the 'forcibly repressed'. Anxiety at disapproval is a later factor in ego-development. It is preceded by anxiety at simple rejection, and the unconscious is built up in the first place by the infant's struggle in turn to reject his bad object.

Sullivan does in fact recognize an unconscious part of the personality in a more radical sense but he does very little about it. After explaining the way in which the infant very early forms two distinct 'personifications' of the mother—the good tender mother and the bad anxiety-producing mother—he proceeds to describe a parallel development in the formation of two distinct 'personifications' of the self—'good-me' and 'bad-me'. To these he adds a third 'personification' of the self which he calls 'not-me'. Here he says :

We are in a different field—one which we know about only through certain very special circumstances, and these special circumstances are not outside the experience of any of us. The personification of not-me is most conspicuously encountered by most of us in an occasional dream while we are asleep; but it is very emphatically encountered by people who are having a severe schizophrenic episode, in aspects that are to them most spectacularly real. As a matter of fact, it is always manifest—not every minute, but every day, in every life—in certain peculiar absences of phenomena where there should be phenomena; and in a good many people . . . it is very striking in its indirect manifestations (dissociated behaviour), in which people do and say things of which they do not and could not have knowledge, things which may be quite meaningful to other people but are unknown to them. . . . It is from the evidence of these special circumstances—including both those encountered in everybody and those encountered in grave disturbances of personality . . .—that I choose to set up this third beginning personification . . . of not-me. (1955b, pp. 162–3.)

One would conclude from this that the discovery of ways of investigating this ever-present and so influential area of personality, this *not-me* would be a psychiatric priority. That was certainly Freud's view. However, Sullivan leaves it there as something we cannot know anything about. He writes :

The not-me component is, in all essential respects, practically beyond discussion in communicative terms. Not-me is part of the very 'private mode' of living. But . . . it manifests itself at various times in the life of everyone after childhood . . . by the eruption of certain exceedingly unpleasant emotions in what are called nightmares. (1955b, p. 164.)

In a stimulating chapter on 'Sleep, Dreams and Myths' in *The Interpersonal Theory of Psychiatry* (1925b, ch. 20) he speaks of 'powerful motivational systems' being 'dissociated' so that 'it is impossible to abandon enough of the self-system function so that one can have deep and restful sleep' (p. 331). This again seems to challenge resolute investigation, but Sullivan concludes :

there is an impassable barrier between covert operations when one is asleep and covert operations and reports of them when one is awake. If the barrier is passable at all, it is only by the use of such techniques as hynosis, which are so complex as to produce data no more reliable than the recalled dream, so that in essence the barrier *is* impassable. (1955a, p. 331.)

Sullivan thus abandons the attempt which Freudian psychoanalysis perseveres in, to arrive at a depth-psychology, an elucidation of the mystery of this so influential if unconscious *not-me* component of personality. This is the counterpart of the concentration of all the 'culture-pattern' theorists on the investigation of the socially adapting ego.

We must now examine Sullivan's theory of anxiety. It rests on the fact that the infant and child who is accepted and approved, experiences a sense of well-being which Sullivan speaks of as *euphoria*, and that when he is disapproved he loses this sense of well-being and experiences a sense of discomfort qualitatively different from pain and fear which Sullivan calls anxiety. The entire self-system is built up on the principle of avoiding this experience of anxiety.

Two points need to be made about this. As already noted, it is guilt as much as simple anxiety about which Sullivan is speaking, and it is not satisfactory simply to subsume guilt under anxiety. There is a more primitive form of anxiety than this 'anxiety of disapproval'. Sullivan implies that, when he describes anxiety as originating in the first place as a not-understood state of disturbance *empathized* from the anxious mother. Anxiety at disapproval is a distinctly later development. Primitive anxiety lies closer to *fear* in the simple sense, but it persists as a permanent undercurrent in the personality, as a reaction to the highly disturbing figures which persecute repressed portions of the ego in the unconscious. This more hidden anxiety is something Sullivan does not take into account. It constitutes the deep anxiety of early infantile origin against which the conscious ego builds its defences. All the 'culture-pattern theorists' assume that the anxiety that dominates the disturbed person is that which arises out of conflict with the outer cultural environment. The truth is that conflict with the outer world calls forth anxiety of disruptive intensity only because it involves the sense of loss of external support, and leaves the individual alone and at the mercy of his internal dangers. It is when external anxieties arouse internal ones that breakdown occurs. If the inner world at deep levels is relatively anxiety-free, a great deal of conflict with, and isolation from, the outer world can be born.

One further point calls for examination, Sullivan's theory of 'parataxic distortion'. He here approaches but fails to recognize the all-important fact of 'internal psychic objects' without which no proper account of the dynamic unconscious can be given. We may state Sullivan's views in Thompson's summary of them. She writes :

Interpersonal relations as understood by Sullivan refer to more than what actually goes on between two or more factual people. There may be 'phantastic personifications' such as for instance the idealization of a love-object, or one may relate to a non-existent product of the imagination, e.g. 'the perfect mate'. Also one may endow people falsely with characteristics taken from significant people in one's past. An interpersonal relationship can be said to exist between a person and any one of these more or less phantastic people, as well as between a person or group evaluated without distortion. This brings us to Sullivan's concept of parataxic distortion, which is not identical with Freud's transference, although it includes the latter. Parataxic distortion occurs whenever in an interpersonal situation at least one participant is reacting to a personification existing only or chiefly in his phantasy. . . . Parataxic distortion, therefore, would be any attitude towards another person based on phantasy or identification of him with other figures. (1952, pp. 215–16.)

This passage refers to the distortion of perception of the outer world by unconscious projection into it of the inner world. Such externalizing of the unconscious inner world may be extensive or confined for the moment to a single figure. But it is inadequate to speak of these inner figures simply as 'phantasies' or as 'non-existent products of the imagination'. It is only from an outer and rationalistic point of view that they can be so described. Psychologically considered they have *psychic-reality*, they have actual and continuing existence as persisting structural aspects of the total psyche, most of all when they are bad, sinister figures. They are the internal psychic objects which have become so important in British psycho-analytical developments, but which American analysts of both the orthodox and the cultural schools have so far shown little evidence of understanding.

The whole school of 'culture-pattern' theorists are in the predicament of having discarded the orthodox instinct theory (which at any rate did make it possible to describe the deep dynamic unconscious in some approach to structural terms) while they have not yet possessed themselves of its true alternative, internal-objects theory. Thus they are left with no concepts capable of accounting for the unconscious in that deep and dynamic sense which is demanded by so many clinical facts. Their study of the moulding pressure of the cultural milieu on the conscious ego is extremely valuable, and an important corrective of biological theory. But as it stands, their theory is psychologically superficial. They have but supplied the antithesis to Freud's thesis, and for a synthesis we must look to the 'object-relations' theory now developing in British circles out of Freud's own work. Of Sullivan we may say that he goes no farther than the study of the Freudian ego, in its relation to the super-ego, and has no real theory of the unconscious.

One important general question is raised by Sullivan's theory. Having abandoned Freud's attempt to make psychology a science by basing it firmly on biology and neurophysiology, he seeks to make it a science by another method. His theory is, strictly speaking, a 'process theory'. 'Psychiatry is the study of processes that involve or go on between people.' In spite of all the differences due to his sociological orientation, in this fundamental respect his theory is of the same type as Freud's metapsychology. In substituting the term 'dynamisms' for the Freudian 'mechanisms', and in using such a term as 'self-system' in some way as parallel to Freud's 'psychic apparatus', Sullivan is not really getting any closer to a psychology of man as a person. He is only substituting one type of impersonal terminology for another. He is still constructing a scientific process theory and dealing not really with 'persons-in-relationship' but rather 'groupings-of-interpersonal-processes-in-a-cultural-field'.

The 'person' somehow eludes us in Sullivan's writings. He writes:

A personality can never be isolated from the complex of interpersonal relations in which the person lives and has his being. . . . The unique individuality of the other fellow need never concern us as scientists. (1955a, p. 11.)

Nevertheless the *person* does exist as a basically unique individual *within the* field of interpersonal relations, and it is with this person that we *are* concerned in psychotherapy. Since the practical purpose of psychodynamic theory is to provide a basic understanding usable as a guide in psychotherapy, the theory must somehow take account of the person as something more than a collection or focus of processes in the field of interpersonal relations; otherwise the very term 'inter*personal*' relations loses its significance. From this point of view Sullivan cannot be regarded as having moved even as far as half-way beyond Freud towards a theory of object-relations that could do justice to personality.

British developments are more successful in this respect in no small degree because they retain a fundamental Freudian concept of which Sullivan makes no use. He altogether lacks the concept of a dynamic *libido*, a term in which Freud conceptualized the basically object-seeking nature of the human being. Sullivan traces out the infant's development of personifications of the good mother and the bad mother, and of the good-me, the bad-me and the not-me: he explores thoroughly the detailed processes of learning by anxiety, and of the acculturation and socialization of the conscious ego (the self-dynamism). But he has nothing to say about the basic indissoluble libidinal attachment of the infant-person to his personal love-objects which is the foundation of all human psychology, persisting in the unconscious depths of the personality. The 'self' that Sullivan deals with is a 'pattern of energy transformations', a mosaic of safe patterns, and we feel the lack of a dynamic 'whole self' which cannot be imprisoned in that 'pattern' or 'envelope' which presents only 'insignificant differences' from the cultural norm.

A note may be added about the goal of psychotherapy. The books of Fromm and Horney, written for the general public, are widely read in America and this country, and they tend to convey a somewhat moralistic idea of psychotherapy as simply the correction of bad character traits so as to make possible true self-realization.

H. V. Dicks, in a paper 'In Search of our Proper Ethic' (1950, pp. 4–5), regards the goal of therapy set up by the psychotherapist as of great moment to the sociologist. He points out that this may be viewed as either Adjustment, Self-realization or Integration. Horney's early statement that 'neuroses are deviations from the normal pattern of behaviour' implies an adjustment goal. Dicks writes: 'I find the concept of adjustment highly suspect. . . . Adjustment implies that someone who has revolted and will not play the game according to society's rules must be brought round to accept his social obligations. Psychiatrists are often, not without reason, accused of acting on behalf of current social norms. . . . I cannot regard normality, i.e. the average fitting into the current culture patterns as synonymous with mental health. . . . Any therapy, individual or social, based on the conscious or unconscious strategy of moulding a child, a patient or a group, like a lead pipe until it fits, seems to be fraught with dangers. . . . The valid component in the concept of adjustment is the hope that where a person or a group had falsely projected hostile or dystonic feelings to the larger environment which demanded conformity, therapy directed to the removal of the subjective distortions would enable the patient to become *reconciled* to the reality situation. . . . Reconciliation is to reality and is not the equivalent of mere acquiescence of the patient in a social or personal *status quo*.'

As to the goal of self-realization, which Horney emphasized later, Fromm stressed, and Jung made a key concept, Dicks writes :

Another commonly held therapeutic goal is that of 'finding the self', individuation and the like—terms which seem to stress somewhat the opposite of adjustment. Self-realization seems to me an introverted value with considerable narcissistic undertones. . . . At its highest the concept denotes a working through culturally imposed obstacles which had falsified the person, towards an autonomy strongly differentiated from group or collective norm pressures. . . . I do not deny its value, for if it were successful it could profoundly change people's relations to the object-world. Only it seems too narrow and world-denying to stand as a goal for divers personalities.

Dicks advocates the goal of integration as capable of including the antagonistic ideas of adjustment and self-realization, leading to a new concept of 'mental health' as a new value.

A Note on Carl Jung

Jung need not detain us long at this point, for though he, too, strongly emphasizes the present, and still more the future, as important for understanding human problems, he also discards the depth-psychology of Freud with its all-important revelation of the way the child lives on in the unconscious. He substitutes a depth-psychology of his own, a highly speculative theory of an hereditary racial unconscious which dominates behaviour through the activation of 'archetypes' which are, it seems, deposits of racial memory. In virtue of them we deal with present-day problems and situations, not so much in the light of the way we dealt with our environment when we were infants, but in the light of the way our ancestors dealt with environments of untold thousands of years ago. Whatever may be the fate of this theory, it seems scientifically preferable to deal with more accessible material from the research point of view, and exhaust that first.

Jung has not made a marked contribution to sociology, perhaps because the goal of his theory is the narcissistic goal of individuation. The writer can only repeat here what he wrote elsewhere in 1949 :

Jung has put his finger on a really determining motive in the psychic life of a human being. It is the inescapable and ineradicable urge to become, and to fulfil oneself as, a person. Unfortunately, however, Jung's treatment of this is too subjective : he does not show how integration is necessarily bound up with good object-relationships.

Jung's theory of integration or individuation is of profound significance for the psychology of religion, but it does raise two difficulties. Jung either does not see, or does not deal with, the question of personal relationship as the medium in which ultimately integration is achieved. The importance of this is apparent in Macmurray's treatment of 'mutuality' as of the essence of personality. One gets the impression that Jung regards integration as an esoteric and wholly internal process, in achieving which we end up inside our own psyche. A condition of psychic self-sufficiency would surely be a state of spiritual isolation which contradicts the very nature of the personal life. He also seems to treat integration as a process largely confined to the second half of life, whereas we see integration as the dominating need from the very earliest moment that conflict arises, and as the inner meaning of psychological growth through every phase of our life-course. Integration within ourselves and personal relationship with other people proceed *pari passu*. (1949, pp. 208–9.)

On two points, however, Jung was a forerunner of the culture-pattern theorists whose views we have just examined. He early recognized that psycho-analytical therapy was an interpersonal situation which involved the personality and reactions of the analyst as well as the patient : and in a more subtle and personal sense than is allowed for by the Freudian theory of transference and counter-transference.

Further, his theory of the Persona is a description of a most important way in which an individual is moulded, so far as his visible social self is concerned, by the pattern of his cultural milieu. It is a social mask, typical for the individual's class or profession which protects and hides his inner self. It is therefore a socially determined ego-defence.

PSYCHODYNAMIC THEORY OF THE 'PERSON'
AND PERSONAL RELATIONS

CHAPTER X

THE RELATION OF MELANIE KLEIN'S
WORK TO FREUD
(THE DEVELOPMENT OF MELANIE KLEIN'S CONCEPTIONS)

THIS study of the development of psycho-analytical theory has so far traced the first two phases of a dialectical pattern. The original *thesis* of psychobiological theory, postulated by Freud, provoked an *antithesis* of psychosociological theory which really began with Adler in the first decade of the twentieth century, and developed from around 1930 in America into an elaborate challenge to Freudian orthodoxy. Both thesis and antithesis flourish together side by side to-day, but they call for a further development towards a true *synthesis*. In this, both emphases must be reconciled in one more specifically *psychological* theory. What this might mean can be seen from Fairbairn's view that the proper object of psychological investigation is the person, not the organism, especially if we add, 'nor the cultural community'. Psychodynamic theory calls to be developed in such a way as distinguishes it from both biology on the one hand, and from sociology and social psychology on the other. It is the present writer's view that such a synthesis has already begun to emerge in British psychoanalysis, in the work of Melanie Klein and W. R. D. Fairbairn.

The danger that the two earlier points of view could be set in unfruitful opposition was recognized by Otto Fenichel. He writes:

There is no 'psychology of man' in a general sense, in a vacuum, as it were, but only a psychology of man in a certain concrete society.
. . . In the endeavour to investigate the relationship between biological

needs and external influences, one or the other of these two forces may be over-estimated. The history of psycho-analysis has seen both types of deviation. Certain authors in their biologistic thinking have entirely overlooked the role of outwardly determined frustrations in the genesis of neuroses and character traits, and are of the opinion that neuroses and character traits might be rooted in conflicts between contradictory biological needs in an entirely endogenous manner. Such a point of view is dangerous even in therapeutic analysis; but it becomes entirely fatal if it is assumed in applications of psycho-analysis to sociological questions. Attempts of this kind have sought to understand social institutions as the outcome of conflicts between contradictory instinctual impulses within the same individuals, instead of seeking to understand the instinctual structure of empirical human beings through the social institutions in which they grew up. But there are also certain authors at the other extreme who reproach psycho-analysis with being too biologically oriented, and who are of the opinion that the high valuation of the instinctual impulses means that cultural influences are denied or neglected. They are even of the erroneous opinion that the demonstration of their importance contradicts any instinct theory. Freud's own writings contain, essentially, descriptions of how instinctual attitudes, objects, and aims are changed under the influence of experiences. (1945, p. 6.)

Fenichel's view, however, like Freud's, of the kind and extent of social influence on the individual does not go deep enough. He writes :

certainly not only frustrations and reactions to frustrations are socially determined; what a human being desires is also determined by his cultural environment. However, the culturally determined desires are merely variations of a few biological basic needs. (*Ibid.*, p. 6.)

The character of men is socially determined. The environment enforces specific frustrations, blocks certain modes of reaction to these frustrations, and facilitates others; it suggests certain ways of dealing with the conflicts between instinctual demands and fears of further frustrations; it even creates desires by setting up and forming specific ideals. Different societies, stressing different values and applying different educational measures, create different anomalies. (*Ibid.*, p. 464.)

The environment is here, however, still seen only as something external which facilitates, obstructs, deflects and distorts instinctive drives. There is no recognition of the all-important fact of the psychic internalization of the environment as an inner world in Klein's and Fairbairn's sense.

A psychodynamic theory is now emerging which takes into account the fact that man lives in two worlds at the same time, inner and outer, psychic and material, and has relationships with two kinds of objects, internal and external. Here 'depth psychology' and the sociological orientation merge in a synthesis. It is a formidable task to discuss 'internal objects' psychology with any but specialists in psycho-analysis. Classic Freudianism appeared to many people to give an alarmingly complex view of the nature and working of the human mind. Yet all forms of pure instinct theory give a picture of mental development in infancy and childhood which is simple by contrast with the complexities revealed by investigation of 'internal objects' and the unconscious as an inner world. Melanie Klein speaks of 'the bewildering complexity of the processes which operate, to a large extent simultaneously, in the early stages of development'. (1952, p. 198.)

There is, however, no particular reason why we should expect to find mental phenomena simple and easy to understand. Had they been so, they would surely have been elucidated, and human nature understood, long ago. The scientific investigation of 'matter' began with the common sense prejudice in favour of a simple, solid substance, and has arrived at the complexities of atomic physics which, though completely beyond the comprehension of all but the expert few, plainly represent realities or they would not confer on man the ability to harness atomic energy.

It seems that the scientific investigation of 'mind' is following a similar course. Starting with such straightforward, common-sense assumptions as that of the simple unity of the soul and its warfare with bodily appetite, thus resolving all problems into one of moral responsibility, psychodynamic theory has arrived at an almost frighteningly complex picture of the developmental history of the human mind in its early formative years. Any appearance the adult mind may have of being relatively simple and straightforward in character and functioning, turns out, under the psychoanalytical microscope, to be a complete illusion. Repression, and unconsciousness of all of the structure and a great part of the functioning of the human mind, create and maintain the illusion of simplicity.

Mankind in general can afford to consign atomic physics to the physicist and leave the experts to apply atomic power to our practical needs. We cannot in the same way leave psychodynamics so entirely to the expert, since in our daily life we must deal with other human beings, and we will do so more successfully if we have some accurate and reliable insight into human nature. Not that everyone must become a psycho-analyst, but all who are practically concerned with the fact that living is a matter of human relationships need to grasp the significance of at any rate the essential discoveries contained in the new developments of psychoanalysis to which we now turn.

1. *The Early Development of Mrs. Klein's Conceptions*

Since psycho-analysis traces the origin of the fundamental personality problems back to infancy, it is most appropriate that its further development should be brought about by discoveries made in the analysis of children. Freud opened up the prospect of the analysis of children as early as 1909 in his *Analysis of a Phobia in a Five-year-old Boy*. Adler early developed psychotherapeutic treatment of children on an extensive scale. Not till shortly before 1920, however, was the treatment of children undertaken systematically by psycho-analysts, first by Hug-Hellmuth, and then by Anna Freud and Mrs. Melanie Klein. Hug-Hellmuth and Anna Freud both held that the classic psycho-analytical technique needed to be modified to be more supportive and educational in order to be applied to children. Mrs. Klein, by using the child's play in all its forms, games of impersonation, drawing, cutting out, using water, etc., as a substitute for the purely verbal free association of the adult patient, gained direct access to the unconscious of the child as young as $2\frac{3}{4}$ years. Material from the phantasy life of the pre-verbal period was made accessible and in due course the child would become able to verbalize its conflicts within the limits of its vocabulary, which Mrs. Klein held to be necessary for radical analysis. This was a purely psycho-analytical technique.

In the Preface to the First Edition of *The Psycho-Analysis of Children* (1932, 3rd Ed., p. 7, 1948) Mrs. Klein described her results as 'a contribution to the general psycho-analytic theory of the earliest stages of the development of the individual'. Ferenczi suggested to her that she had an aptitude for child-analysis, and she developed her play technique in 1922–3. Her first three published papers belong to this period: 'The Development of a Child'; 'The Role of the School in the Libidinal Development of the Child'; and 'Infant Analysis'. These papers do not show any specific formulation of her characteristic later concepts but they certainly foreshadow them. They are implicit in the type of material she discovered.

In 1924–5 Mrs. Klein had a fourteen months' analysis with Karl Abraham. She quotes Abraham as saying in 1924, 'The

future of Psycho-Analysis lies in Play Analysis.' In 1925 Ernest
Jones invited her to lecture and then to settle in London, and we
may regard the period from then up to the publication of *The
Psycho-Analysis of Children* in 1932 as laying the foundations of
her distinctive contribution. The book was based on lectures given
in 1925–7. Though her theory made further developments after
1932, she wrote in the third Edition in 1948, 'this book as it stands
represents fundamentally the views I hold to-day' (p. 13).

It is interesting to watch the gradual emergence of the main
Kleinian ideas in the early papers. They are a storehouse of early
childhood phantasy material. Phantasies that work through only
slowly and very partially, and often heavily intellectualized and
disguised, in the dreams and free associations of adults, come out
with startling directness and detail when played out openly by the
small child. Mrs. Klein's later views are implicit in the material as
presented even in the three earliest papers (1919–23). Their main
theme is that of the influence of sexual libidinal impulses and of
sexual curiosity on the character, intellectual development and
ego-activities of the small child. Yet already the themes of *sadism*
and *anxiety* are in the forefront.

Her general theory at this time was orthodox. Libidinal and
sexual are equated. Her emphasis on anxiety is clear but is not yet
related specifically to aggression. She takes for granted Freud's
'instinct theory' which had just assumed its final form as 'life and
death instincts' in 1920, though the death instinct, on which Mrs.
Klein later insisted so strongly, is not mentioned in her writing
prior to 1932. (1932, p. 180.) Repression is regarded as aimed
essentially against pleasure-toned sexual libidinal impulses.
Anxiety is converted, frustrated, sexual libido, and Sublimation is
the sexual cathexis of ego-instincts, activities and interests. On the
basis of this theoretical position she shows how play, phantasy and
intellectual development in the very small child are inhibited by
the repression of sexual curiosity and set free by its release. This
curiosity develops over four questions : (1) Where do babies come
from? (2) What are babies made of (food, faeces, etc.)? (3) What
is the difference between male and female? (4) What part does the
father play in the making of a baby?

Mrs. Klein's case material (Fritz, aged 5 years) shows that it is
the fourth problem that presents by far the gravest difficulty to
the child, so that he cannot even consciously recognize and ask his
own question without much help. This help, however, is hard to
give because he resists enlightenment in the most unyielding way.
It is evident that a specially intense anxiety maintains a heavy
repression on this disturbing matter of the father's role in the

genital sexual relationship between him and the mother, i.e. the Primal Scene. Mrs. Klein did not, at this early date, go into the causes of this peculiarly powerful resistance and repression, but it becomes clear that it is due to the factor which was to emerge as basic for her theory, namely anxiety and/or guilt concerning aggression.

As little Fritz consciously accepted and absorbed the knowledge of the father's sexual role, his Oedipus complex became fully conscious, bringing out a flood of aggressive phantasies in this hitherto very unaggressive little boy. A soldier calls the king a dirty beast and is imprisoned and beaten. Fritz is an officer, a standard bearer and a trumpeter, and he says: 'If papa were a trumpeter too and didn't take me to the war, then I would take my own trumpet and my gun and go to the war without him.' (1948, p. 45, cf. pp. 40 ff.) Oral, anal and genital sadism and general aggressiveness were exposed against his father and symbolic father-figures in his phantasies, followed by clear primal scene phantasies in which Fritz showed himself to be involved in identifications with, and displacings of, both parents. As anxiety mounted he began to put a stop to aggressive games and re-experienced his earlier night-terrors, while in phantasy he took up the homosexual position in the form of a fear of his father's penis and of castration. It is evident that the child must be victim, not aggressor, in face of his own anxiety and guilt. Finally it emerged that it was anxiety over his mother's fate in the sadistic heterosexual situation that dictated his flight into the homosexual position. For ultimately the fear of the castrating mother emerged from behind the fear of the punishing father, related to the child's own hate and aggression against his mother which he turned back on to himself.

All the material required for Mrs. Klein's later theoretical developments is set forth in her first paper (1919–21). Anxiety and guilt are manifestly due to aggression rather than to sexuality *per se*, arising from the development of sadistic parental images which persecute and punish the child for his own aggression with monstrous ruthlessness. Mrs. Klein observes thus early that the origin of complexes lies far back in the pre-verbal period. (1948, p. 62.) From this starting-point she gradually proceeds to the employment of Freud's new super-ego concept for the explanation of these persecuting parental imagos, an explanation which developed in course of time into the theory of internal objects, and carried back the origin of both the super-ego and the Oedipus complex from the Freudian genital phase to the anal and oral phases in the second and first years of life. As her theory came to centre more and more on aggression, she adopted in the most uncompromising way Freud's theory of the death instinct as its basis, though that was by no means a necessary step.

In her second paper Mrs. Klein showed how the unconscious sexualization of school, teacher, work and sport created inhibitions and problems for the child after it had emerged from infancy; for all activity that is unconsciously sexualized tends to arouse 'castration-anxiety' to put a stop to it, and this can be avoided only by finding acceptable 'sublimations' of the repressed sexual component drives, oral, anal and genital. It is already clear in her clinical material, as it later became in her theoretical formulations, that sexuality becomes a source of disturbance to the child not because it is sexuality but because it has become sadistic. There could be no motive for the suppression of a purely pleasure-toned impulse in the absence of external deprivation and frustration-rage. A sexuality that is unconsciously determined by the sadistic conception of coitus embodied in the repressed primal scene phantasy has become a permanent source of internal conflict, and incapable of straightforward, conscious assimilation into the experience of the growing child. The future of Melanie Klein's work lay in the detailed analysis of the way in which intense aggression is aroused in the infant at such an astonishingly early age, and fused with his sense of personal need particularly in the form of infantile sexuality, to create a sadistic emotional life which makes the infant terrified both of himself and of the fate of his love-objects, and fills him with persecutory anxiety over their phantasied retaliation against him.

Her third paper, 'Infant Analysis' (1923), deals with anxiety, inhibitions, symptoms and sublimations. It falls before Freud's monograph on *Inhibitions, Symptoms and Anxiety* in 1926. Already Mrs. Klein's attention had become concentrated on anxiety and its causes and manifestations. She wrote:

Anxiety is one of the primary affects . . . [and] the ego tries in the different neuroses to shield itself from the development of anxiety. . . . There is probably not a single child who has not suffered from *pavor nocturnus* . . . [and] in all human beings at some time or other neurotic anxiety has been present in greater or lesser degree. (1948, p. 89.)

Children often conceal from those around them considerable quantities of anxiety . . . some primary anxiety is always hidden behind the amnesia of childhood and can only be reconstructed by an analysis which penetrates really deep. (*Op. cit.*, p. 89, note.)

In these early papers her main *emphases* on aggression and anxiety and their relation to the Oedipal conflict have not yet led to new *theoretical formulations*. As these emerged she rightly regarded them as true developments from and beyond Freud's own theory. She has, however, never fully recognized that her work involves not only a development but also a revision of some of Freud's basic ideas. Mrs. Klein's first five papers coincide with Freud's second great revolutionary and creative period (1920–26), and, as the impact of the 'structural theory' that he originated in that period spread throughout the psycho-analytical world, its stimulating influence became a major factor in Mrs. Klein's thinking. Had Freud himself recognized the extent to which his ego-analysis and structural theory demanded a far-reaching revision of his earlier instinct-theory, Mrs. Klein would have been helped to the clearer conceptualization of her own discoveries and spared the controversies that arose out of a widespread feeling that she was unorthodox, a singularly misplaced accusation to make against scientific work. As it was, she held to the orthodox, classic Freudian theory with one hand while putting a new patch on the old garment with the other. This must have hampered her thinking about her own clinical work, where her original genius lay in her capacity for direct understanding of the unconscious in the very small child.

This problem is shown by the orthodoxy of her view at the outset that primary libidinal-sexual pleasure 'draws repression upon itself, for *repression is directed against the tone of sexual pleasure* associated with the activity and leads to the inhibition of the activity or tendency' [present writer's italics]. (1948, p. 88.) The idea that repression is directed against what is pleasurable could only be maintained by appealing to the Oedipus conflict as orthodoxly conceived, i.e. the child's sexual activity calls forth castration-anxiety because of its fear of the jealousy and punitive interference of the parent of the same sex. In fact, Mrs. Klein's analysis of sadism shows that this view is far too simple, that the repression of sexuality is secondary to the repression of aggression, and that simple attraction and rivalry is far from being an adequate account of the complex phenomena that comprise the ramifications of the so-called Oedipus complex. By 1932, in *The Psycho-Analysis of Children*, she finalized a definite change of viewpoint in this matter.

The excessive sense of guilt which masturbatory activities arouse in children is really aimed at the destructive tendencies residing in the phantasies that accompany masturbation. (1932, pp. 164–5.)

Concerning sexual activity between children she writes:

Whether its effect will ultimately be good or bad . . . seems to depend on the quantity of sadism present . . . where the positive and libidinal factors predominate, such a relationship has a favourable influence upon the child's object-relations and capacity for love; but where . . . destructive impulses, on one side at any rate, and acts of coercion dominate it, it is able to impair the whole development of the child in the gravest way. (*Ibid.*, p. 175.)

This view that it is not sexuality *per se* but aggression, or rather the fusion of aggression with sexuality to form sadism, that is primarily subjected to repression, implied that the sense of guilt, and the feeling of anxiety, also relate to aggression rather than to sexuality. Mrs. Klein's conclusion in 1926 that 'impulses of hatred and aggression are the deepest cause and foundation of guilt' (1948, p. 26, footnote) is reaffirmed in 1932 in the words: 'the child's early anxiety and feelings of guilt have their origin in aggressive impulses connected with the Oedipus conflict'. (1948, p. 26.)

In the Preface to the third edition of *The Psycho-Analysis of Children* Mrs. Klein summarizes the position she had reached in 1932, when the book was first published; the 'essential hypotheses' were as follows:

In the first few months of life infants pass through states of persecutory anxiety which are bound up with the 'phase of maximal sadism'; the young infant also experiences feelings of guilt about his destructive impulses and phantasies which are directed against his primary object—his mother, first of all her breast. These feelings of guilt give rise to the tendency to make reparation to the injured object. (1932, p. 11.)

To this we may add her statement on page 28 that:

The Oedipus conflict sets in as early as the second half of the first year of life and . . . at the same time the child begins to modify it and to build up its super-ego.

In Part 2 of the book she reviewed all her findings concerning the early developmental stages of the infant as dominated by the central factor of aggression originating at first in the frustration of oral needs. Thus her theory came to concentrate on the analysis of the earliest stages of super-ego formation, and the significance, and effects on development of the ego, of the earliest anxiety-situations. It was the still closer analysis of these early anxiety-situations that later led her to distinguish an early paranoid position of the first three to five months, and a depressive phase from the sixth to the eight month, the early stages of the Oedipus complex being then correlated with the depressive and ambivalent position. Thus emerged her important distinction between persecutory and depressive anxiety.

Melanie Klein's theory amounts at this stage to a reorientation of psycho-analysis on the basis of aggression rather than libido as the pathogenic factor arising in response to libidinal frustration. Libidinal development takes place under the dominance of aggression and frustration-rage, and is turned into sadism in the hate-motivated infantile psyche. A complex anxiety is evoked in the child by his destructive impulses, an anxiety made up of his fear of being himself destroyed by their violence, and the fear of destroying his objects together with the projection of his sadism on to them and the fear that they will retaliate destructively on him. Since the super-ego is the carrier of this aggression turned inwards against himself, the analysis of the early anxiety situations and of the formation of the super-ego must proceed together. The importance of this approach is seen from Mrs. Klein's view of psychotherapy as the mitigation of the severity of the super-ego together with the strengthening of the weak ego of the child. (1932, pp. 19 and 35.) Anxiety and guilt aroused by the sadistic super-ego press upon the immature ego. 'There are always present not only wishes but counter-tendencies coming from the super-ego.' (1932, p. 34, footnote.) Anxiety and guilt constitute the core of the neurosis, i.e. interference with active ego-functioning, and the psycho-analytic situation has come into existence when contact has been made with the child's deep, repressed anxiety and guilt. (1932, p. 96.)

Mrs. Klein first analysed the early anxiety phases and super-ego stages in the phenomena of the successive oral, anal and genital levels of development, as revealed in early phantasy. She was confronted with an abundance of phantasies in which her child patients fought with or were persecuted by soldiers, burglars and robbers, fierce wild animals, giants, bizarre creatures and symbolic parent-figures of many kinds. The weapons and means of combat and destruction included sucking, biting, eating, cooking and devouring, emptying, wetting, dirtying, stealing body contents and cutting off organs, penetrating, stabbing and so on. The symbolism is easily recognized as falling into the oral, anal and genital categories already established by Freud from adult analyses.

Ernest Jones, in his Introduction to Mrs. Klein's *Contributions to Psycho-Analysis, 1921–1945* has written :

Freud had shown that the child's mind contained in its depths much besides the innocence and freshness that so entrance us. There were dark fears of possibilities that the most gruesome fairy tale had not dared to explore, cruel impulses where hate and murder rage freely, irrational phantasies that mock at reality in their extravagance. Mrs. Klein's unsparing presentation of the cutting, tearing, gouging, devouring phantasies of infants is apt to make most people recoil. . . . She went further than this by maintaining that the Cimmerian picture Freud had drawn of the unconscious mind of a three-year-old was at least as valid of an infant of the first months of life. . . . Devouring or cannibalistic phantasies had been observed and traced to perhaps the age of three. But Mrs. Klein ruthlessly maintains that they occur during the so-called cannibalistic stage of infancy itself, which after all seems what one would have expected. (1948, pp. 10–11.)

Those who have played freely with little children will need little convincing about this. The little child has not yet learned the trick of abstracting his mind from his body and setting up that strange dichotomy which enables adults to shelve many personal problems. The child is an intensely 'embodied person', and Mrs. Klein's material shows him to be emotionally preoccupied with 'embodied persons'. His phantasies are all of bodies, attacks on bodies, getting something out of one body and into another body with fears of retaliatory reversals of this procedure, of robbing and injuring bodies and healing and repairing the damage done to them. This begins with oral hunger for the breast where 'coitus' between child and mother is in terms of sucking, biting, eating, greedily devouring. A pattern of relationships is created in the child's feeling and phantasy which is then applied in turn to urethral, anal and genital functions and relationships, to feeding, cleanliness training and genital coitus between parents (not seldom witnessed or heard, but sooner or later always phantasied), *and to all kinds of personal relationships.* Coitus in the primal scene is felt by the child and interpreted on the analogy of the original coitus of child and mother at the oral stage, and the child experiences rage and jealousy (in proportion as he has already become insecure) due to the fact that he feels that his parents are getting something from each other (by exchange and incorporation of bodily substances and organs—the only terms in which the infant can experience anything) while he himself feels excited, stimulated with needs and longings, but left out, ignored and left unsatisfied. He usually reacts with bodily expressions of his rage such as wetting and dirtying, while in phantasy he attacks the parents who seem to be combined against him.

In due course as the child develops, sexual curiosity emerges within the total personality, and in so far as this immature personality is already disturbed by lack of satisfaction of vital needs and hence by frustration-rage, so that its fundamental libidinal life of feeling and phantasy has turned sadistic, this curiosity but adds one more activity over which to feel guilt and anxiety, and over which to institute repression. The resulting inhibitions may damage intellectual development as thoroughly as the earlier repressions damage emotional spontaneity in personal relationships. Basically Mrs. Klein's view is that it is oral, anal and genital sadism that are the source of anxiety and the targets of repression under the force of anxiety and guilt. The super-ego, which incorporates the infant's sadism turned against himself, includes oral, anal and genital components as may be seen by the pre-genitally symbolized attacks under which the infant suffers in his phantasy and play. This super-ego takes the form of an internalized version of the child's loved and hated parental objects on to whom his own aggression has been projected and thus used up in his own punishment for his phantasied attacks on them.

Two comments call to be made about Mrs. Klein's conclusions up to this point. Firstly, Mrs. Klein is so busy analysing the endopsychic situation in the child that the child's environment seems to be taken only cursorily into account. Generalized references to oral frustration occur, particularized as 'unfavourable conditions of nutrition'. (1932, p. 180.) The traumatic effect of witnessing the primal scene is specifically taken account of. But the case-histories of the child patients do not contain much information of a more detailed kind concerning the parents. The mother of the patient Rita is stated to have been suffering from a severe obsessional neurosis. (1932, p. 24.) The birth and activities of siblings are reckoned into the picture. But one misses more subtle characterizations of traumatic environmental factors such as Winnicott's mention of 'erratic mothering', or the existence of unconscious hate and rejection of the child in the mother, or the effect of maternal types on the quality of mothering given to the child. An impression grows that in the main the child's troubles are for the most part internally generated, the environment supplying only an initial 'push'. Thereafter neurosis develops by an almost wholly endopsychic process and inner conflicts are automatic and self-generated developmental phenomena. Perhaps this trend is incidental to the necessary concentration on the endopsychic problem in the early stages of its more intimate analysis, but is dangerous if it persists into the realm of final conclusions. In *The Psycho-Analysis of Children* Mrs. Klein writes:

In my judgment, reality and real objects affect the child's anxiety-situations from the very earliest stages of its existence, in the sense that it regards them as so many proofs or refutations of its anxiety situations, which it has displaced into the outer world. (1932, p. 302.)

This amounts to the view that our experience of outer reality is from the start secondary and subordinate to internal experience, a highly controversial view.

Secondly, Mrs. Klein's discussion of anxiety is vitiated by her use of the speculative concept of the death instinct. E. Jones called attention to this as one of his points of disagreement with, or at least doubt about, her views. Thus Mrs. Klein regards oral-sucking as libidinal and oral-biting as sadistic; 'the polarity between the life-instincts and the death-instincts is already coming out in these phenomena of early infancy, for we may regard the force of the child's fixation at the oral-sucking level as an expression of the force of its libido, and, similarly, the early and powerful emergence of its oral sadism as a sign of the ascendency of its destructive instinctual components'. (1932, p. 180.) She quotes with approval a passage of Therese Benedek : 'Anxiety, therefore, is not a fear of death but the perception of the death-instinct that has been liberated in the organism—the perception of primary masochism.' (*Todestreib und Angst*, 1931.) Some analysts had already uncritically accepted the death instinct as an established fact rather than a questionable speculation. (1932, M. Klein, p. 183.) It implies the view rejected by O. Fenichel that neurosis is caused by a purely innate 'conflict between contradictory biological needs in an entirely endogenous manner'. (Quoted on p. 193.) This led Mrs. Klein to rely on an innate and primary sadism which set up an equally innate primary masochism operating alongside of the libidinal drives. This in turn obscured the fact that her own analysis pointed to aggression as being a reactive development in face of bad objects, and being internally aimed as a result of, and indeed in the process of, the internalization of bad objects. Her work should lead to an equal emphasis on parental impacts on the child and on the subjective elaboration of the bad object situation in the child's experience.

Mrs. Klein considers this question in the light of Freud's views. She writes:

Concerning the formation of the super-ego, Freud seems to follow two lines of thought, which are to some extent mutually complimentary. According to one the severity of the super-ego is derived from the severity of the real father whose prohibitions and commands it repeats. According to the other . . . its severity is an outcome of the destructive impulses of the subject.

Psycho-analysis has not followed up the second line of thought. As its literature shows, it has adopted the theory that the super-ego is derived from parental authority and has made this theory the basis of all further enquiry into the subject. Nevertheless, Freud has recently, in part, confirmed my own view, which lays emphasis on the importance of the impulses of the individual himself as a factor in the origin of his super-ego and on the fact that his super-ego is not identical with his real objects. (1932, pp. 196–8.)

Thus, while Freud leaned too heavily towards the side of the external origin of the super-ego, Mrs. Klein risks leaning too far over in the opposite direction till at times the super-ego as inwardly directed aggression seems to become a purely subjective development of the death instinct in spite of the fact that her work provides a fully satisfactory developmental analysis of sadism and masochism without any need to call in this so-called instinct.

This point provides a suitable opportunity to look more closely at the relationship of Mrs. Klein's work to that of Freud. With a group of co-workers, of whom the best known were Susan Isaacs, Paula Heimann and Joan Riviere, she created from the later 1920s a theoretical development of classic Freudian psycho-analysis round which much controversy has raged. Some of the ultra-orthodox such as Edward Glover regard it frankly as a 'deviation' from Freud. This has caused a number of British analysts of recent years to state explicitly that theory cannot stand still with the death of Freud. In any case the term 'deviation' specifically used by Glover is one that savours more of political differences from the Party-line than of scientific discussion, in which connection it ought to be regarded as inadmissible. American psycho-analysts, apart from Bibring, do not appear as yet to have made a serious attempt to get to grips with Mrs. Klein's work, while Bibring's critical examination of it is too limited in scope to touch the really critical issues. There is evidently considerable resistance and guilt felt about departures from the Founder's system.

However, the charge that Kleinian theory is a deviation of a type that deprives it of the right to be called 'psycho-analysis' cannot be regarded as proved. Her work is a true development of Freud's insights. Perhaps the most astonishing thing about Freud is that he himself provided practically all the initial insights and observations which were starting-points to enable later workers to think their way beyond the positions he formulated. The student is bound to acquire a competent knowledge of Freud before he can begin to understand the work of Melanie Klein, and subsequently Fairbairn. Her theory rests on such basic concepts as Freud's theory of libidinal and aggressive (destructive) instincts, the classical theory of the complex nature of sexual development through oral, anal and phallic phases to the goal of libidinal integration and maturity at the genital level, the phenomena of repression, inhibition, symptom formation and sublimation, the Freudian theory of psychic structure—i.e. the id, ego and super-ego, by means of which psychic conflict and the arousal of anxiety and guilt are made manifest—and finally the operation of the ego defence mechanisms.

The most important Kleinian literature comprises three books by Mrs. Klein; *The Psycho-Analysis of Children* (1932), *Contributions to Psycho-Analysis* (1948), her collected papers, and *Envy and Gratitude* (1957), two comprehensive symposia, *Developments in Psycho-Analysis* (1952) by Melanie Klein and others, and *New Directions in Psycho-Analysis* (1955) edited by M. Klein, P. Heimann and R. Money-Kyrle: also a small book, *Love, Hate and Reparation* (1937, reprinted 1953) by Klein and Riviere. *Developments in Psycho-Analysis* is a publication, with modifications and additions, of contributions to private 'Discussions' of the Kleinian theory held by the British Psycho-analytical Society in 1943–4. *New Directions in Psycho-Analysis* reproduces, with additions, the birthday number of the *International Journal of Psycho-Analysis* in honour of Mrs. Klein in 1952. (Vol. XXXIII, Pt. 2.) Four important studies of her theories have appeared: by Ed. Glover, 'An Examination of the Klein System of Child Psychology' (1945); by Ed. Bibring, 'The So-Called English School of Psycho-Analysis' (1947); by Marjorie Brierley (1951, ch. 3) and by J. O. Wisdom (in a review in *The British Journal for the Philosophy of Science* (1956)). Glover is hostile, Bibring is critical, Brierley and Wisdom are sympathetic.

Perhaps the question of 'instinct' is the most convenient matter over which to raise the apparently vexed issue as to whether Mrs. Klein's work is a deviation from that of Freud. We have stated our view that on general grounds the charge fails, yet the critics of Klein have sensed something they have not clearly stated. Joan Riviere successfully rebuts the charge by showing that Melanie Klein developed hints and suggestions embodied in Freud's own writings, thus carrying his work farther at those very points where Freud left an open invitation to further research. When, in addition to that line of argument, Riviere bases her vindication of

Klein's loyalty to Freud on the ground that, above all, her work demonstrates and develops the truth of Freud's theory of the death instinct, that notably controversial issue in psycho-analysis, one feels that Kleinian writers, immersed in the massive details of their analysis of infancy, have not seen the wood for the trees. In fact, their work is essentially a supersession of instinct-theory in Freud's sense. Mrs. Klein retained so much of classic Freudian theory, and in particular instinct theory, that she did not recognize that her discoveries outmoded important parts of the classic 'psychobiology', providing, in fact, the material for a more consistently psychodynamic theory. *Mrs. Klein's 'deviation' from Freud consists, in fact, of the radical development of Freud's own greatest deviation from himself.* She has elaborated Freud's theory of the super-ego into a fully psychological view of mental development, while retaining Freud's own blindness to the fact that this constitutes a theory different in principle from the earlier instinct-theory.

2. *The New Emphasis on Aggression*

Freud himself had, after at first concentrating almost entirely on libidinal problems, begun to bring 'aggression' more and more to the front, and Mrs. Klein carried further that trend. Apart from the background of general theory, the developments arising out of Mrs. Klein's pioneer analysis of children by play-technique rest upon the use of such basic Freudian concepts as identification, introjection, projection (borrowed from psychiatry), psychic reality, phantasy, anxiety, and the super-ego as an internalized version of parent-figures. *These are, however, all purely psychodynamic concepts owing nothing at all to psychobiology and instinct-theory.* She goes beyond Freud in the tracing out of types of primitive phantasy, the development and types of infantile anxiety, the internal phantasied and felt situations in which anxiety rises, and the formation of a whole inner world of psychic (i.e. mental or imaginary) objects, good and bad, on the model of the super-ego. All this springs from the fact that just as Freud made an analytical investigation into the development of the libidinal aspects of psychic life, so Melanie Klein took over from him and carried on the task of making a truly psychodynamic analysis of the development of aggression, particularly in its anti-libidinal aspect. She shows how the arousal of aggression and its development as a persisting feature of the psychic life, through the agencies of projection and introjection and internal-object formation, creates chronic anxiety and determines the whole complex process of the evolution of the inner psychic world.

Thus, when Mrs. Klein and her associates hold on to instinct-theory with grim tenacity, they obscure the bearing of their own work. We repeatedly find that a searching analysis of some problem of aggression is given in terms of the developmental processes of infancy, and then, at the end, the whole phenomenon is suddenly referred to the death instinct. Often this appears to be an afterthought, for 'death instinct' turns up in brackets, thus: '. . . under the pressure of intense anxiety (ultimately deriving from the death instinct).' (1952, p. 35.) It forms a kind of biological mysticism, an epiphenomenon which adds nothing to the real substance of the work, a guarantee of Freudian orthodoxy that obscures the importance of new ways of thinking. Mrs. Klein and her associates still talk the language of 'instinct and impulse-psychology', while their really creative thought is in terms of 'object-relations psychology' and of Freud's analysis of ego-structure.

Joan Riviere, referring to new varieties of psycho-analysis, writes:

one feature is common to all these; they have all disputed or denied the basic source and origin of human psychology, as postulated by Freud, in the instincts with their bodily organs and aims. Freud's approach was biological from the start. . . . Melanie Klein's work retains this fundamental relation of psychology to the biological core of the human organism, its function as a vehicle of the instincts, which Freud recognized. (1952, p. 6.)

On the next page she contradicts this statement.

The most important instance of Freud's own indecisive attitude about his theories is that of his postulation of the life and death instincts . . . he was careful not to make it a first principle of psycho-analysis. (*Op. cit.*, p. 7.)

Yet two pages later she reverts to the first position again.

Freud put forward the duality of the life and death instincts as the fundamental antithesis in the unconscious . . . after which he constantly and repeatedly referred to it as the foundation of intra-psychic conflict. (*Op. cit.*, p. 9.)

In elaborating this view Riviere says:

The enormity, to our adult minds, of the destructiveness and cruelty . . . in babies ceases to be such an insoluble mystery when, as (Klein) shows, Freud's hypothesis of a destroying force in our minds, always in interaction with a life-preserving force, is allowed its due

significance. This concept of a destructive force within every individual, tending towards the annihilation of life, is naturally one
which arouses extreme emotional resistance. (*Op. cit.*, pp. 2–3.)

Emotional resistance is felt surely to the fact of deep repressed
aggression, and not to any particular theory of it. One cannot
argue, as Riviere does, that this resistance is the cause of the
neglect by psycho-analysts of Freud's theory of a death instinct.
The concept has been legitimately criticized on theoretical grounds
as we have seen in an earlier chapter, and it is possible to accept
Melanie Klein's disturbing analysis of infantile aggression and at
the same time to feel that the idea of a death instinct adds no
further illumination of the problem. Nor can the claim be accepted
that no theory is properly psycho-analytical unless based on
Freud's theory of instincts. Freud himself did not lay down any
such criterion. In his paper in 1914 *On the History of the Psycho-
Analytic Movement*, he wrote :

The doctrine of repression is the foundation stone on which the
whole structure of psycho-analysis rests . . . the theory of psycho-
analysis is an attempt to account for two observed facts that strike
one conspicuously and unexpectedly whenever an attempt is made
to trace the symptoms of a neurotic back to their sources in his past
life : the facts of transference and resistance. (*C.P.*, I, pp. 297–8.)

The criticism of all types of instinct-theory with respect to their
adequacy for psychological explanation is to-day far too radical
and widespread to admit of such a claim.

In point of fact, Mrs. Klein's success in achieving a thorough-
going and purely clinical analysis of the early development of
aggression as a function of bad-object relationships, makes it the
more plain that the speculative idea of a death instinct does not
represent anything that is actually clinically presented but something that, from the clinical point of view, is an *a priori* assumption.

Thus Joan Riviere remarks :

Many psychic manifestations show that a threat from the death
instinct produces a strong uprush of Eros, and we may fairly conclude that the aim of this process is to counteract the destructive
forces felt to be within. (1952, pp. 52–3.)

But such terms as 'death instinct' and 'Eros' are vague mysticisms
which have no exact scientific connotation, whereas we are on the
solid ground of observable clinical phenomena when it is said that
intense sexual impulses may arise as a craving for a protective

union with a good object in the outer world because the individual is suffering from imagined destructive attacks by bad objects (often visible in nightmares) in the inner world; or in a more general and comprehensive way when Melanie Klein says that sexual relationships can function 'as a disproof by means of reality of [the] fear of [one's] own sexuality and that of [one's] object as something destructive'. (1932, p. 305.)

The enormous aggression and cruelty developed in babies, as revealed in infantile phantasies of biting, tearing in pieces, etc., is adequately accounted for by Melanie Klein as a developmental phenomenon, and does not need the postulate of an innate, permanent aggressive drive working always towards destruction. It is sufficiently explained by the fact of the infant's defective or immature sense of reality, and its lack of developed ego-control to moderate the rapid increase of emotional tensions to dangerous extremes : a vicious circle of frustration, anger, fear and increased tension spirals upwards. The infant's inexperience of objective reality and his incapacity to recognize either his own exaggerated interpretation of his frustrations or the effects of aggression, leaves him unprotected against the blind interaction of the projection of his own rage on to his objects, and the introjection of his objects as he now sees them coloured by his aggression in addition to their own. He is then at the mercy of phantastically violent internal persecutors, and this means that his emotions cannot be kept at realistic and appropriate levels.

Melanie Klein's work, being in the first place an analysis of aggression as a post-natal development, has no specific bearing on the theory of a death instinct and neither proves nor disproves it. But it does provide us with a means of accounting for personality phenomena as clinically presented without need to have recourse to instinct-theory except in the quite restricted, purely biological sense of initial, innate potentiality prior to development. This fact is probably the basis for the feeling among orthodox analysts that the Klein system is a deviation from Freud. If it is, the deviation was unwittingly started by Freud himself. Melanie Klein's is a theory of personality development and structuring in a purely psychodynamic sense.

An oft-repeated criticism of Melanie Klein is that she reads back into the first two years what belongs to later stages of development, in particular with respect to genital sexual and to super-ego phenomena. This may be considered here in the form in which it is made by Bibring in an article entitled 'The So-called English School of Psycho-Analysis'. (1947, pp. 69–93.) He states that Mrs. Klein set herself to fill the gap left unexplored by Freud between

birth and the second or third year, the pre-Oedipal stage, including the vicissitudes of the neglected aggressive drives and the
development of the primitive ego. However, he narrows down his
critical examination of her view mainly to one issue, the problem
of the sources of sexual excitement in childhood. This was stated
by Freud in physiological terms, in the *Three Contributions to
Sexual Theory* and *The Economic Problem of Masochism.* Sexual
excitement arises as a secondary effect of other internal processes
when they reach a certain degree of intensity. Mrs. Klein, says
Bibring, sought a solution of this problem not on physiological but
on purely psychological grounds. Early anxiety situations starting with oral frustrations, intensify needs and arouse angers which
fuse into oral sadism. This becomes an internal obstacle to the
satisfaction of needs, which makes existing external frustration
worse, in a vicious circle. The infant feels his sadistic impulses
threaten him with extermination internally, as well as threaten
his object with destruction. The pressure of anxiety forces the ego
to mobilize defence mechanisms, i.e. to develop. Too early and
violent arousal of oral sadism constitutes *a premature excitation
of sexual tensions.*

Defences such as projection, introjection, the spreading of
damned-up tensions to urethral, anal, muscular, genital and other
bodily functions lead to the creation of an imaginary or hallucinated world of inner mental experience, according to Freud's
hypothesis that the infant hallucinates fulfilment when frustration
is prolonged. The particularly important view of Mrs. Klein,
according to Bibring, is that intense oral tensions can and do
prematurely arouse, and cause a precipitate unfolding and development of genital tensions in a way that leads to unconscious
knowledge of genital functions. The receptivity of the mouth to
the breast leads on to that of the vagina needing to receive a penis,
the teeth biting and penetrating the breast lead on to the penis
penetrating a hole in the body, via intermediate linking experiences including anal ones. (One of my own hysteric patients
said, 'I want a breast in my mouth and a penis in my vagina
all at the same time.') As a result of this, primal scene phantasies,
not only of oral and anal but of genital kinds, come into
being. Mrs. Klein's is a theory of genetic continuity of development without gaps or breaks, in an ever-elaborating phantasy
life which involves premature development of even genital experience, sensation and symbolism in the first year of life. She places
the origins of both the super-ego and the Oedipus complex in that
early period.

Bibring writes :

An entirely new developmental factor appears at this point, a vague 'knowledge' (in whatever form it may exist) about external facts such as the complementary sex organs, arrived at with the help of internal data like obscure reference sensations and impulses. Since this 'knowledge' is in a way a constituent part of the impulses and sensations in question, I propose to call it 'sensation or impulse' knowledge (p. 79).

He quotes Mrs. Klein thus:

Oral frustration arouses in the child an unconscious knowledge that its parents enjoy mutual sexual pleasures. (1932, p. 188.)

Thus in the first years the infant enters into the painful early Oedipal conflicts similar to those of a child of two to three years.

Bibring regards the Kleinian scheme as resting on two fundamental concepts: first, this theory of development (premature activation and precipitate development), and second, the theory of innate unconscious knowledge of sex. He criticizes the theory of development on the grounds that not enough account is taken of limitations set by biological maturation, and of causes to be looked for in further and continuing environmental experience; that too much is attributed to premature over-stimulation; that development is more than a defence mechanism, and the 'motors' of development are more than tensions and anxieties. Concerning this last objection it may be said that Mrs. Klein is referring to psychopathological development in the main rather than normal development, though she believes that *all* infants undergo this disturbed development to some degree.

Concerning Bibring's other criticisms, the relationship between endopsychic development and biological maturation is a matter for much further detailed research and Mrs. Klein's theories have forced this matter to the forefront. We may be content to regard her work at this point more as a challenge to further investigation than merely as a target for criticism. We have already made substantially the same criticism as Bibring of Mrs. Klein's tendency to minimize if not actually to ignore, the environmental factor in favour of a too-exclusively endopsychic view of development. Bibring writes: 'There is no substantiation for the conception of a development nearly exclusively from within' (p. 85), or for a 'development that is to a very large extent endopsychic and independent of any appropriate external stimulation' (p. 85). Yet it may well be that Mrs. Klein, under pressure of her pioneer exploration of the subjectively conditioned aspects of 'inner world' development, is guilty only of an error of over-emphasis on her own immediate approach. Her work has made it far easier to understand how it is that human beings, in proportion as they are more seriously mentally ill, do in fact live more and more subjectively, and interpret outer reality more and more in terms of their inner phantasy. Her work has led in fact to a deeper study of the way in which human beings live in two worlds at once, an outer and an inner world, and how the two are constantly confused even while they also have a separate and independent existence relative to each other.

We shall not here attempt a detailed examination of Bibring's criticism of Mrs. Klein's theory of innate and unconscious knowledge. It is another point at which her work is first and foremost a challenge to further exact research. Rather we would emphasize that whatever the final verdict may be on these detailed aspects of her total theory, her main contribution is not touched by criticism of these points. The science of biological evolution is the tracing of intermediate links and the overcoming of the older view that nature grew by jumps and gaps. We would expect continuity of development from birth to the genital Oedipal period to be true in principle, however much difference of opinion is legitimate about details, pending further research. Mrs. Klein found that in patients as young as the second half of the third year elaborate systems of phantasy of a sexual nature, concerning the relations of the mother and father to each other and to the child, were already in existence and full activity, and determining serious anxiety and guilt. Symptoms of this state of affairs, such as *pavor nocturnus*, were recognizable at a still earlier age, showing that all this could not spring up fully developed and suddenly into the mind of the child of two years and six months onwards. Such phenomena were bound to be already an end-product of processes in the second and first year, as was evident from their anal and oral components. Mrs. Klein sought to trace out this early history and arrived at the conception of a period of maximum sadism at weaning time, the development of persecutory and depressive positions, and the formation of internal objects (the super-ego) arousing persecutory anxiety and guilt, all in the first year of life. Her theory of the super-ego makes it a blanket-term covering all internal objects, good and bad, so that her theory of the internal objects world is a development of Freud's theory of the super-ego. In play, the child from the third year gives unmistakable representations of these internal objects and of their relations with one another and with himself, so that his play is an acting out of his phantasy life. In tracing the evolution of this state of affairs from the first through the second year, is Mrs. Klein reading back the phenomena of the third into the first year, or is she following the carrying forward of oral patterns into later phases in ways that determine the later unfolding?

That is the question concerning her theory of development, the only part of her theory that Bibring examines. Suppose he is right that her views imply a biologically impossible precipitation of development too far in advance of biological maturation, and that she reads back too much too early. We are still left with the fact that by the second half of the third year the child's emotional make-up finds expression in a most complicated sexual phantasy life which he plays out in the form of conflicts between himself and his bad objects against whom he seeks the help of good objects. These situations also duplicate the relationships which he phantasies as existing between his objects themselves. These objects, good and bad, already bear little actual relationship to his real parents, and are phantasied internal figures created somehow in the first two years, and now forming the structural basis of his personality. Bibring does not deal with the real psychodynamic contribution of Mrs. Klein, her 'internal objects' structural theory arising out of her far more detailed analysis of the 'super-ego'. If her views of the detailed course of development in the first two years are open to criticism, still her theory of endopsychic structure in terms of internal objects opened the way to a new approach to psychodynamic theory in general, making it a true theory of personality. In Mrs. Klein's work the phantasy life of the third year is (1) a clue to the child's previous emotional history, and (2) a clue to the present and subsequent structural organization of his personality. The first is her theory of early development, the premature activation of genital experiences in the oral stage, leaving little place for regression from genital to oral in Freud's sense, and envisaging an 'oral-genital' phase *in* the oral phase itself leading on later through anal to true genital phenomena. Bibring says: 'Mrs. Klein has retrojected into the earlier stages of development much that belongs to later stages. However, many suggestions made by Klein and others with regard to early experiences will probably be of great value' (p. 92). In the opinion of the present writer that is already proving to be an understatement, considering the far-reaching issues raised by the second part of her theory concerning internal objects and endopsychic structure.

Chapter XI

THE PSYCHODYNAMIC THEORY OF
MELANIE KLEIN

WE have traced the gradual emergence in Mrs. Klein's work of a central emphasis on aggression, especially on that fusion of sexuality and aggression known as sadism. This she found to be entrenched in the Freudian super-ego and operating in the Oedipal situation, the origins of both of which she traced back into the first year of life. We saw how this was referred even farther back into the hereditary constitution, in terms of Freud's innate conflict between Life and Death, or libidinal and destructive, instincts. J. O. Wisdom remarks that

(It appears to be a non-object-relation theory for her as for Freud.) There is just as much difficulty in seeing what clinical bearing or explanatory power it has with her approach as with Freud's; just the same difficulty in understanding why it is regarded as needed at all; and just the same difficulty in admitting it to the status of a scientific theory. (1956, p. 108.)

Wisdom further remarks that 'hers is throughout an object-relations theory' (*op. cit.*, pp. 108–9), thus stressing its incompatibility with instinct-theory. We agree with Wisdom that her work is 'definitely incompatible with Freud's theories of primary narcissism and libido and ... require[s] revision of ego-theory.' (*Op. cit.*, p. 109.) The view we have taken is that her work is a development from and beyond Freud's ego-analysis and his structural theory. This we must now study in more detail.

Clinically her orientation is dominated by emphasis on anxiety, theoretically by the development of her structural concept of the internal object. The central position she accorded to aggression links these two, for she regards it as the main cause of the infant's anxiety on the one hand and the dynamic drive leading to structural differentiation in terms of internal objects on the other. Joan Riviere writes:

Anxiety, with the defences against it, has from the beginning been Melanie Klein's approach to psycho-analytical problems. It was from this angle that she discovered the existence and importance of the aggressive elements in children's emotional life, which led her to her present formulations about persecutory and depressive anxieties and the defences used by the early ego against them. (1952, pp. 8–9.)

The title of chapter 10 of *The Psycho-Analysis of Children*, namely 'The Significance of Early Anxiety-Situations in the Development of the Ego', is itself a kind of summary of her theory. This is one of psychic development in the early and most formative years as dominated by *anxieties of two kinds, persecutory and depressive*. These are caused by aggression which, in the course of development, builds up an internal psychic world full of bad objects which menace and endanger both the ego and its necessary good objects inside and out. It is in this development that aggression itself elaborates and becomes a permanently active factor in the psyche. It can only be understood, therefore, not as an innate but as a developmental phenomenon, arising out of bad-object relationships inside as well as outside the psyche.

Thus Klein carries object-relationships right back through the Freudian so-called narcissistic and autoerotic phases to the beginning of the infant's separate bodily life. It is the importance, not of instinct but of the earliest experiences in object-relationship, not of innate factors but of developmental experiences in the first two years, which her work emphasizes. Her detailed factual analysis of this situation led both to the 'internal objects' theory and the differentiation of persecutory and depressive anxieties. The structural theory clarifies the 'early anxiety-situations' out of which these two types of anxiety arise.

Summarizing Mrs. Klein's theory thus far, Wisdom writes:

Freud and Ferenczi had introduced introjection into analysis, where it played an important though minor role. Mrs. Klein gives it a dominating position : she holds that all sorts of objects are introjected, i.e. that there are 'internal objects' resulting from the introjection or phantasied incorporation of either of the two parents or parts of them. A part of a person (such as a breast) is called a 'part-object'. These introjected (or internal) objects, whether whole or part, are felt to be either good or bad because the child projects his own feelings into them. This is the main structural hypothesis. Disturbances are held to be due to one or other (or both) of two things (a) loss or destruction by the self of internal good objects, and (b) persecution of the self by internal bad objects. These disturbances are experienced respectively as depressive-anxiety and persecutory-anxiety. Thus they result from attacks by or on the self. Aggression therefore plays at least as important a part as sexuality; it is given a central position which it hardly occupies in Freud's theory. (*Op. cit.*, p. 105.)

The change of emphasis to aggression is, however, greater than is suggested by the comment 'at least as important a part as sexuality'; for whereas in Freud's original theory sexuality was itself the source of pathological developments, now aggression has definitely taken over that role. *Persecutory anxiety* arises if one is under direct attack oneself, if aggression goes against the ego. It is fear for one's own safety. Kleinians, parting company here with Freud, believe that the internal dangers to which the ego can feel exposed in the unconscious may be so great as to develop into a fear of death, a terror of extinction and annihilation. Such persecutory anxieties can be easily observed in fear dreams in later life, where the dreamer is being attacked by wild animals, burglars, concentration camp torturers, sinister evil figures, or bombs and impersonal agencies of destruction. This persecutory anxiety is apt to dominate the first three months of life.

Depressive anxiety is a fear, not for oneself but for one's love-objects. It develops later than persecutory anxiety, which belongs to the earliest stage in which good and bad part-objects (breasts) are not recognized as belonging together. When the mother begins presently to be experienced as a whole person and the good and bad parts, aspects or phases of her dealing with the infant are brought together, an ambivalent relationship to the mother arises to replace the earlier 'splitting' of the object into unrelated good and bad objects. In the earlier position the infant could feel desire towards the good object and terror towards the persecuting bad one, without these two reactions influencing each other. Now that love and hate can be felt towards one and the same changeable object, the anxiety arises that in hating one's object as bad one may destroy it as good. Depressive anxiety is, therefore, a pathological version of grief and mourning, and is particularly likely to be aroused in later life by the loss of emotionally important persons by parting or death. It is essentially a separation-anxiety accompanied by severe guilt. But depressive anxiety also involves direct danger to oneself, since, through identification with the love-object who is the victim of one's hate and aggression, one becomes involved in the fate of that object. This serves as a punishment for aggression by turning it against oneself internally. Thus depressive anxiety can take up persecutory anxiety into itself, or, from a different point of view, persecutory and depressive anxiety develop into persecutory and depressive guilt.

Thus Mrs. Klein envisaged the early infantile anxiety-situations as comprising a whole series of events of the nature of active object-relationships repeatedly enacted and re-enacted in the phantasy and feeling life of the small child, both conscious and unconscious; and as continuously lived through in a way that came to be more and more unrelated to the child's external world. His psychic life grows into a second and wholly internal world, the patterns of which come to be blindly imposed on external persons and situations. The neurotic process consists of this interior life, while the therapeutic process consists of drawing the individual out of it and back into realistic contact with the outer world. We are thus introduced to a group of highly important concepts: the internal object, the inner world, phantasy and psychic reality.

1. *Psychic Reality*

We will begin the consideration of these concepts with that one which is most indisputably of Freud's own creation. *Psychic Reality* is one of his own most important ideas. The mind or psyche has a reality of its own, separate and distinct from the reality of the outer material world. It has its own permanencies, its own energies, and its own enduring and not easily alterable organization. The psyche has, one might almost say, a kind of solid substantiality of its own which we cannot alter at will, and which we have to begin by accepting and respecting. Thus, we cannot ourselves, by wishful thinking, become anything we would like to be, we cannot by an effort of will make ourselves *feel* differently from the ways in which we discover that we do feel. We do not choose what we shall feel, we simply discover that we are feeling that way, even if we have some choice in what we do about its expression. Our feelings are instantaneous, spontaneous and at first unconscious reactions which reveal the psychic reality of our make-up. At any given moment we are what we are, and we can become different only by slow processes of growth. All this is equally true of other people who cannot, just because we wish it, suddenly become different from what they are. Psychic reality, the inner constitution and organization of each individual mind, is highly resistant to change, and goes its own way much less influenced by the outer world than we like to think.

Our conscious mental operations do not convey the full force of this stubborn durability of psychic reality, since it is relatively easy to change our ideas, to alter our decisions, to vary our pursuits and interests, and so on; but we can do all that without becoming very different basically as persons. Our mental life appears to be a freely adaptable instrument of our practical purposes in the outer material world, as no doubt it should be. The closer, however, we get to matters involving the hidden pressures of emotions, the more do we recognize the apparent intractability of psychic reality. The infatuated man cannot subdue his infatuation, the person who worries cannot stop worrying, the hyper-conscientious person who works to death cannot relax, the man with an irrational hate cannot conquer his dislike, the sufferer from bad dreams cannot decide not to have them. This is conspicuously the case with neurotic persons, who manifest a marked helplessness towards their own psychic reality and emotional life. This Freudian concept of psychic reality becomes a much more striking and arresting one as a result of the work of Mrs. Klein.

2. *Internal Objects and Psychic Structure*

The theory of *psychic structure* evolved from Melanie Klein's clinical findings was to the effect that it consisted of phantasied or imaginary ego-object relationships which had become persistent, almost permanent, organizational features of the deeper psychic life. These *'internal object-relations'* were only 'imaginary' from the point of view of external reality; they possessed 'psychic reality' to a very high degree, as becomes apparent when we try to change them. Mrs. Klein's descriptions of the *'internal object'* gather force and clarity throughout her early papers and *The Psycho-Analysis of Children*. The distinction between the child's real external objects and its internal and phantasied versions of them forced itself on Mrs. Klein's notice. In 1926 she wrote concerning the patient Rita, who could not play with dolls with any pleasure at two and a half years and felt prohibited from being the doll's mother, that

the prohibition . . . no longer emanated from the *real* mother, but from an introjected mother, whose role she enacted for me in many ways and who exercised a harsher and more cruel influence upon her than her real mother had ever done. (1948, p. 144.)

This difference between the external and the internal object, the outer real object and the inner, subjective image of it, was emphasized again in 1927 in 'The Symposium on Child-Analysis' when Mrs. Klein wrote :

The analysis of very young children has shown me that even a three-year-old child has left behind him the most important part of the development of his Oedipus complex. Consequently, he is already far removed, through repression and feelings of guilt, from the objects whom he originally desired. His relations to them have undergone distortion and transformation so that the present love-objects are now *imagos* of the original objects. (1948, p. 165.)

This introjection of parents, which Mrs. Klein regards as a kind of mental incorporation as a parallel to physical, oral incorporation, with subsequent internal elaboration of the parent images into 'imagos' differing widely from the real parents, takes place under the stress of aggression. This, Mrs. Klein thinks, is even as early as the oral stage largely the infant's reaction to the primal scene, the sexual union of parents from which the infant is excluded and about which it invariably feels the most intense excitement and rage. This Oedipal development proceeds through the oral and anal phases to the genital phase so that the phantasied attacks on parents employ both oral and anal means. Mrs. Klein originally held that the Oedipus complex begins under the influence of the phase of maximum sadism at about three to five months; but she later came to feel that the depressive phase was the crucial one. In 1948 she wrote concerning the early stages of the Oedipus complex:

I still believe that these begin roughly in the middle of the first year. But since I no longer hold that at this period sadism is at its height, I place a different emphasis on the beginning of the emotional and sexual relation to both parents. Therefore, while I suggested . . . that the Oedipus complex starts under the influence of sadism and hatred, I would now say that the infant turns to the second object, the father, with feelings both of love and of hatred. I see in the depressive feelings derived from the fear of losing the loved mother—as an external and internal object—an important impetus towards early Oedipus desires. This means that I now correlate the early stages of the Oedipus complex with the depressive position. (1932, Preface to Third Ed., p. 13.)

The following quotation shows how the internalization of objects and the formation of imagos under the influence of aggression leads to the development of an elaborate inner world embodying the infant's early anxiety-situations.

The early infantile situation . . . of fundamental importance [is] . . . the attack on the mother's body and on the father's penis in it. . . . Now what weapons does the child employ in this attack on his united parents? . . . the weapon which very little children have at their disposal: namely the device of soiling with excrement. [There are] other weapons of the child's primary sadism, which employs his teeth, nails, muscles and so on. . . . When the objects are introjected, the attack launched upon them with all the weapons of sadism rouses the subject's dread of an analogous attack upon himself from the external and the internalized objects. . . . Freud's hypothesis is that there is an infantile danger-situation which undergoes modification in the course of development, and which is the source of the influence exercised by a series of *anxiety-situations*. Now the new demand upon the analyst is this—that analysis should fully uncover these anxiety-situations right back to that which lies deepest of all . . . he says that a complete analysis must reveal the primal scene. This latter requirement can have its full effect only in conjunction with that which I have just put forward. (1929, *Infantile Anxiety-situations Reflected in a Work of Art*; 1948, pp. 228–30.)

Thus we see how a neurosis is conceived as a repressed inner world of internal object-relationships constituting anxiety- or danger-situations of both a persecutory and depressive order, in which the ego launches phantasied attacks by oral, anal and ultimately genital means on its parent-imagos, and fears retaliatory attacks in turn from them.

The interaction between this internal world of psychic reality and the external world of material reality is of the highest importance. Mrs. Klein writes:

As far as can be seen, there exists in the small child, side by side with its relations to real objects but on a different plane as it were, relations which are based on its relations to its unreal imagos both as excessively good and excessively bad figures. Ordinarily, these two kinds of object-relations intermingle and colour each other to an ever increasing extent. (1932, p. 213.)

[The child] attaches to its imaginary objects not only feelings of hatred and anxiety but positive feelings as well. In doing this it withdraws them from its real objects, and if its relations to its imaginary objects are too powerful, both in a negative and a positive sense, it cannot adequately attach either its sadistic phantasies or its restitutive ones to its real objects, with the result that it undergoes disturbance of its adaptation to reality and of its object-relationships. (1932, p. 192, note.)

The full significance of the child's development along these lines is seen in one further passage of Mrs. Klein.

In those cases in which the significance of reality and real objects as reflections of the dreaded internal world and imagos has retained its preponderance, the stimuli from the external world may be felt to be nearly as alarming as the phantasied domination of the internalized objects, which have taken possession of all initiative and to whom the ego feels compulsively bound to surrender the execution of all activities and intellectual operations. (1948, p. 263.)

Thus Mrs. Klein outlines the development of the infantile mind in the first few years as the creation of a phantastic and intensely emotional internal world of bad, aggressive, destructive ego-object relations, counteracted by an equally phantastic inner world of ideally good-object relations, both more and more removed from realistic relationship with outer reality, yet increasingly influencing the child's and finally the adult's perception of outer reality, and hence behaviour towards it. This is the essence of neurosis, and also the content of psychic structure. Her work leads to a theory of living in two worlds at the same time, an inner mental world which forms the structure of the psychic personality and is revealed functionally in phantasy of all types, and an outer material world : there are ego-object relationships in both these worlds and also interaction between them.

Neurosis is seen to be not merely a phenomenon of disturbed emotions. If it were, it could be relieved simply by abreaction as was at first hoped. It is a phenomenon of pathological personality-structuring. The neurosis is the way the personality has grown, organizationally, and this is what we see made conscious in phantasy. Only in this light can we understand why neurosis is so hard to cure. Absolute cure would involve radical re-growing of the total personality structure, if such a thing be possible.

3. *Phantasy*

Psychic Reality, and its structuring in terms of internal objects and internal object-relations, is made manifest in Phantasy, of which day and night dreams and the play of children are the most clinically relevant examples. With these, however, we must link other forms of phantasy, the myths and legends of primitive peoples, folk-lore, and the imaginative creations of literature and art in all ages which together constitute a continuous revelation of the phantasy-life of the human race, and throw tremendous light on the workings of the Unconscious. All these taken together display an inventive, creative, imaginative activity of the human mind which is not, like science, concerned with the accurate portrayal of the outer material world by intellectual activity, but rather with an expression, every bit as accurate, of the inner mental world, the world of emotional events which forms the inner hard core of personality-functioning. The prosaic mind may dismiss all that as 'mere imagination' or as 'fantasy' or even as

'fantastic nonsense' and—to come back to our starting-point—
dreams. The practical mind is apt to contrast 'hard facts' like
money and guns with the 'useless' products of the imagination,
'such stuff as dreams are made of'. The dreamy person with his
head in the clouds is despised. It is true the dreamer is orientated
inwards rather than outwards and may become disorientated in
outer reality, at a loss and useless in practical affairs. But the so-
called hard-headed, practical man is usually just as helpless in face
of emotional realities. His evaluation of the products of emotion
involves a two-fold error. He believes that he is free from phantasies and dreams, whereas he is only unconscious of what goes on
in his inner world and is phantasy-ridden without knowing it.
This is usually discernible at least in such forms as confident
prejudice and narcissistic self-evaluation. Further, he believes
dreams and phantasies can be contrasted with hard facts as unreal,
and dismissed as of no importance. But these same products of
imagination are themselves 'hard facts' in a psychological sense, of
a peculiarly inescapable kind, having 'psychic reality'.

In this scientific age men continue as much as ever to produce
their phantasies, often, it is true, disguised as political ideologies
and even as scientific theories, but also as religious, artistic and
literary symbolism, and tale-telling—that immemorial, perennial
interest of human beings. Men continue to dream and day-dream,
and those who find day-dreaming has a strong hold on them are
not seldom frightened by their inability to stop it. In fact, this
world of the imagination, which we cannot either eliminate or
suppress, is the eruption of precisely that 'psychic reality' which
Freud and Melanie Klein have so stressed, a psychological 'hard
fact' which we are obliged to take into account. When it develops,
as sometimes happens, to the full force of the disintegrating and
even homicidal delusions of the insane we can no longer under-
estimate its power.

Psycho-analysis has, especially in the work of Melanie Klein,
singled out the phantasy life in such a way as to recognize its
special status. As Susan Isaacs put it :

The psycho-analytical term 'phantasy' [spelt with a 'ph' and used
as a technical term : present writer's note] essentially connotes *unconscious* mental content. . . . Psycho-analysis has shown that the quality
of being 'merely' or 'only' imagined is not the most important
criterion for the understanding of the human mind. When and under
what conditions 'psychical reality' is in harmony with external
reality is one special part of the total problem of understanding
mental life as a whole. . . . Freud's discovery of *dynamic psychical*

reality initiated a new epoch of psychological understanding. He showed that the inner world of the mind has a continuous living reality of its own, with its own dynamic laws and characteristics, different from those of the external world. In order to understand the dream and the dreamer, his psychological history, his neurotic symptoms or his normal interest and character, we have to give up that prejudice in favour of external reality, and of our conscious orientations to it, that undervaluation of internal reality, which is the attitude of the ego in ordinary civilized life to-day. . . . A further point of importance . . . is that unconscious phantasy is fully active in the normal, no less than in the neurotic mind. . . . The difference between normal and abnormal lies in the way in which the unconscious phantasies are dealt with, the particular mental processes by which they are worked over and modified; and the degree of direct or indirect gratification in the real world and adaptation to it, which these favoured mechanisms allow. (1952, pp. 81–2.)

To sum up in Isaacs' words : 'Phantasies are the primary content of unconscious mental processes.' (*Op. cit.*, p. 82.) The term '*unconscious* phantasy' may be thought to raise problems. It is certainly true that feeling can be active but unconscious, as, for example, when it is discharged in the form of a physical symptom. Patients frequently say : 'I didn't know I felt so angry when I came in.' But can phantasy be unconscious? The complex emotional state which would find expression, if it is expressed, in consciousness in a specific phantasy can be unconscious, but it would seem that phantasy is the form in which we express unconscious emotion when it becomes conscious. Phantasy is a psychic structure in action in consciousness, a conscious expression of the fact that our deep-down complex emotional and impulsive activity at the moment is the same as it would be if in outer reality we were having a relationship of a certain kind with a person of a certain kind, as imagined in the phantasy. This can be expressed only by a 'story' either 'seen' in the mind's eye, i.e. hallucinated, as in a dream, or consciously thought through as in day-dreaming. It is always a story of some form of ego-object relations in which the 'object' is imagined, and is in fact an 'internal object' in the sense already made clear. It seems preferable to say, then, that the primary content of the unconscious mental processes is an emotionally active psychic structure, and that phantasy is its emergence into consciousness.

4. *The Inner World*

If we consider a novel, say *Wuthering Heights*, an elaborate phantasy which has been given literary form and an existence independent of its creator, we see at once that a phantasy is a world inhabited by persons and its action consists in their relationships to one another. Such places as Wuthering Heights and such persons as Heathcliffe and Cathy and the other characters of the story have a tremendous vitality of their own, and make a powerful and living impact on us. If, now, we consider a phantasy in an unsophisticated form, in its immediate mental form as we see it in a disturbing dream that wakes us up while its action is still in progress in our minds, we recognize these same characteristics. The dream as we perceive and experience it *is*, so to speak, a place, and it *is* a number of people or animals or other figures in active relationships. So real is all this that the half-awake dreamer starts up and looks about the room expecting to see the sinister figure who frightened him in his dream. The dream, at the moment of dreaming, has hallucinatory vividness and reality, though its reality lies in the fact that we are experiencing it as our own personality make-up in action, and not in its having outer material reality.

Freud considered, and psycho-analysts of all types agree, that *hallucination* is the earliest infantile form of mental experience and activity in response to delay in the satisfaction of needs, so that the world of the dream, unlike our conscious intellectual processes, goes back to the very beginnings of the dreamer's individual life. This dream-world apparently has access to the stored memories and information of a lifetime, and things beyond conscious recall can reappear in dreams, and emotional states and experiences of earliest infancy beyond conscious revival in the ordinary way can be re-lived in dreams. The inner world of 'unconscious' phantasy into which dreams give us a peep, is the world of the past, just as our conscious and waking mental life of perception and reasoning is the world of the present.

But this unconscious psychically real and powerful inner world is the past as we emotionally experienced it perpetuated as an ever-active and persistent internal present. Past aspects of our 'self' and our past objects of impulse and feeling live on inside us as a repressed unconscious present. To express it differently, the object-relationship situations of past years back to infancy, in which we were bound together with the important persons who were the chief objects of our needs and desires, loves and angers, have entered into our mental make-up, albeit elaborated and distorted by our own emotions as to the mental images we formed of them. They are preserved within us as dynamic parts of the hidden structure of our personality. They are endowed with psychic reality and in that sense continue to exist long after the original real figures have materially ceased to be, as in vivid dreams of long dead parents.

We live in these two worlds at the same time, one mental and the other material, the one a perpetuation of the past and the other an exploration of the present, and we are involved in both of them in situations and relationships which rouse in us excitements, emotions and impulses of all kinds. It is impossible to keep the two worlds of outer and inner reality, of conscious and unconscious mental life, entirely separate. They interact and overlap in everything we do. If, however, the overlapping of outer by inner reality is too crude and uncontrolled, our perceptions of the outer world become badly distorted; and therefore our reactions to it become falsified in disturbing and even dangerous ways. This happens in neurosis and still more in psychosis. Events in the outer world play upon, stir up and draw upon themselves projections of the phantasied events and situations that form parts and aspects of our inner world—often to our own and other people's exceeding discomfiture. Melanie Klein writes:

The young child's perception of external reality and external objects is perpetually influenced and coloured by his phantasies, and this in some measure continues throughout life. External experiences which arouse anxiety at once activate even in normal persons anxiety derived from intrapsychic sources. The interaction between objective anxiety and neurotic anxiety—or, to express it in other words, the interaction between anxiety arising from external and from internal sources—corresponds to the interaction between external and psychic reality. (1952, pp. 289–90.)

The figures with whom we have relationships in our phantasies are called appropriately, by Melanie Klein, 'internal objects' because we behave with respect to them, emotionally and impulsively, in the same ways as we do towards externally real persons, though in more violent degrees of intensity than would be socially permissible. The formation of this inner world of internal objects and situations proceeds from the very beginnings of life. Its basic figures or 'inhabitants' date from so early a time as before the baby could grasp in perception the wholeness of its parents as persons. We must presume that at first all the baby knows or experiences is a breast (a 'part-object') and that it takes time and development for the baby to become aware of the mother in her completeness (a 'whole-object').

Accordingly we find the dream and hallucinatory experiences of adult patients 'peopled' not only with completely personal figures, but also with 'part-objects' in the form of detached breasts, penises or bodily parts, or their symbolic representations in the form of animals or inanimate objects. Thus one patient, as she was dropping off to sleep, would start wide awake as a result of the frightening experience of seeing an unattached penis coming at her. During her analysis she learned to drive a motor-car and then for a time she would see, instead of a penis, a motor-car rushing at her as she dozed off. That it represented the penis, however, was clear from the fact that in the act of starting awake she would find that she was clutching her vagina to protect herself. Several times in dreams the penis was represented by a snake or a rat on the bed, while one male patient saw himself in a dream attacked by a penis on which the glans had a rat's mouth and eyes. Here we see a series of graduated representations from the penis, through the penis-rat, the rat and snake, to the inanimate motor-car. A further series is indicated by the dream of yet another patient, who saw a breast with a penis instead of a nipple and on another occasion dreamed of a breast with a snake for a nipple. The resolution of a penis into a breast pure and simple as the part-object corresponding to the infant's earliest experience always occurs ultimately in any analysis that goes at all deep. It should be added that the so-called 'part-object' is not a part-object to the infant but a whole-object. It is only from the adult observer's point of view that we recognize that the infant's first object is only a part of the whole mother.

As the infant's experience expands to the taking in of the whole of his mother, he does not necessarily lose his earlier partial mental representations of her. They lie under increasing repression, and in the unconscious at a later stage part-objects and whole-objects both exist in a psychically active way. Moreover, the whole-objects become more and more complex. Phantasied persons in the inner world, representing at bottom aspects of parents, become complicated by the addition of aspects of other early and later experienced significant persons. These internal 'parental' figures are not, of course, exact and truthful copies of the real parents. They represent dissociated aspects of parents and others seen through the medium of the baby's emotional experience of them. They are doubly falsified in that they are both partial, and also distorted by the baby's own feelings. An internal image of an angry parent has no redeeming features as the real parent had, and also it is built up in the baby's mind by his own emotional tensions into a monster or devil. One patient, in a nightmare, saw his mother's face, at first in its ordinary aspect, and then gradually growing redder, angrier, larger, more and more threatening, till it seemed to fill his world and overwhelm him in a volcanic eruption of accusing rage out of which shot the words: 'What have you done?' He woke with violent palpitation and profuse perspiration. In fact his mother was a much-enduring woman who worked hard to help him get an education while her husband was in a mental hospital. Yet the dream represented an intensification of one aspect of his actual experience of her.

This inner world is for the most part a world of terrors. Its objects are built up, according to Melanie Klein, by projection and introjection. The baby, faced with an angry or unloving mother and a frustrating breast, projects his own anger on to the mother, and then introjects her, takes her in mentally, endowed with his own aggression as well as hers. Another way of putting this is to say that our expectations of other people's behaviour to us is greatly influenced by our fear that they will retaliate for the aggression we feel against them: and it is in this light that the infant internalizes parents. The unconscious inner world is peopled, at deep mental levels, by frightful persecutors who are exaggerated out of all realistic proportions into monsters, devils, sinister figures and wild beasts of the most violent kind, such as terrify us in nightmares and have been enshrined in myth and folk-lore from earliest times. All personal and sexual relationships in this deep unconscious inner world are of a sado-masochistic character. Even when our emotional reactions are evoked by events in our outer present-day world, the tone and intensity of the emotion is, to a far greater extent than is generally known, determined by our reactions to these 'bad' figures in the unconscious. This is why very emotional people so often behave unrealistically.

We are now in a position to see where the endopsychic persecutory and depressive anxieties come from. Violent attack and counter-attack, suffering and turning the tables, goes on between the infantile ego and its internal bad objects. When the ego feels itself to be attacked in its phantasies, it feels persecutory anxiety. When it succeeds in a phantasied turning of the tables, then it rapidly begins to appear that the objects destroyed are much-needed parents and love-objects, and depressive anxiety supervenes. In actual details, in the imaginative phantasying of these violent scenes, all the biological possibilities open to the infant are made use of. Phantasies of tearing in pieces, sucking out, biting, eating, swallowing and devouring belong to the earliest oral level. A little later phantasies of destroying by urination and defecation occur, and later still sadistic versions of genital sexual destructiveness develop. These phantasies express what Melanie Klein calls the 'early anxiety-situations' of the infant. Thus one patient, a young married woman who had been exceptionally severely neglected by her mother as a child, became afraid of a sudden impulse to strangle me, remembered she had always felt hungry as a child, and reported a dream in which a slimy black lizard came at her to eat her. She then went back to an incident of very early life which she had previously reported, namely an occasion when she had defecated in her cot and jumped out of it and run downstairs. She now added further details, that she had looked at the black bits of excreta in the bed and suddenly felt they were alive and would eat her, and she climbed out of the cot in fear. Clearly the excreta represented to her bad internal objects that would retaliate on her, the terrifying internalized breast that would eat her because she wanted hungrily to eat it. This patient, who had never heard of Melanie Klein or of oral sadism, herself remarked : 'I wanted to eat everything as a child. I expect I wanted to eat my mother.'

An important aspect of Mrs. Klein's views is that not only is anxiety always at bottom due to unconscious phantasied aggressive and destructive relationships, but also that anxiety and guilt over internal and external aggression is counteracted by reparative phantasies and activities. Injured love-objects must be restored and made whole again if the personality is to be at peace. This simplified version of Melanie Klein's teaching aims simply at bringing out its salient features. An *internal object* is an *imago*, a mental image of a particularly fundamental kind, which defined psycho-analytically is an unconscious psychic image of a person or part of a person as if the object had been taken into the mind, developed within the inner mental world, repressed and elaborated from infancy onwards, and heavily loaded with emotion. As Susan Isaacs says :

Such images draw their power to affect the mind by being 'in it', i.e. their influence upon feelings, behaviour, character and personality, upon the mind as a whole, *from their repressed unconscious somatic associates* in the unconscious world of desire and emotions ... and which do mean, in unconscious phantasy, that the objects to which they refer are believed to be inside the body, to be incorporated. (1952, pp. 105–6.)

Commenting upon Melanie Klein's work, Fairbairn writes :

On the basis of the resulting concept of internal objects there has been developed the concept of *a world of inner reality* involving situations and relationships in which the ego participates together with its internal objects. These situations and relationships are comparable with those in which the personality as a whole participates in a world of outer reality, but the form which they assume remains that conferred upon them by the child's experience of situations and relationships in the earliest years of life. It should be added that the world of inner reality is conceived as essentially unconscious; but this does not preclude its manifesting itself in consciousness in the form of dreams and phantasies. Morbid anxiety, irrational fears and psychopathological symptoms of every kind are also conceived as having their source in the unconscious world of inner reality. Indeed, it follows that human behaviour in general must be profoundly influenced by situations prevailing in the inner world. The fact is that, once the conception of inner reality has been accepted, every individual must be regarded as living in two worlds at the same time—the world of outer reality and the world of inner reality; and, whilst life in outer reality is characteristically conscious, and life in inner reality is characteristically unconscious, it will be realized that *Freud's original distinction between the conscious and the unconscious now becomes less important than the distinction between the two worlds of outer reality and inner reality.* (1952, p. 124.)

The only disputable aspect of Mrs. Klein's clinically based account of the Inner World is that it owes more to the projection and re-introjection of innate sadism than to external bad handling of the infant.

5. *The Super-Ego and the Internal Object World*

We have seen how the development of ego-analysis steadily brought to light the complexity of the super-ego. Freud introduced the concept at first as a development from that of an ego-ideal, and spoke of the super-ego as a differentiating grade within the ego. Gradually the super-ego, standing as it were over the ego with often terrifying authority, came to take on the aspect of an internal object, the representative of the parents within the psyche. Freud recognized both paternal and maternal components in the super-ego. Its complexity was further apparent in the difference between its early sadistic forms and its later ego-ideal character, a complexity that could not be properly conceptualized in terms of Freud's id-ego-super-ego scheme.

The work of Melanie Klein from the start bore directly on super-ego analysis.

She carried back the Oedipus complex, and with it the early stages of super-ego formation to the period from six months on into the second year, whereas for Freud the super-ego was 'the heir to the Oedipus complex' and came into being only after the Oedipus conflict had been overcome at about the fifth year. It became apparent that her early super-ego was identical with the extremely sadistic super-ego and could hardly be called an 'ego-ideal' in any sense of the term that implied genuine moral values. It was a phenomenon of fear, aggression and hate in which the infantile ego suffered acute persecutory anxiety in relation to its internalized bad objects. The super-ego had now become, as a result of Mrs. Klein's work, a blanket-term covering the complexity of the whole endopsychic world of internalized objects, for the world of inner reality as Mrs. Klein presents it is a scene in which the ego seeks the aid of good objects in its struggle with its persecuting bad figures. We must now regard the super-ego as standing for the whole complex process whereby the pristine ego undergoes the beginnings of structural differentiation under pressure of the external environment. The resulting psychic development has two aspects which Freudian and even Kleinian terminology do not yet enable us to conceptualize clearly. An 'internal environment' is created in which the ego feels to be living under the shadow of powerful parental figures who are cruel persecutors at the deepest mental levels but steadily take on the aspect of ruthless punishers and guilt-inducers in later stages of development. But at the same time this complex structural differentiation includes a function of self-persecution and self-punishment in which the ego identifies with its internal enemies. One may say that the bad objects who arouse our rage in outer reality then become necessary to us to enforce control on our impulses; we can then forestall their punishment-cum-persecution by taking over their repressive functions ourselves. This entire process is duplicated in inner reality. If, for the moment, we exclude this function of self-judgment which is properly called 'conscience', whether primitive or matured, we may then say that the super-ego covers the whole world of internal objects, good and bad.

It is thus clear that for Mrs. Klein the super-ego covers a confusing multiplicity of good and bad internal objects, persecutors and pseudo-, semi- and fully-moral figures, some inducing terror and some inducing guilt (i.e. fear of death or of castration on the one hand, and fear of punishment and disapproval on the other). Her work is thus a challenge to still closer analysis. This complexity is plainly set forth by her.

I believe that . . . early phobias contain anxiety arising in the early stages of the formation of the super-ego. The earliest anxiety-situations of the child appear round about the middle of the first year of its life and are brought on by an increase of sadism. They consist of fears of violent (i.e. devouring, cutting, castrating) objects, both external and introjected; and such fears cannot be modified in an adequate degree at such an early age.

The difficulties small children often have in eating are also closely connected, according to my experience, with their earliest anxiety-situations and invariably have paranoid origins. In the cannibalistic phase children equate every kind of food with their objects, as represented by their organs, so that it takes on the significance of their father's penis and their mother's breast and is loved, hated and feared like these. Liquid foods are likened to milk, faeces, urine and semen, and solid foods to faeces and other substances of the body. Thus food is able to give rise to all those fears of being poisoned and destroyed inside which children feel in relation to their internalized objects and excrements if their early anxiety-situations are strongly operative.

Infantile animal phobias are an expression of early anxiety of this kind. They are based on that ejection of the terrifying super-ego which is characteristic of the earlier anal stage . . . the displacement on to an animal of the fear felt of the real father. . . . The fact that the anxiety-animal not only attracts to itself the child's fear of its father but also its admiration of him is a sign that the process of ideal-formation is taking place. Animal phobias are already a far-reaching modification of the fear of the super-ego; and we see here what a close connection there is between super-ego, object relationship and animal phobias. (1932, pp. 219–21.)

We will pass over here the problem of Mrs. Klein's somewhat loose use of terms, to which Edward Glover takes strong objection (as exemplified in the phrase 'ejection of the super-ego' which taken literally is impossible), and note that in this passage the theory of the super-ego has taken up into itself the whole range of phenomena now called 'fear of internal objects' and also needs felt towards them, as manifested in food and animal phobias and ideal-formation, i.e. all the child's experiences of reaction to the object-world as duplicated internally in its mental organization.

One fact needs to be stressed if a somewhat crude approximation to the idea of devil-possession is to be avoided, though in fact the traditional idea of devil-possession was a non-scientific recognition of the phenomena of 'internal objects'. Though these internal psychic objects appear to us in dreams and are experienced by us as if they were independent entities owning their own aggression and expressing their own hostility against us, they are in reality structural parts of our own psyche. The anger that animates these *dramatis personae* on the stage of our internal psychically real world is, and can only be, our own anger. They are the expression of the internal processes by which a human being can turn against himself the anger that really he feels against those who frustrate him. It is our own disturbed emotion that both constitutes and perpetuates this persecutory inner world. A vicious circle is set up by which anger is aroused by our bad objects, we turn it on to our self, thus arousing in our 'self' still greater anger, in the light of which our original bad objects appear even more bad, and so on. One patient who was addicted to violent hitting of her own body used to say: 'When anyone makes me angry someone has got to be hit, and it had better be me.' By this means, both physically and mentally, her rage against her factually bad mother was expended in self-persecution. She could alternate quickly between feeling identified with the persecuting, punishing mother in rage against herself and all girl children, and having anxiety-attacks which corresponded to dreams of her bad mother coming to murder her.

Mrs. Klein's work takes us deep into the problems of early structural development and, just as Freud's work paved the way for her investigations, so her work urgently called for further theoretical clarification of the problems of endopsychic structure.

CHAPTER XII

MELANIE KLEIN: THEORY OF EARLY DEVELOPMENT AND 'PSYCHOTIC' POSITIONS

1. *The Depressive and the Paranoid-Schizoid Positions*

MELANIE KLEIN'S work on the early years of childhood led, not only to a theory of psychical structure based on the concept of the 'internal object', but also to new clinical concepts of early infantile development. Abraham's important paper on the 'Theory of Libido Development' in 1924, the year Mrs. Klein began her analysis with him, no doubt represents her position at that date. It was the theory of a psyche at first objectless and auto-erotic, which developed through oral, anal, phallic and genital phases; these determined its object-relationships, as its originally auto-erotic and narcissistic libido and aggression became extraverted. Fixations at these stages accounted for the various psychoses and neuroses. The early oral fixation gave rise to schizophrenia, the late oral fixation led to depressive psychosis, the early anal to paranoia, the late anal to obsessional neurosis and the phallic to hysteria.

In 1934 Melanie Klein read a paper entitled 'A Contribution to the Psychogenesis of Manic-Depressive States'. (1948, p. 282.) E. Glover regards that as marking a 'second phase' in her views, and quotes her statement that in her opinion 'the infantile depressive position is the central position of the child's development'. He comments: 'The publication of this paper marked the commencement of an entirely new orientation in psycho-analysis in a section of the British Society. The trend of discussions at subsequent meetings and the content of various papers soon indicated that a school of thought was developing based exclusively on a new hypothesis of development. Thus . . . Joan Riviere . . . in a subsequent paper on "The Genesis of Psychical Conflict in Earliest Infancy" . . . endeavoured to establish a systematic metapsychological basis for the new views. Clinically, the most significant point in this paper was contained in a footnote where she committed herself to the explicit statement. "We have reason to think since Melanie Klein's latest work on depressive states that all neuroses are different varieties of defence against this fundamental anxiety, each embodying mechanisms which become increasingly available to the organism as its development proceeds." ' (E. Glover, 1945.) He compares this with 'Rank's deviation'. 'Instead of Rank's birth trauma, we have offered us a "love trauma" of the third month, which, it is maintained, is as fateful for subsequent development as Rank thought the birth trauma to be. . . . In my considered opinion the concept of a three-months-old love-trauma due to the infant's imagined greedy destruction of a real loving mother whom it really loves is merely a matriarchal variant of the doctrine of Original Sin.' (*Op. cit.*, p. 43.)

In the judgment of the present writer the clinical evidence is against Glover's adverse opinion. It is not possible to analyse any neurosis deeply without finding that as its symptoms and defensive character traits are worked through, one comes upon intense fear of oral sadistic needs, and both anxiety and guilt over the phantasied loss of love-objects. If at that stage actual harm befalls a loved person in real life, serious depression is the usual result, while, as Fairbairn points out, the schizoid person is so afraid of love-impulses as destructive that he dare not love at all. One patient of mine who showed a marked liability to produce paranoid reactions as a defence against repressed guilt and depression, had the following dream : 'Mother and I and others were in a room and we knew that downstairs was a horrible monster that we were barricading against. Then mother went down and presently I knew she was dead, and I saw the monster and it was all made of teeth.' Soon after this dream in which she was dissociating herself from her oral sadistic need of her mother, a greatly loved friend was discovered to be dying of a hidden disease. He had recently given her valuable comfort and she began to feel that he was dying because she had drained away his life. She turned with an intense sense of need to me and rapidly began to become very solicitous for my health and safety, a reaction mixed with a growing conviction on her part that I was pressing analysis in a way that hurt her and made her worse and she could not carry on. Then the feeling of intense anger emerged against her friend because he was dying and leaving her. At the point where she could not face any more her intense repressed guilt over her oral sadistic needs towards both of us, she took refuge in the paranoid defence of the conviction that we were bad objects to her and that her anger was justified. Here in a nutshell are both of the main points of Mrs. Klein's view that Glover so criticizes: guilt and depression over a love-trauma created by the patient's 'imagined greedy destruction of a real loving mother' and a resort to a paranoid technique as a *defence* against this 'fundamental anxiety'. (Riviere.)

If Melanie Klein is to be charged with having produced a doctrine of Original Sin, it could only be on the ground that she persists in regarding the infant's sadism as innate by treating it as a manifestation of Freud's death instinct. It is Freud, not Mrs. Klein, who gives us a doctrine of Original Sin. If, on the other hand, she had stressed more clearly what is in fact the real outcome of her work—namely that sadism and neurotic aggression are post-natal phenomena in reaction to inadequate and unsatisfying mothering, felt by the infant as real frustration of the need for either or both food and tenderness—Glover's criticism would clearly be pointless. As for her views constituting a new and deviating metapsychology, the only thing that could interest us scientifically is whether they are clinically justified. It was already orthodox psycho-analysis to hold that the psychoses were developments of the oral level, while psychoneuroses were phenomena of the post-oral phases of development. It does not in fact seem to be a deviation but a further development of this theory if it be now discovered that the later developed psychoneuroses are *defences* against the more serious dangers of the earlier psychotic conditions. Fairbairn adopted Mrs. Klein's view on this point.

Presumably, Glover's criticism, in so far as it is based on purely theoretical grounds, rests on the fact that Freud regarded the Oedipus complex of the third to fifth year as the 'central position' in the child's development and held also that the infantile psyche in the earliest phase was objectless and autoerotic. But clinical phenomena forced Mrs. Klein to recognize the conflicts typical of the Oedipal phase at a far earlier age than three to five years. This of itself undermined the hitherto accepted view that the infant psyche was to begin with objectless and autoerotic, for the depressive phenomena which, she believed, arose as early as the infant's first developing perception of mother as a 'whole-object' in the early months of life are object-relations phenomena. Hungarian analysts in the Ferenczi tradition (Alice Balint as early as 1933, Peto and M. Balint 1937, *Int. J. Psych. An.* Vol. XXX, Pt. 4, 1949) were discarding Freud's view that the earliest stages of psychic life were objectless. This is one of the points at which Freud's own views most needed correction. Mrs. Klein and her co-workers in child-analysis realized that the infant is object-related to the mother's breast from the beginning, and that during the first year of life his development proceeds in the setting of external object-relationships of the Oedipal situation, duplicated within by the creation of internal objects and the early anxiety-situations arising from internal object-relations. As a result, the two kinds of anxiety come into being, persecutory anxieties and depressive anxieties. The persecutory anxieties she regards as paranoid and as the basis of all phobias of menace and danger to the ego from its bad objects. In her paper 'Notes on Some Schizoid Mechanisms' (1952, pp. 292–320) she wrote in a footnote on page 293. 'When this paper was first published in 1946, I was using my term "paranoid position" synonymously with W. R. D. Fairbairn's "schizoid position".' [i.e. for this 'persecutory phase' of the first few months. Present writer's note.] 'On further deliberation I decided to combine Fairbairn's term with mine and throughout the present book I am using the expression "paranoid-schizoid position".' This 'position' she held to precede the 'depressive position', in which the infant becomes anxious on behalf of its love-objects and not merely for itself, and guilt arises. Mrs. Klein writes :

If persecutory fears are very strong, and for this reason (among others) the infant cannot work through the paranoid-schizoid position, the working through the depressive position is in turn impeded. This failure may lead to a regressive reinforcing of persecutory fears and strengthen the fixation points for severe psychoses (that is to say, the group of schizophrenias). . . . While I assumed that the outcome of the depressive position depends on the working through of the preceding phase, I nevertheless attributed to the depressive position a central role in the child's early development. For with the introjection of the object as a whole the infant's' object-relation alters fundamentally. The synthesis between the loved and hated aspects of the complete object gives rise to feelings of mourning and guilt which imply vital advances in the infants emotional and intellectual life. This is also a crucial juncture for the choice of neurosis or psychosis. To all those conclusions I still adhere. (1952, p. 294.)

Thus Mrs. Klein regards these psychotic persecutory and depressive anxieties as originating in early infancy, while the psycho-neuroses of the post-oral phases constitute defensive struggles to master these deeper disturbances. In this same paper she writes explicitly :

I have often expressed my view that object-relations exist from the beginning of life, the first object being the mother's breast which to the child becomes split into a good (gratifying) and bad (frustrating) breast; this splitting results in a severance of love and hate. (Ibid., p. 293.)

As a result of this the view grew among Kleinian writers that the ego itself was a whole entity from the beginning, and was not to be regarded as growing together piecemeal by the synthesis of 'ego-nuclei' (E. Glover) or other components. In spite of the fact, however, that her work led away from the more usual Freudian conceptions of an atomistic development, it is a logical development along the main line of Freud's own interest. His super-ego theory marked a change of direction in his interest away from Hysteria where he began, and towards Obsessional neurosis and Depression and the part played by aggression and guilt in these conditions. The direction in which Freud's own views changed from 1920 onwards really implies Mrs. Klein's conclusion that it is the depressive position that is central for development. This conclusion is certainly in a line of continuous development from her earlier work on aggression and sadism, and her analysis of the super-ego in terms of internal persecutory and depressive object-relations. Her paper on manic-depression in 1934 was the culmination of a development of interest beyond psychoneurosis to psychosis and criminality which can be traced from at least 1929, where her earliest written reference to child-psychosis occurs in the paper on 'Personification in the Play of Children'. (1948, p. 223.)

In 1948 Mrs. Klein summarized this development in the Preface to the Third Edition of *The Psycho-Analysis of Children*.

In the years that have elapsed since this book first appeared, I have arrived at further conclusions—mainly relating to the first year of infancy—and these have led to an elaboration of certain essential hypotheses here presented. . . . The hypotheses I have in mind are as follows : In the first few months of life infants pass through states of persecutory anxiety which are bound up with the "phase of maximal sadism"; the young infant also experiences feelings of guilt about his destructive impulses and phantasies which are directed against his primary object—his mother, first of all her breast. These feelings of guilt give rise to the tendency to make reparation to the injured object.

In endeavouring to fill in the picture of this period in greater detail, I found that certain shifts of emphasis and time relations were inevitable. Thus I have come to differentiate between two main phases in the first six to eight months of life, and I describe them as the 'paranoid position' and the 'depressive position'. (The term 'position' was chosen because—though the phenomena involved occur in the first place during early stages of development—they are not confined to these stages but represent specific groupings of anxieties and defences which appear and reappear during the first years of childhood.)

The paranoid position is the stage when destructive impulses and persecutory anxieties predominate and extends from birth until about three, four, or even five months of life. . . . The depressive position, which follows on this stage and is bound up with important steps in ego development, is established about the middle of the first year of life. At this stage sadistic impulses and phantasies, as well as persecutory anxiety, diminish in power. The infant introjects the object as a whole, and simultaneously he becomes in some measure able to synthesize the various aspects of the object as well as his emotions towards it. Love and hatred come closer together in his mind, and this leads to anxiety lest the object, internal and external, be harmed or destroyed. Depressive feeling and guilt give rise to the urge to preserve or revive the loved object and thus to make reparation for destructive impulses and phantasies. . . .

This concept (i.e. the Depressive Position) also throws new light on the early stages of the Oedipus complex. I still believe that these begin roughly in the middle of the first year.

Since by that time Mrs. Klein now regarded the period of maximal sadism as having been already passed, she came to hold that the infant turns to the father with an ambivalent attitude of both love and hate, and says: 'I now correlate the early stages of the Oedipus complex with the depressive position.' The comment of J. O. Wisdom is pertinent at this point:

To see how the theory of the structure and function of internal objects gives rise to the Oedipus-situation requires an additional piece of theory. This is the theory of the 'paranoid-schizoid position' and of the 'depressive position'. (*Brit. J. for the Phil. of Sc.*, Vol. III, No. 25, 1956, p. 107.)

2. *The Primary Unity of the Ego*

Mrs. Klein's work has led to the view that the ego is a whole entity in its own right from the beginning. The conclusion is clearly at variance with Freud's theory of the id and ego. The inadequacy of Freud's id-ego-super-ego scheme has been revealed already through the criticism of its individual terms. It is also possible to discuss the inadequacy of Freud's scheme from another point of view, in the light of Melanie Klein's findings. It is incomplete as a scheme of internal ego-object relationships. If, to simplify the discussion for the moment, we use the term ego-ideal for the conscious part of the super-ego, this would appear to be an internal object with which the Freudian ego sustains a relationship. If the sadistic and mainly unconscious part of the super-ego is likewise taken to be an internal object, it has no corresponding ego with which an internal object-relationship can be sustained, for such an ego must by definition be 'repressed' and unconscious to function as such; whereas Freud's scheme makes no provision for such a repressed ego or part of an ego. It cannot be found in the id, for if it is to partner the sadistic super-ego it must be against the id. The id itself is neither ego nor internal object and is an anomalous entity; however, since it is essentially 'libidinal energy', we have already seen reason to think it ought to be regarded as itself a libidinal ego rather than as energy in a formless and totally unstructured state. At best then, Freud's scheme gives us (1) an internal object-relationship between the ego and the ego-ideal; (2) a sadistic part of the super-ego as an internal object without an ego to partner it, and (3) the id as an ego without an internal object to partner it. Mrs. Klein's work has already suggested the internalized good object, the introjected maternal breast as satisfying, to partner the id if this were treated as an ego, and though she speaks of the id she has really already transcended that idea in the concept of the original unity of the infantile ego.

This realization of the need for a revision of structural theory was not reached by Mrs. Klein and her colleagues, and the problem of an ego needed to correlate with the sadistic unconscious super-ego was not even glimpsed. Meanwhile it had become apparent to Kleinian writers that Freud's distinction between id and ego, in his sense, is artificial and needed to be transcended. Writing of the differentiation of the Freudian ego from the id, Paula Heimann observes:

We can define the beginning of the ego with the first introjections of another psychological entity. By virtue of his needs and his utter helplessness, guided by his oral instincts, the infant turns to the outer world and makes contact with another human being. He sucks at his mother's breast. This simple process can be defined in several ways: as a direct expression of instinctual needs, that is an id activity (since by definition the id is the seat of the instincts); or, since, again by definition it is the surface part of the id, i.e. the ego which performs the contacts with the outer world, as an activity of the ego. *The burden of the argument is this: when we consider the earliest processes we cannot make a sharp distinction between the id and the ego,* because in our view the ego is formed from experiences. The earliest contacts (introjections and projections) start this process. *The infant's first sucking is then neither an id-activity nor an ego-activity—it is*

both, it is an activity of the incipient ego. [Present writer's italics.]
(1952, p. 128.)

Heimann is in process of outgrowing the id concept. There does
not exist at the beginning a mere id. Its activities have an ego
aspect, and this primitive ego manifests so-called id-activity, i.e.
libidinal impulses towards the maternal breast. Energy and structure are all one, as was really implied by the criticisms of Hartmann, Kris and Loewenstein and F. Alexander. The Freudian ego
is a later development which arises out of the splitting of the
original ego into two egos. The so-called id is the primary libidinally needy self and the Freudian ego is a self that seeks adjustment
to outer reality (in the trends to conformity of which H. S. Sullivan
made so much). The libidinally needy self, as it strives for satisfaction, comes to be opposed and repressed. Freud discovered it in
the unconscious and mistook it for an impersonal id because it was
not a conscious ego. Had he held to the phenomena of hysteria
with its dissociations and repressions, he might have come to base
his structural scheme on the concept of a fundamental splitting of
the unity of the original ego. Kleinian writers took the first steps
to a revision of structural theory in arriving at the concept of the
mental splitting of the object in the course of internal-object
formation, and of the primary unity of the ego.

The primary libidinal id-ego is as much an ego, a self, as any
later developed ego-aspect of the psyche. It has an object, the
breast, and it can introject its object. Heimann says that the ego
begins with the first introjections but that is self-contradictory. It
implies that the id is already functioning as an ego, having an
object and introjecting it, in order to start up ego-development.
Heimann speaks of :

processes of adding something new to the self or ridding it of something of its own which have an inestimable share in the modification
of the original id into an ego. (M. Klein *et al.*, 1952, p. 126.)

But, surely, introjection and projection make sense only when
they are seen as activities of an ego in dynamic relations with
objects. The literal implication of her words would be that the id
functions as an ego in order to give rise to the ego. Such confusions
are due to the fact that Kleinian writers did not recognize that
Freud's structural theory and id-instinct theory are incompatible.
It is far simpler to see that a new theory of endopsychic structure is needed as a result of Melanie Klein's work and of the
already existing criticisms of Freud's structural scheme, a new
theory which, in fact, Heimann almost explicitly states without

recognizing it. The unreality involved in the Kleinian preservation of the id-concept is clear from the way in which Susan Isaacs and Joan Riviere accept the existence of an ego from birth. Susan Isaacs writes :

Some measure of 'Synthetic function' is exercised upon instinctual urges from the beginning. The child could not learn, could not adapt to the external world (human or not) without some sort and degree of control and inhibition, as well as satisfaction, of instinctual urges progressively developed from birth onwards. (M. Klein *et al.*, 1952, p. 110.)

Joan Riviere discusses the orthodox criticism by Anna Freud of the Kleinian theory of ego-development. Anna Freud wrote :

It is a controversial matter whether clashes between opposing instinctual urges of the love-hate, libido-destruction series can come into being before a central ego has been established with power to integrate the mental processes, or only afterwards. (Quoted in M. Klein *et al.*, 1952, p. 13.)

Joan Riviere adds in a footnote that 'Anna Freud stated that the period before such a central ego has been established extends roughly over the first years of life.' (*Ibid.*, p. 113.) To this Riviere replied :

Klein's view is that in accordance with the genetic character of development we may postulate an ego which has some rudiments of integration and cohesion from the beginning and which progresses increasingly in that direction ; further, that conflict does arise before ego-development is much advanced and power to integrate mental processes is established at all fully . . . libido itself (Eros) is defined by Freud as a force serving the purpose of preservation, propagation and unification; i.e. its function is a synthetic one; we do not understand the view that at any period of life there could be no synthetic function in operation. In our view struggle and conflict of various kinds, integrating and disintegrating forces, exist and operate from the very beginning in human life. (*Ibid.*, pp. 13–14.)

The disagreement between Anna Freud and the Kleinians on this point is, however, largely the result of the id-theory and instinct-theory. Anna Freud cannot recognize that there are synthetic functions at work from the beginning because she cannot admit that the so-called id is the primitive libidinal ego sustaining a definite object-relation to the breast from birth, and that so-called instinctive id-impulses are, even at this stage, activities of a self with synthesizing functions, reactions of a primitive dynamic ego-structure to objects. Kleinians recognize that the ego, in however rudimentary a form, is there from the first, and is involved in object-relationships from the very beginning. But they have not realized that the primacy of ego-object relations, external and internal, and the fact that instinctive reactions never occur except as reactions of a dynamic ego-structure to objects, renders the id-concept and the classic instinct-theory superfluous.

It will be well to make it clear that Kleinian theory, departing from classic Freudian theory, carries object-relations as well as the ego back to the very beginning. Freud is explicit and insistent that the earlier phases of development are autoerotic and narcissistic and that this means that they are objectless. Melanie Klein and her followers at first carried on this piece of orthodox theory. Speaking of earliest infancy, Joan Riviere wrote in 1936 :

This narcissistic world of the psyche is one of 'hallucination', based on sensation and ruled by feelings (under the sway of the pleasure-pain principle), entirely autistic, not only lacking in objectivity, but at first without objects.

But she added a footnote later to this :

1950. I should now correct this to : 'At the very first without awareness of external objects.' (Ibid., pp. 40–41.)

Paula Heimann states clearly the primacy of object-relations, when she writes concerning the development of differentiations in endopsychic structure, that :

The differentiations are brought about by the fact that the in-dividual exists in a world on which he is dependent by virtue of his instincts : his wish to keep alive, his desire for pleasure and his fear of destruction. It seems evident that an organism which depends to a vast extent on other organisms and powers outside itself for attain-ing its purposes, must become influenced and changed by such con-tacts. (Ibid., p. 122.)

Joan Riviere quotes Anna Freud as saying :

I consider that there is a narcissistic and autoerotic phase of several months' duration, preceding object-relations in the proper sense, even though [Riviere's italics] the beginnings of object-relation are slowly built up during this initial stage. . . . Freudian theory allows at this period only for the crudest rudiments of object-relation-ship and sees life governed by the desire for instinctual gratification in which perception of the object is only achieved slowly. . . .

Riviere comments :

Here she makes a distinction between 'object-relation in its proper sense', on the one hand, and 'the crudest beginnings of object-relation built up during the initial stage' on the other. There can be no such distinction, since the 'beginnings' and so on are the object-relation appropriate and proper to the earliest stage of development. At each stage of instinctual primacy the character or degree of object-relation is proper to that stage. (Only if 'object-relation proper' were understood to mean fully developed adult object-relation could such a distinction be made.) (M. Klein *et al.*, 1952, p. 12.)

In view of this it seems that she makes an unnecessary concession to the older theory when she still held that the infant is at first 'without awareness of external objects', for surely the beginnings of awareness appropriate to that stage must be present with the beginnings of object-relationship. Autoeroticism and narcissism are, of course, clinically observable phenomena and are explained by Kleinians as overlapping and co-existing with object-relations. They turn out to be a matter of disguised relationships with objects internal to, and identified with, the self.

We may now attempt some general assessment on the controversial question of whether the Kleinian system is a deviation (or heresy) from Freud. Kleinians retain Freud's unsatisfactory theories of the life and death instincts and of endopsychic structure, the distinction of the id and ego, and his hedonistic or pleasure theory of motivation. Yet their title to the name 'psycho-analyst' is more safely rested on their basically psycho-analytical orientation and method in dealing with human nature, and on their development of the most progressive psychodynamic aspects of Freud's theories rather than on their retention of his earlier psychobiology and structural terminology. For they are undoubtedly in process all the time of outgrowing the implications of his instinct-theory and substituting for it an object-relations theory which calls for a revised structural theory. Their explicit disavowal of his theory of autoeroticism is a case in point. They are true psycho-analysts in spirit and have continued and developed Freud's own work in new and profoundly important ways. But their discoveries necessitate a far bigger break with the early psychobiological Freud than they have recognized, and point the way to more far-reaching revisions of the theories of the later psychodynamic Freud than they themselves have made. This is the core of truth in the charge of 'deviationism'.

It appears to the present writer that the work of Freud in the 1920s paved the way for that of Melanie Klein in the 1930s.

Freud's creative contributions may be regarded as ending with *Inhibitions, Symptoms and Anxiety* in 1926, or possibly with *Civilization and its Discontents* in 1930, apart from the outstanding essay *Analysis, Terminable and Interminable* in 1937 which is, however, more a contribution to therapy than theory. He must surely rank for all time among the greatest of scientific pioneers, and it is the first steps in discovery that are the hardest to take. But the honour must be accorded to Melanie Klein of having made those decisive developments of Freud's work that make it possible for psycho-analysis to become a true psychodynamic theory of the human being as a person. Her 'deviationism' is 'developmentalism', and simply shows that psycho-analysis does not stand still.

Some aspects of Mrs. Klein's latest work, on 'projective identification' and 'envy', we shall consider in chapter XVI, after we have dealt with the views of Fairbairn.

CHAPTER XIII

THE RELATION OF FAIRBAIRN'S WORK TO FREUD: FAIRBAIRN'S APPROACH TO PSYCHO-ANALYSIS

1. *Fairbairn and Freud*

PSYCHO-ANALYSIS itself implies that different types of theoretical orientation will be developed by different types of personality. Brierley warns us that 'The form of any hypothesis is always influenced by unconscious determinants, since we can only apprehend things in ways permitted by the specific structure of our individual minds.' (1951, p. 96.) This is a factor that can either facilitate insight or falsify it. One type of mind is liable to see certain things otherwise than as they are; we all to some extent project our own mental structure on to the outer world. Another person can recognize those same things as they are, in a way that other thinkers may miss. Probably more in psychology than in other scientific studies, the initial approach of an investigator is determined by his mental make-up and his previous education and experience of living. A comparison of the personalities and work of, say, Pavlov, J. B. Watson, Janet, McDougall, Spearman and Freud shows that each investigator studies those phenomena that his type of mind is most ready to accept as significant, and is liable to undervalue or even deny the reality of other parts of the total field that others see clearly enough.

Within the narrower field of psychotherapy and psycho-dynamic theory, the differences of approach to the complex problem of human nature likely to be made by different types of personality, is exemplified by the hypnotist and suggestionist, Adlerians, Jungians, Freudians and the Objective Psychological Testers. For our present purpose, within the still narrower field of psycho-analytical theory, one feels a difference of mental atmosphere and attitude in the writings of Freud and Fairbairn. This is partly due to the different cultural climates of the 1880s and the

1920s and 1930s, and partly to a difference between the two men as human beings.

Fairbairn has stated that it was out of definite personal conviction that he followed the line of Freud and not that of Jung. He has written:

I cannot say that I entertain any regrets over the fact that my researches have been conducted under the auspices of the Freudian rather than the Jungian tradition. When I first became interested in problems of psychopathology, I had no controversial axe to grind; and if, on reaching the cross-roads of thought, I chose to follow the path mapped out by Freud instead of that mapped out by Jung, this was certainly not because I considered Freud invariably right and Jung invariably wrong. It was because, on comparing Freud's basic conceptions with those of Jung, I found the former incomparably more illuminating and convincing, and felt them to offer an infinitely better prospect of solving the problems with which psychopathology is concerned. If some of the conclusions which I have subsequently reached involve no inconsiderable divergence from Freud's views, I still feel that, in taking Freud's views as my starting-point, I was building upon a more solid foundation than would otherwise have been the case. (1955, p. 144.)

Fairbairn's earliest writings show him thoroughly rooted in the orthodox psycho-analytical concepts. Yet one becomes aware of a type of mind that is radically different from that of Freud, even though sharing so much that is fundamental with him.

It is a perilous business trying to describe the difference, but some attempt must be made. Freud and Fairbairn put their primary emphases in different places. It is, perhaps, a rough approximation to say that with Freud, whilst he was an eminently human being in his family and private life, in his work the human being was absorbed into the scientist. This would have mattered little in any other branch of scientific work, but in psychology it led him to evolve a distinctly impersonal type of theory, tied as we have seen to the thought-forms of physical science, and also an impersonal therapeutic technique. Fairbairn is as scrupulously careful in his scientific work as was Freud. His scientific conscience is as exacting as Freud's, but always he is first and foremost, not 'the scientist', but a human being using scientific enquiry to further his understanding of other human beings in their struggle to live. A young professional social worker, after reading his book for the first time, remarked: 'My most general impression is that Fairbairn writes about human beings.'

Freud was first 'the scientist'; the anatomist, physiologist and

neurologist who would have preferred a life devoted to laboratory
research and was not primarily interested in being a healer. He
had to be pushed by events into the field of psychological investigation in which he then proved to possess powers amounting to
genius. In his work Freud was a scientist turned 'humanist'. By
contrast, Fairbairn is a 'humanist' turned scientist. His classical
education and graduation in Mental Philosophy in Edinburgh
were followed by intensive studies in Hellenistic Greek, and in
religious, philosophical and psychological subjects, both in Great
Britain and Germany. But he was at the same time greatly attracted by medicine and, when he finally turned to that as a
career, it was with the specific aim of specializing in psychological
medicine. The human interest dominated the purely scientific
interest throughout. He has stated that his interest in Freudian
psycho-analysis was aroused by the fact that he felt it could throw
light on the profoundly human problems of anxiety and guilt.

It was not, then, an accident that Freud evolved a biological
psychology founded on the concept of instinct and never quite
realized how far he was driven away from his basic assumptions
by the need to embark on the analysis of the ego in terms of human
object-relationships. Neither is it an accident that Fairbairn
quickly realized the far-reaching importance of Melanie Klein's
analysis of endopsychic structure in terms of object-relations and
proceeded further than Melanie Klein herself in developing a full
psychodynamic 'object-relations' theory of the personality. In
revising psycho-analytic theory in terms of the priority of human
relations over instincts as the causal factor in development, both
normal and abnormal, Fairbairn was also expressing his own
mentality which is of a type to facilitate his seeing correctly the
objective facts in this matter. He does not, of course, by any means
stand alone to-day in recognizing the need for this change of
emphasis, but more thoroughly than anyone else so far he has
reformulated theory to conform to this newer insight.

2. The Attitudes of Freud and Fairbairn to Science and Religion

The difference between Freud and Fairbairn comes out clearly
in their respective attitudes to science and religion. Freud shared
the late nineteenth-century overvaluation of science in an
emotional sense as the proper substitute for religion. For him the
Weltanschauung or 'philosophical world view' of psycho-analysis
was simply that of the scientific rationalism of his day. He looked
to the 'still small voice' of scientific reason for the ultimate solution
of all problems, practical as well as theoretical. For Freud, Science

with a capital 'S' was Truth with a capital 'T', in the sense that science alone, throughout all its changing and developing theories, was working towards that goal. Hence for Freud, as scientist and rationalist, religion was at worst nothing but superstition, and at best infantile phantasy. He was not only biased but hostile to both religion and philosophy. We have dealt with Freud's 'philosophy of science,' and the changes that have come about in this field of thought since his day, in chapter VII.

Fairbairn, on the other hand, having had the benefit of the critical examination of the claims of science to represent 'Truth' that has gone on since Freud's day, is less prepared to 'bow the knee to the scientific Baal' and has a more critically independent attitude. In his paper 'Schizoid Factors in the Personality' (1940) he writes :

Intellectual pursuits as such, whether literary, artistic, scientific or otherwise, appear to exercise a special attraction for individuals possessing schizoid characteristics to one degree or another. Where scientific pursuits are concerned, the attraction would appear to depend upon the schizoid individual's attitude of detachment, no less than upon his overvaluation of thought processes : for these are both characteristics which readily lend themselves to capitalization within the field of science. The obsessional appeal of science, based as this is upon the presence of a compulsive need for orderly arrangement and meticulous accuracy, has, of course, long been recognized; but the schizoid appeal is no less definite. (1952a, p. 6.)

The scientific attitude of complete unemotional detachment from the facts investigated is essentially schizoid. It is not a psychopathological state if it is an attitude of mind voluntarily adopted for the specific purpose of investigation. But schizoid intellectuals are bound to be attracted to science as an escape from the pressure of personal emotional relationships which the schizoid person finds difficult. Any analyst who has treated University staff members cannot fail to realize how important the schizoid factor is in their problems. It has played an important part in the controversy between science and religion. This controversy was most obviously due to the fact that, dating from the pre-scientific era, religious tradition had come to usurp the functions of science, and its thinkers mistakenly regarded its dogmas and symbols as being statements of the same kind as scientific statements of fact. But many a schizoid scientist, in rejecting religion, made exactly the same mistake. Science is primarily intellectual investigation of impersonal phenomena, and religion is primarily emotional experience of personal relationships, from which the schizoid person is detached and which he often consciously dislikes and has little capacity to understand. It is not therefore surprising that the overwhelmingly scientific trend in Freud's theory and therapeutic technique should have shaped both in a markedly impersonal way. Freud said that he employed the couch technique because he could not stand being looked at by his patients for eight hours a day, and he seems to have disliked 'regressed' patients who cannot so easily be treated by impersonal methods. It was natural for his theoretical interest to switch over from hysteria to obsessional problems. He showed fairly clear signs of a resistance against the 'human closeness' involved in the kind of work for which at the same time he had such extraordinary gifts. Fairbairn has observed that a schizoid trend can confer marked intellectual insight into psychological realities, no doubt because any degree of outer emotional detachment involves living more in the inner world. Only a man of an introspective intellectual type could have developed psycho-analytic theory out of a self-analysis, and probably for this reason Freud's theory and technique bore the impersonal stamp of the 'pure science' point of view. Freud must have had some personal reasons for overvaluing the impersonal scientific method, as also for his hostility to religion.

In his paper on 'Observations in Defence of the Object-Relations Theory of the Personality' (1955) Fairbairn has stated explicitly his view of science.

It would be truer to say that I regard . . . psycho-analysis as a *scientific discipline* than that I regard it as a 'natural science'. In other words, I regard it as a legitimate field for the harnessing of scientific method to the task of exact conceptualization. At the same time I do not regard it as either necessary or desirable for the analyst who aspires to be scientific to adopt the particular method appropriate to *physical* science. Thus I consider that, as in the case of all forms of psychological research, *the investigations of psycho-analysis should be conducted at the level of personality and personal relations* [Present writer's italics] (p. 151).

Here is a radical difference of outlook from that of Freud, which played a great part in determining Fairbairn's substitution of an object-relations theory of the personality for the orthodox psycho-biological instinct-theory. It is also the ground on which he rejects 'process theory' as an unsuitable type of terminology for the psychological study of the 'person'. He writes :

My conception of science is that it is essentially an intellectual tool and nothing more. I do not regard it as in any sense providing an (even approximately) accurate picture of reality as it actually exists, still less a revelation of ultimate truth : and if asked to define the nature of scientific truth, I should describe it as simply *explanatory truth.* . . . *The picture of reality provided by science is an intellectual construct representing the fruits of an attempt to describe the various phenomena of the universe, in as coherent and systematic a manner as the limitations of human intelligence permit, by means of the formulation of general laws established by inductive inference under the conditions of maximum emotional detachment and objectivity on the part of the scientific observer. (Ibid.,* p. 154.)

Concerning science as nothing more than an intellectual tool, Fairbairn says :

It is possible, of course, to make this intellectual tool the basis of a philosophy of life—and even of a form of religion; and there is a prevalent tendency in the age in which we live, especially among the intelligentsia, to exploit science in this way. However, I do not happen to be one of those who adopt such an attitude. It seems obvious to me that the analyst is not primarily a scientist, but a psychotherapist; and it seems equally obvious that the adoption of a psychotherapeutic role *ipso facto* involves a departure from the strictly scientific attitude. (*Ibid.,* pp. 154–5.)

Psychotherapy rests on a broad basis of human value-judgments quite different from the purely *explanatory* values of science. To the therapist it is *better* for the patient to be well than ill. To the scientist *qua* scientist health and sickness are alike merely phenomena to be explained. Fairbairn holds that the possession of

a scientifically based and explanatory psychological system is a tool of inestimable value in the hands of the psychotherapist. (*Ibid.,* p. 155.)

Its use, however,

apart from such inherent justification as it may possess as a means of satisfying curiosity . . . can only be justified in so far as it is made to serve human and personal values transcending any purely scientific value. (*Ibid.,* p. 155.)

Fairbairn here raises fundamental problems concerning science, psychology and psychotherapy that Freud did not, and in his time probably could not, begin to discuss. Psychotherapy uses science but is not itself a scientific activity. Freud set out simply as a scientific investigator and naturally sought to fashion psychology and psychotherapy so as to 'make them scientific', not realizing that the attempt was a contradiction in terms in the case of psycho-therapy, and in the case of psycho-analytic theory could not succeed if science was to mean 'natural science'. This difference of standing-ground between Freud and Fairbairn is simply funda-mental. Fairbairn adds two further important comments.

Personally I consider that a psychology conceived in terms of object-relations and dynamic structure is more compatible with the recognition of such human and personal values as psychotherapy serves than is any other psychology hitherto available. It is not for this reason that I have adopted such a psychology, but for the purely scientific reason that its correspondence to the facts and its explana-tory value seem to me greater than those of any other psychology, e.g. a psychology conceived in terms of 'impulse' and 'instinct'. (*Ibid.*, p. 155.)

Because of Fairbairn's difference from Freud in type of mind and basic approach, he recognized the priority of object-relations over instincts as causal factors in personality growth, in a way that Freud did not.

This same basic difference gives Fairbairn a different attitude to religion from that of Freud. Even while he regards scientific ex-planatory truth as an indispensable guide in psychotherapy he writes:

It is the verdict of history, and particularly of religious history, that effective psychotherapy can take place in the absence of all scientific knowledge. . . . I consider further that what is sought by the patient who enlists psychotherapeutic aid, is not so much health as salvation from his past, from bondage to his (internal) bad objects, from the burden of guilt, and from spiritual death. His search thus corresponds in detail to the religious quest. . . . I am convinced that it is the patient's relationship to the analyst that mediates the 'curing' or 'saving' effect of psychotherapy . . . the development of the patient's relationship to the analyst, through a phase in which earlier pathogenic relationships are repeated under the influence of trans-ference, into a new kind of relationship which is at once satisfying and adapted to the circumstances of outer reality. (*Ibid.*, pp. 155-6.)

In spite of the concept of transference being common to both, Freud and Fairbairn are here in different worlds of thought and feeling; and the question of religion, to which Freud could adopt only a negative and hostile attitude, is a touchstone of the dif-ference. Fairbairn recognizes in the religious terminology of 'salvation' an expression of the natural, naïve and unreflective way

in which human beings spontaneously felt about their personality problems. Such terminology is not peculiar to any one
religious creed. With cultural differences and variations it is
shared by all forms of religion, and is close to man's actual, immediate experience of himself. Thus for Fairbairn religion is an
impressive activity and experience of human beings throughout
the centuries, and is to be approached not with hostility as a mere
nuisance, irrelevance and brake on progress, but with sympathetic
insight in order to understand what human beings have actually
been seeking and doing in their religious life.

In the result Fairbairn finds that religion provides a more
illuminating analogy to the aims and processes of psychotherapy
than either science or education do. He even recognizes no inconsiderable part of psycho-dynamic theory implicit, if not yet
scientifically formulated, in religious concepts.

The relevance of this is seen in Professor John Macmurray's
definition of the sphere of religion as the sphere of human relationships. Fairbairn's interest in the psychology of religion is one expression of his fundamental concern with 'object-relationships' as
the substance of human living, and the key to the understanding
of all personality phenomena.

The earliest of Fairbairn's published papers (1927) is 'Notes on
the Religious Phantasies of a Female Patient'. (1952a, pp. 183–
96.) It was written before Melanie Klein's work had advanced
very far and shows no trace of her influence. It shows how easily
and naturally the personal quest for a good object as the primary
psychic motivation flows into the religious channel. The patient, a
spinster aged thirty-one years presented hysterical symptoms covering a profound schizoid disturbance. The central fact of her history
was that, though her father was alive, she had never seen him,
since her parents separated soon after her birth. Her entire psychopathological development revolved around her profound need to
satisfy her craving for a father. The case recalls the 'protesting cry
of a patient' Fairbairn quoted years later, in affirming his principle
that libido is not primarily pleasure-seeking but object-seeking,
namely, 'You're always talking about my wanting this and that
desire satisfied; but what I really want is a father.' (1952a, p.
137.)

At the time of her first breakdown, she felt cravings for male
attentions, was sexually enlightened by her doctor as a precaution
and medically examined by another doctor; from then on
masturbation became a distressing habit which she regarded as
the chief factor in aggravating her illness. But she ultimately became 'a complete devotee of masturbation; and the experience

accompanying the act was described by her as "exquisite beyond belief"'. (*Ibid.*, p. 195.) It represented the satisfaction of her need for a father, being often accompanied by phantasies about medical men who had become father-figures for her, and who had focussed her life-long craving for a father in sexual phantasy and masturbation. In a second breakdown at twenty-two years of age, she began to have religious visions and phantasies in which she felt herself to be identified with either the Mother of Christ, or Christ Himself, or the Bride of Christ. This phantasy life was an alternative satisfaction of her longing for a father, since, (*a*) as the Mother of Christ she was specially chosen by the Father, and (*b*) as Christ Himself she was the special child of the Father, and (*c*) as the special child (daughter) of the Father, only the Son could be worthy of her as His Bride; and in addition she is again the beloved of a male person, a phantasy registering her fixation on her brother as a father-substitute. She once woke from a dream with the words 'Perhaps I shall marry father' in her ears.

The final result of this case is startling in its implications. The patient, who had discontinued analytic treatment, fell into a condition of increasing neurasthenic weakness for which no cause in organic disease could be found, while she remained perfectly rational and orientated in space and time. Fairbairn was called and saw her on her death-bed, and he records his view that 'she died in a state of sexual desire; and when I left her moribund on the occasion of my final visit, almost her last words were, "I want a man".' (1952a, p. 196.)

The implication would appear to be that so basic is the object-relations need that a human being can even die in consequence of the complete frustration of the primary libidinal need for a basic (parental) good-object relationship during the development period. The symptoms of her illness represented the phases of her tortured personal, emotional and sexual need for this vital object-relation.

Such a case as this at an early stage must have exercised a profound influence on a thinker of Fairbairn's outlook, preparing for the shaping of his thought towards the formulation of 'object-relations' theory. He stated thus early his view of the problems of the psychology of religion. He is not prepared to 'explain away' the phenomena of the cultural life of human beings by reference to their psychological origins, while he preserves a proper place for the scientific investigation of those origins. He writes:

Personally, I am very far from being one of those who considers that higher values can be accounted for wholly in terms of their psychological origins; and, indeed, if it were so, it would be a poor outlook for human culture. Nevertheless, psychological origins provide a legitimate field for investigation on the part of psychological science. (*Ibid.*, p. 189.)

Thus he is prepared, in a way that Freud was not, to allow for the existence of a normal cultural, and in this case religious, experience along with its psychoneurotic counterpart. Concerning the case under discussion, he says :

It is plain that we are not here dealing with the normal religious experience of the devout person orientated in reality, but with experiences of an unusual and grandiose character in which the imagination has been exalted at the expense of the facts of real life. It is not a case of the ordinary Christian experience . . . but of an actual dramatization within the individual of the themes underlying the religious experience. (1952a, p. 188.)

He pointed out that the patient did not feel herself to be a worshipper, but to be the actual principal figure in the religious mysteries : a schizoid failure to distinguish between phantasy and reality. Yet, this very psychopathological intensification and distortion was a revelation of the terrific power resident in the primary need and search of the human child for a good father. So overpowering was this need for good-object relationship that it seized possession of the patient's entire life, world and available energy, ultimately destroying her physical existence in its utterly uncompromisng struggle to gain satisfaction. From the point of view of the psychology of religion, the true inference would seem to be that, though this patient's religion was neurotic, religion *per se* is not necessarily neurotic. Religious experience is so much an expression of human nature as rooted in the primary need for good personal relationship that it became a natural channel in which the patient's starved need should flow, albeit to find distorted and psychopathological expressions. Study of the psychological origins of religious, as of moral and aesthetic, values, does not, then, settle the question either for or against their truth and validity. It simply contributes data that must be taken into consideration in a wider enquiry. It is, of course, important that manifestations of guilt and anxiety in moral and religious experience should be studied psycho-analytically, but when one considers that human behaviour in art, marriage, sport, hobbies, money-making and even science—in short, any and every form of human behaviour—can be similarly affected by the same motivation, it is clear that there is more to be said than psycho-analysis can say. Especially with reference to religion, Freud and most analysts have used psycho-analytical considerations simply to explain away. Fairbairn uses psycho-analytical considerations as one factor among others in helping to determine the nature and function of religion in human life.

I have stated elsewhere what seems to me to be the correct view of the relationship of religion and science as bearing on psychotherapy, though this does not cover the whole problem of the nature of religion. If the therapeutic factor in psychotherapy is to be found, as Fairbairn holds, in the object-relationship of patient and analyst, then :

The fundamental therapeutic factor in psychotherapy is more akin to religion than to science, since it is a matter of personal relationship rather than of the application of impersonal knowledge and technique. Bertrand Russell once defined the good life as 'the life inspired by love and guided by knowledge' (*What I Believe*, p. 28, 1925), which provides a neat formula for relating the scientific and religious factors in psychotherapy and in human life generally. Religion has always stood for the saving power of the good object-relationship. *Religion is distinguished from science as the historical form under which the therapeutic factor for personality ills has been recognized and cultivated.* Unfortunately it has so often lacked the accurate knowledge which science could supply of the nature of the problems and how best to apply the remedy. *Science* stands for the discovery of the necessary knowledge without which love may be ineffective. (Guntrip, 1953, p. 116.)

Fairbairn states the position so far as the strictly psycho-analytical study of religion is concerned as follows :

The characteristic standpoint of the psycho-analytical school is to look for the sources of the religous need in the dynamic unconscious of the individual. It is, of course, in the same direction that this school of psycho-analytical thought looks for the source of artistic inspiration and of all the achievements of human culture in general —the guiding principle being that cultural phenomena represent the symbolic and sublimated expression of repressed wishes of a primal character. . . . Where the psychological sources of the religious need are concerned there are two factors in the dynamic unconscious to which special importance is attached. . . . These are (1) persistence of the original attitude towards parents prevailing during early childhood, and displacement of this attitude towards supernatural beings from its attachment to human parents under the influence of disillusionment regarding their powers and capabilities to provide unlimited support; and (2) the persistent influence of a repressed

Oedipus situation accompanied by conflict, and an inner need to obtain relief from the attendant guilt. (1952a, pp. 188–9.)

Of these two points one would have to say, first, that they prejudge the question of whether religion is infantile *per se*, and rule out the possibility of religious experience in the mature personality; but second, that they do make it very clear that religion is *about* the human being's innate need to find good object-relationships in which to live his life.

The Kleinian emphasis generally, seems to be on good-object relations as a defence against anxiety. Brierley writes: 'The conception of psychic life as mastery of anxiety is only a modern version of Freud's original conception of the psyche as an apparatus for the regulation of instinct-tension.' (1951, p. 42.) But since anxiety itself is a secondary thing a reaction to the thwarting of the primary libidinal 'will to live', Fairbairn's emphasis is the fundamental one, namely, that the drive to good-object relationships is itself the primary libidinal need. Good-object relations have an intrinsic and not merely a defensive value. Thus Fairbairn's first paper was very markedly 'object-relations orientated', even though he had not yet begun to theorize on the question of the relative importance of object-relations and instinct.

3. *Fairbairn's Early Writings*

Fairbairn's original theoretical writings began with his paper on schizoid phenomena in 1940. Prior to that date he wrote a number of papers which fall roughly into two groups, before and after 1933–4. From 1927–33 he was exploring the ramifications of psycho-analysis in many directions and tracing out its relations to academic psychology, physical phenomena, psychosis, religion, dentistry and sexual-legal problems. This coincides with his period as lecturer in the Department of Psychology, Edinburgh, till 1935, and Psychiatry 1931–2. From 1934 onwards he continued to pursue the implications of psycho-analysis in wider fields, in problems of politics, war, art and University teaching; but now the influence of Melanie Klein becomes important, leading on to his period of original work from 1940 onwards.

This early work of Fairbairn is of interest in two ways. First it shows how thoroughly rooted in orthodox Freudian instinct-theory he was to begin with. That is important because those who have the best right to make a critical appraisal of a theory are those who have first tested it by full acceptance in practice, and so have discovered where and how it calls for further development. Both Melanie Klein and Fairbairn began in the orthodox camp. Fairbairn's early papers show here and there some reservations at points where one can see now that he was destined to explore new avenues of thought. But it was not till 1937 that he produced two papers on Psycho-analysis and Art which suddenly rose above all his earlier work and showed his power of original thought, though this was not yet turned to the critical re-thinking of the whole field of psycho-analytic theory. By 1940 his paper on schizoid problems began his real work as a theorist. One has the impression of an unconscious process of deepening insight silently maturing and then suddenly beginning to break surface. Thought is a socially conditioned phenomenon and Fairbairn did not develop in a vacuum. Of the external influences stimulating his mind, he regards that of the growing work of Melanie Klein as the most important and dates it definitely from hearing her read her paper on the 'Psycho-genesis of Manic-Depressive States' in 1934. He quotes her in papers written in 1936–7. Between 1934 and 1940, a revolution in his psycho-analytical thinking was going on, creating a climate of thought in which ideas put forward in an earlier paper in 1931, 'The Analysis of a Patient with a Genital Abnormality', could come to fruition. 1927–34 was the Freudian period, 1934–40 the Kleinian period, 1940 onwards the Fairbairnian period.

His earliest paper, in 1927, we have dealt with. It was followed by 'Fundamental Principles of Psycho-analysis' (1929, *Edin. Med. J.*), a clear and persuasive statement of orthodox theory. But at one point the independent thinker breaks through to foreshadow a later point of view. He writes:

One cannot help feeling that Freud would have been better advised to describe the satisfaction which the child derives from sucking as 'sensuous' (i.e. 'of the senses') rather than as 'sexual'. The pleasure derived from childish activities such as sucking is essentially due to the satisfaction of appetite, in the sense in which psychologists use this word. In the psychological sense of the word, 'appetite' is not restricted to the food-seeking tendency, but applied to all tendencies demanding immediate bodily satisfaction. All pleasure afforded by the satisfaction of appetites is essentially sensuous pleasure, whatever the nature of the appetite concerned. Since the fundamental activities of the infant are all appetitive, the satisfaction derived from their indulgence may be described as sensuous. To call it sexual, as Freud does, involves a mistaken narrowing of the conception concerned. The truth seems to be that in infancy sensuous satisfaction is undifferentiated, and that it is only as development proceeds that it becomes differentiated into sexual, alimentary and other forms. For similar reasons the 'libido' . . . should be regarded as the biological life-impulse, from which, in individual development, the sex-instinct is differentiated, rather than as something strictly sexual from the start. Freud, however, regards the libido as sexual from the outset, because the adult sex-instinct develops from it. It is for the same reason that he regards the appetitive activities of childhood as sexual, namely, because they are later integrated into the sexual impulse. . . . We may accept the continuity of development upon which Freud lays emphasis, while reserving judgment as to his use of the word 'sexual'. (*Edin. Med. J.*, June, 1929, pp. 340–1.)

This suggestion would avoid the confusions arising out of Freud's broadening of the term 'sexual' until in the end it denotes a mystical entity, 'Eros'. Fairbairn regards sex as but one form of libidinal experience, and the way in which an individual uses his sexuality as depending upon his character and personality as formed by his experiences in object-relationships. He reverses Freud's view that character and personality type depend on sexual development. Further he regards 'libido' as the basic, positive, all-inclusive life-urge, which he now defines as the urge to good-object relations, while the sex-drive is but one of its manifestations, one channel along which it flows. Thus Fairbairn does not now hypostatize THE LIBIDO as a sexual entity or energy in itself, but regards it as the energy-flow of the 'person' in action seeking the satisfaction of his primary needs. There is no such thing as THE libido driving the person, but a person who is libidinally active. As early as 1929 Fairbairn dissented from Freud's use of libidinal and sexual as synonymous.

The year 1929 saw also the publication of a paper, 'Some Points of Importance in the Psychology of Anxiety' (*Brit. J. Med. Psych.*, Vol. IX, Pt. 4, pp. 303–13). Here he discusses the problem of instinct, making use of academic psychology as well as of psychoanalysis. It was a subject to which he repeatedly returned till he evolved a new approach. Here his position is orthodox with some hints of critical questioning. He writes :

The reason why anxiety is such a constant feature of psychopathological states is that the dreaded danger is of internal origin. It has its source in the instinctive endowment of the individual concerned . . . the libido is ever striving for expression, it thus constitutes an ever-present menace (p. 305).

To this orthodox psycho-analytical view he adds the comment :

The suggestion may be hazarded that anxiety over an internal menace is not necessarily fear of the libido. Fear may be occasioned theoretically by any internal tendency which presents itself as a menace. Psycho-analytical investigation appears to show, however, that, of all the tendencies which constitute the instinctive endowment of man (the 'id'), those related to the sex-instinct (the 'libido') are, as a matter of fact, specially prone to occasion neurotic anxiety. Every psycho-analysis of a neurotic patient seems to reveal the libido as the danger from which escape is sought by a flight into illness. . . . The reason why it is libido from which escape is sought is that the libido conflicts with the child's early identifications with parents as frustrating figures. As Freud points out in *The Ego and the Id*, this identification of the child with frustrating figures forms the nucleus of the psychical organization to which he gives the name of 'super-ego'. . . . It is because of the conflict between the super-ego and the libido that repression is called into being. . . . The super-ego may come to constitute a source of danger to the ego . . . the object of fear for the neurotic personality. It would thus appear that morbid anxiety may be determined not only by the menace of the libido, but also by the menace of the super-ego (p. 306).

This way of presenting the problem expresses that particular way of sensing the realities of the endopsychic situation that ultimately led to his resolving the speculative theory of life and death instincts into a clinically factual statement of two observable factors, libidinal and anti-libidinal. The anti-libidinal factor is a turning against the self which owns the libidinal needs, and this aggression is found to operate in and through what Freud had termed the super-ego. Fairbairn mentions here one patient 'in whom the super-ego was particularly aggressive' (p. 307). The Freudian 'reality-ego' fears the upsurge of libidinal needs because that triggers off the internal, anti-libidinal counter-attack.

In these early papers Fairbairn has a mode of selection, statement and emphasis in presenting orthodox theory which already foreshadows his later views. In the second half of this paper he discusses neurotic anxiety in a way which hovers close to internal object-relations theory. He criticizes E. Jones for speaking of an instinct of fear. Fear is an emotion, and the instinct with whose activity it is associated is that of escape. Fairbairn agrees here with McDougall's view that the instincts are 'the prime movers of all human activity' (*Soc. Psych.*, 12th Ed., p. 38), and adds 'the primitive instinctive endowment, which McDougall postulates, [is] identical with what Freud describes as "the id" ' (p. 308). But with regard to the theory of emotion he prefers Drever's view that the affective element in instinctive experience is not one specific individual motion to each instinct, but a non-emotional 'instinct-interest' which becomes intensified into emotional excitement when the instinctive activity is specially obstructed or facilitated. 'All affective experience is bipolar (i.e. all affective experience finds a place on the pleasure-unpleasure scale)' (p. 310). 'The emotional phase of affective experience develops' towards the negative pole of unpleasure, sorrow, when the activity of an instinct is particularly thwarted, and towards the positive pleasure, or joy, pole when it is markedly facilitated. In the case of the instinct of Escape, this means *Fear* at the negative pole and a *Sense of Relief* at the positive pole. The reason why anxiety is so prominent in neurosis is that the danger is internal. 'The constant presence of a powerful endopsychic menace is certain to lead to situations in which the means of escape are inadequate' (p. 312), i.e. the 'defence mechanisms' or, as Fairbairn here prefers to call them, 'escape mechanisms' fail in the presence of a danger that is really inescapable because it is internal.

At this point Fairbairn falls back on the orthodox view that 'owing to the fact that the menace proceeds from the innate, instinctive endowment, final escape is impossible' (p. 313). The danger is the libido. If, however, he had followed up the other point he had already made, that menace proceeds from the superego (which is not part of the instinctive endowment but an internalized version of the child's object-relations with parents), he would have been very near stating the view that neurotic anxiety is due to an endopsychic situation in which there seems no escape for the ego from a menacing, internalized bad-object relationship.

A paper of 1931 entitled 'Features in the Analysis of a Patient with a Physical Genital Abnormality' (1952a, p. 197 ff) closes with an important foreshadowing of his later re-formulation of the theory of endopsychic structure. The patient's neurosis was not caused by her physical genital abnormality which apparently involved 'at least the absence of the vagina and uterus' (p. 220), but was caused by whatever determined her personality development along the lines of a fierce internal conflict between her libidinal needs and a 'titanic super-ego'. 'The dominant figure in the home was the patient's mother—an energetic and efficient woman, for whom the welfare of her family was all-important. She belonged to the type of good mother who is only too liable to instigate the formation of an exacting super-ego in her children' (p. 210). The patient's physical abnormality, when she learned of it, was simply fitted into this already-existing inner conflict. She felt relief at knowing that she could not play the normal feminine sexual role, and this must have been due to the fact that she felt correspondingly freed from persecution by her super-ego over sexual activity. Her breakdowns occurred in the period when, as a teacher, her super-ego was entirely dominant and she was driving herself with undue conscientiousness by perfectionist standards. She was living in and through her super-ego all the time, both in her attitude to herself and in her discipline of the children she taught. Just as she antagonized them, so she unconsciously also antagonized her own natural self. As the tempo of inner revolt and increased super-ego repression grew greater, exhaustion and breakdown became a recurring inevitability.

So far Fairbairn's presentation of this case followed orthodox lines. He was not yet influenced by Melanie Klein's concepts about 'internal objects'. The passage where he writes 'The nucleus of the super-ego is pre-genital in origin, belongs to an oral level and must therefore become established during the oral stage' (p. 221) arose out of his own observations on this case. He uses Freud's scheme for the analysis of psychic structure, the id, ego and super-ego. The importance of this paper historically emerges, however, at the end where he discusses the patient's strongly marked tendency to 'personify various aspects of her psyche' (p. 216). It is clear that in 1931, thirteen years before the publication of the paper on 'Endopsychic Structure Considered in Terms of Object-Relationships', his independent examination of Freud's tripartite scheme in the light of clinical evidence had begun.

This will best emerge against the background of the diagnosis of the case, which Fairbairn presents as an Obsessional Drive to duty in her period as a teacher, masking and defending against a Manic-Depressive inner situation. This manic-depressive condition he sees in terms of a conflict between her libidinal needs and her maternal super-ego. Her father was not a particularly significant figure, and the two influential adults in her early life were her mother and her maternal grandfather. The first phase of her analysis brought 'endless memories of early childhood concerned mainly with the patient's grandfather and the estate with which he was connected . . . endless days of happy play' (p. 205). Fairbairn writes :

She re-entered the paradise of her childhood, which had become all the more elysian through the operation of unconscious phantasy during the intervening years. In the background, however, there was always the menacing shadow of a mother-figure . . . who seemed to stand like a sinister figure in the background, frowning disapproval. In the earliest phase of analysis, however, her super-ego was largely in abeyance. It was the happy memories and phantasies of childhood that predominated. She was re-united to her grandfather in phantasy and played gaily with him in the elysian fields. Re-pressed emotional experiences of a libidinal nature thus broke through the trammels of the years; and she re-discovered what she came to describe as her 'infantile self', which had remained for long repressed in her unconscious. This break-through of repressed emotional experiences was accompanied by the emergence of sexual sensations, which at first appeared to her entirely novel, but which eventually revived memories of sensations experienced on swings and see-saws in her early days . . . they conformed to the clitoris type (p. 205).

'The sudden release of pent-up libido which analysis had effected' (pp. 205–6) resulted in her becoming markedly sexually attractive to men and led to what she called 'adventures' in her train journeys to analysis. Before she worked through this phase, she developed for a time somewhat grandiose delusions about pos-sessing a capacity to 'affect' people which could be used for the benefit of humanity as a whole. A mild manic phase emerged as an expression of the break-away of her early libidinal self from the oppression of her maternal super-ego. This early libidinal self, or what she called her 'infantile self', is clearly what later on Fair-bairn came to designate 'the Libidinal Ego', and in her analysis it emerged in more than one 'personification'.

Over against this 'libidinal self' in her personality was her maternal super-ego frowning upon it. The release of her libidinal self led, in the second stage of the analysis, to the appearance of a strong oral sadistic attitude to the envied penis, and so in the third stage to the parallel emergence of anal and oral elements in her super-ego. The dominance of her super-ego always led to a swing away from the mild manic libidinal position to depression. We may now consider the 'personifications' to which reference has been made. These appeared first in her dreams but came to be consciously adopted. The two chief were 'the mischievous boy' and 'the critic'. Two secondary but important personifications were 'the little girl' and 'the martyr'. 'The mischievous boy' was pre-adolescent, irresponsible, poked fun at the adults, and was regarded by her 'as representing her own childish self; and end-less play seemed to constitute his sole object in life, as was actually the position in her own case during childhood' (p. 216). He repre-sented also her penis envy and her mildly maniacal behaviour. Opposed to him was 'the critic', 'characteristically represented by a serious, formidable, puritanical and aggressive woman of middle age . . . who uttered public accusations against the dreamer . . . "the critic" was characteristically a figure endowed with maternal authority; and not uncommonly the patient's own actual mother played the part without any disguise' (p. 216–17).

'The little girl' and 'the martyr' played subordinate roles, but it is clear that the 'little girl', who was constantly pictured at the age of five years, antedated 'the mischievous boy' and was a representation of 'herself as she would fain have been in childhood—a natural, but innocent self, to whom no exception could have been taken on the part of the super-ego' (p. 217). Thus 'the little girl' is an earlier or an alternative aspect of her libidinal self as compared with 'the mischievous boy'. 'The martyr' is obviously this same libidinal self under persecution by the super-ego.

Fairbairn's application of these clinical data to the problem of endopsychic structure must have been the beginning of his gradually evolved reformulation. He writes :

The two figures just described were regarded by the patient as fundamentally antagonistic; and it is interesting to note from their descriptions how closely 'the mischievous boy' and 'the critic' correspond to the elements in the psyche described by Freud as 'the id' and 'the super-ego'. It should be added that there occurred dreams in which the 'I' of the dream was herself represented as playing the part of 'the mischievous boy' and there were also frequent teaching dreams, in which the 'I' of the dream always played the part of 'the critic'. Usually, however, the dreaming consciousness played the part of an independent onlooker, whose sympathies were sometimes on the one side, sometimes on the other. The dreams in which these personifications figured thus provided the scenes of a moving drama in which the leading actors played parts corresponding significantly to those ascribed by Freud to the ego, the id and the super-ego in the economy of the human mind (p. 217).

Fairbairn as yet regards these data as supporting Freud's theory of structure, and so indeed in a broad sense they do, but he also begins to be aware that it points towards a more complex formulation. He writes :

The conformity between the three leading actors in this patient's dreams and Freud's tripartite division of the mind must be regarded as providing striking evidence of the practical validity of Freud's scheme. It must be recorded, however, that the dream-figures so far mentioned by no means exhaust the personifications appearing in this patient's dream life (p. 217).

He then cites 'the little girl' and 'the martyr', and though we may now recognize them as roles of what he ultimately designated 'the Libidinal ego', at that date he wrote :

Their validity as personifications seemed in no sense inferior to that of 'the critic' and 'the mischievous boy'. This fact raises the question whether Freud's tripartite division of the mind has not led us to regard the ego, the id and the super-ego too much in the light of entities. . . . It is a question whether any topographical representation whatsoever can hope to do justice to all the complexities of mental structure (p. 218).

What is already evident is that, like Melanie Klein, Fairbairn now saw the mental life of this patient as a veritable 'inner world', a drama of a highly personal nature. We are not confronted with impersonal 'instincts' and 'mental mechanisms' but with 'personi-fications' or 'leading actors' in the scenes of this moving drama, corresponding to Freud's ego, id and super-ego. Fairbairn refers to Freud's term 'the id' but he does not use it himself. Instead he notes

that there occurred dreams in which the 'I' of the dream was herself represented as playing the part of 'the mischievous boy' (p. 217).

In fact he already regards the 'person' represented by the term 'I' as the basic underlying reality who operates in turn or even simul-taneously through the 'personifications' of 'the critic', 'the mis-chievous boy' and the onlooker. He is here envisaging the splitting of the unitary ego by reason of its operating through differing and even antagonistic mental structures. Here is the origin of one-half of his later theory of endopsychic structure, the ego-structures.

Moreover, in tacitly abandoning the id-concept by regarding it as personal, as an ego-structure, he has already set up his concept of 'dynamic structure', which he expresses at this date, 1931, by the term 'Functioning structural units'. He writes:

The data provided by the case under discussion seem to leave no doubt about the existence of functioning structural units correspond-ing to the ego, the id, and the super-ego; but the same data seem equally to indicate the impossibility of regarding these functioning structural units as *mental entities*. After all, the general tendency of modern science is to throw suspicion upon entities; and it was under the influence of this tendency that the old 'faculty psychology' perished. *Perhaps the arrangement of mental phenomena into func-tioning structural groups is the most that can be attempted by psycho-logical science.* [Present writer's italics.] At any rate, it would appear contrary to the spirit of modern science to confer the status of entity upon 'instincts'; and in the light of modern knowledge an instinct seems best regarded as a characteristic dynamic pattern of behaviour. Similar considerations apply to Freud's tripartite division of the mind—which must accordingly be taken to represent a characteristic functional grouping of structural elements in the psyche. That the ego, the id and the super-ego do represent characteristic functioning structural units seems to be indicated by the facts of the case before us; but the facts of the case also indicate the possibility of other functioning structural units arising (p. 218).

The fact that a different and more 'personal' type of thinking than that of Freud's is at work here, is evident from the complete absence of any reference to 'the pleasure principle' in what Fairbairn says about 'the mischievous boy'.

Fairbairn does not regard this point of view as applicable simply to the case in hand, but as representing something that is universally valid in the analysis of the human psyche. After considering the phenomena of multiple personality, he says :

It would also appear that multiple personality is a product of the same processes of differentiation which lead to the isolation of the ego, the id and the super-ego. Evidence of the differentiation of these structures is found so constantly in analytical work that their presence must be regarded, not only as characteristic, but as compatible with normality. It must be recognized, however, that the differentiation of the id and the super-ego from the ego achieves its maximum expression in abnormal individuals; and the question arises how far these structures would be capable of isolation at all in the theoretical case of a completely integrated personality, whose development had proceeded without any hitch (p. 219).

Here, again, is the essence of Fairbairn's later and ultimate view that the human psyche begins as a pristine, personal, unitary ego, and that, contrary to the view of Freud that the ego is a superficial phenomenon differentiated out from the id, the id (or libidinal self) and the super-ego are differentiated out from the primary ego as a result of disturbed development. This paper really laid down the concepts of *dynamic structure, ego-splitting* and the existence of *ego-structures* in a basically *personal psyche*.

A paper on 'Medico-Psychological Aspects of the Problem of Child Assault' (*Mental Hygiene*, No. 13, April 1935) only concerns us in that it presents the orthodox Freudian social psychology of instinct versus repression as the key to culture.

Civilization is a complicated and precarious mechanism for controlling man's various instinctive tendencies—particularly, perhaps, those of sex and aggression (two tendencies which come to simultaneous expression in the act of sexual assault). These instinctive tendencies, if allowed uncontrolled expression, would of course render social life as we understand it quite impossible; and it is only through the operation of inhibition and repression—mental agencies which function as barriers to the natural expression of instinctive impulses—that social redirection of these impulses can possibly occur. Part of the price we have to pay for the advantages of living in a civilized society is our constant exposure to the risk of a break-down of repression, accompanied by a breakthrough of primitive impulses in the case of either social groups or individuals. When such a breakthrough occurs in the case of an individual, society regards him as a criminal; and he becomes a criminal either (a) because character-formation has been so weak and repression so inadequate as to leave the primitive tendencies insufficiently tempered, or (b) because repression has been so excessive as to deny all expression to primitive impulses until they reach a state of explosive tension. (*Op. cit.*, pp. 65–6.)

Fairbairn was by this time, however, approaching the period of Melanie Klein's decisive influence. He came to see that the theory of antisocial instincts was misleading, and failed to explain the excitement and frustration that goes on in a vicious circle in the inner world of internal bad-object relationships.

4. *The 'Kleinian' Period*

From 1934 to 1939 the influence of Melanie Klein became a dominant factor. Fairbairn recalls (in a personal communication) the great impression made on him by her 1934 paper on manic-depressive problems. Her work brought home to him, as it did to many others, the tremendous part played from earliest infancy by aggression, and it also brought to him concepts of internalized objects that matched his already conceived view of the split ego forming distinguishable 'ego-structures'. While this 'inner world' psychology helped the development of his own distinctive point of view, the emphasis on aggression in some respects held him back, since it compelled him to grapple with aggression in the particular form in which Melanie Klein presented it, as an innate, instinctive factor, the death instinct, a view that militated against an 'internal objects' psychology. In every paper between 1934 and 1940 the subject of aggression stands in the forefront. The period begins with two papers written in 1934 and 1936 on 'Communism' (*Brit. J. Med. Psych.*, Vol. XV, Pt. 3, 1935, and *Edin. Med. J.*, Vol. XLIV, p. 433, 1937), both covered by the paper on the subject included in *Psychoanalytic Studies of the Personality* (p. 233). Fairbairn's approach was determined by Freud's 'demonstration of the part played by aggression no less than libido within the economy of the individual mind' (p. 233), and his 'ego-ideal' or 'super-ego' theory according to which 'external social agencies [are] organized into an internal psychical structure' (p. 233). Thus he later states his view that 'all sociological problems are ultimately reducible to problems of individual psychology . . . "group psychology" must be regarded as essentially the psychology of the individual in a *group*' (p. 241). This is not an attempt to undercut 'social psychology' but rather an expression of the fact that *all* psychology is both individual and social. The individual and his objects—i.e. his human environment—are the two inseparable elements in object-relationship.

The paper, 'The Effect of a King's Death Upon Patients Undergoing Analysis' (1936, see 1952a, pp. 223–9) takes the definite step of including the *internal-object structures* of Melanie Klein's theory in addition to the ego-structures of his own 1931 paper. Here for the first time Fairbairn quotes Mrs. Klein directly. The three patients he referred to were all characterized by marked oral sadism and strong tendencies to oral incorporation. Of one of them, Fairbairn writes :

He felt as if a war were being waged inside him and sensed the presence of some antagonistic and dangerous force at work within his body. . . . It was evident that the war inside him was a war between his own oral-sadistic ego and an internalized father-figure, whom he had endowed with oral-sadistic attributes. The King's death represented a consummation of his oral-sadistic designs against his father, whose incorporation became responsible for his sense of a destructive force within. (*Ibid.*, p. 225.)

Of a second patient, who had a dream representing the wholesale destruction of his entire family, Fairbairn writes :

The act of destruction was really an act of oral-sadistic incorporation—an act, moreover, involving mortal danger to the patient himself. The anxiety-symptoms precipitated by the King's death would thus appear to have been mainly due to the dangerous qualities with which the patient had endowed the internalized object. (*Ibid.*, 224.)

He describes the third patient as 'internalizing the libidinal object in order to save the real person from being destroyed by oral-sadistic impulses'. (*Ibid.*, p. 225.) Comparing this with attacks of depression *after* the death of a real person (the patient's brother and also the King), he says :

Perhaps the truth lies in Melanie Klein's statement that every experience which suggests the loss of the real loved object stimulates the dread of losing the internalized object too. (*Ibid.*, p. 229.)

In 1937 he contributed a paper to *The Liverpool Quarterly* (Vol. 5, Jan., No. 1) entitled 'Arms and the Child'. It shows that although the concepts of internal object-relations psychology were becoming his real tools of psychodynamic thinking, Fairbairn was still held back by the earlier tie to instinct theory. He writes :

The ultimate source of war lies in the incorrigible aggression of mankind. The truth is that the hereditary endowment of man includes powerful aggressive instincts which, being hereditary, are for all practical purposes incapable of modification (p. 28).

The study of functional nervous and mental disorders has provided us with evidence to show that the aggressive instincts are profound biological urges which surge up inside human beings and seek expression in destructive behaviour. Worse than that, there is evidence to show that these destructive urges are present in the child from birth (pp. 28–9).

Since the child is born with aggressive instincts which demand expression, the ultimate source of war can never be removed (p. 29).

Knowing his later work, it seems strange to read such words from Fairbairn's pen, words almost identical with those quoted in chapter V from Marie Bonaparte in their Freudian fatalism. The strong emphasis on aggression as an instinctive phenomenon that characterizes Fairbairn at this period shows the influence of Melanie Klein as clearly as does his adoption of 'internal objects' terminology. His writings from 1934–9 show an increasing stress on aggression as the pathogenic factor, and from 1936 in Mrs. Klein's own terms, and Freud's, of an innate, instinctive drive. He only does not adopt the idea of the death instinct. But after 1940 Fairbairn, without losing sight of aggression, began to take up again his own earlier, and Freud's original, emphasis on the primacy of libido.

In 1938, Fairbairn's two papers on Art, though not widely known, must rank as the first of his papers of outstanding originality. They belong, however, to the psychology of aesthetics rather than to psychodynamic theory, and we are only concerned with them in that they show the deepening influence of Melanie Klein. In the first paper, 'Prolegomena to a Psychology of Art' (1938a), he described the super-ego in Kleinian terms, thus : 'The replacement of external by internal objects has been shown by Freud to constitute the essence of super-ego formation' (p. 303). Throughout the paper he uses Mrs. Klein's theory of Restitution to explain creative art. He regards the artist as expressing the deep springs of human emotion, and as drawing therefore on the repressed, deep-level phantasy life of the unconscious.

It is to deal with the anxiety and guilt engendered by destructive phantasies regarding love-objects that repression is originally instituted in childhood; and it is owing to the persistence of such phantasies in the unconscious that it is maintained in adult life. (*Ibid.*, p. 296.)

Art relieves repression by giving symbolic expression to both the libidinal and destructive elements in the unconscious phantasies. He goes on to remark :

No investigator has done more to enlighten us regarding the prevalence and strength of destructive phantasies in the unconscious than Melanie Klein; but Melanie Klein has also shown that these destructive phantasies are characteristically accompanied by compensatory phantasies of restitution. These phantasies of restitution arise as a means of alleviating the guilt and anxiety engendered by destructive phantasies. (*Ibid.*, p. 297.)

Thus the destructive phantasies must be cancelled under super-ego pressure by restitutive phantasies, and the work of art presents in varying degrees the 'broken object' made whole again.

In the second paper, 'The Ultimate Basis of Aesthetic Experience' (1938b), he continues this line of thought, illustrating it by reference to the Surrealist theory that the work of art is a 'found object' which the artist so frames as to bring out the significance he sees in it. This object, however, reveals itself to be also a 'restored object' according to Fairbairn. In over-formalized art, the restitutive drive has eliminated too much of the experience of the destructive drives by over-symbolization. In Surrealist art the opposite tends to be true, the destructive drives break through too nakedly because of under-symbolization, and the needed restitution is not achieved.

'Psychology as a Proscribed and as a Prescribed Subject' was a paper read at St. Andrews University Philosophical Society in 1939, and published in *Psychoanalytic Studies of the Personality* in 1952. It is a discussion of the reasons why psycho-analysis is not taught at Universities. So far as theory is concerned it contains further evidence that, in this period, Fairbairn was very much in the process of digesting Melanie Klein's primary emphasis on aggression, and innate aggression at that, as the pathogenic factor in neurosis. He writes :

In the earlier days of psycho-analysis, when repression of sexual wishes was the phenomenon upon which attention was almost exclusively focussed, it appeared as if it were the presence of repressed sexual tendencies that men sought above all to deny. In the light of further investigation, however, it has become evident that what man seeks to deny more unreservedly is the intensity of his own aggression, and his attempts to deny the extent of his own sexuality is in no small measure due to the association of his sexual tendencies with aggressive attitudes on his part. It would thus appear that the exclusion of psycho-analytical theory from the academic curriculum represents an attempt to keep the veil drawn over a side of human nature which is the occasion, not only of guilt in the individual, but also of a taboo on the part of society. (1952a, pp. 250–1.)

The paper, 'The Psychological Factor in Sexual Delinquency' (*Mental Hygiene*, April, 1939), contains a distinction between the sexual and reproductive (i.e. genital) functions that reminds one of the distinction Fairbairn made earlier between the sensuous and the sexual. There, 'sensuous' concerned appetitive needs in general and sexual stood for genital drives. Here he employs the characteristic Freudian terminology, using 'sexual' as the wider term to include all appetitive and bodily needs and sensuous gratifications, while still separating out the 'genital' by means of the term 'reproductive functions'. He comments : 'It was Freud who first pointed out the real significance of such sexual activities as have no reproductive aim' (p. 2). The real distinction underlying both ways of stating it, is that between 'personal needs' expressed by means of the body in general, and the more narrowly defined sexual or genital needs. This distinction was important for Fairbairn's later views. In this paper he adopted the Kleinian distinction and terminology of 'part-objects' or organs, and 'whole-objects' or persons, and he stresses again the intimate connection between sex and aggression. Finally, he not only employs the Kleinian concept of the 'internal object' but in stressing the repression of the superego he foreshadows his later theory that it is internal objects rather than impulses that are primarily repressed.

Roughly one may say that the 1930s were for Fairbairn a decade of the conflict of old and new ideas, while the 1940s were the creative period of the working out of the object-relations theory of the personality. In the 1950s his attention has been turned more and more to the application of his theoretical views in the field of psychotherapy. It would seem that in 1939 the traditional Freudian instinct-theory fought a last rearguard action in his thinking, in the paper 'Is Aggression an Irreducible Factor?' (*Brit. J. Med.*

Psych., Vol. XVIII, Pt. 2, pp. 163–70, 1939.) It is a clear statement of orthodox Freudian instinct-theory, and reads strangely in the light of the 1931 paper of eight years earlier. He then called for a psychology, not of mental entities of the type of instincts, but of the arrangement of mental phenomena into functioning structural groups; and he regarded 'an instinct' simply as a 'characteristic dynamic pattern of behaviour'. Now, he concluded the 1939 article with the view that mitigating frustrations 'offers no prospects of exercising any influence upon primary aggression, which represents a fundamental and inborn instinctive tendency in human nature' (p. 120). This paper, however, is valuable in that it shows how firmly rooted in Freudian orthodoxy Fairbairn was at first, and how slow and cautious he was in abandoning it under the pressure of new ideas. He seems here to be making a specific effort to cast up accounts with Freud's views on instinct, especially in the form presented by Melanie Klein, stating them as clearly and arguing for them as powerfully as possible.

He compares the instinct theories of McDougall, Drever and Freud, before turning finally to consider the work of Melanie Klein on aggression. For McDougall an instinct is a 'reactive tendency; i.e. a characteristic mode of response to more or less specific situations'. Drever recognized a further group of instincts which he described as 'appetitive tendencies', aiming at the relief of internal biological tensions. Fairbairn observes that in psycho-analytical theory 'no place is found for "reactive tendencies" in the strict sense' (p. 164).

The two groups of instincts recognized in (Freud's) final formulation are (1) the life instincts comprehensively designated as 'the libido', and (2) the death instincts or destructive instincts. . . . In recent years . . . there has been a tendency among psycho-analysts, particularly those of the British school, to regard aggression as the primary psychological manifestation of the death instincts (pp. 164–5).

In 1946 Mrs. Klein expressed the view that Fairbairn 'underrated the role which aggression and hatred play from the beginning of life'. (1952, p. 295.) She could hardly have made that criticism if she had read or remembered this article from 1934–9. Referring to the treatment of aggression as a manifestation of the death instincts, and in plain reference to her work, he wrote:

This view is in part determined by the psychotherapeutic necessities arising out of the consideration that the psychoneuroses and psychoses represent the expression of death-impulses. Nevertheless it finds therapeutic support, not only in the deep analysis of the adult, but also in the analysis of children. Undoubtedly, the most remarkable, if also the most disconcerting, finding of psycho-analysis in recent years is the enormous part played by aggression in infancy and childhood. The disposal of aggression is the chief problem which the child is called upon to face in the course of his emotional development; and it is largely by the direction of aggression inwards that a solution of the problem is attempted. . . . It has thus the effect of obscuring the part played by aggression in human affairs (p. 165).

Fairbairn proceeds to treat aggression, as did Freud and Mrs. Klein, as an innate factor which is on the same footing in all respects as libido. It is regarded by psycho-analysis, not on the pattern of McDougall's 'reactive tendencies' but more on the pattern of Drever's 'appetitive tendencies'. From this point on, however, it begins to be clear that two different principles of explanation are competing in Fairbairn's mind for the right to explain the persistence of aggression in human nature, the principle of innate instinct and the principle of internal object-relations. The issue is not decided in this paper, for he had not yet moved beyond Mrs. Klein's own position, which was to retain both without recognizing any inconsistency.

This problem emerges in the consideration of phantasies, of which he here observes that they are 'phenomena which are left almost entirely out of account by the psychology of the reactive tendencies' (p. 166). That is because they cannot be accounted for as reactions to direct external stimuli, but psycho-analysis accounts for them by reference to internal causes which, for orthodox psycho-analysis, could only mean instincts. They 'represent an exploitation of experiential data for the satisfaction of inner needs . . . and they can only be satisfactorily interpreted as the product of internal tensions created by the pressure of biological drives' (p. 166).

Although at this date Fairbairn was familiar with the Kleinian concepts of internal object-relations, he does not, any more than Melanie Klein herself, yet raise the question of whether they provide an alternative explanation to the problem of 'internal stimulus'. He stated that :

Considered from the psycho-analytical standpoint . . . the instincts are fundamental biological drives or urges. . . . The 'reactive tendencies' described by such psychologists as McDougall are thus simply common patterns in the manifestation of the primary instinctive urges, and not in any sense irreducible instinctive tendencies themselves. . . . What is significant, therefore, is not the pattern of the behaviour itself, but the extent to which the primary instinctive drives are represented in it (pp. 166–7).

He rejected Jung's attempt to reduce aggression to a manifestation of libido and held that 'There is no alternative but to regard aggression as a primary instinctive tendency, and therefore as an irreducible factor in the economy of human nature' (p. 168). This acceptance of aggression and libido as innate drives, mental entities of the same type, existing prior to experience and specific behaviour patterns, is surprising considering that he had repudiated this view in 1931 in favour of what was really the dynamic-structure view of the psyche, with instinct as simply a 'characteristic dynamic pattern of behaviour'. The reason, however, is clear. Melanie Klein had not pursued her work upon internal object-relations to the point of realizing that they represented dynamic structural phenomena which accounted for the persistent internal arousal of aggression as a reaction to persistent internal frustration of all libidinal aims, without calling in the idea of aggression as an innate drive. Nor had Fairbairn yet reached the point of recognizing that, so for the moment he had to fall back on instinct theory. It is probable that there was also a personal reason for this last, and major attempt to come to terms with the orthodox theory. It was common knowledge among Fairbairn's associates that, during the five years or so preceding the writing of this paper, he had become the target of considerable personal hostility in psychological and psychiatric circles in Edinburgh on account of his connection with the psycho-analytical movement. Thus he knew from his own experience what Freud himself had to face. This may well have led him, in a paper read at a meeting of the British Psychological Society held in Scotland, to defend accepted psychoanalytical views of which he was already becoming critical. In due course he was to reach the position that internal tensions are always the tension of object-seeking drives, which does away with the difference between appetitive and reactive tendencies. Innate needs and reaction to libidinal objects are parts of one whole, but aggression can now take a secondary place as simply a reaction to the frustration of libidinal needs, and not a permanent drive or mental entity *per se*. In fact, aggression is intensified self-assertion in face of some danger. When Fairbairn writes, in this paper, that 'as the individual develops, . . . it is found that his thoughts and behaviour continue to be influenced at the unconscious, if not at the conscious, level by phantasies persisting from his early childhood' (p. 166), one can see that sooner or later his earlier critical ideas about instincts and his acceptance of the Kleinian view of the 'inner world' and of 'internal object-relations' would come together to produce a new view of both internal stimulation and of endopsychic structure. The following year, 1940, saw the writing of the first paper that ranks as part of his reformulation of psychoanalytical theory.

CHAPTER XIV

FAIRBAIRN: A COMPLETE 'OBJECT-RELATIONS' THEORY OF THE PERSONALITY

(1) LIBIDO THEORY

WE have seen in Fairbairn's early writings the signs of a particular point of view, implicit in his emphasis on object-relations rather than instincts, and becoming explicit in his development of a concept of endopsychic structure based on ego-splitting as a result of object-relations in infancy. The development of this point of view was hindered by the need to deal with the problem of aggression. He needed Mrs. Klein's concepts of the 'internal object' and the 'inner world' to complete his own concepts of ego-splitting in such a way as to make possible a full theory of endopsychic structure in terms of internal object-relations, i.e. a psychodynamic theory of the personality that would be genuinely 'personal'. The issues, however, were obscured by the fact that aggression was presented, by both Freud and Mrs. Klein, as a problem of instinct, as an innate drive in the same sense as libido. A sharp intellectual conflict must have developed as a result of the struggle to reconcile 'Instinct psychology' and 'Internal-objects psychology', and it was borne in upon him that this was an impossibility. At the same time his attention was more and more arrested by the deep psychopathological significance of schizoid processes. These two factors coinciding in his thought about 1939–40 cleared the ground for an outburst of original and creative thinking. In five papers from 1940 to 1944 (see 1952a, p. 1) he achieved a far-reaching reformulation of the main body of psycho-analytic theory which changes it from a psychobiology based on the instinct-concept, into a truly psychodynamic theory of the development of the personality in and through the medium of personal object-relationships: (1) 'Schizoid Factors in the Personality', 1940, a primarily clinical paper which was unfortunately not published at the time; (2) 'A Revised Psychopathology of the

Psychoses and Psychoneuroses', 1941 (*Int. J. Psych-An.*, Vol. XXII, Pts. 3 and 4); (3) 'The Repression and Return of Bad Objects', 1943 (*Brit. J. Med. Psych.*, Vol. XIX, Pts. 3 and 4); (4) 'The War Neuroses, Their Nature and Significance', 1943, then published, again unfortunately, only in a much abbreviated form in the *British Medical Journal*, 13 Feb., 1943; a clinical paper; (5) 'Endopsychic Structure Considered in Terms of Object-Relationships', 1944 (*Int. J. Psycho-Anal.*, Vol. XXV, Pts. 1 and 2). It was an unhappy circumstance, first that the two clinical papers, which were essential to support the three theoretical ones, were not available to readers, and second that the entire body of material was produced in wartime when there was so much to distract people from calm thought.

The change of theme and atmosphere from the 1938–9 papers to 'Schizoid Factors in the Personality' in 1940 is striking. One is suddenly in a new world of thought and clinical orientation, yet it is one which links with the Fairbairn of 1927–31 whose first paper concerned a patient whose hysterical symptoms masked 'a more profound disturbance of a definitely schizoid nature'. (1952a, p. 183.) Fairbairn explicitly attributes his theoretical reconstruction of this period to the influence of his study of schizoid problems. In 1944 he wrote: 'It is the schizoid position that constitutes the basis of the theory of mental structure which I now advance.' (*Ibid.*, p. 107.) In 1941 he had stated more fully:

Within recent years I have become increasingly interested in the problems presented by patients displaying schizoid tendencies. . . . The result has been the emergence of a point of view which, if it proves to be well-founded, must necessarily have far-reaching implications both for psychiatry in general and for psycho-analysis in particular. My various findings and the conclusions to which they lead involve not only a considerable revision of prevailing ideas regarding the nature and aetiology of schizoid conditions, but also a considerable revision of ideas regarding the prevalence of schizoid processes and a corresponding change in current clinical conceptions of the various psychoneuroses and psychoses. My findings and conclusions also involve a recasting and reorientation of the libido theory, together with a modification of various classical psychoanalytical concepts. (*Ibid.*, p. 28.)

The classic concepts affected were those of instinct, motivation, repression and endopsychic structure, resulting in a psychodynamic theory that parted company with the earlier Freud, but carried to fruition the work of Freud from 1920–6 and the work of Melanie Klein. Of the originality of this achievement, Ernest Jones has written thus:

Dr. Fairbairn's position in the field of psycho-analysis is a special one and one of great interest. . . . Dr. Fairbairn's originality is indisputable. . . . If it were possible to condense Dr. Fairbairn's new ideas into one sentence, it might run somewhat as follows. Instead of starting, as Freud did, from stimulation of the nervous system proceeding from excitation of various erotogenous zones and internal tension arising from gonadic activity, Dr. Fairbairn starts at the centre of the personality, the ego, and depicts its strivings and difficulties in its endeavour to reach an object where it may find support . . . a fresh approach in psycho-analysis. (*Foreword to Fairbairn*, 1952a, p. v.)

With Fairbairn psycho-analysis ceases to be a psychobiology of the organism with an ego-psychology tacked on, and becomes a psychodynamic theory of the person developing and fulfilling himself or being frustrated in his personal object-relationships. It was the schizoid problem that convinced him that this was the true and proper approach to man. It was a patient under treatment in 1939 who brought his latent insights to a head and whom he quoted in 1946. He wrote:

The ultimate principle from which the whole of my special views are derived may be formulated in the general proposition that libido is not primarily pleasure-seeking, but object-seeking. The clinical material on which this proposition is based may be summarized in the protesting cry of a patient to this effect—'You're always talking about my wanting this and that desire satisfied; but what I really want is a father.' It was reflection upon the implications of such phenomena as this that formed the real starting-point of my present line of thought. (*Ibid.*, p. 137.)

The subject of schizoid phenomena itself involved a departure from Melanie Klein, whose main emphases were then on aggression and depression and for whom the fundamental position in psychic development was the depressive position. Fairbairn, having taken meanwhile too complete an account of aggression to be in danger of overlooking its importance, here moves back to the original Freudian emphasis on libido. Mrs. Klein's main interest in oral phenomena lay in the fact of their being to such a remarkable extent *sadistic*, which she explained as due to the death instinct in the end. Fairbairn came to the conclusion that this was a secondary phenomenon, that aggression was a reaction to the frustration of libidinal needs, and his attention was centred on the fact that this sadism was basically *oral* (even when later disguised as anal and genital) and represented not a death instinct but the infant's angry disturbance in the face of deprivation and lack of satisfaction of his need to 'take in' from the mother. Thus he moves back from Freud's later preoccupation with Obsessional Neurosis and Depression to his earlier stress on Hysteria, and beneath that to the schizoid problem of the earliest oral phase.

1. *The Rejection of Biological Psychology*

Fairbairn holds that intellectual disciplines ought to be kept separate and not mixed together in ways that confuse their respective concepts. Let physiology be physiology, and biology be biology, and let psychology be a true psychology and not an attempt to reduce psychic phenomena to some supposed lower denominator thought to be had in common with phenomena of quite different kinds. Psycho-analysis ought to deal with *psycho-dynamic* events, the activities of the personality as such, and its fate in normal or abnormal development of the psychic self. Its basic potentialities and primary needs are given in its biological inheritance and psycho-analysis must take this innate or 'instinctive' factor as its starting-point, and then trace out how the personality as we know it in the child and the adult comes about. Thus Fairbairn's theory is one of the developmental psychogenesis of personality structure in terms of the object-relationships that are the primary causes of internal psychic differentiations. It is an ego-psychology, but the ego is not the superficial, adaptive ego of Freud (or of H. S. Sullivan) formed on the surface of a hypothetical impersonal id as its adjustment to outer reality. Fairbairn's 'ego' is the primary psychic self in its original wholeness, a whole which differentiates into organized structural patterns under the impact of experience of object-relationships after birth. It is not a synthetic whole whose patterns are put together mosaic-wise by the integration of separate and at first unrelated ego-nuclei. He writes :

(1) The pristine personality of the child consists of a unitary dynamic ego.
(2) The first defence adopted by the original ego to deal with an unsatisfying personal relationship is mental internalization, or introjection, of the unsatisfying object. (1954, p. 107.)

From that starting-point the original unitary psyche goes on developing in complex ways, and in varying degrees loses its unitary nature. It undergoes processes of ego-splitting in which its conflicts take on a relatively permanent, internal, structural form. But Fairbairn does not regard his ego-structures, or Melanie Klein's 'object-structures', as drawing their energy from some separate and unorganized source. Every part of the complex, total structural pattern of the personality is a developed aspect of the original 'unitary dynamic ego', and is endowed with its own inherent energy. Structure and energy do not represent the ego *versus* psychobiological instinct; they are simply distinguishable but not separable aspects of the active and organized psychic self.

Fairbairn's criticism of Freud's instinct-theory arises over this fundamental issue. He writes:

I had already become very much impressed by the limitations of 'impulse psychology' in general, and somewhat sceptical of the explanatory value of all theories of instinct in which the instincts are treated as existing *per se*. . . . 'Impulses' cannot be considered apart from the endopsychic structures which they energize and the object-relationships which they enable these structures to establish; and, equally, 'instincts' cannot profitably be considered as anything more than forms of energy which constitute the dynamic of such endopsychic structures. (1952a, pp. 84-5.)

If 'impulses' cannot be considered apart from objects, whether external or internal, it is equally impossible to consider them apart from ego-structures. . . . 'Impulses' are but the dynamic aspects of endopsychic structures, and cannot be said to exist in the absence of such structures. . . . Ultimately, 'impulses' must be simply regarded as constituting the forms of activity in which the life of ego-structures consists. (*Op. cit.*, p. 88.)

Thus ten years before the work of Colby, Fairbairn discards Freud's divorce of energy and structure, involved in differentiating between an id as the source of instinctive energies and an ego as the organized structure of controls. He proposes instead a theory of *dynamic structure* in which energy and structure are not treated as separate factors, but 'instincts' are the 'forms of energy', and ' impulses' are the 'forms of activity' which 'constitute the dynamic of endopsychic structures'. This theory avoids the now outmoded 'atomistic' type of theory. He writes:

The conception of erotogenic zones is based upon an atomic or molecular conception of the organism—the conception that the organism is initially a conglomeration of separate entities, which can only become related and integrated as a result of a process of development. Within the functional sphere, a corresponding atomism has given rise to a tendency to describe dynamic processes in terms of isolated impulses and isolated instincts. It has led to the common practice of hypostatizing 'libido' by endowing it with the definite article, and describing it as '*the* libido'. . . . Such atomism seems to me a legacy of the past quite alien to modern biological conceptions, in accordance with which the organism is regarded as functioning as a whole from the start. (*Op. cit.*, pp. 138-9.)

After noting that Freud's divorce of energy and structure arose out of his Helmholtzian atomistic physics, he adds:

So far as psycho-analysis is concerned, one of the unfortunate results of the divorce of energy from structure is that, in its dynamic aspects, psycho-analytical theory has been unduly permeated by conceptions of hypothetical 'impulses' and 'instincts' which bombard passive structures. . . . From the standpoint of dynamic structure, 'instinct' is *not the stimulus* to psychic activity, but itself consists in characteristic activity on the part of a psychical structure. Similarly 'impulse' is not, so to speak, a kick in the pants administered out of the blue to a surprised, and perhaps somewhat pained, ego, but a psychical structure in action—a psychical structure doing something to something or somebody. (*Op. cit.*, p. 150.)

Thus Fairbairn envisages

A replacement of the outmoded impulse psychology, which, once adopted, Freud had never seen fit to abandon, by a new psychology of dynamic structure,

in which instincts as mental entities are discarded and

the instinctive endowment of mankind only assumes the form of general trends which require experience to enable them to acquire a more differentiated and rigid pattern. (*Op. cit.*, p. 157.)

Nor are the differentiated dynamic structures to be hypostatized either. He refers to

The impossibility of regarding these functioning structural units as *mental entities*. After all, the general tendency of modern science is to throw suspicion upon entities; and it was under the influence of this tendency that the old 'faculty psychology' perished. *Perhaps the arrangement of mental phenomena into functioning structural groups is the most that can be attempted by psychological science.* [Present writer's italics.] At any rate, it would appear contrary to the spirit of modern science, to confer the status of entity upon 'instincts'; and in the light of modern knowledge an instinct seems best regarded as a characteristic dynamic pattern of behaviour. (*Op. cit.*, p. 218.)

The concepts of modern physics may still provide us with a starting-point in the hypothesis that reality as we experience and perceive it consists, not of particles of immutable matter operated on by a separate energy, but of *events* the material, spatial and temporal nature of which for our perception are relative to our position and motion as observers. In the 'event' structure and energy appear not as separate 'things' but as logically distinguishable aspects of one whole which is at once organized and active, a happening rather than a thing. This may be set forth in terms of 'processes' but either way it forms a much more helpful starting-point for psychology, provided we make the initial distinction between impersonal events or processes and personal events or processes. The distinction is a fact of observation and is the datum from which we start.

2. *The Schizoid Problem and Object-Relations*

As we have seen, it was schizoid problems that finally forced Fairbairn to abandon physiological and biological psychology in favour of a personal and structural theory of a whole ego divided by its relationships with internal objects. Schizoid problems forced themselves on his notice, not as problems of the control of instincts but as pre-eminently problems of the need for good-object relationships, and of the desperate struggle to achieve good-object relationships in the face of acute internal difficulties. *Schizoid Factors in the Personality*, 1940 (1952, pp. 3–27), is a clinical study of great importance. He shows the essential characteristics of the schizoid condition to consist *structurally* in an early splitting of the ego, *aetiologically* in a reaction of intense oral sadistic libidinal need in the face of deprivation of mother-love, *dynamically and emotionally* in a refusal to risk libidinal object-relations in the outer world because of the terrifying dangers felt to be involved in loving and seeking love, and hence a radical introversion of libido to the inner world.

The tragic dilemma of the schizoid person is that his specially intense need of a good love-object is matched by an equally great fear of object-relationship, so that his love-hunger is hidden from the outer world beneath his mask of detachment, aloofness and emotional apathy. His libidinal object-relationships become confined to his inner world and his dealings with his internalized objects. Whereas the depressed person is afraid of harming and destroying his love-objects by his hate—i.e. the problem that arises in the late oral biting stage—the schizoid person is afraid of harming and destroying his love-objects by his love, the deeper problem of the early sucking stage, the earliest stage of all.

To suck at the mother's breast is 'the individual's first way of expressing love' (1952, p. 24), and the effect of deprivation is to impart 'an aggressive quality to his libidinal need' (p. 24). Intense anxiety arises about the danger of sucking out, emptying and destroying the breast and then the mother herself. The patient referred to on p. 37 expressed this in a general way by saying, 'I can't make moderate demands on anyone so I don't make any at all.' She would long all day for her husband to come home and as soon as she heard him enter she would lose all feeling and desire for him, but feel hungry for food instead as a symbolic substitute. She would then get a meal and the moment she sat down to eat her appetite would vanish, so much so that severe anorexia developed. At the same time, however, she would dream of enormous meals that never ended. Clearly, she felt that her needs for love just had not to be expressed in action either directly or symbolically. Fairbairn writes of the schizoid person : 'He keeps his love shut in because he feels that it is too dangerous to release upon his objects' (p. 26). As a substitute he sometimes 'becomes subject to a compulsion to hate and be hated, while all the time he longs deep down to love and be loved' (p. 26). The schizoid person is afraid to want, seek, take from or give to objects in outer reality. If he gives, he feels he will empty himself and his gift will prove harmful; if he takes, he fears he will empty his love-object; so he cannot risk any kind of libidinal object-relation in his outer life. His libidinal need can only flow inwards into the cathexis of internal objects in his inner world, where he lives in terror, in relationships which are all of a consuming and devouring kind.

Fairbairn regards the schizoid position as the fundamental position in the development of the emotional life of the psyche, antedating Mrs. Klein's depressive position. The problem concerns so basically the need for good-object relationships at the very start of life, that he was constrained to revise the orthodox libido theory of ego-development on the basis of object-relations rather than on the basis of erotogenic zones, and phases of instinct maturation. He is close to the Kleinian point of view in stressing the primary unity of the ego, and in carrying object-relations back to the very start of post-natal life, though he has expressed these principles more explicitly in the context of a coherent theory. On the other hand, Melanie Klein's emphasis on the inner world is generally felt to carry with it an under-emphasis on environmental factors which, in her view, play a very secondary role in comparison with endopsychic processes. Fairbairn, however, is quite

explicit in viewing the causal starting-point of disturbed developments as definitely environmental, while all through childhood
growth the outer and the inner world are seen by him as interacting in the closest possible way, each being accorded its full
reality and influence.

Thus there emerges from his writing what one may call a major
aetiological formulation which he repeats and stresses again and
again : one which was not in any comparable fashion so clearly
stated and recognized by other analytical writers. Disturbed
development results when the mother does not succeed in making
the child feel she loves him for his own sake and as a person in his
own right. This, he holds, is at the bottom of all psychopathological processes. Limitations in the mother's personality and her
emotional conflicts, amounting in some cases to open rejection and
hate of the baby, though more often to unconscious and over-
compensated rejection, influence her handling of it to all degrees
of traumatic seriousness. The tone of voice, the kind of touch, the
quality of attention and interest, the amount of notice, and the
total emotional as well as physical adequacy of breast feeding, are
all expressions of the genuineness or otherwise of the mother's personal relationship to the infant. From the moment of birth Fairbairn regards the mother-infant relationship as potentially fully
personal on both sides, in however primitive and undeveloped a
way this is as yet felt by the baby. It is the breakdown of genuinely
personal relations between the mother and the infant that is the
basic cause of trouble. That is the factor that dominates all other
and more detailed, particular issues such as oral deprivation, anal
frustration, genital disapproval, negative and over-critical discipline and so on.

This is a more radically personal formulation than Melanie
Klein's oral frustration viewed as activating sadistic instincts, for
the mother who is orally frustrating is usually the one who cannot
really love her baby. Melanie Klein's way of seeing the problem
led her to recognize the facts concerning the internalizing of bad
objects and the creation of 'persecutory anxiety' at this earliest age.
Fairbairn's way of seeing the facts led him to grasp the total fundamental personal relationship problem as revealed in *the schizoid
position* with its catastrophic threat to the possibility of sustaining
any object-relations at all. He is here consciously indebted to Mrs.
Klein for her valuable theory of the depressive position which
points the way to his own further theory of the schizoid position.
These concepts worked out by Mrs. Klein and Fairbairn of fundamental, internal, structural psychic positions, which, once formed,

are operative in every subsequent stage as determinative of personality type, are more basic than Freud's theory of the Oedipus complex which rather concerns detailed psychic content by means of which basic emotional positions can be expressed. We present Fairbairn's view in his own words:

the tendency of those with schizoid characteristics [is] to treat libidinal objects as means of satisfying their own requirements rather than as persons possessing inherent value; and this is a tendency which springs from the persistence of an early orientation towards the breast as a partial object. Here it may be remarked that the orientation towards partial objects found in individuals displaying schizoid features is largely a regressive phenomenon determined by unsatisfactory emotional relationships with their parents, and particularly their mothers, at a stage in childhood subsequent to the early oral stage in which this orientation originates. The type of mother who is specially prone to provoke such a regression is the mother who fails to convince her child by spontaneous and genuine expressions of affection that she herself loves him as a person. Both possessive mothers and indifferent mothers fall under this category. Worst of all perhaps is the mother who conveys the impression of both possessiveness and indifference—e.g. the devoted mother who is determined at all costs not to spoil her only son. Failure on the part of the mother to convince the child that she really loves him as a person renders it difficult for him to sustain an emotional relationship with her on a personal basis; and the result is that in order to simplify the situation, he tends regressively to restore the relationship to its earlier and simpler form and revive his relationship to his mother's breast as a partial object. (1952a, p. 13.)

The failure of a mother, who would not by observers have been regarded as a bad mother in any gross or obvious sense, to give a properly personal love-relationship to a daughter is evident in the case of a mother who used at times to say to her younger daughter: 'You don't know how ill I was when I was having you, but I made up my mind that it was my duty to go through with it, to give your sister a companion.' The patient felt she had never been wanted for her own sake, and in fact was always treated in subtle ways as if she were there for the family's convenience. These subtle attitudes of rejection on the mother's part which are interwoven with all that goes on, form the commonest serious traumatic factor. Winnicott puts this very clearly when he pinpoints erratic mothering as the bad-object situation *par excellence,* and describes psychosis as an environmental deficiency disease. (1958, p. 246.)

He writes: 'Psychotic illness is related to environmental failure at an early stage of the emotional development of the individual.' (1958, p. 286.) In his review of Fairbairn's book he wrote:

Fairbairn's most valuable contribution is the idea that at the root of the schizoid personality is this failure on the part of the mother to be felt by the infant as loving him in his own right as a person. (1953, p. 331.)

Some mothers fail to satisfy the infant at the breast. But even with mothers who were able to offer the baby a good breast, it not seldom happens that the mother is unable later to offer him a good personality which would enable him steadily to achieve a growing capacity for object-relationship on a genuinely personal level. In some cases this may be due to the fact that the mother is disturbed by the father. The resulting chronic frustration of all the infant's expanding needs as a rapidly developing 'person', needs not only for tenderness and appropriate, sufficient bodily contact but more and more for interest, understanding, supporting encouragement for self-expression, proofs given of his being valued and wanted for himself—the frustration of these needs drives him back into a regressive reinstatement of the early oral sucking attitude, and even of the original feeling of identification; but now intensified by deprivation into an angry hunger to devour. The schizoid problem is thus set up, for the anxiety felt over this fundamentally greedy, consuming, destructive way of feeling basic needs, as a craving to incorporate and possess utterly the whole of one's love-object, turns into a fear of loving and a withdrawal from effective emotional relationship with the outer world. Dealings with the outer world at best are carried on in an automatic way with no real feeling put into anything, a far commoner condition than true depression, and found, as Fairbairn holds, in all people with recognizable tendencies to introversion in varying degrees.

Thus, whatever Fairbairn has to say about endopsychic structure and internal object-relations, in furtherance of the work begun by Melanie Klein, he keeps it all in close touch with the external facts of the child's real-life object-relations as the true causes of disturbed development of personality. One does not so much get the impression one receives from Kleinian writings, of a purely endopsychic process going its own way, and merely helped on by outer events which are interpreted, ultimately, in the light of an innate conflict of libido and the death instinct.

3. *Theory of Motivation and Developmental Phases*

Fairbairn presents the above aetiological formulation as a revised theory of motivation when he writes : 'The ultimate goal of libido is the object', and works out 'a theory of development based essentially on object-relationships'. (1952a, p. 31.) Schizoid problems were decisive in bringing to a definite focus Fairbairn's implicit emphasis on and interest in object-relations because the schizoid person's major internal frustration is an inhibition by acute anxiety of the power to love. The more the need to love is frustrated, the more intense does it become and the unhappy person oscillates between an overpowering need to find good objects and a compulsive flight into detachment from all objects, under pressure mainly of the terror of exploiting them to the point of destruction ; for the destruction of the love-object feels then to involve also the loss of the helplessly dependent ego which is in a state of emotional identification with the object. Love-object relationships are the whole of the problem, and the conflicts over them are an intense and devastating drama of need, fear, anger and hopelessness. To attempt to account for this by a hedonistic theory of motivation, namely that the person is seeking the satisfactions of oral, anal and genital pleasure, is so impersonal and inadequate that it takes on the aspect of being itself a product of schizoid thinking. One of my patients dreamed that she was physically grafted on to a man who represented to her a good father-figure (on to whom was displaced an original umbilical relation to the mother). She would say that whenever anyone important to her went away, she felt the bottom had dropped out of her own self, and her emotional history was a long series of infatuations with older men who stood to her *in loco parentis*. She had grown up quite specially love-starved in an affectionless home. To try to reduce such problems to a quest for the pleasure of physical and emotional de-tensioning of sexual needs is a travesty of the personal realities of human life. As Fairbairn's patient protested : 'What I want is a father.' So Fairbairn concluded that 'the ultimate goal of libido is the object'.

The orthodox libido theory developed by Abraham on the basis of Freud's work was one of development through successive stages determined by so-called erotogenic zones—oral, anal and genital—which became active in succession as a result of biological maturation. At each stage the infant was said to be motivated by the quest for pleasure, the pleasure of oral, anal or genital detensioning. Philosophers have often exposed the fallacy of hedonism or the pleasure motive. When pleasure is primarily sought and directly aimed at, it is not found, for pleasure is not a 'thing-in-itself'. It is the affective tone of a satisfying experience with an object, the sign that a good relationship with the object has been achieved, the accompaniment of getting something other than itself. The object is what is directly sought. In practice the life of the pleasure-seeker always ends in disillusionment, for pleasure, treated as itself the aim, is a will o' the wisp which eludes one's grasp in the absence of a worthwhile object. If one finds pleasure in a good book, beautiful landscape or satisfying companion, one's attention is centred on the book, the landscape or the companion. If one switches attention away from the object to the pleasure of the object-relationship experience, the object is lost sight of, the experience of a satisfying object-relationship is lost and the pleasure soon evaporates. Those who seek pleasure only find the unpleasurable kind of excitement of the continuing tension of a never satisfied quest.

Translating the above insight into terms of psychodynamic theory, Fairbairn regards the aim of libido as not pleasure but the object. His revision of theory starts with this basic assumption, and he writes :

It must be recognized, however, that in the first instance erotogenic zones are simply channels through which libido flows, and that a zone only becomes erotogenic when libido flows through it. *The ultimate goal of libido is the object.* (1952a, p. 31.)

It follows from this in principle, though it is also evident from observation of human living, that pleasure-seeking is a deteriorated form of behaviour that arises out of the breakdown of good-object relationships and despair of their possibility. He says :

Explicit pleasure-seeking represents a deterioration of behaviour. . . . Explicit pleasure-seeking has as its essential aim the relieving of the tension of libidinal need for the mere sake of relieving this tension. Such a process does, of course, occur commonly enough; but, since libidinal need is object-need, simple tension-relieving implies some failure of object-relationships. The fact is that simple tension-relieving is really a safety-valve process. It is thus, not a means of achieving libidinal aims, but a means of mitigating the failure of these aims (pp. 139–40).

Freud's impersonal 'pleasure-principle' treated the object as a mere means to the end of a purely subjective and impersonal tension-relieving 'process' and not as sought for its intrinsic value in a relationship. That is something which can be represented only by 'personal theory'.

From this point of view Fairbairn subordinates the pleasure-principle to the reality-principle, which is now seen to be the object-relationships principle; whereas Freud regards the reality-principle simply as a delayed pleasure-principle. He regards Freud's pleasure-principle as an immature, infantile reality-principle in the first place, operating at a time when the baby's appreciation of reality is as yet elementary and defective. Yet so far as it goes it is a reality-principle quite as much as that which guides the adult's cautious balancing of pros and cons; for to the infant at first reality is the breast which answers to his needs. What he seeks is the breast, and pleasure is his enjoyment of it, the effective accompaniment of a successful application of the reality-principle in object-relations. That is the meaning of pleasure in dealing with the object-world whether in infancy or adult life. Of the reality-principle, Fairbairn writes:

If, however, libido is primarily object-seeking, it follows that be-haviour must be oriented towards outer reality, and thus determined by a reality-principle from the first. . . . What the child lacks above all is experience of reality; and it is this, rather than any lack of orientation towards reality, that gives the adult observer the im-pression that the child's behaviour is primarily determined by a pleasure-principle. It must be recognized, of course, that with the child's inexperience goes a tendency to be more emotional and im-pulsive, i.e. less controlled, than the adult; and this, combined with the amount of frustration which he encounters, leads him to be more prone than the adult to resort to tension-relieving behaviour. In my opinion, however, it is erroneous to conclude that his be-haviour is primarily determined by a pleasure-principle which has later to be replaced by a reality-principle. No such distinction be-tween principles of behaviour can be drawn in the case of animals. . . . Characteristically the child's sense of reality is of low degree compared with that of the adult; but he is none the less actuated by a reality sense from the beginning, even if he is all too liable, in face of frustration, to stray into tension-relieving side-tracks (pp. 140–1).

It is only in so far as conditions of adaptation become too difficult for the child that the reality-principle gives place to the pleasure-principle as a secondary and deteriorative (as against regressive) principle of behaviour calculated to relieve tension and provide compensatory satisfaction (p. 157).

Concerning erotogenic zones Fairbairn writes:

The conception of fundamental erotogenic zones constitutes an unsatisfactory basis for any theory of libidinal development because it is based on a failure to recognize that the function of libidinal pleasure is essentially to provide a signpost to the object. According to the conception of erotogenic zones the object is regarded as a signpost to libidinal pleasure; and the cart is thus placed before the horse. Such a reversal of the real position must be attributed to the fact that in the earlier stages of psycho-analytical thought, the paramount importance of the object-relationship had not yet been sufficiently recognized. (1952a, p. 33.)

An erotogenic zone does not originate libido as such, in Fairbairn's view: it is a channel through which libido flows to the object. Libido is the primary object-seeking life-drive, and an erotogenic zone is any part of the body that is being used, i.e. libidinized, for the time being as a means to object-relationship, but the 'ultimate goal of libido is the object'. Just because zones are made erotogenic by being used for object-relationship, they can just as well be de-eroticized, when the personality refuses so to use them. Furthermore, organs, areas and the whole body can as well be used to provide a channel for aggression as for libido, and then they become either unusable for good-object relationships (i.e. the mouth in anorexia, the genitals in impotence and frigidity, the hand or foot in hysterical paralysis, and so on), or else usable only for sadistic object-relationships. He regards concentration on an 'erotogenic zone' as a conversion hysteria symptom (1954). What is important is not the channel but the nature of the personal emotional attitude, libidinal, sadistic, merely destructive or inhibited. Thus Fairbairn revised the classic theory of libidinal development, basing it not on erotogenic zones and biological considerations, but on the changing, over-all libidinal attitudes, infantile, transitional and mature, of the ego to its objects, i.e. upon the quality of dependence (of the ego) upon the object. (1952, p. 34.) Biological maturation places organs and functions at the disposal of the developing 'person' for his use in conducting the main business of his existence, the sustaining of relationships with the people around him. How he uses those biological functions will depend on how far he is being helped by those with whom he has to deal, to develop a satisfactory, non-anxious, loving and self-confident personality of his own and so to grow out of his original infantile dependence on the mother.

Libidinal development is the process whereby the infantile psyche becomes, through various stages of growth, a sufficiently mature 'person' to be capable of sustaining adult and non-neurotic personal relationships in which also he can find self-fulfilment allowing for the fact that maturity is never more than relative, and 'normal' persons all have some neurotic traits. The beginning and end of the process is thus given by definition : the starting-point of infantile dependence and the goal of maturity, or mature dependence. *Infantile dependence*, Fairbairn holds, is characterized by a persistence of both *primary identification* (the emotional state of the infant in the womb) and the *oral incorporative or 'taking in' attitudes* (contributed by breast-feeding) as the infant's chief means of object-relationship after birth. It is an object-relationship stage in which the mouth is the main and natural libidinal organ and the maternal breast the libidinal object. The infant is not immature because he is oral; he can as yet be no more than oral because he is immature, and at first capable only of taking without giving.

Mature dependence is characterized by full differentiation of ego and object (emergence from primary identification) and therewith a capacity for valuing the object for its own sake and for giving as well as receiving; a condition which should be described not as independence but as mature dependence. It is therefore expressed physically by a capacity for truly genital relationships which represent the co-operative mutuality and giving of two equal partners. Thus the adult is not mature because genital, but is capable of proper genital relationships because mature. (Neurotic genitality, which is compulsive, expresses oral sadistic rather than truly genital attitudes.) Fairbairn says : 'The development of object-relationships is essentially a process whereby infantile dependence upon the object gradually gives place to mature dependence.' What this involves he further describes :

This process of development is characterized (*a*) by the gradual abandonment of an original object-relationship based upon primary identification, and (*b*) by the gradual adoption of an object-relationship based upon differentiation of the object. The gradual change which thus occurs in the nature of the object-relationship is accompanied by a gradual change in libidinal aim, whereby an original oral, sucking, incorporating and predominantly 'taking' aim comes to be replaced by a mature, non-incorporating and predominantly 'giving' aim compatible with developed genital sexuality. (1952, pp. 34-5.)

In between the earliest, infantile dependent (oral) stage and the final, mature (including genital) stage, there is *a transitional stage* during which all the problems of achieving this development are encountered. It is a stage in which all neurotics, and in varying degrees most people, have remained to some extent arrested in their development. Fairbairn writes :

The relationship involved in mature dependence is, of course, only theoretically possible. Nevertheless, it remains true that *the more mature a relationship is, the less it is characterized by primary identification*; for what such identification essentially represents is failure to differentiate the object. It is when identification persists at the expense of differentiation that a markedly compulsive element enters into the individual's attitude towards his objects. This is well seen in the infatuations of schizoid individuals. (1952a, p. 42.)

The transitional stage is much characterized by the use of anal symbolism and techniques for representing and dealing with internalized objects, mentally incorporated in the oral stage, with which the ego is still in various ways identified. But the anus is only an artificial, not a natural, libidinal organ, just as faeces is only a symbolic, not a real, libidinal object. Usually anal functioning is endowed with emotional significance because the mother forces it into the centre of her relationship with the child. Since the transitional stage consists of the struggle to outgrow infantile dependence on the mother primarily, it oscillates between rejection and retention of objects, both processes being easily symbolized anally. The way in which defecation can acquire this significance is clear in the case of a small boy who could defecate only if his mother was kneeling in front of him and he could clasp his hands round her neck. If he felt likely to pass a motion when his mother was not there to hold on to, he would jump up screaming, 'It won't come.' Fairbairn rejects the idea of a biological anal phase, and regards anal phenomena as simply dramatizations of conflicts concerning internalized objects in the transitional stage.

The *psychoses* represent fixation in, or rather regression to, infantile dependence, characterized by the oral sucking and biting stages, and in the absence of later ego-defences : they constitute the basic psychic dangers. The *psychoneuroses* (phobic, hysteric, obsessional and, for this purpose, paranoid reactions) are defensive techniques adopted in the transitional stage for dealing with the internal bad objects incorporated in the earlier oral phases, in relation to which the ego may suffer the catastrophe of a schizoid or depressed state of mind.

It is no exaggeration to say that *the whole course of libidinal development depends on the extent to which objects are incorporated and the nature of the techniques which are employed to deal with incorporated objects.* (1952a, p. 34.)

This theory of the way in which human beings develop from birth to maturity strikes one as eminently realistic and comprehensible by comparison with the classic theory. That character and personality should be shaped by the kind of personal relationships the child finds it possible to have with parents, as it struggles to grow out of its original totally dependent state towards an adult personality, capable of both self-reliance and good relations with other people, impresses one as self-evident once stated. Likewise it seems equally self-evident when we are studying human beings as 'persons' and not just as biological organisms, that what we do at each developmental stage with bodily organs such as the mouth, anus and genital is determined by the quality of our personality and personal relations at each stage, rather than vice-versa. The working out of this phasic development in detail, in terms of relationships with internal as well as external objects (i.e. in a theory first of libidinal development and second of endopsychic structure), does not involve anything new in principle but is forced on us by Mrs. Klein's discoveries about the nature of the mental constitution as it grows. It simply carries deeper into the unconscious, hidden structure of the psyche, the principle that personality is formed in the matrix of personal relationships. Fairbairn's theory is closer to the actualities of life than the classic theory.

About the theoretical goal of mature dependence there can be little difference of opinion. Maturity is not equated with independence though it includes a certain capacity for independence. The nature of this is best appreciated by reference to emotional identification which so involves the infantilely dependent person with other people's fates that he rises and falls with his love-object; and cannot disentangle himself from his infatuation so as to remain stable by his own inner strength, which has not developed. But the independence of the mature person is simply that he does not collapse when he has to stand alone. It is not an independence of needs for other persons with whom to have relationship: that would not be desired by the mature. The importance of this scheme lies in the light it throws on the difficulties of arriving at maturity through earlier stages, i.e. on the various ways in which the process of development can be arrested and distorted. These give rise to the psychotic conditions which are held to have their psychological roots in the earliest, oral phase of infantile dependence, and to the psychoneuroses which are transitional-phase phenomena arising as defences against the dangers of relapse into the orally conditioned states. Melanie Klein and Fairbairn agree in broad principle here, whatever differences exist in detail.

4. *Theory of Psychoneurosis*

Though Mrs. Klein's work came to involve the view that psychoneuroses are defences against psychoses, she did not attempt to revise Abraham's theory, which treated the various psychoses and psychoneuroses as due to fixations at the oral, anal and phallic phases, culminating in hysteria as a phallic fixation. It is now recognized, however, that hysteria cannot be the latest psychoneurotic development, for it yields clearer evidence of oral fixation than the other neuroses. Fairbairn wrote in 1941 : 'I have yet to analyse the hysteric, male or female, who does not turn out to be an inveterate breast-seeker at heart.' (1952a, p. 124.) Referring, in 1954, to an hysteric whose mother 'combined in a big way the roles of exciting and rejecting object for her', he found in this type of mother-infant relation 'the explanation of the fact that the libidinal ego of the hysteric is found to contain so powerful an oral component'. (1954, p. 113.) He regards the so-called phallic phase as an artifact like the anal phase. Whereas in anal phenomena the child's faeces have been used to symbolize its libidinal object, in the phallic phenomena of hysteria the penis has been used to symbolize the breast (with the vagina taking on the role of a mouth). Hence genitality is rejected and then discovered to be operative under repression in such a state as to justify Fairbairn's further comment : 'whereas the sexuality of the hysteric is at bottom extremely oral, his (or her) basic orality is, so to speak, extremely genital.' (1954, p. 114.)

In accordance with the point of view here adopted, paranoia and the obsessional neurosis are not to be regarded as expressions of a fixation at the earlier and later anal phases respectively. On the contrary, they are to be regarded as states resulting from the employment of special defensive techniques which derive their pattern from rejective excretory processes. (1952a, p. 36.)

The paranoid technique is simply to reject outright, to eject or project. The obsessional technique is more developed, since it treats excretion not simply as the rejection of an object regarded as bad, a persecutor, but also as parting with an object that is regarded as contents that can be given but also lost, so setting up a need to control the object and obtain mastery over it. The internalized object may be regarded as bad, but, whereas the paranoid treats it as externalized, the obsessional retains it within and seeks to master it. By comparison with these techniques the phobic reaction, like the paranoid, is to externalize the object, to treat it as existing in the outer world, but not in order to direct hostility towards it but rather to fly from it. The hysteric, like the obsessional, on the other hand treats the bad object as internal, but does not seek to master it; rather, like the paranoid he rejects it, which he does by means of repression or dissociation. Since the object is identified with the genital organ, this leads to a rejection of the genitals and so to hysteric impotence or frigidity.

The full distinction between these techniques emerges when their reaction to the potentially good object is taken also into account. Ambivalence arises as a result of the splitting of the image of the object into two, corresponding to its partly satisfying and partly unsatisfying aspects. The bad object is rejected and the good object accepted. Fairbairn thus regards these four transitional defensive techniques as involving both the accepted and the rejected object, in the following manner. The obsessional retains and seeks to master both as internal objects, the phobic treats both as externalized and seeks to fly from the bad object and take refuge with the good one. The paranoid externalizes the bad object to hate and attack it, but accepts the good object as internalized and remains identified with it, thus becoming convinced that he is perfectly in the right. The hysteric does the opposite; he externalizes and clings to the good object in his outer world, while internalizing and rejecting his bad object in his inner world. These techniques do not arise at fixation points, but are usable interchangeably throughout the transitional period.

Fairbairn's views about internalization differ somewhat from those of Mrs. Klein, and have also undergone a development in one particular. Mrs. Klein regards the infant as internalizing both good and bad objects from the beginning, because it is by nature incorporative, mentally as well as physically. Kleinians hold that only the internalization of good objects from the start enables the infant to achieve good ego-development. Fairbairn at first held that only the bad object was originally internalized in an attempt to gain mastery over it because as an external object it could not be mastered. He saw no reason for the original internalization of the good object. It is satisfying in real life and good ego-development results from good object-relations. He writes:

In my opinion, it is always the 'bad' object (i.e. at this stage the unsatisfying object) that is internalized in the first instance; for I find it difficult to attach any meaning to the primary internalization of a 'good' object which is both satisfying and amenable from the infant's point of view. There are those, of course, who would argue that it would be natural for the infant, when in a state of deprivation, to internalize the good object on the wish-fulfilment principle;

but, as it seems to me, internalization of objects is essentially a measure of coercion and it is not the satisfying object, but the unsatisfying object, that the infant seeks to coerce. (1952a, pp. 110–11.)

In 1951 he introduced a modification in one particular. He now regarded the original internalization as appertaining not simply to the bad object, since in the pre-ambivalent early oral stage the bad and good objects have not yet been separated in the infant mind. Rather, it must be the pre-ambivalent object that is at first internalized, for the reason that, while it is in some measure satisfying, it is also in some measure unsatisfying, which creates the need to internalize it in an attempt to make it more satisfactory, i.e. to deal with the problem 'in the mind' because it cannot be dealt with in outer reality. Only after internalization is it split into a good object and a bad object in the inner phantasy world, and therewith ambivalence arises. The good object is then desired, while the bad object is hated and rejected. The stage is now set for the manipulation of these internal objects by the psycho-neurotic techniques of the transitional period. The internal objects are, for both Mrs. Klein and Fairbairn, creations of the oral period. Fairbairn writes :

From the phobic point of view the conflict (of the transitional period) presents itself as one between flight from and return to the object. From the obsessional point of view, on the other hand, the conflict presents itself as one between expulsion and retention of the object. (1952a, p. 44.)

He regards the phobic technique, therefore, as predominantly passive and masochistic, while the obsessional technique is predominantly active and sadistic. Further :

In the hysterical state . . . the conflict appears to be formulated as simply one between acceptance and rejection of the object. Acceptance of the object is clearly manifested in the intense love relationships which are so typical of the hysteric; but the very exaggeration of these emotional relationships in itself raises a suspicion that a rejection is being over-compensated. This suspicion is confirmed by the propensity of the hysteric to dissociative phenomena. . . . If the paranoid and the hysterical states are now compared, we are confronted with a significant contrast. Whereas the hysteric over-values objects in the outer world, the paranoid individual regards them as persecutors; and, whereas the hysterical dissociation is a form of self-depreciation, the attitude of the paranoid individual is one of extravagant grandiosity. The *paranoid state* must accordingly be regarded as representing rejection of the externalized object and acceptance of the internalized object—or, alternatively, externalization of the rejected object and internalization of the accepted object. (1952a, pp. 44–5.)

The hysteric position is the opposite of this; the accepted object is sought in the outer world and the rejected object is regarded as being inside.

5. *Criticisms of Fairbairn's Views*

(*a*) *Winnicott and Kahn's Review of Fairbairn's Theory*. The chief critical study so far of Fairbairn's work has been made by D. W. Winnicott and M. Kahn in a review of Fairbairn's book in *The International Journal of Psycho-Analysis*. (1953, pp. 329– 33.) They examine his views on internalization, on the inherently object-seeking nature of libido and on the relationship of 'primary identification' to the 'object-relations principle'. The real point of their criticism is by no means clear or convincing, and it is a little difficult to see why Winnicott seeks to make it in view of the fact that his own writings imply an unformulated theoretical revision of Freud that is very close to that of Fairbairn. They state that they 'share many of Fairbairn's dissatisfactions' but are 'left with the feeling that Freud's developing ideas provided and still provide a more fertile soil than the developed theory of Fairbairn' (p. 333, col. 1). It is, however, 'Freud's developing ideas' that have gone on being developed in both Melanie Klein and Fairbairn, both of whom have met with criticism from the standpoint of Freud's more static ideas. Certain remarks in the review suggest that the reviewers have been unable to escape from their own original Freudian frame of reference, though Winnicott's views about the 'true and false self' imply a position far removed from that of Freud. They write :

Fairbairn makes a definite claim . . . that Fairbairn's theory supplants that of Freud. If Fairbairn is right, then we teach Fairbairn and not Freud to our students. If one could escape from this claim we could enjoy the writings of an analyst who challenges everything, and who puts clinical evidence befóre accepted theory, and who is no worshipper at a shrine (p. 329).

However, one does not challenge things as an enjoyable exercise merely, but to replace inadequate theories by more adequate ones. The same claim is implied in certain parts of Melanie Klein's work and will be implied in any genuine development beyond Freud. The point is irrelevant to scientific progress. The last part of the quotation describes the true scientific approach, except for its expressed wish to escape from the consequences of 'putting clinical evidence before accepted theory' if it appears to outmode accepted theory. The alternative of 'teaching Fairbairn' or 'teaching Freud' has nothing to do with science, which, in this case, should be concerned only to 'teach psycho-analysis' as a developing theory of which Freud, Melanie Klein, Fairbairn and others as yet unborn will represent stages of progressive clarification. One would not represent physics as a choice between 'teaching Newton' and 'teaching Einstein'. This emotional standing-ground of Winnicott and Kahn appears to impose on them a kind of duty to criticize this 'new theory' with which, in fact, Winnicott at least has much in common.

They state that 'it is hopeless to try to correlate these [i.e. Fairbairn's] statements with those of Melanie Klein', make a gratuitous assumption that Fairbairn is not sufficiently familiar with her writings and say : 'This is but a caricature of Klein's theory, if it is related to that theory at all, which seems doubtful except that the terms overlap' (p. 332). Again, 'It is a pity that terms are used which suggest familiarity with work such as that of Klein in respect of what she named the "positions" in emotional development, the "depressive", "paranoid" and "schizoid" respectively' (p. 331). However, since Fairbairn's views do not claim to represent Klein's but to be based on independent observations, they cannot be a 'caricature', and in the interests of accuracy it must be stated that 'schizoid position' is not a Kleinian term : by her own express statement she adopted Fairbairn's term to amplify her conception of the 'paranoid' into the 'paranoid-schizoid' position. Fairbairn would be the first to acknowledge that he learned much that was fundamental to his new views from Mrs. Klein. He writes explicitly :

The time is now ripe for a psychology of *object-relationships*. The ground has already been prepared for such a development of thought by the work of Melanie Klein; and indeed it is only in the light of her conception of *internalized objects* that a study of object-relationships can be expected to yield any significant results for psychopathology. (1952a, p. 60.)

But Fairbairn's theory is the result of independent thinking, as all true theoretical work should be, and must be evaluated as such.

Coming to specific criticism, one of the most important is the following :

This internalizing to coerce is surely a defence mechanism. . . . Fairbairn is thus considering introjection as a specific defence mechanism, and not as a primary process as such, nor as a kind of object-relationship. It is difficult to see how the human being could build up inner sources of strength, or the basic stuff of the inner world that is personal and indeed the self, simply on the taking in of 'bad' objects through the operation of a defence mechanism (p. 332).

In the first place Fairbairn himself regards the term 'defence mechanism' as invalid because it is mechanistic and impersonal. One must speak rather of defensive activities of the ego in relation to bad objects. Thus the statement that Fairbairn treats introjection as a defence mechanism and not as a kind of object-relationship is incorrect. Fairbairn treats introjection as a defensive reaction of an ego in relation to a bad object, the purpose of which is to master the bad object inside the psyche because it cannot do so in external reality. The result is to set up an internal bad-object relationship. The important point, however, in Winnicott and Kahn's criticism is that Fairbairn does not treat introjection as a 'primary process' as such, while Winnicott and also Kleinian writers do. That does pinpoint a specific difference between Fairbairn and Klein and raises an ultimate issue.

Introjection is admitted to be a defensive operation which, as the reviewers say, 'has been well described and accepted in analytic literature'. Is it also a primary process? Kleinians say 'Yes', and hold that only by primary internalization of good objects can the infant get a start in good-ego development. Fairbairn says 'No'. He regards introjection as concerned, not with good-ego development, but with the creation of the psychopathological unconscious, the inner world of bad objects in the first place, which in turn calls for the creation of internal good objects as a protection. Introjection is in itself a schizoid withdrawal from external object-relations in real life, and is the chief agent in creating the inner dream world which Fairbairn regards as a universal schizoid phenomenon based on fundamental splitting of the ego. He treats good ego-development as a function, not of introjection, but of good ego-object relationships in the outer world. This view seems to be closer to the facts. It is, in any case, difficult to see how good ego-development could be secured by any sort of good-object relations, external or internal, in face of a death instinct working within.

Winnicott and Kahn note that Fairbairn introduced a modification of his original views on introjection, in 1951, and their critical reaction to this is curious. They write that Fairbairn 'himself . . . found this state of affairs unsatisfactory' (p. 332). This, however, was not over the issues that they had just raised, concerning which Fairbairn's view remained unaltered. They write:

He [Fairbairn] seeks to correct himself by harking back to the 1941 paper, and by writing: 'The object which is originally internalized is not an object embodying the exclusively "bad" and unsatisfying aspect of the external object, but the pre-ambivalent object. . . . The internalization of the pre-ambivalent object would then be explained on the ground that it presented itself as unsatisfying in some measure as well as in some measure satisfying. On this assumption ambivalence will be a state first arising in the original unsplit ego in relation, not to the external object, but to an internalized pre-ambivalent object.' But this lands the author in other and possibly worse contradictions, and in any case it would seem that if this new turn to his theory be true, then his main point (which is that libido is object-seeking) is no longer a good one (p. 332, col. 1).

It is still, however, Fairbairn's view that it is on account of its 'bad' aspects that the pre-ambivalent object is internalized, to be subsequently split into good and bad objects which are then manipulated in the psychoneurotic techniques for the defence of the ego against internal bad objects. It is, moreover, still Fairbairn's view that it is not in this direction that we should look for the causes of good ego-development, but to good object-relationships in real life. In terms of his later theory of endopsychic structure, this is a Central Ego process.

We turn to Winnicott and Kahn's view that the 1951 modification 'lands the author in other and possibly worse contradictions. . . . If this new theory be true, then his main point (which is that libido is object-seeking) is no longer a good one.' The argument by which they seek to prove this is unconvincing, and had in fact already been refuted by Joan Riviere in another connection. They seek to prove that the infantile ego cannot be primarily libidinally object-seeking because it is in a state of primary identification with the mother, a characteristic of what Fairbairn calls 'infantile dependence'. Quoting Fairbairn's definition of primary identification 'to signify the cathexis of *an object which has not been differentiated* [the reviewers' italics] (or has only been partly differentiated) from himself by the cathecting subject (p. 145)' (p. 332), they lay it down that 'if an object is not differentiated it cannot operate as an object. What Fairbairn is referring to then is an infant with needs, but with no "mechanism" by which to implement them, an infant with needs not seeking an object, but seeking de-tension, libido seeking satisfaction, instinct-tension seeking a return to a state of rest or un-excitement; which brings us back to Freud' (p. 332). It certainly does and would cancel out Melanie Klein as well as Fairbairn.

In the first place this argument, which is really a piece of special pleading, ignores the fact that Fairbairn in this definition is contrasting primary with secondary identification. Primary identification characterizes the infant in the womb. Secondary identification is a regression back to identification after some amount of differentiation has begun to develop. In between them lies the problem of the point at which the process of differentiation gets a start. Presumably the first point that we can with confidence choose as the beginning (or as creating the possibility of the beginning) of the disruption of primary identification is the process of birth. This is the problem already raised by Mrs. Klein's work, as to how far object-relations go back into infancy, and whether, as Kleinians concluded, the original Freudian theory of autoeroticism is not now disproved. Winnicott and Kahn evidently stand by the orthodox Freudian view of an original autoerotic and narcissistic stage when the ego is objectless (or is that Kahn, for it is hardly consonant with Winnicott's writings). It is apposite here to recall the Kleinian reply to this (which we set forth fully in chapter XII, pp. 240–4 by Paula Heimann and Joan Riviere. Winnicott and Kahn write :

The provision of a way out by the mother is not a part of the infant's mental activities, but something that may (or may not) be *given* to him. That *if all goes well* the individual infant may develop to a point at which he can begin to relate the object to his need, to seek it, to create it, to coerce it, etc., is well known (p. 332).

This plainly confirms Fairbairn's view that object-relation is the basis of development. Of course, at first, the object must come to the infant from without and be *given* before it can become in any sense a mental possession or creation. From the moment of birth there is a separate object to be *given* to the infant in just that way. The opposite of their general line of argument was implied by Heimann, when she wrote :

The differentiations are brought about by the fact that the individual exists in a world on which he is dependent . . . an organism which depends to a vast extent on other organisms and powers outside itself for attaining its purposes, must become influenced and changed by its contacts. (1952, Klein *et al.*, p. 122. Quoted in ch. XII, p. 276.)

As a result of the infant's separation from the mother at birth, the effect of which is that the physical basis for complete primary identification now no longer exists, the infant in fact is now an entity in himself seeking a relationship with a separate object in however blind a way, and in a way that was not the case prior to birth. It has become, in Heimann's words, 'an organism which depends . . . on other organisms . . . outside itself', and this is now the physical basis for a disruption of the ante-natal state of primary indentification, even though this normally yields only slowly to the impact of object-relationships. If, as Freud held, the process of birth is itself the first anxiety-creating experience, then this experience enforces a disturbance which promotes the dissolution of primary identification. Winnicott and Kahn's argument that 'the provision of a way out by the mother is not a part of the infant's mental activities' seems to be beside the point. It is Fairbairn's view that if the mother is a good object, the dissolution of primary identification under the experience of good object-relationship will proceed at a normal pace. If the mother is a 'bad' or unsatisfying object, then separation will threaten to dissolve primary identification all too rapidly and separation-anxiety will dictate a flight backwards into secondary identification with an internalized object.

Joan Riviere, as we have seen, refers to Anna Freud's view that

There is a narcissistic and autoerotic phase of several months duration preceding object-relations in the proper sense, *even though* [Riviere's italics] the beginnings of object-relation are built up during this initial stage. . . . Freudian theory allows at this period only for the crudest rudiments of object-relationships. (Quoted ch. XII, p. 243.)

Joan Riviere points out that Anna Freud distinguishes between 'object-relation in its proper sense' and 'the beginnings of object-relation' or 'the crudest rudiments of object-relationship . . . slowly built up during this initial stage'. She rightly replies :

There can be no such distinction, since the 'beginnings' and so on are the object-relation appropriate and proper to the earliest stage of development. At each stage . . . the degree of object-relation is proper to that stage. (Only if 'object-relation proper' were understood to mean fully developed adult object-relation could such a distinction be made.) (Klein *et al.*, 1952, p. 12. Quoted in ch. XII, p. 244.)

This incidentally disposes of Winnicott and Kahn's criticism that Fairbairn's view implies 'an equation of the infant with the adult individual he is going to be' (p. 330). That is not so. Fairbairn's view implies no more, in this case, than the Kleinian view does, namely, that certainly from the moment of birth primary identification is challenged by another process, the emergence of object-relations experience in however rudimentary a form at first. As Joan Riviere says: 'At each stage the character or degree of object-relation is proper to that stage', and Fairbairn holds that primary identification is not 'objectless' but the most primitive form of object-relation.

The facts seem to be as follows: the infant is an organically separate object from the mother after birth and has in fact therefore an object-relation to the breast. Birth is the experience that makes the first disrupting impact on the untroubled bliss of primary identification. After that, the experience can never again be absolute. Some undefinable difference has been made that is in fact the first step towards the differentiation of the object and the ego. As yet the infant's separate individuality is potential and his task is to achieve mental realization and development of his own separate existent self. The mother-child relation is, at birth, an organically actual, and a psychologically potential, object-relation, and the first phase of growth is the development of an explicitly conscious object-relation out of the already ruptured primary identification. Feelings of identification and object-relation must war together with ever-sharpening intensity as time goes on, the first slowly fading as the second increases in strength. But they must co-exist for a long time and the infant must have some vague, elementary experience of both at the same time. This is common ground to both Klein and Fairbairn. It is not the case, as Winnicott and Kahn aver, that Fairbairn does not 'consistently maintain the view by which the infant is always a separate entity, seeking objects, from within his own entity experience' (p. 331, col. 1). It is rather that the infant finds it difficult not to oscillate between identification and differentiation. Nor is it the case that 'if the object is not differentiated it cannot operate as an object' (p. 332, col. 1). Rather, it is because the object is an object and operates in fact as an object, and the infant's nature is basically object-seeking, that it is psychically possible to get a start at all in the process of differentiating the object. Fairbairn writes:

It may be claimed that the psychological introjection of objects and, in particular, the perpetuation of introjected objects in inner reality are processes which by their very nature imply that libido is essentially object-seeking; for the mere presence of oral impulses is in itself quite insufficient to account for such a pronounced devotion to objects as these phenomena imply. (1952a, pp. 82–3.)

Fairbairn's view is that the process of differentiation proceeds smoothly if the first object-relations are good. Winnicott and Kahn apparently agree. They write : 'That *if all goes well* the individual infant may develop to a point at which he can begin to relate the object to his need . . . is well known' (p. 332, col. 2). Their case against Fairbairn (and also against Klein on this point) amounts to little more than an implication that it is difficult to pin-point the moment at which identification is broken into by explicit object-relations experience. That is no justification for arguing that Fairbairn lands in Freudian objectless autoerotism as the first phase after birth.

Fairbairn's further view is that it is bad-object relations that impede the development of differentiation by creating insecurity and anxiety through lack of satisfaction of libidinal needs. This causes (1) an intensification of oral-incorporative attitudes to the breast, and also (2) a deep, unconscious repression or flight backwards to identification again, thus creating secondary identification in the place of the primary identification that has already been disturbed. Hence the two fundamental features of Infantile Dependence, sadistic oral-incorporative trends and secondary identification with incorporated (i.e. internalized) objects, come to fuse into a complex whole.

(*b*) *Balint's Criticism of 'Libido as Object-seeking'.* Dr. M. Balint, in a paper entitled 'Pleasure, Object and Libido. Some Reflections on Fairbairn's Modifications of Psychoanalytic Theory' (1956, pp. 162–7), and also in 'Criticism of Fairbairn's Generalization about Object-Relations' (1957, p. 323), makes two criticisms. It is difficult to decide how far he really presents them as criticisms, since in both cases he retains Fairbairn's view but yokes it with a qualification. To the present writer, however, the qualification appears to be too incompatible with Fairbairn's view to be capable of travelling in this double harness.

The first criticism concerns Fairbairn's view that libido is primarily object-seeking rather than pleasure-seeking. Balint holds that because Freud originally chose the term 'libido' to denote the intensity factor in sexual striving, it should be restricted to that sense, at least in that it should be regarded as basically pleasure-seeking (i.e. seeking de-tensioning). He thinks that Fairbairn has been misled into forgetting that original meaning, by the increasing use of the term as a 'barely sexual, almost mythical, hazy conception' (1956, p. 163), and that if he had remembered it, he would have had 'to invent a new term for what he now calls libido'. (1956, p. 163.) That, however, ignores the very point of Fairbairn's theory. He regards animal as well as human nature as primarily object-seeking; and the view of libido as primarily pleasure-seeking, as a quest simply for de-tensioning, as resting on mistaken factual observation. He regards tension as specifically the tension of object-seeking needs, and he would reply that even animal psychology would disprove the idea that 'had the translators used "lust" instead of "libido" [Fairbairn] could never have said "lust is not pleasure-seeking" since this would have been obviously self-contradictory'. (1956, p. 163.) Balint himself appears to fall into semantic confusion here over the meaning of 'lust'. The term was not used by the translators, because in English it had acquired 'the overtone of sinfulness' (1957, p. 323), but it is in this rejected sense that lust is pleasure-seeking and regarded by Fairbairn as a phenomenon of deterioration and failure of object-relationships.

Balint states Fairbairn's position as follows : 'Libido is not pleasure-seeking : it is object-seeking.' (1956, p. 162.) That way of putting it suggests that Fairbairn wishes to deny the existence of pleasure in libidinal object-seeking, and to treat pleasure and objects as mutually exclusive goals. In fact, his view is that 'pleasure is the signpost to the object', but the object is the goal, and libido is only reliably pleasure-finding in proportion as it is object-seeking. By becoming purely pleasure-seeking, the ego in the end loses both the object and the pleasure. Fairbairn himself has replied to Balint thus :

I should now prefer to say that it is the *individual in his libidinal capacity* (and not libido) that is object-seeking. This reformulation is designed to avoid any appearance of hypostatization of instincts . . . there is no question of my denying the importance of the role played by pleasure in the mental economy. What is at issue is the particular role which it plays; and my contention would be that, whilst there can be no doubt that under certain conditions it can become an 'end', its natural function is that of a 'means'. (1957, p. 335.)

Balint has ignored the fact that for Fairbairn psychodynamic theory is a theory of man as a 'person', and that his purely organic and tension-relieving processes acquire an entirely new significance when seen as personal libidinal activities. Balint apparently retains psychobiology and adds object-relations psychology as an appendix. Fairbairn lifts psychodynamic theory out of psychobiology into object-relations theory.

Thus Balint writes :

It is a pity that Fairbairn takes the view that libido is not pleasure-seeking but object-seeking. If I am right the correct way to describe his clinical experience would have been something like this : in addition to the hitherto well-studied quality of libido, i.e. its pleasure-seeking tendency, clinical observations have proved beyond doubt that its object-seeking tendency is at least equally important, especially in patients while under analysis. The further problem arises now how to evaluate the relative importance of the two tendencies of the libido—pleasure-seeking and object-seeking. (1956, p. 167.)

That is exactly what Fairbairn does not mean and is concerned to deny. The way Balint slips into the use of the term THE libido shows that he is still under the influence of the earlier sub-personal level of conceptualization. Fairbairn explicity repudiated this hypostatization of THE libido, and speaks, as we have just seen, only of 'libido' as the striving of a person for good object-relationships, in which the experience of pleasure accompanying success is a signpost to the object. The problem of the comparative evaluation of pleasure-seeking and object-seeking is dealt with very explicitly by Fairbairn. The failure to achieve good object-relationships on a properly personal level leads to a deterioration of the libidinal quest to the level of pure pleasure-seeking or tension-relieving. This partakes of the nature of hysterical symptom formation (sexual compulsions, for example, counteracted by sexual inhibitions), the substitution of a bodily process for a personal-relations problem. (Cf. Fairbairn, 1954.)

We note further that Balint does not deny that libido is object-seeking, but he seeks to limit this by the qualification 'especially in patients under analysis'. This is the substance of his second criticism. He writes :

To a large extent we would all agree with [Fairbairn] if only we could be allowed to qualify his conclusions by adding that they are valid only so far as the limitations of the analytic situation and Fairbairn's individual technique go. (1956, p. 166.)

If this were true it would apply to all psycho-analysis of any description and could be held to make objective psychological science impossible. In fact, however, it is impossible to maintain that the primary importance of object-seeking is restricted to the psycho-analytic situation. It is written too plainly over the whole of life. Balint suggests that Fairbairn overlooks the fact that transference phenomena belong to the field of two-person psychology, and treats them as belonging to the field of one-person psychology. It is, however, the essence of Fairbairn's point of view that he would deny the existence of the field of one-person psychology in any sense that could be meaningful for psycho-analysis. Even

purely autoerotic tension-relieving activities turn out to be relationships with internalized objects. He regards the object-relationship of the patient and analyst as fundamental alike for theory
and therapy, and holds that the psycho-analytic sessions provide a
proper field for the objective and scientific study of two-person
relationship phenomena. He writes :

The contrast between past and present (like that between uncon-
scious and conscious) has come to be largely subordinated to the
contrast between inner reality and outer reality; and the influence of
inner reality upon the behaviour of the patient in outer reality has
come to occupy the focus of the analyst's attention. In conformity
with this fact, the analysis of the transference situation has tended
more and more to become the primary aim of psycho-analytical
procedure . . . the psycho-analytical method has largely ceased to
be a historical method involving a reconstruction of the patient's
past, and has largely become a method for investigating the influence
of (characteristically unconscious) situations and relationships in
inner reality upon contemporary experience and behaviour. (1952b,
p. 127.)

This view of transference is kept by Fairbairn in its true context
in the total 'object-relationship' between patient and analyst. He
says :

What mediates the 'curing' or 'saving' process . . . is the development of the patient's relationship to the analyst, through a phase in
which earlier pathogenic relationships are repeated under the influence of the transference, into a new kind of relationship which is
at once satisfying and adapted to the circumstances of outer reality.
(1955, p. 156.)

The aim of the analytic session is thus to give the patient an opportunity to grow out of his emotionally infantile inner world into an
ability to relate himself realistically to the analyst as a real person
of the present-day outer world, and as a consequence to become
able so to relate himself with realism to all other persons. To make
this possible the analyst himself must be a real person to the
patient. In doing this he gives the patient just what was missing
in childhood to enable him to become a real person himself. It is
because of this that psycho-analysis is a window opening out on
to the whole of human life. Fairbairn can hardly be charged with
forgetting that psycho-analysis is a two-person relationship.

Balint holds, however, that this patient-analyst relation is of
necessity frustrating, especially in that while some gratifications
are allowed inevitably, they must stop short of bodily orgiastic

pleasures. This, he regards, as resulting in a forcing to the front
of object-seeking on the level of a quest for personal relations. Fairbairn sees the analytic situation as having precisely the opposite
effect. He writes :

It must be recognized that, since the patient, *qua* patient, may be
presumed to have suffered severe deprivations in childhood, he
comes to the analytical situation with an intense craving for object-
relations already present in him, and that, since the conditions of
the orthodox analytical situation impose upon him a severe deprivation of object-relations with the analyst, they have the effect of
reproducing the trauma of deprivation from which he originally
suffered. . . . But, contrary to Balint's contention, the effect of the
artificially induced trauma is to compromise such capacity for object-
relations as the patient possesses, to provoke in him actively the
'regressive' phenomena to which Winnicott has drawn attention, . . .
and to compel him to fall back upon the pleasure-principle. . . . The
effect of the orthodox psycho-analytical method is thus to confer an
exaggerated importance, not upon object-seeking phenomena, but
upon phenomena of a pleasure-seeking nature. (1957b, pp. 334–5.)

It is Fairbairn's view that bodily gratifications early became for
the patient the 'area' into which he was forced back for solving
his problems of unsatisfied needs for genuinely personal relations
to parents. The patient will only be cured as he gets out of that
and deals with the real problem, which is always that of finding
someone with whom a properly personal relationship is possible,
so that the maturing of the patient as a 'total personality' can be
achieved.

(c) *Markillie's Criticism of the 'Status' of Internal Objects.* In a
review in the *British Journal of Medical Psychology* (1956, pp.
169–71) Markillie raises an important point, which will be better
appreciated in the light of the next chapter on Fairbairn's theory
of endopsychic structure. He writes :

The sharp definition Fairbairn gives to objects and structures in
the personality at times gives the impression of too great sophistica-
tion in these structures. For example, although he talks quite specifically about ego-development, it is difficult not to conceive of his
original pristine unitary ego, which becomes split into three parts, in
far more sophisticated terms than would appear to be warranted.
The clarity of his objects is perhaps the product of abstraction rather
than of actual experience, though localization of feelings into specific
identifiable objects as in fairy stories and myths is one of the ways of
defending against the much more threatening anxieties that the

immature ego must experience . . . when he talks of the return of bad objects, it is difficult not to feel that they have achieved a life of their own, that, for instance, the aggression in their persecution is theirs and not the subject's own aggression (p. 170).

Sutherland has remarked, in similar vein, that Fairbairn's 'structures give the impression of a greater degree of organization than appears to be the case, at least in some patients', and suggests that 'the anti-libidinal ego in many severe hysterics . . . has active substructures'. (*Brit. J. Phil. Sc.*, Vol. 7, No. 28, 1957, p. 332.) No doubt, the exigencies of clear conceptualization give this impression, especially in the initial stating of new concepts. Fairbairn writes :

I find no difficulty in accepting the proposition that the internal objects are composite structures; and indeed it would be my contention that this is so. Thus the internal objects which I envisage may be composed of maternal and paternal components in all proportions and in all degrees of integration. . . . As contrasted with these internal objects, the three ego-structures which I describe would seem, characteristically, to be much more definitely organized and differentiated—a phenomenon which may be attributed to the simple fact that they are ego-structures. (1957b, p. 338.)

He regards the anti-libidinal ego as the most rigid, the libidinal ego as somewhat less so, and the central ego as the most loosely organized, which accounts for patients often not knowing who or what they really are.

A lengthy study of Fairbairn's views was made by Abenheimer in the *British Journal of Medical Psychology*, Vol. XXVIII, Pt. I, 1955, pp. 29–41. This, however, hardly concerns us here since it is made entirely from the Jungian point of view, and has been replied to at length by Fairbairn himself, in 'Observations in Defence of the Object-Relations Theory of the Personality' (1955).

6. *Theory of Psychosis and the Psychopathology of Infantile Dependence*

Edward Glover regarded Mrs. Klein's theory of a 'depressive position' as different in principle (a new metapsychology) from Freud's theory of the Oedipus complex, as the basis of psychoneurosis. Fairbairn has adopted Mrs. Klein's point of view rather than Freud's in seeking the basis of psychoneurosis not in one particular aspect of the environmental problem, but rather in the endopsychic development of a particular, fundamental 'emotional position in object-relations' that will operate as a general factor in the psychic life. Mrs. Klein pushed the Oedipus situation back into the oral period in seeking to account for 'super-ego' phenomena or internal persecutors at that early time. Yet the Oedipus situation was still regarded as basically biologically conditioned. This is extremely doubtful. The criticisms of the 'culture-pattern' writers cannot be ignored on this point. Neurotic factors in the parents play a great part in determining whether a given child will develop an actual and marked libidinal fixation on the parent of the opposite sex coupled with hatred of the parent of the same sex. Subtle differences in the respective types of the mother and father and their resulting relationship lead to endless varieties in the actual patterns of Oedipus complex found in patients. Even with respect to the two main varieties, the Oedipus and the Inverted Oedipus situations, children will oscillate between them while they play off the mother and the father against each other. The final result, an Oedipus complex—an internally felt and phantasied situation that has become a persisting structural feature of a given individual mind—by no means corresponds exactly to the real outer parental situation. It is more akin to a final summary form in which the problem relationships of the child's infancy-life come to be preserved in his mental make-up. It would be better to call it the 'Family Complex', the inner representation of what the child ultimately comes to feel about his position *vis-à-vis* both parents and taking up into itself, as it does, his relationships with siblings as well. This leaves it open to discover in each individual case the precise form which the Family Complex has taken. But as regards psychoneurosis, one would have to say that this Family Complex, together with the symptoms that arise from it, constitute the substance of the neurosis rather than its cause.

Psycho-analytic investigation had to begin with the detailed description of the immediately presented neurotic phenomena. Thus, in working out piecemeal explanations, first of symptoms and then of the states of mind that achieved expression in them, cause and effect became confused together, particularly when any attempt to go beyond the descriptive picture to some ultimate factors only led to references to 'instincts'. What was needed for the understanding of psychoneurosis was to see man as a 'person' whose nature and life consisted essentially in his relationships with other persons so that a study could be made of the fundamental difficulties and forms of personal relationship from the beginning, and of their effects in producing the basic trends and types in human personality. Such matters as sadism and masochism, sexual symptomatology whether oral, anal or genital, the primal scene in the unconscious, the castration complex, the Oedipus complex in any of its forms, and so on, concern the ways in which these fundamental trends and types of personality manifest themselves. When Mrs. Klein outlined her theory of the 'depressive position' she described something that was ultimate, a consolidated position of the psyche in its emotional life in object-relations, which would determine its reactions throughout all stages of emotional development within, and human dealings without. On this basis it was possible to differentiate meaningfully between the neurotic and the mature person (relatively) as psychogenic types. It seems that Mrs. Klein did not recognize as clearly as E. Glover did that she had made a definite departure from Freud at this point. She kept the Oedipus Complex and the Depressive Position side by side as casual concepts.

Fairbairn saw that the Oedipus complex now needed to be evaluated differently. He writes :

I have departed from Freud in my evaluation of the Oedipus situation as an explanatory concept. For Freud, the Oedipus situation is, so to speak, an ultimate cause; but this is a view with which I no longer find it possible to agree. So far from agreeing, *I now consider that the role of ultimate cause, which Freud allotted to the Oedipus situation, should properly be allotted to the phenomenon of infantile dependence.* [Present writer's italics.] In conformity with this standpoint, the Oedipus situation presents itself, not so much in the light of causal phenomenon as in the light of an end-product. It is not a basic situation, but a derivative of a situation which has priority over it not only in the logical, but also in the temporal sense. This prior situation is one which issues directly out of the physical and emotional dependence of the infant upon his mother, and which declares itself in the relationship of the infant to his mother long before his father becomes a significant object. (1952a, p. 120.)

As compared with the Oedipus complex, the truly fundamental nature of Mrs. Klein's 'depressive position' may be judged from Fairbairn's view of the development of the Oedipus complex. He regards the infant as becoming ambivalent first of all to the mother alone, then when the father is taken into the picture the infant repeats this ambivalence with the father and so has two ambivalent objects both of which are split into good and bad objects ; gradually by layering and fusion internal good and bad objects are formed in which there are both maternal and paternal components, and finally the infant elects to regard one parent as the good and the other as the bad object, so arriving at the stage of constituting the Oedipus situation for himself. (1952a, pp. 119–25.) Mrs. Klein's 'depressive position' concerns the early formation of a genuinely basic emotional position in object-relationship *vis-à-vis* the mother, which can and will be repeated in all future object-relations as a fundamental characteristic of the individual in question. This 'depressive position' is, in truth, an aspect of that infantile dependence which Fairbairn regards as the true cause of psychoneurosis.

Fairbairn differs from Mrs. Klein with respect to the importance to be attached to the 'depressive position' by comparison with the phase that precedes it at the stage of infantile dependence. He regards the 'schizoid position' as the real foundation of all later psychoneurotic and indeed psychotic developments. It seems that Mrs. Klein has gone at least a long way towards accepting the validity of Fairbairn's contention though she still regards her 'depressive position' as the 'central' one in the child's development. This depends on the precise meaning we attach to the term 'central' and it might be said that in fact infantile dependence involves two distinguishable emotional positions: the *schizoid position*, which is *fundamental* in the sense that all psychopathological developments spring from it; and the *depressive position*, which is *central* in the sense that its achievement marks the point at which the infant begins to emerge from the pre-moral into the moral, or as Fairbairn would also put it, the civilized position.

It is a clinically observable phenomenon that a patient can oscillate between the two positions, using each in turn as an escape from and a defence against the other. Thus Mrs. Klein, writing of an actual case in 1934, says:

Paranoid fears and suspicions were reinforced as a defence against the depressive position which was overlaid by them.

But she immediately goes on to say:

I must again make it clear that in my view the depressive state is based on the paranoid state and genetically derived from it. (1948, pp. 295–6.)

Her later paper, 'Notes on Some Schizoid Mechanisms', in 1946, reprinted in *Developments in Psycho-Analysis,* 1952, contained the already mentioned footnote, in which she adopted and combined Fairbairn's term with her own, as 'paranoid-schizoid' position. This footnote was appended to a paragraph in which Mrs. Klein stated that failure to work through the 'paranoid-schizoid position' could prevent the working through of the 'depressive position', leading to regression to the earlier position again. (Cf. ch. XII, p. 237.) If the term 'central' means 'standing at the crucial juncture of development where vital advances are made to the moral and civilized level', as the above passage implies, then there appears to be no difficulty from Fairbairn's point of view in regarding Mrs. Klein's 'depressive position' as 'central'. On the other hand, Mrs. Klein herself in this passage makes it clear that the earlier 'schizoid position' of Fairbairn is fundamental for all later pathological developments.

Fairbairn himself deals with both the schizoid and depressive states as aspects of the psychopathology of the infantile dependence which he regards as the basic causal concept for psychoneurosis. (1952a, pp. 46–58.)

We find ourselves confronted with two basic psychopathological conditions, each arising out of a failure on the part of the individual to establish a satisfactory object-relationship during the period of infantile dependence. The first of these conditions, viz. the schizoid state, is associated with an unsatisfactory object-relationship during the early oral phase; and the second of these conditions, viz. the depressive state, is associated with an unsatisfactory object-relationship during the late oral phase. It emerges quite clearly, however, from the analysis of both schizoid and depressive individuals that *unsatisfactory object-relationships during the early and late oral phases are most likely to give rise to their characteristic psychopathological effects when object-relationships continue to be unsatisfactory during the succeeding years of early childhood. The schizoid and depressive states must, accordingly, be regarded as largely dependent upon a regressive reactivation, during subsequent childhood, of situations arising respectively during the early and late oral phases.* [Present writer's italics.] The traumatic situation in either case is one in which the child feels that he is not really loved as a person, and that his own love is not accepted. (1952a, p. 55.)

Fairbairn holds that trauma in the early oral sucking period leads to 'a reaction conforming to the idea' that the infant's love, his libidinal need of his love-object, the mother's breast, is bad and destructive, so that he becomes afraid to love and is precipitated into the characteristic schizoid state. At a slightly later stage, trauma in the late oral biting period provokes 'a reaction conforming to the idea' that the infant is not loved because his hate is bad and destructive. Thus he becomes afraid of loving for fear of hating and is precipitated into a depressive state. These two conditions Fairbairn regards as the ultimate psychic catastrophes against which the psychoneuroses or techniques of the transitional period are attempted defences. In common with all psychoanalysts he regards these states as forming the psychological basis and content of the psychoses, so that we may say that *psychosis is a direct manifestation of infantile dependence, while psycho-neurosis is a defence against that condition.*

The extent to which Fairbairn regards these facts as represent-ing the psychological ultimates in the realm of personality may be gauged from the following :

It must be recognized, of course, that no individual born into this world is so fortunate as to enjoy a perfect object-relationship during the impressionable period of infantile dependence, or for that matter during the transition period which succeeds it. Consequently, no one ever becomes completely emancipated from the state of infantile dependence, or from some proportionate degree of oral fixation; and there is no one who has completely escaped the necessity of incorpor-ating his early objects. It may consequently be inferred that there is in everyone either an underlying schizoid or an underlying depressive tendency, according as it was in the early or in the late oral phase that difficulties chiefly attended infantile object-relationships. We are thus introduced to the conception that every individual may be classified as falling into one of two basic psychological types—the schizoid and the depressive. (1952a, p. 56.)

He regards this as the truth underlying Jung's classification into 'introvert' and 'extravert' types, and Kretschmer's classification into 'schizothymic' and 'cyclothymic' types. We could construct a triangle in which the two bases represent the extreme schizoid and depressive states while the apex represents theoretical perfect maturity. In such a diagram every conceivable position—psy-chotic, psychoneurotic and relatively mature—could be plotted, in-cluding the possibilities of mixed types in which oscillations be-tween many different ultimate and defensive reactions occur in the struggle towards maturity.

It remains to make clear that the two chief general character-istics of infantile dependence are secondary identification and oral incorporativeness. Secondary identification is a regressive reactiva-tion, in face of later difficulties, of the state of feeling of the unborn infant's primary emotional identification in the womb with the mother of whom it is actually a part. This kind of feeling in later life gives rise to what may be called 'the safe inside policy' and it can produce striking clinical manifestations. The agoraphobic patient particularly seeks to set up an equivalent of being 'safe inside' the protective mother. Agoraphobia is a flight back to the womb and fear of being reborn, so that the patient is afraid to venture out of the house or far from something supporting to hold on to. This tendency of identification leads to the swallowing up or absorbing of the personality in that of other people. One patient,

who has a ferocious hate of her own—i.e. her mother's—sex,
vilifies and physically attacks her own body. But in her deep feelings her body represents to her the mother's body and she feels like
a tiny thing imprisoned inside it. A patient previously cited
dreamed of being physically grafted on to a father-figure, and
commented that whenever anyone important to her went away,
she felt as if the bottom had dropped out of her. Thus, this state
of identification with another person so that it seems impossible to
live without that other person leaves the patient extremely vulner-
able and at the mercy of whatever happens to the 'parent-figure'.
Identification may be supportive so long as the other person is
secure, but it undermines as soon as the other person is absent, fails,
is ill or dies. Then the utter incapacity of the patient to feel that
he has any life in himself that is properly his own is thrown into
stark relief. But identification may be just as undermining in
another way when the other person is not being lost. For it is not
an unusual thing to find that patients who suffer from strong
feelings of identification in their infantile dependence on parents
lose all trace of any personality of their own when they are in the
presence of the parent with whom they feel identified. They will
report that as soon as they go home they become lifeless, silent,
tired and a nonentity.

So identification comes to represent not only a flight to safety
(expressed by one man as a longing to retire from business to a
quiet lonely little hotel in the Lakes), but also being swallowed up
by and in another person. Thus one male patient began to develop
a good friendship with another man in a hostel where he lived,
and then suddenly felt a violent aversion from him and avoided
him. He then had a dream in which he was pursued by a monstrous mouth which swallowed him and he fought and cut his way
out again. Infantile dependence includes not only the factor of
identification which originates before birth, but also the factor of
oral incorporation from the breast which is added to identification
after birth. These two mingle and alternate. Identification with
the mother is felt to be both the mother swallowing the infant and
the infant swallowing the mother. All relationships are felt as both
a mutual swallowing and a mutual merging, and the patient is
never quite sure at any given moment whether he feels most as
if he is being swallowed or doing the swallowing. A male patient
remarked that the sexual relationship between him and his wife
was so intense that it felt like mutual cannibalism. Thus the patient
in a state of marked infantile dependence is always both inor-
dinately possessive towards the love-object and yet feels helplessly
dependent and loses personality to the love-object. A great deal of

aggressive reaction comes out of a struggle not to surrender to infantile dependent relationship with its dangers to the adult self. One ought rather to say dangers to the adult role, for the patient is in the position all the time of having to force himself to the maintenance of an adult role while feeling like a child inside.

The agoraphobic patient who is 'safe inside' and afraid to be born may alternate with the claustrophobic patient who feels smothered inside and is in such a hurry to be born that he repudiates all dependencies whatsoever. Thus a male patient had a long series of dreams in which he was in prison and overpowering his guard and breaking out to be free, only to be retaken and put back in prison again. The series culminated with a big dream of being in prison in an ancestral castle; a young man (another part of himself) came and gave him a file to cut the window bars and escape, but he said, 'I don't need that. The doors are not locked.' The visitor said, 'Then why don't you escape?' He answered, 'Look out of the window, see how dangerous it is out there; how would I be if I found myself out there all alone', and at that moment he became aware of his mother standing behind him as the jaileress. But she was not holding him; he was staying with her, and yet all the time longing to break away. This fundamental conflict between dependent and independent needs in the immature personality is regarded by Fairbairn as the ultimate conflict.

The essence of psychopathology in Fairbairn's view may be summarized as follows: it is essential that a child should be helped to develop a self-confident and strong individuality of his own, as a person in his own right capable of entering into relationships with other persons without danger to his own integrity as a person. Whatever hinders this development to mature adulthood forces the child to seek security in dependence on some other person instead of being able to feel secure in reliance on the sense of growing adequacy and ability in himself. He is driven back into a regressive revival of his original infantile dependence on his parents—and at bottom his mother—in his deeper feelings, and identification and oral incorporativeness dominate his unconscious reactions thereafter in all personal relationships. In order to cope at all with the day-to-day necessities of his outer life as he continues to grow up under the pressure of others' expectations of him, he is forced to construct in consciousness an apparently adult self or role, and drive himself by unremitting self-control to maintain it. This over-compensation for the infant within cannot, however, be stable because it does not grow from deep roots in mature emotional development. Fear of the break-through of the 'child underneath', with his utter need and demand for absolute support to the accompaniment of infantile greed and hate, precipitates strong tendencies to develop either schizoid or depressed states of mind, and sets going the defences of psychoneurotic techniques —obsessional, paranoid, hysteric or phobic—in proportion as straight repression fails. Underlying all is the deep unconscious dread of parting with, losing, the internalized bad objects because they represent the parents whom it is impossible to do without; this is a factor that causes the final resistance to all efforts to effect a 'cure' of the total condition. All the phenomena which psycho-analysis has investigated in such wealth of detail, the oral, anal and genital phantasy and symptomatology, the sadistic and maso-chistic trends, the castration and Oedipus complexes, the defence 'mechanisms', resistances, transferences, dreams, 'acting out' and behaviour disorders along with psychopathological character traits and types, all these are in fact but details of the fundamental problem in its working out, the struggle of the infant to grow out of his starting-point in total dependence on the mother, and in face of the frustrations, deprivations and bad-object relationships incidental to inadequate parenthood to grow to an adult person-ality. Fairbairn's theory of libidinal development from infantile dependence to mature dependence in the setting of object-rela-tionships orders and simplifies the whole complex field of psycho-pathological phenomena.

One further matter must be mentioned. Melanie Klein brought aggression to the fore as *par excellence* the pathogenic factor and traced it through sadistic component instincts to the death instinct. While retaining all the discoveries concerning the endopsychic operations of aggression, Fairbairn returned to the original Freud-ian view that libidinal need is the primary drive. Thus he writes :

According to my view, ambivalence is not itself a primal state, but one which arises as a reaction to deprivation and frustration. Thus I do not consider that in the absence of frustration the infant would direct aggression spontaneously towards his libidinal object. Accord-ingly, whilst I regard aggression as a primary dynamic factor in that it does not appear capable of being resolved into libido, I also regard it as ultimately subordinate to libido, and essentially representing a reaction on the part of the infant to deprivation and frustration in his libidinal relationships—and more particularly to the trauma of separation from his mother. It is thus the experience of libidinal deprivation and frustration that originally calls forth the infant's aggression towards his libidinal object and so gives rise to ambival-ence. (1952a, pp. 171–2.)

As we shall see in the next chapter, aggression turned inwards plays a great part in producing the internal differentiations that result in endopsychic structure : though the libidinal self is the foundation of everything.

7. *Comparison with Rank's 'Birth Trauma' Theory*

Since, superficially, there may appear to be some similarity between Fairbairn's theory of Infantile Dependence as the cause of neurosis, and Rank's theory of Birth Trauma, it may be well to deal with this here. The essentials of the problem posed by Rank's theory are clearly set forth by Ernest Jones. (1957, pp. 60–81.) Concerning Freud's paper, 'The Dissolution of the Oedipus Complex' (1924) Jones remarks : 'Ferenczi assumed from the strong word *Untergang* in the title that Freud was combating *Rank's tendency to replace the Oedipus Complex by the Birth Trauma as the essential aetiological factor in the neuroses*' (p. 114). [Present writer's italics.] Freud regarded the painful process of birth as creating the basic pattern of anxiety reactions and Rank proceeded to treat this as the primary trauma which created neurosis. The rest of life was one long struggle to undo or overcome its results, and psycho-analysis could be shortened by concentrating on unmasking this birth trauma. Treatment and cure would then appear as a process of rebirth. In a letter to Abraham, 15th February, 1924, Freud wrote :

> I do not hesitate to say that I regard this work as highly significant, that it has given me much to think about, and that I have not yet come to a definite judgment about it. We have long been familiar with womb phantasies and recognized their importance, but in the prominence that Rank has given them they achieve a far higher significance and reveal in a flash the biological background of the Oedipus complex. To repeat it in my own language : some instinct must be associated with the birth trauma which aims at restoring the previous existence. One might call it the urge for happiness, understanding there that the concept 'happiness' is mostly used in an erotic meaning. Rank now goes further than psychopathology, and shows how men alter the outer world in the service of this instinct, whereas neurotics save themselves this trouble by taking the short cut of phantasying a return to the womb. (Jones, 1957, p. 64.)

Freud regarded the obstacle to this neurotic, phantasied regression to the womb as part of the general barrier against incest, and as arising from the prohibition of the father—i.e. Oedipal guilt and anxiety—whereas Rank regarded 'the anxiety opposing incest as

simply a repetition of the anxiety at birth'. (*Ibid.*, p. 64.) Freud
further added : 'It is not clear to me how the premature interpreting of the transference as an attachment to the mother can contribute to shortening the analysis.' (*Ibid.*, p. 65.) In a further letter
to Abraham, 3rd March, 1924, Freud wrote :

Let us take the most extreme case, that Ferenczi and Rank make
a direct assertion that we have been wrong in pausing at the Oedipus
complex. The real decision is to be found in the birth trauma, and
whoever had not overcome that would come to shipwreck in the
Oedipus situation. Then instead of our actual aetiology of the
neuroses we should have one conditioned by physiological accidents,
since those who became neurotic would be either the children who
had suffered a specially severe birth trauma or had brought to the
world an organization specially sensitive to trauma. (*Ibid.*, p. 67.)

Freud's criticisms of the Birth Trauma theory were decisive and
Rank's views failed to convince. What was important, however,
was that they had taken much fuller account than hitherto of pre-
Oedipal and earliest infantile material. After the publication of
Freud's *Inhibitions, Symptoms and Anxiety*, 1926, Jones wrote to
Freud : 'You were wise enough to do what none of us others could
do : namely to learn something from it all by allowing Rank's
views to work on you in a stimulating and fruitful way.' (*Ibid.*,
p. 75.)

Since those days the tendency has gathered increasing strength
to seek farther back than the three to five years Oedipal phase for
the origins of psychopathological developments. Melanie Klein's
work was the major move in that direction so far as clinical investigation was concerned. Fairbairn has drawn the necessary theoretical inferences from this shift of emphasis from the genital Oedipal
to the oral infantile stage. Like Rank he holds that Freud was
'wrong in pausing at the Oedipus complex' in search of the aetiology of neurosis. But, unlike Rank, he has not arbitrarily picked
out one fact, such as the process of physical birth, as the cause of
all later troubles. He has rather surveyed the detailed processes of
development throughout the whole infancy period to discover the
fundamental pattern of disturbance. The Oedipus complex falls
into place as the late and fairly elaborately developed form of
trouble that began earlier, at a stage when the good and bad, or
exciting and rejecting, objects were not the mother and father, but
two aspects of the mother herself.

The material with which Rank dealt, such as phantasies of a
return to the womb and of rebirth, and the agoraphobic and
claustrophobic anxieties associated with them, is explained by

Fairbairn not by means of an unproved reference to a physical birth trauma, but in a fully psychological way, by reference to emotionally traumatic object-relations. The infant, having been born, begins to take the first and natural steps in the development of his own personality, a process which he is well able to accomplish provided he has a secure emotional environment in which to grow. If, however, as childhood proceeds he becomes more and more insecure, and is driven to find safety not in growing inner strength through good-object relationships but in clinging to parents as a protection in the midst of bad-object relations and his own highly disturbed reactions to them, then healthy development is frustrated and the child is pushed into regressing more and more at deep unconscious levels to a revived state of infantile dependence on the mother. This whole complex inner situation thereafter remains under repression as the root cause of all psychopathological developments. Fairbairn's Infantile Dependence with its implications is the correct answer to the problems with which Rank's Birth Trauma theory first sought to grapple.

Emotional involvements in Oedipal relationships are the form taken by Infantile Dependence on parents (and basically on the mother) at the post-oral period. The urge to 'restore the previous existence' is not an 'instinct' but a regression to find security when the path of forward development is blocked by bad-object relationships in reality. The child who cannot overcome this revival of or return to 'Infantile Dependence' will 'come to shipwreck in the Oedipal situation'. Womb phantasies may well, in the last resort, represent 'the biological background of the Oedipus complex', but their clinical importance lies in the fact that they represent an immediate expression of a profound active infantile dependent trend involving the quest for security by identification with and absorption into another personality, and often in real life the espousal of a passive policy of longing for 'security inside' in any obtainable shape or form.

One point in which Fairbairn has nothing at all in common with Rank is the latter's superficial idea that such deep matters could be quickly brought to consciousness in a short analysis of a few months by what could only be merely intellectual explanation.

CHAPTER XV

FAIRBAIRN: A COMPLETE 'OBJECT-RELATIONS' THEORY OF THE PERSONALITY

(2) THEORY OF ENDOPSYCHIC STRUCTURE

W E have traced how Fairbairn worked out a full-scale revision of the classical libido theory, or theory of psychodynamic development, on the basis of the view that libido was primarily and inherently object-seeking, not pleasure-seeking. For Freud, pleasure meant basically the experience of organic de-tensioning, so that Fairbairn shifted the emphasis from the organism to the person, and from psychophysical processes to personal relationships. He presented the problem of normal development as that of growing out of the starting-point of infantile dependence on the mother to a capacity for the mature dependence of 'equals' in an adult relationship. Correspondingly the problems of psychopathological development are seen to represent various kinds of failure to outgrow infantile dependence, so that the physically and intellectually 'grown up' person is compelled to struggle to sustain an adult role with emotional equipment of an insecure child.

At this point a further problem arose. By what means, and in what form, does this infantile dependence persist in the psyche after infancy itself is past? This represents the problem of mental organization or *Endopsychic Structure* as the necessary complement to the *Libido Theory* which represents the nature of emotional development. He turned to this further problem in the two papers of 1943-4, 'The Repression and the Return of Bad Objects' (1952a, ch. III) and 'Endopsychic Structure Considered in Terms of Object-Relationships' (1952a, ch. IV.) The material used by psycho-analysis is mental content presented mainly in the form of phantasy, but this has an enduring basis in the structural organization of the psyche, which it represents. It was Melanie

Klein's contribution to explore infantile phantasy and to recognize from that material the fact that the ego had relationships with mentally internalized objects both good and bad. Here were the beginnings of a revision of the theory of endopsychic structure, but Mrs. Klein did not consider the bearings of her discoveries on the orthodox id-ego-super-ego theory. Ernest Jones writes :

> In spite of the basic contributions Freud made to the study of the origins of the super-ego it has proved more complex than was at first expected. When I reviewed the problems a few years later (E. Jones, 'The Origin and Structure of the Super-ego', *I.J.*, 1926, VII, 303–11), Freud wrote to me : 'All the obscurities and difficulties you describe really exist. But they are not to be improved even with the points of view you emphasize. They need completely fresh investigations, accumulated impressions and experiences, and I know how hard it is to obtain these. Your essay is a dark beginning in a complicated matter. (1957, p. 308.)

We have traced the beginnings of criticism by orthodox writers of the original concepts of the id, the ego and the super-ego. The 'completely fresh investigations', however, that Freud called for began with the work of Mrs. Klein and were carried to the point where Fairbairn could bring another fresh mind to the problem and using 'internal-objects theory' could revise Freud's structural theory. Mrs. Klein had concentrated on 'phantasy' which was expounded by Susan Isaacs as the direct representative of instinct. That kind of approach no doubt explains why Kleinian writers did not re-consider endopsychic structure theory afresh, since if phantasy is simply the direct representative of instinct, then it is an 'id-phenomenon' and as such fits neatly into the Freudian scheme. Fairbairn, however, applying Kleinian views more radically than Kleinians themselves had done, states :

> Unless it is assumed that internalized objects are structures, the conception of the existence of such objects becomes utterly meaningless. (1952a, p. 95.)

On this view, phantasy is primarily a revelation of endopsychic structure.

His first step was to reconsider the theory of repression in the light of the priority of object-relations over instincts. His approach was determined by his fundamental assumptions, namely (1) that 'The pristine personality of the child consists of a unitary dynamic ego' (1954, p. 107); (2) that this whole ego is motivated by its primary libidinal need of good-object relationships; (3) that in so far as it obtains these, good-ego development results, but that

(4) bad-object relationships, leading as they do to internalization of objects, set up processes of inner differentiation and thereby structural development and organization of the psyche. The problem, then, was to show in what way the relationships of the ego with its internalized objects created a basic pattern of endopsychic structure by means of which the experiences of infancy were perpetuated in the psyche and the problem of infantile dependence in later life made intelligible. By 1931 Fairbairn had realized the importance of the loss of unity in the ego. His attention now turned to the internalized objects to seek light on this problem, in the 1943 paper, 'The Repression and the Return of Bad Objects'.

He directed psychopathological enquiry not now upon impulse or the ego but upon the object, in the way that Mrs. Klein's theory of internal objects made possible. He came to the conclusion that

what are primarily repressed are neither intolerably guilty impulses nor intolerably unpleasant memories, but intolerably bad internalized objects. If memories are repressed, accordingly, this is only because the objects involved in such memories are identified with bad internalized objects; and, if impulses are repressed, this is only because the objects with which such impulses impel the individual to have a relationship are bad objects from the standpoint of the ego. Actually, the position as regards the repression of impulses would appear to be as follows. Impulses become bad if they are directed towards bad objects. If such bad objects are internalized, then the impulses directed towards them are internalized; and the repression of internalized bad objects thus involves the repression of impulses as a concomitant phenomenon. It must be stressed, however, that what are primarily repressed are bad internalized objects. (1952a, pp. 62–3.)

This conclusion involves two others of far-reaching importance. First, since impulses are not isolated entities within the psyche but are the impulses of the ego, they can be repressed only by repressing part of the ego whose impulses they are. This involves the splitting of the ego, and its basis is the ego's cathexis of the bad internalized objects which are repressed. Since internalized objects are themselves formed by the splitting up of the mental representation of the external object into bad and good imagos, we arrive at the position that it is the internalizing and splitting of objects that leads to the splitting of the ego, and what the theory of endopsychic structure must aim at is to clarify the fundamental pattern, however complex, of the internal relationships of the disunited ego with its internalized objects. This will be equivalent to an explanation of how infantile dependence is perpetuated in the psyche, and of the emotional constitution of the personality as rooted in its need-systems.

Secondly, if what are primarily repressed are bad internalized objects, then the dynamic of repression is the aggression felt in the first place against the bad external object. Repression was originally regarded as due to the fact that certain impulses were not acceptable to the conscious ego and were rejected at the instance of guilt. Fairbairn, however, arrived at the view that repression originates in a more primitive situation than that, one in which there can as yet be no question of the rejection of what is not approved by the socialized self on the moral or civilized level; rather, it is a situation in which the primitive ego angrily rejects what is not satisfying to itself, what is simply unpleasant, intolerable, bad in the purely emotional sense. Thus Fairbairn's theory of repression envisages two levels or stages, the earlier and more primitive of which is pre-moral, and the later is moral or civilized. We shall deal with these two stages in the above order.

1. *The Pattern of Endopsychic Structure*

Just as internal objects became observable to Melanie Klein when, in treatment, she succeeded in releasing the phantasy-life of the child in various forms of play, so the basic pattern of this life of internal object-relations was recognized by Fairbairn in dreams, the secret mental play of the adult patient. Here the disunities and conflicts of the inner world come to view, and give us a picture of the psychic forces that are played out in real life in symptom-formation and in disturbed behaviour. Since theory is an abstraction from clinical data, it may be as well first of all to represent in concrete form the loss of internal unity that we seek to understand in structural terms. Integration has always been one of the key words in setting forth the aims of psycho-analytic therapy. The theory of endopsychic structure seeks to give an account of the fundamental pattern of disintegration with which psychotherapy has to deal.

We may illustrate this by the phenomenon long known as 'split libido'. The commonest example of this is the case of the man who feels no sexual attraction towards a wife whom he loves in an affectionate manner, and is only capable of feeling sexually excited by a woman he does not truly love and whom he may in fact hate, despise and treat with varying degrees of aggressive behaviour. His relationship with this woman may vary from pleasurable sexual excitement, through different degrees of sadistic fusion of sexual and aggressive feeling, to frank disgust, bad treatment, hate and rejection, but none of these reactions disturb his relationship with his wife whom he does respect and love, albeit in a calm and much more neutral way. A variation on this 'split libido' theme is provided by a case I have quoted elsewhere.

A male patient reports that his relationship with his wife is one of constant rows and antagonism, while he finds another woman at work sexually exciting; but neither of them are his ideal woman for a wife. His ideal wife is clearly described in terms of the internal ideal object who is perfectly supporting but in no way emotionally disturbing. His actual wife is the rejecting object and the other woman is the exciting object. Hereby he reveals the tripartite split in his own ego setting up needs for three quite different types of women. (1956a, p. 98.)

In fact the relationship was more complicated than that, for he could change round his objects, so that at times his wife was the sexually exciting woman and the woman at work roused his anger. Since he felt marked guilt and anxiety concerning aggressiveness, sexual or otherwise, towards a woman, he at least lessened that difficulty by keeping up a sharp separation between the woman towards whom he felt sexual and the woman towards whom he felt aggressive. Always both of them had to be quite separate from his phantasied ideal wife. All variations on this theme disclose, when carefully studied, the same threefold division, though sometimes it takes the form, not of real life relationships with two or three different types of woman, but the alternation of three different moods or reactions towards the same woman, who is seen in turn as the woman to be sexually excited by, the woman to hate and the woman to be affectionate towards. Thus it is a commonly recognized fact that many men will turn with disgust from the woman as soon as they have had a sexual relationship with her, while in other cases a couple may have to quarrel violently before they can feel sexual towards each other. Always, however, there is the third type of relationship, of respect, consideration and duty without any strong emotion.

Now these common clinical phenomena cannot any longer be called merely 'split libido' problems, for on the basis of object-relations theory, we must think of 'libido' as the libidinal quest of an ego for an object. If the libidinal striving is 'split', then it can only be because the ego itself is 'split' and has lost its unity. We are, in fact, presented here with a case of a tripartite split in the libidinal object which is matched by a similar split in the ego. The Freudian Oedipus situation and complex is one of the forms taken by this threefold splitting of ego and object. The mother of the male patient will enter into his dreams as the woman who is sexually exciting, while the father will emerge as the hated punishing aggressor; on the conscious level an attitude of dutiful affection without strong feeling towards both of them is preserved. One such patient remembered clearly how as a small boy he was for ever following his mother about asking her if she loved him and feeling most intense longings for her, while he remembers his father mainly as a stern, angry man, a memory by no means realistic or fair to the father in question. But this same patient also, in one dream, suddenly found himself face to face in his boyhood home with his mother frowning at him in an irate and frightening way. It is often possible to discover the figure of the angry, rejective mother hidden behind the angry, rejective father in Oedipus dreams, making it the more easy to recognize that these images of the exciting and angry or otherwise rejective figures were originally aspects of one and the same person who has been split in mental representation. Oedipus and inverted Oedipus complexes, and homosexual relationships and dreams, are all susceptible of reduction to this basic pattern of a threefold splitting of the object-relationship life.

We can observe in the phantasy-life how the ego is split into three different egos, which accounts for the fact that the dreamer very commonly enters into the dream in more than one role at the same time. Each of these egos is to be found reacting to its own appropriate object, and these objects similarly turn out to be different aspects of one and the same object in outer reality in their origin. In a very close and detailed analysis of one striking dream, Fairbairn has shown how these internal ego-object relationships exist together and interact on the stage of inner psychic reality. (1952a, pp. 94–105.) In order to systematize and clarify these inner complexities of psychic constitution, he was forced to evolve a terminology that differed from Freud's by now too simplified ego-id-super-ego scheme. As we have seen, that terminology only allows for one internal object-relationship, that between the ego and the super-ego. The id, being impersonal, cannot be dealt with as either ego or object but merely as unstructured raw psychic material, an impossibility on the theory of 'dynamic structure'. This scheme is no longer adequate to cover all the complexities of psychic functioning, and has been regarded by many writers, including Freud himself, as requiring further development. Fairbairn's terminology constitutes a revised theory of endopsychic structure called for by fuller clinical data. The first stage in the development of this theory was Freud's concepts of the ego and super-ego. The second stage was Melanie Klein's work on the

multiplicity of internal objects, making plain the as yet ill-under-
stood complexity of the super-ego. The third stage is Fairbairn's
contribution of a full object-relations theory of endopsychic
structure in which he correlates the splittings of the ego and the
object in the internal development of the infant psyche, producing
what he terms 'the basic endopsychic situation'. (1952a, p. 106.)
His theory eliminates the anomalous and impersonal 'id', reduces
to fundamental order Mrs. Klein's multiplicity of internal objects,
and shows how the internal organization of the psyche proceeds as
the infant struggles to grow out of his original total dependence
upon the mother under the influence of such good, bad or indifferent parental and familial object-relationships as are available
to him.

Fairbairn writes:

It is necessary for us to remind ourselves of the importance of the
part played by an incorporative attitude at the stage (i.e. of Infantile
Dependence) from which transition is being attempted. This incorporative attitude manifests itself, not only in the ingestion of milk,
but also in the psychological internalization of objects, i.e. the psychological incorporation of representations of objects into the psychical structure. (1952a, p. 146.)

His definition of 'the psychological internalization of objects',
namely as the process whereby 'the psychological incorporation
of representations of objects into the *psychical structure*' [present
writer's italics] takes place, is important for making clear just
how and where his theory makes an advance on the work of Mrs.
Klein. He writes:

Melanie Klein has never satisfactorily explained how phantasies
of incorporating objects orally can give rise to the establishment of
internal objects as endopsychic structures—and, unless they are such
structures, they cannot be properly spoken of as internal objects at
all, since otherwise they will remain mere figments of phantasy.
(1952a, p. 154.)

Of Mrs. Klein's work in general Fairbairn remarks that 'in certain
important respects she had failed to push her views to their logical
conclusions'. (1952a, p. 154.) These 'important respects' he regards as including her retention of Freud's hedonistic libido story
and impulse-psychology, and Abraham's theory of libidinal development. To these must also be added her not applying her
'internal-objects theory' to the revision of the theory of psychic
structure.

The internal developments in infancy which result in the

elaboration of a complex structural pattern for which Fairbairn
sought a more adequate descriptive terminology proceed according to his view as follows: in so far as good-object relationships
lead to strong ego-development, the infant passes from infantile
to mature dependence on his objects, including passing from an
oral incorporative to a genital co-operative attitude to his heterosexual object. In any complete sense that is an unattained ideal, a
theoretical perfection only to be approximated in practice. In
reality, all human infants encounter varying degrees of bad-object
relationship, and developments on the basis of disturbed emotional
reactions take place. The maternal object, on account of her unsatisfying aspects, is internalized mentally, and split into an
accepted and a rejected object, thus giving rise to ambivalence.
The rejected object is further split into two separate imagos in
virtue of her having both an exciting and a rejecting aspect. The
mother's capacity to excite the child's needs is, however, here
associated with her rejective failure to satisfy them, so that both
the exciting and the rejective objects are bad objects. The child's
realistic anger and aggression against the mother who excites
needs which she does not meet, then becomes the dynamic of the
child's internal struggle to reject the bad object whom he feels
rejects him; i.e. his aggression becomes the dynamic of his *repression* of both the Exciting Object and the Rejecting Object (E.O.
and R.O.). The remainder of the original object, shorn of its disturbing, exciting and rejecting aspects, is then retained as a good
object in an idealized form at the level of consciousness, and is
called by Fairbairn the Ideal Object (I.O.). While the E.O. and
R.O. are repressed into the unconscious as bad figures, the I.O. is
projected back into the real external objects, and every effort is
made to see the actual mother (and later father and other external
objects) as a good, undisturbing figure in the outer world. The real
parent is 'idealized' in equal proportion to the badness of the bad
parent figures who have been repressed.

Corresponding to this tripartite splitting of the internalized
object, there inevitably follows a similar tripartite splitting of the
originally whole and unitary ego. The ego at first cathects the
whole object, and continues to cathect the parts into which it is
split; but this involves the ego in disunity, conflict, division. When
the E.O. is repressed, part of the ego which remains attached to it
by reason of the libidinal need which it excites becomes repressed
with it. It is appropriate to call this the Libidinal Ego (L.E.), since
it is that part of the ego in which is chiefly concentrated the ego's
primary urge towards the good object. This L.E. is, however, in a
constant state of unsatisfied desire, so that its need becomes ever

more aggressively orally incorporative and it is drawn back ever more deeply into the revival of the original primary identification with the mother in proportion as no satisfying objective relationship is obtained in reality. It is in the repressed L.E. that Infantile Dependence persists most obviously as an undermining undercurrent in the adult personality.

Furthermore, when the R.O. is repressed, that too remains cathected by a part of the ego which also goes into repression along with it. If the relationship between the L.E. and the E.O. is a double one, consisting partly of oral incorporative desire and partly of identification, the relationship between the R.O. and that part of the ego which still cathects it under repression is predominantly one of identification. Little else is permitted by the rejective nature of the object. Direct libidinal desire could at best only take the form of distant admiration of the 'ruthless strength' of the R.O. Identification is always an alternative to and a substitute for object-relationship, when it is revived in its secondary form. By reason of this identification, the part of the ego that still sustains under repression a relationship to the R.O. itself takes on rejective characteristics. In real life it manifests itself as the tendency to reproduce all the undesirable characteristics of the cold, harsh, domineering, aggressive, neglectful or otherwise 'bad object' aspect of the unsatisfactory parent. Thus, when it predominates in the personality it crushes out all manifestations of libidinal desire and affectionate feeling and sabotages the love-life of an aggressive character. For that reason Fairbairn at first called it the Internal Saboteur (I.S.) a descriptive rather than scientific term, which is, however, extremely valuable in clarifying the actual role that this part of the ego plays. Fairbairn now calls this secondary ego the Anti-Libidinal Ego (Anti-L.E.), an accurate term that has the advantage of making clear the fact that this part of the personality plays a persecutory role in relationship to the L.E. It is, in fact, the sadistic super-ego of Melanie Klein and Freud, arousing sheer terror in the primary libidinally needy part of the personality (L.E.). Infantile Dependence is secretly present in, though outwardly repudiated by, the Anti-L.E.

Repression, however, is in the first place carried out by that remainder of the original ego as it rejects the L.E. and Anti-L.E. which are split off. This remainder Fairbairn terms the Central Ego (C.E.), and he regards it as cathecting the I.O. whom it takes as the model of its Ego-Ideal. It is aggressively rejective to the E.O. and R.O. and also to the L.E. and Anti-L.E., using its own original aggression against the external object in real life as the motive force of its power to repress. We have, therefore, three pairs of object-relationships embodied in the structure of the personality. A C.E. projects its I.O. into outer reality, while two subsidiary egos cathect the E.O. and R.O. in the unconscious and feel hungry love and hate. Both of these are repressed by the C.E., and in addition the L.E. is further repressed by the bitterly antagonistic Anti-L.E. (or I.S.). This latter phenomenon Fairbairn calls *indirect repression*. It is a persecutory repression in terms of terror. One can see this in operation in the case of one patient who became excessively anxious and afraid to show any weakness in a crisis of great need, and attacked both herself and me angrily in the words: 'I'm not going to come creeping and crawling to you for help. Damn you, I'll show you I can do without you.' It is not by any means obvious to the patient in such a state of mind that this violent 'negative transference' against the analyst actually involves an unconscious terrifying attack upon his or her own libidinal self. The repression of both the L.E. and the Anti-L.E. by the C.E. is then further elaborated on a later developed, moral and civilized level, in terms of guilt.

2. *Analysis of the Super-Ego*

To whatever extent a given individual has not attained sufficient maturity and integration to be capable of carrying on his everyday life and its normal human relationships without tensions arising from internal disturbance, he seeks to make life as emotionally workable as possible by endeavouring to relate himself to significant persons as I.O.s. The C.E. is the self of everyday life. Fairbairn writes:

The central ego's 'accepted object', being shorn of its over-exciting and over-rejecting elements, assumes the form of a desexualized and idealized object which the central ego can safely love after divesting itself of the elements which give rise to the libidinal ego and the internal saboteur. It is significant, accordingly, that this is just the sort of object into which the hysterical patient seeks to convert the analyst —and the sort of object into which the child seeks to convert his parents, usually with a considerable measure of success. It now seems to me, therefore, that this is the object which forms the nucleus of the super-ego as I have come to conceive it (in contrast to 'the internal saboteur'). It would, however, seem more appropriate to the nature of this object to describe it as 'the ego-ideal' rather than 'the super-ego' (and thus to revive the earlier term). (1952a, pp. 135–6.)

Fairbairn is here raising the question of the complexity of the super-ego, a problem that was opened up by Alexander, and by

Hartmann, Kris and Loewenstein and considered by Jones and
by Freud himself. So far as Freud's views are concerned Fairbairn
holds that under the heading of repression Freud dealt mainly
with the attack of the Anti-L.E. on the L.E., which Fairbairn
designates 'indirect repression'. He writes that his

differentiation of ego-structure corresponds roughly to Freud's account of the mental apparatus—the central ego corresponding to
Freud's 'ego', the libidinal ego to Freud's 'id' and the internal
saboteur to Freud's 'super-ego'. (1952a, p. 171.)

The difficulty of the Freudian 'super-ego' concept was early seen
to be that it included two quite different elements, both of which
operated as controlling factors in the psyche but one of which was
moral and the other quite non-moral or even immoral in the sense
of being sadistically cruel. In the light of Fairbairn's more detailed
analysis of mental structure it is now possible to recognize that
what he calls the I.S. or Anti-L.E. is the sadistic component included in the Freudian super-ego, while the C.E. deriving values
from the I.O. which functions as an ego ideal is responsible for
the moral component. The sadistic Anti-L.E. is the primitive, repressed and unconscious part of the 'super-ego' and is to that
extent ineducable. The C.E. is open to the influences of education
and can develop a maturing conscience in relation to outer reality.
In practice, what any particular person possesses as a conscience
may be more or less under the influence of either the ego-ideal, or
the Anti-L.E. and the R.O. Thus we may regard the total 'super-
ego' phenomenon as a complex grouping of structures that includes the R.O., the Anti-L.E. and the I.O. (Ego Ideal).

Fairbairn himself would prefer to restrict the term super-ego
to the moral level of psychic functioning, the level at which the
C.E., the conscious self of everyday life, cathects the ego ideal or
I.O.: i.e. to the level of what he terms 'direct repression'. He
writes:

I retain the term 'super-ego' to describe an internal object which
is cathected and accepted as 'good' by the central ego, and which
appears to function as an ego-ideal at a level of organization established subsequently to the basic level. . . . I regard the cathexis of this
object by the central ego as constituting a defence against the cathexis
of internal bad objects by the subsidiary egos, and as providing the
basis for the establishment of moral values in the inner world. (1952a,
pp. 159–60.)

It would certainly make for clarity to adopt this usage, and retain
'super-ego' as the designation of the source of the moral conscience

in the C.E. through its cathexis of the I.O. Here would be found what is usually called 'rational morality', which, however, is not a good way of expressing the point at issue. 'Rational' is largely an intellectualist and schizoid concept, whereas we are concerned with the emotional sources of self-judgment. These may be either objectively or subjectively orientated. As I have written elsewhere:

> The central ego remains in touch with the outer world and is open to continuing educative influences, which is not true of the repressed parts of the personality. This leads to the evolution of two different types of guilt and morality, the one morbid and the other increasingly realistic and mature. Under the attack of the anti-libidinal ego, the libidinal ego develops not only *persecutory anxiety* but, at a slightly later stage, *persecutory guilt*, which is Melanie Klein's 'depressive anxiety'. The morbid guilt of depression is so persecutory in nature that it is clear that the anti-libidinal ego plays the dominant part in its creation. It contains a large amount of what Freud called 'borrowed guilt' (1949, p. 72), and it leads to the development of a pathological morality of an ultra-authoritarian kind: i.e. in Christian terms, a harsh Calvinistic morality of law rather than love. If the central ego has to do with parents who are, even as idealized outer figures, too intolerant of the child's libido and aggression, the 'superego conscience' will develop little beyond the level of the sadistic, persecuting, rejecting object and anti-libidinal ego.
>
> We may comment at this point on the familiar psycho-analytical idea that 'super-ego morality' needs to be replaced by a rational morality. This is better expressed as the replacement of persecutory morality by the morality of love. 'Super-ego morality' is psychopathological since it rests on splitting phenomena. It involves, as Fairbairn's analysis shows, both the sadistic persecution of the libidinal ego by the anti-libidinal ego, and an attempt to control the psyche as a whole by a central ego morality based on the ideal object and so likely to be perfectionist and unrealistic. But since the central ego is the part of the ego which retains the capacity to deal with outer reality it will do this in ever more realistic ways as infantile egosplitting is outgrown. 'The super-ego conscience' involves the attack of one ego upon another. A mature conscience is a function of genuine self-judgment on the part of the central ego by virtue of its possession of an ego ideal which becomes progressively more realistic as re-integration proceeds and as external objects are perceived in their own true nature and not in the light of the projection of an internal ideal object. (1956a, pp. 96–7.)

It is rarely possible to find a dream that gives clear expression to the whole complex pattern of internal object-relationships which

Fairbairn calls 'the basic endopsychic situation'. One reason for
this is the large part that is played by identification in the infantile
emotional life. Owing to this, one figure in the dream often serves
to represent both a part of the ego and the internal object which
it cathects. The following dream is selected in particular because
it gives such a clear representation of the Anti-L.E. at its fell work
of sabotaging the interest of the primary needy L.E. The patient
dreamed that she went to an interview for a job which she was
keen to get. When she got there, there was another woman of the
same age, height and general appearance as herself, also waiting
for an interview. When the dreamer's name was called, the other
woman rushed in and gave such a bad account of the dreamer
that she did not get the job. The dreamer enters into this dream
primarily as the L.E., the self which owns the basic needs. From
that point of view, the interviewing person from whom she seeks
to get what she needs is the E.O. The other woman is plainly the
dreamer's double but is working against her, and is the Anti-L.E.
However, from that point of view, the interviewer who sides with
the saboteur is now the R.O. Moreover, since in real life the
dreamer was very self-depreciatory and always felt that people of
any standing must have a poor opinion of her, the dream-figure
of the interviewer probably also included and concealed both the
I.O. and the C.E., both of which were over-influenced by the
R.O. and the Anti-L.E. Thus all the forces that could be turned
against the dreamer's basic nature within herself were, so to speak,
stacked against her, and it is no wonder that she was actually in-
capacitated to a high degree for carrying on a normally active
life. Whereas in this dream the three aspects of the object are all
included together in one figure, in their original unity, while the
results of ego-splitting are clearly and separately symbolized, in
other dreams the ego will appear only as one figure, while the
object will reveal itself as having been split in mental representation into two or three separate figures. But always, whatever differences are to be found in dreams, symptoms and characters, the
evidence of the basic threefold splitting of object and ego can be
traced.

The distinction Fairbairn draws between a pre-moral and moral
level of the psychic life is of great importance to the understanding of all developmental problems. Schizoid problems belong
wholly to the pre-moral level, depressive problems may be said to
belong to a pathologically moral level, while true morality belongs
to maturity. Guilt, Fairbairn regards, from the point of view of
psychopathology, as a defence against the cathexis of internal

bad objects which are repressed and unconscious; so that guilt operates necessarily as a resistance in psychotherapy. The real causes of psychoneurosis lie deeper down than the level of guilt, where sadistic persecutory bad objects terrify the masochistic L.E., whose need in psychotherapy Fairbairn regards as best expressed in terms, not of medical cure, but of 'salvation' or rescue from the dangers of the internal world. As I have expressed elsewhere :

Fairbairn's scheme has the advantage of being consistently psychological throughout, of answering to clinically observed facts more closely than the original scheme, and of clarifying the two outstanding anomalies in human nature; i.e. the co-existence of a primitive non- or pre-moral level of psychic life with the civilized moral level on the one hand, and on the other the fact that the individual functions as a self-frustrating entity by reason of his being radically divided between libidinal and anti-libidinal factors in his organization. (1956a, p. 98.)

It is never easy to change established usage, and the id-ego-super-ego terminology has been, for over thirty years, 'established usage' in psycho-analytical thinking. A new set of terms, such as Fairbairn proposes, start with the disadvantage of being 'strange', and they have for some time an 'unfamiliar feel' about them. It is, nevertheless, stultifying to continue to use old terms that have become inadequate to the purposes of accurate conceptual analysis. It is to be hoped that such a thoroughly psychologically unsatisfactory term as 'id' will speedily drop out of use. It can only lead to the blind perpetuation of misleading features of Groddeck's and Freud's philosophical outlook. It is also to be hoped that the term 'super-ego' will now be seen to be a blanket term covering quite distinct structural features of the psyche ; and that its use will be consciously modified. The term could be retained for the specific purpose of referring to the combined effects of the various repressing and controlling structures, so long as that is recognized. But in most cases more detailed analysis is required and we should no longer use the term 'super-ego' for both the whole and the parts of what it refers to. Separate and more accurate terms, such as Fairbairn proposes, have become necessary to make clear exactly what we are talking about. It is perhaps significant that fourteen years after the publication of his analysis of endopsychic structure (1958) no one has so far produced any direct criticism of it, though other points in his theory have evoked critical comment. A diagrammatic comparison of the Freudian and Fairbairnian terms may be useful.

The arrows show the direction of repression.

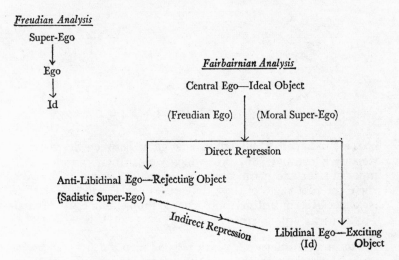

CHAPTER XVI

MELANIE KLEIN AND FAIRBAIRN

S O M E fundamental differences emerge as between the views of Melanie Klein and Fairbairn, which we can now consider. It is important for the clarification of theoretical issues to discover where the root cause of these differences lies. Elizabeth Zetzel in her paper 'Recent British Approaches to Problems of Early Mental Development' (1955) writes:

A theoretical framework which rests on such a definite and controversial premise as that of the death instinct has marked limitations. For this reason, if for no other, Mrs. Klein's theory will not be acceptable to the majority of psycho-analysts in its present form (p. 542).

In 'Notes on Some Schizoid Mechanisms' (1952, pp. 292–320) Mrs. Klein states the points on which she agrees and those on which she differs from Fairbairn. Those on which she differs all arise from her determined retention of the theory of an innate, instinctive force which is specifically destructive in aim and which manifests its specific destructive impulses from the very moment of birth, co-existent with libidinal impulses from the very beginning of life, i.e. Freud's concept of a death instinct.

In her latest book *Envy and Gratitude* (1957) she reaffirms this theory with as much fixity of belief as ever. Mrs. Klein has been entirely uninfluenced by the reasoned criticism of the concept of a death instinct which has led to its rejection by practically all analysts with the exception of Kleinians. Ernest Jones (1957, ch. VIII) states that the book *Beyond the Pleasure Principle* in which the theory was put forward by Freud is

noteworthy in being the only one of Freud's which has received little acceptance on the part of his followers. Thus of the fifty or so papers they have since devoted to the topic one observes that in the first decade only half supported Freud's theory, in the second decade only a third, and in the last decade none at all. (*Ibid.*, p. 287.)

He mentions that the only analysts he knows who still employ the term 'death instinct', even in a clinical sense, are Melanie Klein, Karl Menninger and Nunberg. After a careful survey of the problem Jones concludes :

If so little objective support is to be found for Freud's culminating theory of a death instinct one is bound to consider the possibility of subjective contributions to its inception. (*Ibid.*, p. 300.)

Nevertheless, Mrs. Klein does not even once throughout the entire range of her writings give any hint of the fact that her major premise is generally considered not only highly controversial but invalid. She never once attempts any critical examination or justification of it herself. This is left to Paula Heimann in *Developments in Psycho-Analysis,* pp. 321 ff. Mrs. Klein simply takes the concept over from Freud, and her followers assert that her work on aggression confirms his theory. This appears to be an extraordinary blind spot and, since one is never allowed to ignore the concept, it lends a subtle air of unreality to much Kleinian writing for those who regard it as invalid : just as in a more general way Mrs. Klein's loose and ill-defined use of terms lends an element of confusion and lack of conceptual precision.

As an example of the loose use of terms, one may cite her already noted adoption of the term 'paranoid-schizoid' position. Mrs. Klein first described the early oral period as the 'persecutory phase', and later adopted the term 'paranoid position' (treating the two terms as synonymous). Finally, to mark her agreement with Fairbairn's conclusions concerning schizoid problems and his use of the term 'schizoid position', she adopted the composite term 'paranoid-schizoid' position to denote the characteristics of the period preceding her 'depressive position'. (1952, pp. 293–4.) This composite term has not been accepted by Fairbairn and is in fact inaccurate if the accepted definite meaning of the term 'paranoid' is to be retained. The term 'paranoid' classically has two clear-cut associations which fix its meaning. In the psycho-analytic scheme of libidinal development it applies to reactions coming into being in the *early anal expelling phase*, and is thus marked by the *projection* of bad objects. Mrs. Klein simply transfers it to the earlier oral incorporating and biting phases, and uses it to denote the persecutory anxiety situations felt by the infant internally under menace from non-projected persecuting internal bad objects. This assumes that 'persecutory' and 'paranoid' are simply synonyms, which is not the case, and dilutes the meaning of 'paranoid' so that it would lose its specific application in 'paranoia' to refer exclusively to one particular technique for dealing with internal bad objects by projecting them into external reality while remaining identified with the internalized good object. Persecutory anxiety is present in all psychotic and psychoneurotic states and is not confined to paranoia. Since Fairbairn adheres to the traditional meaning of this term, he does not accept as valid the composite term 'paranoid-schizoid'. Such a term as 'persecutory-schizoid' would be valid but would then call to be paralleled by the adoption of 'guilty-depressive' to denote the two early positions in emotional development. This, however, is unnecessary, and the terms 'schizoid position' and 'depressive position' are adequate and seem to be the correct terms. Mrs. Klein herself writes: 'His [Fairbairn's] term "schizoid position" would be appropriate if it is understood to cover both persecutory fear and schizoid mechanisms.' (1952, p. 295.)

In 'Notes on Some Schizoid Mechanisms' (1952, p. 295) Mrs. Klein states her disagreements with Fairbairn. They are four in number, are intimately linked together and all arise out of her adherence to the Freudian theory of innate destructive drives as manifestations of a death instinct. They are best examined in the setting of her latest work, which shows a marked concentration on schizoid and schizophrenic problems, with the elaboration of the concept of 'projective identification' and a fundamental stress on envy. Mrs. Klein had taken over from Freud his own later dominant interest in depression, and she came to regard the 'depressive position' as central in early development. Nevertheless, she had always been very much aware that psychopathological problems went back behind that to the earliest oral phase. Here arose the 'persecutory anxiety', the isolation of which was a contribution of major importance to the theory of anxiety. She regarded it as preceding 'depressive anxiety'. Her specific acknowledgment of the importance of Fairbairn's work on schizoid problems makes it probable that it was his work on the early oral phase that prompted her to return and pay still closer attention to the pre-depressive experiences of the infant.

However, Mrs. Klein and Fairbairn approach the psychology of the earliest beginnings of mental life with certain fundamental differences in their theoretical assumptions. Mrs. Klein nowhere shows any awareness of the problems constituted by Freud's separation of energy and structure. She merely states that she disagrees with Fairbairn's 'revision of the theory of mental structure and instincts'. (1952, p. 295.) Fairbairn outlines a theory of 'dynamic structure' which is in line with the general trend of present-day scientific thought: and he regards aggression as unlike libido in that it arises as a secondary reaction to frustration. Hence for him the internalization of objects is regarded as a defensive phenomenon, arising out of the necessity for dealing with 'bad objects' which are therefore the first objects to be introjected. Apart from that, libidinal satisfaction (even if it is only an ideal state) would lead simply to good-object relations and good-ego development.

Mrs. Klein, on the other hand, adheres to Freud's instinct-theory and so can only think in terms of aggression as being innate, in the form of specific destructive impulses, just as libidinal drives are innate. The raw, unorganized, internally destructive energy of the death instinct is there from the beginning as a frightful menace to any kind of constructive personality development. This compels her to disagree with Fairbairn on four separate counts. (1) She rejects his theory of instinct as the dynamic pattern of activity of a developing ego-structure, since she regards aggression as active innately before any experience of object-relationships occurs at all, i.e. before there is any structural development. (2) The structural differentiation of the ego has then to be related to the disintegrating impact of this primary death instinct, so that ego-splitting cannot be regarded as primarily due to the repression of internalized bad objects. (3) To meet the internal menace of this death instinct, which is active from the very beginning, it is necessary for Mrs. Klein to postulate the primary internalization of the good object, the good breast, if the weak infantile ego is to have any chance at all of developing inner stability. (4) Finally, while the depressive fear is that of destroying by hate, she cannot agree that the schizoid fear is that of destroying by love—i.e. by the greedy intensity of deprived love-needs in a pre-ambivalent phase—since for her hate exists and is active from the very start. Kleinians at first took over the Freudian theory that hate relations were earlier than love relations, and hate was the infant's primary reaction to objects, though they later modified that to the proposition that love and hate were equally primary.

It is worth while looking at points (2), (3) and (4) more closely.

The Structural Differentiation of the Ego

The choice here is a clear-cut one as between Mrs. Klein's view of structural differentiation originating under the internal, disintegrating operation of the death instinct, a purely speculative view, and Fairbairn's view that structural differentiation originates under the disturbing impact of experience of bad-object relations in real life, a fully clinical view. Mrs. Klein writes :

I would say that the early ego largely lacks cohesion, and a tendency towards integration alternates with a tendency towards disintegration, a falling into bits. I believe that these fluctuations are characteristic of the first few months of life. . . . I hold that anxiety arises from the operation of the death instinct within the organism, is felt as fear of annihilation (death) and takes the form of fear of persecution. The fear of the destructive impulse seems to attach itself at once to an object—or rather it is experienced as the fear of an uncontrollable overpowering object. . . . The anxiety of being destroyed from within remains active. It seems to me in keeping with the lack of cohesiveness that under the pressure of this threat the ego tends to fall to pieces. This falling to pieces appears to underlie states of disintegration in schizophrenics. (1952, pp. 296–7.)

This means that, for Mrs. Klein, in the last resort anxiety is not an object-relations phenomenon but an innate phenomenon. Also object-relations are not really necessary to structural differentiation of the ego as Fairbairn holds, since it will go on any way. It is due to an inherent tendency to internal disintegration of the primary ego under the impact of the death instinct, so that it 'falls to bits'. Such a view would look much more like an explanation of Janet's theory of dissociation than of the purposeful ego-splitting phenomena leading to definite patterns of internal organization that Fairbairn seeks to explain. Mrs. Klein states that 'object-relations exist from the beginning of life' (1952, p. 293), but this seems to be something of an irrelevance; it does not matter much whether they do or not if they are merely incidental to the basic problems. Yet Mrs. Klein in fact rides two horses at once, for she goes on to say :

The question arises whether some active splitting processes within the ego may not occur even at a very early age. As we assume, the ego splits the object and the relation to it in an active way, and this may imply some active splitting of the ego itself. (1952, p. 297.)

This 'may', however, speedily becomes a 'must', for she goes on to say :

I believe that the ego is incapable of splitting the object—internal and external—without a corresponding splitting taking place within the ego. . . . Omnipotent denial of the existence of the bad object and of the painful situation is, in the unconscious, equal to annihilation by the destructive impulse . . . *it is an object-relation* which suffers this fate; and therefore a part of the ego, from which the feelings towards the object emanate, is denied and annihilated as well. (1952, pp. 298–9.)

This passage, written three years after the publication of Fairbairn's paper on 'The Repression and Return of Bad Objects', is pure Fairbairnian theory, and shows the influence of his work. It would, however, appear very questionable whether a weak infantile ego lacking cohesiveness and tending to fall to bits under the menace of a death instinct would have the power to split objects and itself with such definite purposiveness. Mrs. Klein's clinical findings support Fairbairn's views rather than her own theoretical version of Freud's speculative instinct-theory.

Internalization of Good and Bad Objects

Mrs. Klein rejects Fairbairn's view that it is the bad object that is first internalized (the pre-ambivalent object, internalized on account of its unsatisfying aspects). She holds that the good breast must be internalized from the start. Owing to the fact that 'oral-sadistic impulses towards the mother's breast are active from the beginning of life' (1952, p. 297), the frustrating breast is introjected *in bits*, bitten up in phantasy, thus promoting ego-disintegration. That is why Mrs. Klein must have the counterbalancing concept of the good breast introjected whole, also from the beginning, to counteract the inevitable disintegration process.

I hold that the introjected good breast forms a vital part of the ego, exerts from the beginning a fundamental influence on the process of ego-development and affects both ego-structure and object-relations. (1952, p. 295.)

Fairbairn does not need this theory since he does not regard the infant as starting off with destructive reactions to the breast. He holds that the internalized good object is only set up later as a defence against the internalized bad object. It is curious, however, to note that Mrs. Klein herself supports this view in principle, for her theory of the death instinct—i.e. 'fear of the destructive impulse ... experienced as the fear of an uncontrollable overpowering object' (1952, p. 296)—active internally is tantamount to an admission that the bad object is internal before the good object after all. Fairbairn's position is clear. Internalization does not include any and every kind of 'receiving into the mind' and 'influencing of the ego by the object'. The term relates only to the specific creation of a distinct internal object in the structural sense, of a split-off and repressed structure, a defensive procedure. Good-object relations provide no occasion for this procedure, for the good object simply influences good-ego development. The unsatisfying object is internalized in an effort to master it; when it is split after internalization, the good object is created as a defence against the split off and repressed bad objects.

The Schizoid Problem of Love as Destructive

Mrs. Klein rejects this view of Fairbairn, with the accompanying, quite unjustified, statement that he 'underrates the role which aggression and hatred play from the beginning of life'. It is not necessary to believe that aggression is innately active to recognize its earliest factual manifestations. Fairbairn believes that aggression is an instinctive reaction to libidinal frustration and arises as early as libidinal frustration is experienced. The schizoid phase has its own characteristic form of aggression. The frustrated hungry infant does not *aim* to destroy the breast but to possess it. He may, however—and all the evidence is that he does—in phantasy see himself to be destroying it in the act of seeking to possess it. Thus the schizoid anxiety over aggressive needs leads to withdrawal from reality because of destructiveness in phantasy. One of my schizoid patients woke up in terror one night feeling herself to be nothing but one big hungry devouring mouth swallowing up everyone and everything. She had a phantasy of standing with a vacuum cleaner sucking into it everyone who came near. That is the schizoid anxiety, of destroying by love. Depressive aggression, hate, aims to destroy the bad object and so fears the loss of the good object. Schizoid aggression aims to possess the exciting and tantalizing good object with such ravenous need that the loss of the good object is feared through the act of possessing it. The subsequent reactions are also different. In the one case the object is saved by turning destructive hate on to the self. In the other case the object is saved by withdrawing love that has become destructive, and breaking off relationships. Melanie Klein cannot make this distinction because for her, destructive hate, arising out of the death instinct, is there from the beginning.

One cannot but feel that 'instinct theory' has seriously bedevilled psychodynamic investigations and the sooner it is discarded in favour of theories that are based solely on clinical facts without speculative assumptions being imported into them, the better. Fairbairn holds that :

Perhaps the arrangement of mental phenomena into functioning structural groups is the most that can be attempted by psychological science. (1952a, p. 218.)

Two of Mrs. Klein's latest emphases, bearing directly on her analysis of the earliest phases and therefore on her conceptualization of the problems of schizoid and schizophrenic processes, are 'projective identification' and the primary nature of 'envy'. We may deal with these together. In 'Notes on Some Schizoid Mechanisms' (1952, p. 300) she writes :

> The phantasied onslaughts on the mother follow two main lines : one is the predominantly oral impulse to suck dry, bite up, scoop out and rob the mother's body of its good contents. . . . The other line of attack derives from the anal and urethral impulses, and implies expelling dangerous substances (excrements) out of the self and into the mother. Together with these harmful excrements, expelled in hatred, split-off parts of the ego are also projected on to the mother or, as I would rather call it, *into* the mother. These excrements and bad parts of the self are meant not only to injure but also to control and to take possession of the object. In so far as the mother comes to contain the bad parts of the self, she is not felt to be a separate individual but is felt to be *the* bad self. Much of the hatred against parts of the self is now directed towards the mother. This leads to a particular form of identification which establishes the prototype of an aggressive object-relation. I suggest for these processes the term 'Projective identification'. When projection is mainly derived from the infant's impulse to harm or to control the mother, he feels her to be a persecutor. In psychotic disorders this identification of an object with the hated parts of the self contributes to the intensity of the hatred directed against other people.

This piece of clinical analysis throws a flood of light on schizophrenic reactions. We are concerned here, however, not with its clinical bearings but with the theoretical concepts associated. In *Envy and Gratitude* (1957) Mrs. Klein writes :

> Envy is a most potent factor in undermining feelings of love and gratitude at their root, since it affects the earliest relation of all, that to the mother. . . . I consider that envy is an oral-sadistic and anal-sadistic expression of destructive impulses, operative from the beginning of life, and that it has a constitutional basis (p. 1).
>
> The struggle between life and death instincts and the ensuing threat of annihilation of the self and of the object by destructive impulses are fundamental factors in the infant's initial relation to his mother. . . . Together with happy experiences, unavoidable grievances reinforce the innate conflict between love and hate, in fact, basically between life and death instincts (pp. 4–5).

In the paper 'On Identification' (1955, pp. 309–45) she treats of envy as a factor in projective identifications.

In *Envy and Gratitude* Mrs. Klein seems inclined to place a somewhat stronger emphasis on environmental influence (p. 4). Nevertheless, as the previous quotation shows, her belief in innate hate and innate destructive drives is as uncompromising as ever. Whereas, therefore, Fairbairn would presumably seek to understand the motivation and origins of envy, Mrs. Klein treats it as unmotivated and ultimate, and as a basic manifestation of the death instinct. The infant from the start, she holds, feels envious of the good breast of the mother and wishes to destroy it because he does not possess it himself. In that case there seems little hope of love-relationships of a really durable kind coming into being, and it would appear rather that all love must function as a defence against repressed envy and hate. Fairbairn, on the contrary, holds that it is most important to help the patient to recognize that hate is not the ultimate thing and that always love underlies hate if one penetrates deep enough.

On the clinical level it is possible to adopt Fairbairn's view that aggression is not an ultimate in the same sense as libidinal needs, but is rather a reaction to libidinal frustration, and at the same time utilize to the full Mrs. Klein's illuminating emphasis on 'projective identification' and 'envy'. For Fairbairn holds that aggression is aroused as soon as frustration and lack of satisfaction are experienced, and that is early enough to set going almost from the very start the disintegrating processes Mrs. Klein calls attention to. Once aggression is at work, its *ad hoc* analysis is not much affected by whether with Fairbairn we hold that frustration and deprivation originate it, or with Mrs. Klein that they only intensify it as an innate impulse. Further research is needed to determine whether in fact, as Mrs. Klein holds, introjective oral sadism and projective anal sadism do operate together from the very start, or whether the anal phenomena are not somewhat later developments. On this point Fairbairn's view is relevant, that while the mouth is a natural organ of object-relationship the anus is not, and that emotional conflicts centring on anal activity are therefore artifacts and are dependent on the prior internalization of bad objects. To get rid of these internal bad objects the anal function of excretion is then adopted in a symbolic sense. If that is so, then oral introjection antedates anal projection, and one would suppose that 'introjective identification' antedates 'projective identification', which could matter a great deal in actual analyses. It would mean that, as Fairbairn holds, identification with the introjected unsatisfying breast leads to both internal bad objects and bad parts of the self, and that this is the basic process which then leads to projective identification in the working out of the struggle with bad objects, internal and external, and the bad parts of the self which are felt to be bad through cathexis of the bad object.

One final point of comparison. Fairbairn has replaced the unverifiable and speculative concept of a death instinct by the clinically verifiable structural concept of the anti-libidinal ego, to account for the forces at work in human nature which are destructive towards the self, as in suicide, and psychosomatic diseases where frustrated energies locked up inside work havoc with the organism and often end in killing it. These are only the most extreme examples of the remarkable capacity for self-frustration that human beings display, and it was such phenomena that the concept of the death instinct was designed to explain. But instead of explaining them, it only refers them back to an inexplicable and unalterable innate factor.

Fairbairn traces self-destructive impulses to the infant's struggle to cope with internal problems, by using 'a maximum of his aggression to subdue a maximum of his libidinal need', thus turning the full force of the aggression and hate felt against those who deprived him of satisfaction against himself in an attempt to stop himself having any wants that could be denied. This technique of self-suppression is structurally organized and consolidated as a part of the ego, itself split off and repressed—that is, as it were the agent of the rejective object inside the child (like a Vichy government ruling its own country on behalf of an invader).

This anti-libidinal ego operates as an internal saboteur, being devoted to the crushing of the libidinal ego (which is the libidinal aspect of the natural, active, creative primitive psyche in the last resort), and so is the source of all inhibitions, self-attacks, self-punishments and self-destructive impulses. This is not a speculative concept, but a clinically verifiable functioning part of the personality which analysis can lay bare.

Elizabeth Zetzel, whose criticisms of Fairbairn, Balint and Melanie Klein really only amount to the assertion that they are not orthodox, says of Fairbairn :

Instead of attempting to contain his observations within the conceptual framework of Freudian theory, he began . . . to develop a new terminology of his own. He abandoned the classical conception of id, ego, and super-ego, and instead regarded mental development as proceeding from various divisions and splits of an originally unitary ego and of an originally unitary object. . . . His attempt to create a comprehensive conceptual framework to account for certain still unresolved problems regarding the nature of early object-relations and

the development of the ego is praiseworthy. It does not appear, however, that in areas where we are still to a considerable extent working in an unknown territory the introduction of new words or a new
terminology can solve problems which remain unsolved. In short,
Fairbairn's theoretical work consists mainly of an attempt to alter
current analytic terminology. . . . The theoretical framework he has
constructed is highly ingenious and internally consistent. However,
it rests on a number of premises which are highly controversial. It is
extremely abstract and does not readily lend itself to objective validation, and will probably be approached by most analytic readers more
as an intellectual exercise than as a contribution which can be regarded as concurrent with the main stream of analytical development. (1955, pp. 357–8.)

In other words, Fairbairn is unorthodox. This passage is a singularly unconstructive piece of criticism. To begin with, Freud's own
structural scheme introduced new words and a new terminology,
and, just as much as Fairbairn's, was 'an attempt to alter [the
then] current analytic terminology'. Fresh thinking can register
itself only by the employment of fresh terms. Moreover, Freud's
terms, 'id' and 'super-ego', are actually more abstract than Fairbairn's terms 'libidinal ego' and 'anti-libidinal ego'. Fairbairn's
terms have the merit, which Freud's do not have, of conveying an
exact meaning. The functions of the libidinal ego and the anti-
libidinal ego are defined by the terms themselves, whereas the
terms 'id' and 'super-ego' define nothing. As to the terms not lend-
ing themselves to objective validation, the writer finds them more
precisely applicable in clinical analysis than the terms 'id' and
'super-ego'.

This may be illustrated in the case of the anti-libidinal ego,
whose machinations are clearly seen in the following dream. A
minister of religion, who for years, prior to a bad depression, had
lived a life of such extreme self-sacrifice that it amounted to an
obvious campaign of sabotage of his own proper interests, had this
dream. 'I was visiting my flock and trudging from house to house.
Every house I entered was full of sorrow and misery and I left the
people helped and rejoicing. I got more and more weary as I
went on and finally dragged myself into my church and collapsed
and died uttering the words, "Nothing for me".' An anti-libidinal
attitude of one part of the ego to the self is a more intelligible
comment on such a dream than a reference to a death instinct.
This patient had considerable artistic ability and once relieved a
severe depression by starting to paint with no definite aim. Ultimately he found that he had painted a terrible crucifixion scene

in which the lurid surrounding storm colours expressed the rage
and hate expended on the victim. At the side of the cross he
painted a placard on which were the words, 'A penny for the guy'.
The crucified figure he felt was himself, and the whole picture
expressed, first of all his destructive self-hate, and secondly his
bitter resentment at this anti-libidinal drive in him against himself, which led him to make his work·a crucifying self-sacrifice
('Nothing for me'), which had, in fact, been hounding him to
destruction. Happily the process proved to be reversible and the
energies devoted to it were set free for constructive living in a
way which could not have occurred had they arisen from an
innate, instinctive, destructive drive.

We may finally note that the work of both Mrs. Klein and Fairbairn bases psychopathological research definitely on developmental phases earlier than those to which Freud's attention was
mainly given; though it was, of course, Freud's work that led them
on beyond the ground he chiefly explored. In 1944 Fairbairn
raised the cry 'Back to Hysteria' (1952, p. 92) from the over-
emphasis of psycho-analysis on depression, obsessional neurosis
and guilt phenomena. Zetzel writes: 'Fairbairn explicitly recognized earlier than many analysts the close relationship between
hysteria and schizophrenia, which is becoming increasingly accepted by most analysts.' (1955, p. 537.)

To-day, research is going farther back than hysteria into the
aetiology of schizophrenia. Mrs. Klein's researches have recently
centred much more on schizoid than on depressive problems.
Sullivan's work rested almost exclusively on the application of
psychotherapy to schizophrenics. The 18th International Psycho-
analytical Congress in London in 1953 devoted a symposium to
'Therapy of Schizophrenia' (1954, *Int. J. Psycho-Anal.*, Vol.
XXXV, Pt. 2). Schizophrenia has become the advanced front line
of psycho-analytical attack on personality problems. This is what
we would expect if, not the Oedipus complex, but the regressive
reactivation of infantile oral dependence is the root of personality
disturbance.

This is raising urgently the question of the nature and causes of
schizophrenic disintegration of personality. We have three different views of the disintegrated state to which schizophrenics
regress.

(a) *Freud—Ed. Glover—Winnicott: Primary Unintegration.*
There is no ego to start with, but only what Freud calls id-impulses,
Glover ego nuclei, and what Winnicott speaks of as a primary
'unintegrated' state. Concerning this view Fairbairn writes: 'The
idea that there is no ego present at birth, and that the ego is a sort

of special creation which has difficulty in learning to tolerate id-impulses, which are really its own impulses, seems to me fantastic as a piece of conceptualization.' (Personal communication.)

(*b*) *Melanie Klein: Primary Disintegration.* While Mrs. Klein has recently favoured Winnicott's 'unintegrated' primary state, Kleinian writers, as we have seen, hold also to an original unity of the ego. Evidently they have not settled on a consistent theory on this point. However, Mrs. Klein puts forward the view of a primary disintegration of the ego under the impact of the death instinct. She clearly portrays all the destructive forces as present and at work innately from the very start, and needing to be counteracted by internalization of the good breast.

(*c*) *Fairbairn: Primary Integration and Secondary Disintegration.* Fairbairn holds that the ego is from the start in a state of primary wholeness or integration, and that disintegration is a secondary phenomenon, resulting from the persecutory effects of internalized bad-object relationships, i.e. the turning of the infant's aggression inwards against itself. It is the result of the sadistic attack of the anti-libidinal ego on the libidinal ego. This view seems to be more securely based on clinical evidence, while the two other views rest on theoretical presuppositions which invite radical questioning.

Part III

CONCLUSIONS

'The mind is its own place, and in itself
Can make a Heaven of Hell, a Hell of Heaven.'

> Milton ('Paradise Lost', lines 254–5)

'Since the good mother holds me still a child !
Good mother is bad mother unto me !
A worse were better ; yet no worse would I.'

> Tennyson (Gareth in 'Gareth and Lynette',
> lines 15–17, *Idylls of the King*)

CHAPTER XVII

THE BASIC FORMS OF HUMAN
RELATIONSHIP

A. COMPARISON OF FREUD, 'CULTURE-PATTERN' THEORY, KLEIN AND FAIRBAIRN

WE have surveyed the wide sweep of developing psycho-analytical theory from its early classic form to its latest innovations. No science can stand still, and the value of Freud's work lies as much in what he started as in what he himself discovered. The dialectical pattern of development suggested in Part I was not meant to be a rigid form, but it has been useful in ordering the mass of material. There is nothing metaphysical or mystical about a dialectical process. One need not be an Hegelian to observe that the enunciation of a clear-cut theory is likely to provoke fresh minds to the assertion of the opposite, and out of the clash of opposites there will slowly emerge a synthesis of what is true in both. Something like that has been taking place in psycho-analysis. The original Freudian biological emphasis provoked an antithetical sociological and cultural emphasis. This swing of the pendulum of thought had, however, already taken place in Freud himself to some extent, when he turned from his earlier instinct-theory to his later 'super-ego' theory. Even from the very beginnings Freud recognized the part played by the social pressures operating through conscience. Some Americans, or perhaps in the first place Europeans like Horney and Fromm who became domiciled in America, developed the sociological emphasis in a more one-sided manner than did Freud. Meanwhile there was emerging in Britain a third type of theory which quite unintentionally provides a synthesis of the two earlier points of view; for this theory centres in the concept of a 'double environment', internal and external, psychic and material, unconscious and deeply involved in the life of the body and also conscious and deeply influenced by human relationships and all the pressures of the social culture. This type of theory, now known as 'object-relations theory', provides a more complete psychodynamic theory while still taking account of the involvement of the body in the life of the personality. We are now in a position to summarize and compare these three great bodies of psycho-analytical thought.

1. *Freud*

Freud began, as a practising neurologist, with the study of disconnected neurological and psychic phenomena, as his patients brought him their symptoms. He assumed that the emotions and impulses which were active in these states of illness were to be explained by the already current theory of 'instincts' which he adopted and moulded to his requirements. For Freud, this instinct-theory always implied the background of neurophysiological theory. He lighted upon discrete psychic phenomena piecemeal in the investigation of the symptoms of, first Hysteria, and then Obsessions and the psychoneurotic illnesses in general, into the psychoses and psychosomatic illness. He could not at first have realized the extent to which he was opening up an entirely new field of scientific investigation, that of the psychodynamic problem of the personality. He had no particular view of personality as a whole other than that which was implied in his scientific, medical, biological and deterministic approach to man as a patient. He had no particular conception of a unitary psychic ego. His system, as he built it up bit by bit, was as much an atomistic theory of the dynamic psyche as was Associationism of the cognitive psyche. In this he was true to the general scientific outlook of the latter half of the nineteenth century.

Gradually the problem of the *ego* forced itself on Freud's attention, but he thought of it always as something constructed as an apparatus for the control of the dynamic 'instinctive' impulses which he thought of as invading it from an impersonal region of the psyche which did not belong to the ego itself as such. These instinct-derivatives had to be disciplined into conformity with social demands embodied in what he ultimately came to call the super-ego. Thus, Freud's psychology was basically a theory of guilt, a theory of control by psychically internalized social pressures over innate antisocial impulses. This is reflected in his change of interest from Hysteria to Obsessional Neurosis and Depression as the main source of his material. It corresponds with this that he should regard the Oedipus complex as the hard core of psycho-neurosis, and as biologically fated to arise. His was not really a theory of psychic disturbances caused by anxiety pure and simple in its most primitive form, not yet civilized into guilt. Freud for a long time treated anxiety more as a physiological than a psychological fact.

He was too acute an observer not to see deeper down into the pre-Oedipal, pre-genital and primitive levels of psychic life. However, he never specifically sought the basic causes of psychoneurosis there, but regarded the happenings of the earliest phases as preparatory and leading on to the really decisive phase, the Oedipal period, a fully social and conscience-ridden situation. Here, primitive antisocial instincts are at war with cultural and social tradition. The victory of instinct is criminality, the too complete victory of culture is neurosis. This remained the hard core of Freudian thought, which expounded the recalcitrance of man's biological nature to the process of civilization.

Remembering the intellectual climate in which he worked at the end of last century, and the heavily materialistic bias of his neurological education, one is amazed that he was able to break through to so much far-reaching discovery in the realm of purely psychodynamic phenomena. With little beyond the investigations of the hypnotists to stimulate his imagination, he broke into the forbidden regions of the unconscious, the uncomfortable facts of psychic conflicts involving anxiety and guilt. He came upon the embarrassing symptoms and troubles of the sexual life which he found inextricably interwoven with the symptoms of neurosis. Finally he laid the foundations on which all others have been building since, in the erection of a scientific, psychodynamic theory of human personality. However far future science moves beyond his theories, his genius and pre-eminence must be recognized. It is splendidly enshrined in the monumental biography by Ernest Jones.

Nevertheless, his presuppositions hampered his progress. Freud's work produced the first properly psychodynamic study of human personality, but this was obscured by his psychobiological instinct-theory with its consequence, a misplaced emphasis on sexuality. All that Freud discovered about neurotic sexuality so far as the detailed analysis of its symptomatic ramifications is concerned is indubitably true. For all that, it is not fundamental in the causal sense as Freud believed. In neurosis, sexual phenomena are symptomatic of the fundamental and over-all psychic or personality disturbance. The basic thing is the vicissitudes of the 'person', not of his sexuality, which is simply one, however important, of his functions. This was simply expressed by one patient whose neurosis arose out of gross maternal neglect. During a holiday period she found herself experiencing an increasingly intense need for her therapist, and in reporting this said : 'Sexual feelings came into this, but it wasn't a sexual feeling alone, it was a total need.'

Instinct-theory, in all its forms, ancient and modern, has been the major theoretical hindrance to the factual analysis and explanation of human experience and behaviour in psychodynamic terms. The necessary psychodynamic concepts did not exist and were not sought so long as thinkers were content to talk of nothing but expression and control of innate instincts. In spite of this, if Freud's first and greatest claim to recognition lies in the fact that he broke into and opened up the unconscious, his second must be that he really broke away in principle from the instinct-theory that he never formally repudiated. His super-ego theory laid the foundations of true psychodynamic studies.

2. *The 'Culture-Pattern' Theory*

The one-sidedness of the pioneer theory, in which character traits and personality were determined by the fate of sexual component instincts and the death instinct, and, in general, human object-relations were held to be completely dominated by the organic developmental fate of the inherited instinctive drives, brought a reaction, particularly in America, to an opposite and much more one-sided sociological theory. Freud did not ignore cultural phenomena as completely as the 'Culture-Pattern' writers ignored the deep unconscious. They saw human nature as determined solely by 'culture-pattern' pressures and lost many of the fundamental discoveries made by Freud. Beyond calling special attention to the radical importance of human relationships as primary facts for psychology, and carrying out much valuable analysis of character-trends of the social ego, this movement has not made any real contribution to psycho-analysis, i.e. to the profounder analysis of the psychical structure and growth of the human person. It is a kind of nonconformist aside, not in the line of the true development of psycho-analysis from within. For this true development and for the proper synthesis of the two opposites we must turn to Klein and Fairbairn.

3. *Melanie Klein*

Melanie Klein took up the problem at the point where Freud laid it down. She penetrated to the deeper depths below the Oedipus-complex level, into the infantile phases of development in the first three years. The infant cannot directly help us by verbalizing his mental processes at that early period, so that we must depend on external observation, and on interpretation of the infant's emerging phantasy life in the form of 'play' at a slightly later age. Yet the basic causes of psychopathological development are not likely to become first operative at the later Oedipal age only, but must be sought deeper down where Mrs. Klein looked for them. In spite of the fact that Melanie Klein's theory centred so much around depression, like Freud's, the most obvious result of her switch of interest back to the pre-Oedipal years was at first the emergence of a central emphasis on Anxiety. She came to interpret depression as a later form of anxiety which follows after the arousal of a more primitive form, called by her persecutory or paranoid anxiety. Here we see psychopathology going back behind Freud's basic concept of instincts versus conscience.

Utilizing Freud's view of conscience or the guilt-inducing super-ego as a psychic internal object, she showed, by the direct analysis of young children, that by the third year the child is already living in an internal mental world of psychic objects, most of which are terrifyingly persecutory. Its psychic life, conscious and unconscious, is already extremely complex in pattern, and has become, as it were, an internal environment to itself, with grave consequences for its relationships to its external environment. It has come to live in two worlds, one of which is internal and purely psychic and which makes up its mental or personality constitution. The frightening and destructive objects in the inner world turn out to be closely related to the arousal and growth of aggression in the infant mind, and they arouse primarily, not guilt, but persecutory anxiety pure and simple. Here lie the basic causes of neurosis. It is true that Mrs. Klein regards these internal objects as early forms of the super-ego, but it is clear that she has here gone below the moral stratum of the personality on which Freud worked for the most part, to what is truly primitive in man. Her analysis of aggression, anxiety and internal objects is really complementary to and completes Freud's analysis of libido, guilt and the super-ego.

Unfortunately Melanie Klein did not, any more than Freud, overcome the atomistic impulse-theory, and she achieved no real unification of impulse-theory and the theory of ego-structure. Mrs. Klein has truly sewn a new patch on an old garment in retaining Freud's instinct-theory and his particular terminology for endopsychic structure. She did not follow up the implications of her own discoveries. Id and ego remained essentially disparate in nature, and so no true theory of a 'whole' psychic self or of man as a 'person' could yet arise. No adequate general view of the developmental unity and structural differentiation within that unity of the psyche as a whole self was achieved.

4. *Fairbairn*

Fairbairn's work takes this last step. It is an ego-psychology which represents the total psyche or self as the primary ego to which psychic energy belongs, so that at last atomism is overcome, and impulses are seen for what they obviously are, the impulses of the ego itself in reactions to objects. 'Psychology without a Self', which appeared in Associationism in the eighteenth and nineteenth centuries with its congeries of atomic 'impressions' and 'ideas', and reappeared at the end of the nineteenth century in Freud (who was in the middle forties at the turn of the century) with his id-impulses, component instincts, erotogenic zones and mental mechanisms, can be finally discarded. Fairbairn took the step of abandoning the atomistic instinct theory as a biological irrelevance, replacing it by the unity of ego and impulse, structure and energy, in his *theory of dynamic structure*. He based his views on the fact that all psychic *development* is determined by experience in object-relationships which set going processes of structural differentiation within that primary unity of the psyche or ego which Kleinians also held. He saw, therefore, that Melanie Klein's internal objects could not stand alone. They could not be objects unless there are egos to which they stand in relation and for which they are objects. Just as the Freudian super-ego was partnered by the Freudian ego, so the more primitive Kleinian internal objects must be partnered by more primitive and infantile egos. All this structural differentiation takes place within the unity of the basic psychic self. That a multiplicity of internal objects necessarily involves the splitting of the original ego into a parallel plurality of egos is the basis of Fairbairn's theory of endopsychic structure, arrived at through the study of schizoid processes and the dissociation phenomena of hysteria in the first place.

A radical change of outlook has come about. We started with Freud's multiple impulses without an ego and needing to be synthesized into an ego. (Cf. Ed. Glover's 'ego nuclei theory'.) The disintegration that has to be cured in psychotherapy is, from that point of view, an arrest in the early process of integration or synthesis. But we have now arrived at a complete 'ego-object psychology', in which an originally unitary ego is differentiated into multiple egos and internal objects in dynamic relationships. This time, however, the disintegration that psychotherapy has to overcome exists within the basic unity of the whole psyche, whose original unity was shattered by early bad-object relationships in real life. This psyche is now seen, as a result of the ego-splitting processes set going by repression, to be living in two worlds at once, outer and inner worlds on the twin planes of the conscious and the unconscious. The interaction of the two worlds is the source of all neurotic difficulties in real life. This complete 'object-relations theory of the personality' is of far-reaching significance, not only for the understanding of neurosis and personality-disorders, but for sociology, and for the study of every aspect—personal, economic, intellectual, scientific, artistic, moral and religious— of human life.

This Kleinian-Fairbairnian development necessitates a revaluation of the Oedipus complex. The first move was Mrs. Klein's ante-dating of the Oedipus complex to the first year of life. That could hardly be the solution, for Freud's Oedipus complex was essentially a representative of an elaborate social situation which gave rise to moral guilt, and the Oedipus complex loses its original meaning if referred back to the first year. Fairbairn saw that the Oedipus complex was the end-product of the complex pre-Oedipal processes in which the infant psyche lost both its own unity and its capacity to deal with its objects as 'wholes' in a satisfactory way. In fact the Oedipus complex is the finally elaborated form in which the infant's dependent tie to parents is perpetuated in the developing psyche, though this does not eliminate the earlier forms of that infantile dependence at deeper levels in anal and oral relationships. The 'overcoming of the Oedipus complex', of which Freud spoke as the event or process in which the super-ego is formed, is clearly the struggle to repress an elaborate unresolved infantile dependence on parents, and ultimately on the mother, under the pressure of the need to adjust to the demands of outer life on an increasingly grown-up level. Thus Infantile Dependence takes the place, for Fairbairn, of the Oedipus complex as the hard core of psychoneurosis.

B. The Basic Forms of Human Relationships

On the basis of the Klein-Fairbairn 'object-relations psychology' it now becomes possible to give a clearer account of the different fundamental ways in which human beings relate themselves to one another, both as disturbed and as mature persons. This is a matter of importance to sociologists among others. It is generally agreed that the basic forms of human relationship must be determined by psychological analysis. Not all sociologists have turned to psychological science for this, perhaps because psychology has not always had much to offer in this respect. Yet, without help from psychology, the sociologist is not likely to achieve marked success in making, *de novo*, an analysis of his own. This is obvious in the case of Pareto, with his rough-and-ready division of all human actions into logical and non-logical, and the latter into a loose list comprising such vague terms as sentiments, tastes, proclivities, inclinations, instincts, interests, 'residues' and 'derivations'. Ginsberg writes of Pareto : 'His neglect of psychology has resulted in an extremely vague use of terms . . . his conclusions are hardly revolutionary.' (1947, pp. 84–5.)

It is, however, interesting to note that the psychological analysis made by the German sociologist Vierkandt is based on a broadly similar theoretical approach to that of 'object-relations theory'. He adopted the 'phenomenological' method of the philosopher Husserl. Ginsberg described Vierkandt's method as one of :

examining mental functions by direct inspection or intuition of *acts of consciousness as directed upon objects. All such acts are 'of' something. In the phenomenological analysis the consciousness and the object are bracketed together. It is a study of the consciousness-of-objects.* In ordinary experience and in natural science we concentrate on the object. In psychology we concentrate on the subjective act. *In phenomenology we are concerned with the objective reference in so far as it is immanent in the act, and we seek to disentangle the root types of mental functioning or ultimate modes of objective reference.* [Present writer's italics.] (1947, pp. 106–7.)

This is powerful support for the need for an object-relations psychology. In some ways no better description could be given of what is involved in an attempt to set forth the fundamental types of object-relationship as revealed in Fairbairn's psychopathology, in which every reaction of an ego is 'bracketed' with its object. For Fairbairn, psychology no longer 'concentrates on the subjective act' merely, for it is impossible to determine what that is apart from object-relationships. The difficulty with Vierkandt's own list of the irreducible social forms is that they are arrived at in an *ad hoc* rather than in a systematic way. Whatever strikes him on 'direct inspection' as irreducible is included, and we get a collection of psychological attitudes such as self-regard, need for recognition by others, tendency to submission and admiration, attitudes of shyness, embarrassment, love, hate, the feeling of belonging and so on. Why these should be ultimate does not appear, and we are not helped to understand how human beings develop these fundamental reactions to objects. Vierkrandt lacked the key of the subjective fact of internal objects so that he was unable to recognize forms of object-relations as themselves embedded in the subjective make-up of the individual. It is only object-relations theory that enables us to carry out the kind of analysis for which Vierkandt called.

Fairbairn and Klein reveal the true nature of the unconscious as a personal world of object-relations maintained within the psyche and constituting its structural organization. It is an inner world of which we are not directly aware, containing psychically internalized objects with whom infantile parts of the ego are all the time having intensely emotional relationships. Since the parts of the ego which dwell in this internal world are infantile, and the objects inhabiting that same world are, primarily, the ego's objects in infancy and childhood, *the inner world is one in which only immature relationship-patterns exist.* They are the perpetuation within the psyche of the situation of the child *vis-à-vis* parents and other powerful and authoritarian figures with whom the child of necessity had dealings at that time. Nevertheless, the busy life which goes on in the unconscious profoundly affects our feelings and reactions in our conscious outer life. Thus it comes about that the patterns of object-relationship which exist in the unconscious inner world determine the kinds of immature object-relations which people sustain in their outer world. They react repeatedly from the emotional level of inner reality which is immature, and not in ways appropriate to the conscious and adult appreciation of outer reality.

'Determine' is meant literally. Parts of the 'total psychic subject' are 'fixated' in fairly definite situations and types of relationship in inner reality, and these become observable in his dream and phantasy life. So long as the fixation persists, he cannot but feel and react according to those particular patterns of relationship. The integrity of the psyche, the primary unity of the ego, has been disrupted or split up by early experiences of conflict with objects. The central ego is that part of the psyche which is orientated to the outer world, and which classic Freudian theory called the 'reality-ego'. It is, in principle, free to develop, to adjust, to mature and to sustain rational and objectively appropriate relations with external objects. These relations, at the most fully developed and mature 'personal' level, will be characterized by equality, mutuality, spontaneity (lack of compulsion) and stability. On the other hand the infantile parts of the ego in the unconscious inner world are tied down to patterns of childish relations to bad objects, and are not free, so long as they remain repressed, to mature or react in any other way than that which is inevitable in their situation. Mature behaviour in the outer world is therefore constantly interfered with by immature reactions in and from the inner world. From the inner world came the psychic compulsions.

We must differentiate between a functional and a structural splitting of the ego. We are often temporarily 'functionally split' whenever we are 'caught in two minds' about anything. We both do and don't want to do something, or we want two different things and cannot have both. The opposed wishes are both fully conscious and the divided motivation is overcome by a conscious process of balancing and final choice. It is only when objects of ambivalent feelings and wishes are themselves psychically internalized and repressed in early life, and the parts of the ego related to them are split off from the main ego which rejects and represses the entire situation, that the splitting of the ego becomes (relatively) permanent and is preserved in the unconscious structure of the personality. The child grows up into the complex adult world which is organized in such a way that certain broad types of relationships between human beings are already embedded in the social structure. But the child's personality is also organized in such a way that certain types of immature object-relationship are already embedded in its inner psychic structure. *The inner and outer worlds have a two-way causal relationship and reciprocal influence.* The kind of relationships parents set up with the child, complicated by the child's own reactions to the situation, are internalized in the growing psychic structure, and will later on be compulsively externalized again and reimposed on situations in the outer social world, or else they will be spontaneously rediscovered in outer situations which correspond in some way to inner ones. Thus the individual is in the difficult position of being tied down to immature reactions to objects from the unconscious emotional level while at the same time he is doing his best to maintain mature relationships to objects at the level of his conscious reasoning self. Hence the tragic inconsistencies of human beings bewailed all down the ages by saints, moralists, poets and orators. The immature forms of feeling and impulse which surge up from the infantile inner world, coupled with reaction-formations against them imposed by the 'super-ego', in large measure constitute the 'actual' character with which a man enters his human relationships. The reasoned principles of his central ego, the part of his ego with which he is familiar, constitute his 'ideal' character which, in varying degrees, he may deceive himself into confusing with his actual character. In any emotionally stressful situation, and to a greater extent than he realizes in all situations, he will react in terms of compulsions arising from the 'super-ego' and the unconscious repressed parts of the ego rather than in terms of his rational ideals.

We may now, on the basis of Fairbairn's theory of endopsychic structure, set forth the basic forms of object-relationship. These appear to be at least fourteen in number, if we include the original relation of the infant to the mother at a time before any frustration has arisen. This can at any rate be imagined in theory as the starting-point. From the infant's point of view it is a spontaneous, uninhibited, enjoyable, active relation based on sucking at the breast while securely held in the mother's arms. It recaptures, as no other relation can ever do, the security of the womb though only as an approximation, since the disturbing crisis of birth has already been experienced. Some deep-buried memory of the bliss of life in the womb must lie behind all 'Garden of Eden' phantasies of perfect love-relations, all wistful longings for some mystic, unfathomable 'absolute good' which men have experienced in all ages, and all longings for the Golden Age which is always in the past. Its loss must condition what may be called either the futile restless dissatisfaction or else the 'divine discontent' which has always plagued human beings. Since it involves not only possession of, but also complete identification with, the object whence come all satisfactions, it must contribute in idealized form to the mystic's experience of union with the deity, and Plato's vision of the 'Idea of the Good'.

It is the 'oceanic feeling' experienced by one of Freud's friends. Freud writes:

It is a feeling which he would like to call a sensation of 'eternity', a feeling as of something limitless, unbounded, something 'oceanic'. It is, he says, a purely subjective experience, not an article of belief; ... it is the source of the religious spirit and is taken hold of by the various Churches and religious systems, and directed by them into definite channels. . . . One may rightly call oneself religious on the ground of this oceanic feeling alone. (1930, p. 8.)

It is a feeling of indissoluble connection, of belonging inseparably to the external world as a whole. (*Ibid.*, p. 9.)

Freud traces this feeling back to the original symbiosis of the babe and the mother and finds it revived in the experience of love as well.

At its height the state of being in love threatens to obliterate the boundaries between ego and object. Against all the evidence of his senses the man in love declares that he and his beloved are one, and is prepared to behave as if it were a fact. Of the beginning of this experience he says : 'When the infant at the breast receives stimuli, he cannot as yet distinguish whether they come from his ego or from the outer world. He learns it gradually as the result of various exigencies.' . . . Originally the ego includes everything, later it detaches itself from the external world. The ego feeling we are aware of now is thus only a shrunken vestige of a far more extensive feeling —a feeling which embraced the universe and expressed an inseparable connection of the ego with the external world. If we may suppose that this primary ego feeling has been preserved in the minds of many people . . . the ideational content belonging to it would be precisely the notion of limitless extension and oneness with the universe—the same feeling as that described by my friend as 'oceanic'. (1930, pp. 10–14.)

Freud alternately traces the origin of religious feeling to the child's feeling of helplessness and longing for a father. This would be the prototype of religious feeling, not as mystical union with the love-object, but as objective dependence on the powerful parental deity. Both types of religious experience exist, the one going back to the maternal and the other to the paternal relationship. Professor Martin Buber recognized the mystical type clearly, and its connection with the symbiosis of mother and infant, in his metaphysical prose poem *I and Thou*. It describes the part that this primary experience of a relationship, which is as yet, so to say, still embedded in a union or identity, plays in the religious life. He writes :

The ante-natal life of the child is one of purely natural combination, bodily interaction and flowing from one to the other. Its life's horizon, as it comes into being, seems in a unique way to be, and yet again not to be, traced in that of the life that bears it. For it does not rest only in the womb of the human mother. Yet this connection has such a cosmic quality that the mythical saying of the Jews, 'In the mother's body man knows the universe, in birth he forgets it', reads like the imperfect decipherment of an inscription from earliest times. And it remains indeed in man as a secret image of desire. Not as though his yearning meant a longing to return . . . but the yearning is for the cosmic connection, with its true '*Thou*', of this life that has burst forth into spirit. (1937, p. 25.)

Buber's last sentence warns us that purely reductive analytic thinking which believes that anything can be fully explained by discovering its first roots and simplest form may misconceive later developments. But it is clear from this varied testimony that the original relation of the baby to the mother is widely felt to play a

vitally important and continuing part, albeit in hidden, transformed and disguised ways, in all later experience. It is important
sociologically, since no doubt it plays a part in the mystical sense
of identity or unity, not only with God or Church in the religious
community, but also with Dictator, political party, or State, as
experienced by the political fanatic with his pre-moral type of
behaviour and consciousness in that role. It must be the basis of all
kinds of feelings of 'oneness' in both personal and communal
living.

This relationship of simple dependence of the infant on the
mother exists, however, not only in the form of the infant in the
maternal womb, the prototype of all dependence in the form of
mystical union and absorption, but also in the form of the infant
nursed and supported by a mature mother, the prototype of all
truly helpful dependence of the weak, immature or ill on the
strong, mature or healthy. In marriage a sufficiently mature
partner may well be able to protect an immature mate from
nervous breakdown. (We must say 'sufficiently mature', for it can
work the other way and the neurotic partner may break down
the resistance of the not-mature-enough mate.)

However, sooner or later the infant is cast out of the Garden of
Eden, and thereafter has to work his way through all the transitional forms of relationship on the way to full maturity. These
transitional forms of relationship between infantile dependence
and maturity make up the stuff of everyday living. At this point we
may note a matter of fundamental importance, the difference
between psychologically inherently stable and psychologically inherently unstable relationships. The original relationship of the
infant to the mother is relatively inherently stable in a psychological sense, since its absolute bliss is such that the infant can have
no inner motive for wishing to change it, apart from one consideration. It is the extreme of immaturity, and changes are imposed on it by inevitable biological development, from outside the
region of psychological motivation. The state itself is, however, no
doubt internally stable apart from that. At the other end of the
scale of development we come once more upon a psychologically
inherently stable relationship, at any rate in its theoretically complete or perfect form, even though in actual fact human beings
only approximate to it. A relationship between two fully mature,
adult persons is one of equality, mutuality and spontaneity. It
contains no element of compulsion, no striving of either for superiority, no element of distrust or constraint; and therefore there
is no motive arising within the relationship for desiring to change

it. The two are 'on a level' and give and take freely. As Professor Macmurray puts it :

That capacity for communion, that capacity for entering into free and equal personal relations, is the thing that makes us human . . . the personal life demands a relationship with one another in which we can be our whole selves and have complete freedom to express everything that makes us what we are. It demands a relationship with one another in which suppression and inhibition are unnecessary . . . the idea of a relationship between us which has no purpose beyond itself. . . . This is the characteristic of personal relationships. They have no ulterior motive. They are not based on particular interests. They do not serve partial and limited ends. Their value lies entirely in themselves . . and that is because they are the relations of persons as persons. They are the means of living a personal life. (1953, pp. 63, 97–101.)

Clearly only mature persons can sustain such a relationship, which Macmurray characterizes as 'friendship' ; they seek nothing else but to enjoy each other for their intrinsic worth, fulfilling their own respective personalities in the process. There is an easy mutual giving and receiving. It is the relationship we have in mind when we think of 'love'. Such a mature relationship is inherently stable because it contains no motives within itself for wishing for a change, no internal disruptive forces to disturb its serenity and security. Therefore a mature relationship is ideally stable ; it is not capable of change through being reversible for the relationship is the same both ways, irreversible because the attitude of both partners is in principle the same. In proportion as human beings are mature, they are capable of creating such equal and stable relationships, in which differences of type and capacity only enrich the fundamental unity and similarity of emotional attitudes. Such people are factors of stability in a society. The first relatively stable relationship of symbiosis of the mother and infant corresponds to Fairbairn's 'Infantile Dependence' ; the second essentially stable, mature and equal relationship is his 'Mature Dependence'.

In between these two extremes of infantile and mature dependence and stability are eleven *types of relationship all of which are unstable and reversible,* and it is here that all the difficulties of human association are to be found. They represent aspects of the developmental struggle of Fairbairn's 'Transitional Period'. These relationships are essentially unequal, hostile, full of motives for change and 'turning the tables', and lacking therefore in stability. They force life into a constant see-saw pattern of strife in which one person feels his lot can be improved only by weakening the position of some other person in some relevant respect. These relations are essentially competitive and rivalrous. They conform to a general pattern of 'one up and the other down'. The emotions generated in them are always anxious and disturbed emotions such as discontent, frustration, fear, anger, submissiveness, demandingness, longing for love, jealousy, hate. They fall into two groups, of three pre-moral relationships characterized by immature dependence and immature aggression, and two immature moral relationships. They are all unstable, falling short of the goal of mature mutuality. Since these relationships are unequal they each involve two separate individual patterns, that of the inferior and the superior, ten patterns in all. Schizoid withdrawal, or flight from relationship, makes an eleventh pattern.

To make this clear we must refer to Fairbairn's theory of endopsychic structure. The structural organization of the psyche exists on two levels, moral and pre-moral, the moral level being the central ego level. The pre-moral level consists of the deep unconscious where lie repressed the internalized bad-object situations of the earliest phase of development. Expressed structurally in Fairbairn's terms, we have the needed Exciting Object (E.O.) hungrily and angrily longed for by the infantile unsatisfied Libidinal Ego (L.E.). This represents and preserves the original infantile dependent neediness towards the mother, but in a state of frustration and intolerable lack of satisfaction. It is aggressive love-hunger, both emotional and physical (the physical including nutritional and sexual elements), in its earliest forms; the basic libidinal drive towards good-object relationship in the condition of being stimulated and not relieved, meeting with disappointment and being reduced to the pain of a persistent craving which never reaches its object. In the L.E., aggression is in the service of libidinal needs.

This whole libidinal situation is fiercely opposed by the Rejecting Object (R.O.) and the Anti-Libidinal Ego (Anti-L.E., Internal Saboteur) which is that part of the infantile psyche which is identified with the R.O. These two structures together form the early sadistic super-ego of Melanie Klein. It represents the angry despair of the original unitary infantile ego over the non-satisfaction of its libidinal needs and its consequent turning in part against those needs themselves, and against the E.O. that stimulates them. Thus in the Anti-L.E. aggression is now specifically opposed to libidinal needs, and the Anti-L.E. may even monopolize aggression. Thus we have the L.E. craving for the E.O., and the Anti-L.E. and R.O. persecuting both the L.E. and the E.O. But this turning of part of the ego against its own libidinal needs is accomplished by its identifying in part with the R.O., acting, so to speak, as its agent, and this is a dependent relationship which is libidinal in essence even though it is anti-libidinal in form. It represents the infant going over to the side of the rejective parent against himself. If all aggression is absorbed into the Anti-L.E., the L.E. can then only have a suffering, masochistic role.

Here, then, embedded in the unconscious structure of the psyche, there exists *a basic aggressively dependent libidinal situation* involving the child and the exciting mother (with whose mental image are fused later superimposed mother-substitutes), and over against that *a basic dependent aggressive anti-libidinal situation* also involving the child and the mother (with later superimposed anti-libidinal hostile figures) and taking two different forms, persecution of the L.E. and E.O., and also identification with the R.O. The first of these relationships is fundamentally libidinal (L.E. needing E.O.). The second is fundamentally anti-libidinal (Anti-L.E. versus L.E. and E.O.). The third is a mixture of both, a libidinal, dependent attachment in an anti-libidinal form (Anti-L.E. identified with R.O.). Since these relationships are not the same each way, but are unequal and reversible, each comprises two different relationship patterns, that of the subordinate to the superior and that of the superior to the subordinate. Together they make up three pre-moral forms of object-relationship, involving six different patterns of relationship from the point of view of the individual, characterized by immature dependence and immature aggression. They also constitute the world of inner reality at the deepest pre-moral level of the unconscious. The anti-libidinal figures are not as yet moral figures. They do not condemn the L.E. with its urgent needs for satisfaction, and enjoyment of and security-giving possession of its libidinal object. They simply deny, reject and attack. They manifest sadistic rage and cruel destructiveness, much of which is, as it were, lent to them by the baby's own frustration-rage. Melanie Klein has made it clear that the persecuting bad objects of the deepest unconscious, not only represent such anger as the actual external parent may display in the first place against the child, but also embody the infant's own rage against denial, projected on to the object and reintrojected as characterizing the object, from whom it is taken back into the Anti-L.E. In non-technical language, the baby sees his objects as coloured by his own emotions, and internalizes them as such : then by reason of his attachment to the object, his object-hate is turned into self-hate. In these three object-relationships the infant is struggling to solve his problems by keeping in touch with his parents and maintaining such object-relations as he can get even though they are unsatisfactory. If, however, the difficulties are too great, especially in the earliest oral sucking stage, he may give up and express his anger by counter-rejection of parents, by withdrawing, abolishing relationships in real life at the conscious level and developing the pattern of schizoid detachment, a mechanical living without feeling. The pattern of the hungry L.E. is repressed beneath this.

It is common enough, both in treatment and in real life, to find that whenever the intensification of inner needs activates the libidinal patterns (L.E. and E.O.), that is followed by the counter-attacking activation of the anti-libidinal patterns (Anti-L.E. versus L.E. and E.O.; Anti-L.E. and R.O.). This in turn further intensifies needs and a vicious circle or alternation of positive and negative transferences is set up. The six patterns of relationship which emerge from this deep level—two characterized by the exciting of angry needs, two by aggressive hostility to needs, and two by both —will repay close and detailed study. In *the aggressively needy libidinal relationships* the small, weak, needy child has all its desires excited by the big, strong, potentially supporting, satisfying and protective adult. It is very commonly the case that immature people attract one another because their expressions of need for love, their bid for affection by pleasing and friendliness and even self-sacrificing behaviour, may appear like a capacity to give love. In that case a difficult situation is likely to arise between two immature needy people, each of whom is the E.O. to the other but both of whom are in a state of very imperfectly resolved infantile dependence. Each wants to lean on and demands to be looked after by the other, sometimes actively and sometimes passively, and they will oscillate uneasily between the role of the one who wants to be supported and the role of the one who wants to give support. One such couple may 'get along' by being mother and child to each other by turns. Another such couple may quarrel because each is determined that the other must give way and fit in, and both want to be either the mother or the child at the same time. Infatuation, with its aftermath of disillusionment, is the projection of the internal E.O. on to an unsuitable figure in real life.

From this infantile situation, perpetuated into later life as an endopsychic situation, there surge up into adult consciousness compulsive sexual desires of all kinds, demandingness, longings for love in any form such as fussing, praise, approval, recognition, gifts, attention, and also all the compulsions towards compliant, pleasing, submissive and toadying behaviour designed to win some response from another person who is taken to be the indispensable 'needed object' for the time being. Where this condition is very marked, anyone who offers any degree of recognition, friendliness or help at once becomes the E.O. In Fairbairn's view this is conspicuously true of the Hysteric who is constantly seeking good objects in the outer world. The pattern conditions the psychology of much self-effacing 'unselfishness' of a compulsive type, as the basically love-starved person alternates between being the child directly seeking love, and the disguised child indirectly seeking it by filling the role of the unselfish mother-figure who gives it. This oscillation comes about because this type of relationship, characterized by a desperate sense of needy dependence on the object and unsatisfied craving, is *unequal* (as between the one who 'needs' and feels small, weak, helpless, inferior, and the one who is 'needed' and is seen as strong, big and superior); it is also *painful*. It contains inherently, strong motives for a change which can be secured only by reversing the relationship, tipping the see-saw the other way. Now the aim turns into a desire to feel the superior person needed by other weaker, dependent folk, to be indispensable, to lay others under obligation, to collect a retinue of inferior persons among whom one can feel superior and important and by whom one can be looked up to and admired. The longing for love is still there and but thinly disguised. The first situation gives the psychology of all parasitical attitudes, of hero worship and childish admiration, and of infatuations. The second or reversed situation gives the psychology of people who are dependent on being surrounded by others who depend on them, and who break down if they are left alone because they cannot keep going without the help of apparently weaker people who make it easier for them to deny their own repressed dependence. Thus in a basically dependent relationship it is possible to play the roles of either the helpless or the responsible person. This often appears in the case of people who can easily either 'boss' and get all their own way or be ill, go to bed and be nursed. (The mother who rules the family by means of her headaches.) Whether these libidinal relationships are looked at from the angle of the one who directly seeks love, or the one who indirectly seeks it by giving it, sooner or later the basically aggressive character of immature love emerges as a devouring possessiveness, and a ruthless demand for absolute compliance from the partner and angry reactions to the slightest frustration. This is because the whole pattern arises out of original frustration of libidinal needs in infancy. Over-dependent relationships are inherently unstable in adult life because they are painfully humiliating and can be so easily reversed. Very dependent people feel and behave in childish ways because they react from the inner situation which perpetuates childhood.

In the *aggressive anti-libidinal relation* the small, weak, needy child, the L.E., is hostilely rejected or angrily attacked by the big, strong, overpowering, unloving adult, and is reduced to obtaining what satisfaction he can from his sufferings. The L.E. is also persecuted by another part of the total ego that has deserted to the enemy (Anti-L.E.). This inner situation is the prototype of all *sado-masochistic* relationships in adult life, in which aggression is used, not to further libidinal aims, but to suppress them. It can be traced out easily where parents have been addicted to physically beating the child or indulging in mental cruelty to it, situations regularly perpetuated in the inner world and relived in dreams. This relation between an aggressive attacker and a frightened victim, an angry parent and a timid but resentful child, is also unequal, painful and reversible. The victim can escape by turning the tables, if not on the original persecutor, then on some substitute. This gives us the pattern of the person who is meekly enduring towards superiors but harsh and tyrannical towards subordinates, who can alternate between the roles of the sadist and masochist, the harsh boss and the cringing servant. It appears in the child who is submissive out of fear at home, but bites, punches and pushes playmates. It emerges in psychoneurotic form in the person who masochistically endures his own sadism and either suffers severely under hysteric body pains or distressing psychosomatic symptoms, or else reviles and abuses himself with verbal contempt. He may, however, fly into temper outbursts and sudden rages against other people out of sheer need to relieve his internal self-persecution. Aggression is either internalized to produce suffering to oneself, or discharged outwardly to hurt others.

When the desired good objective-relationship with the rejective parent is unobtainable, a substitute for it is found in identification with that parent. The formation of the Anti-L.E. by identification with the R.O. expresses the child's libidinal need of, and increased dependence on, even the unsatisfying parent. Thus the harsh or cold, unloving characteristics of the R.O. are reproduced. The R.O. becomes the model to be admired for toughness, strength, independence. A dependent libidinal relationship is set up which has an anti-libidinal form. Here, also, an alternation of roles sets in, for the person who hero-worships a dictator wants to be a dictator himself over other people. He then craves to be surrounded by inferiors who will slavishly admire him the more domineeringly he treats them. Yet as soon as his own superior comes on the scene, he at once becomes the slave. Thus we see six different roles emerge on this pre-moral infantile level, that of the L.E. to the E.O., of the E.O. to the L.E., of the Anti-L.E. to the L.E. (and E.O.), of the L.E. to the Anti-L.E., of the Anti-L.E. to the R.O., and of the R.O. to the Anti-L.E. These six fundamental ways of relating to another person are clearly recognizable through all their variations from one person to another in real life.

This remarkable see-saw propensity or oscillation of roles in both the immature libidinal and the anti-libidinal relationships is facilitated by the fact that at deep unconscious levels all relationships involve the ego in varying degrees of identification with the object. The psyche includes within itself both ego-structures and object-structures, and it can, as it were, take up its stand in either without ceasing to be the other. Thus the whole activity of the relationship can be carried on within the bounds of the total personality, bodily and mental; i.e. these internal ego-object relationship patterns are acted out either in the inner world of feeling and phantasy to produce neurotic illness and symptoms, or else in the outer world to produce neurotic behaviour disorders. Narcissistic and autoerotic behaviour, taking the form of manifest self-love or self-hate, seems to lie mid-way between the two. In masturbation, for example, the individual is both the comforter and the comforted, both the E.O. and the L.E. In the case of egotistical persons, the individual is both the admirer and the admired, just as in self-hatred he is both the hater and the hated. Some people when angry bang their heads, or punch and hit themselves, and behave as both the attacker and the victim. In milder ways, many people have a prevailing attitude of either nursing or of being hostile to themselves. In the objective relationships with other real persons, the deeply rooted tendencies to identify with the love-object and also with the object of one's aggression constantly lead to the oscillation of roles that we have noted.

In that case the endopsychic ego-object relationship is externalized and some other person in the outer world is forced into the role of either the ego or the object. If he is treated as the object, he will be clung to with a secretly aggressive dependence or else feared as an enemy; if he is treated as the ego, he will be the recipient of compulsive impulses to help, reject or attack him. Either way he cannot be left alone, cannot be allowed any proper independence, which reveals the basically aggressive attitude to the object. It is through this process of externalizing the bad inner situation (which serves for a time to relieve inner tension at the expense of outer peace) that endopsychic relationships come to have such far-reaching sociological significance. The outer environment may help the process by inviting such externalization.

Situations will at times arise in outer reality which parallel to some extent the corresponding situation in the inner world. The result is a disturbing over-reaction to the outer object or event in terms of all that it felt in the inner world. It is because living becomes such a strain when conducting all the ordinary personal relationships and is fraught with so much conflict and anxiety, that refuge may be taken either temporarily or in a more radical and permanent way in schizoid detachment, a method of carrying on the necessary contacts with people in a purely mechanical way without emotion. As one such patient said quite simply, 'It's safer not to feel.' This may be regarded as a ninth, negative pattern.

These inner situations of the pre-moral period all arise around libidinal issues, the infant's frustrated and angry struggle to get his basic love-needs met, and to retain permanent possession of his love-object, good or bad, always in the last resort the breast-mother. At this level 'good' and 'bad' mean *libidinally*, not morally, good and bad, i.e. satisfying, or unsatisfying and frightening. The bad objects which are internalized either excite without satisfying or else actively reject and attack the infantile ego. But from the weaning period onwards through the phase of cleanliness training and socialization, parents turn into figures who deny the child the original intimate libidinal relationships as disciplinarian moral authorities who train the child to reject its own wishes (i.e. libidinal needs for the good-object relationship in which his own personality can flourish) and to do what other people wish and require instead. The issue is no longer solely that of the child's needs for the 'libidinally good' but the parents' demands for the 'morally right', even when, realistically, the parents' demands are so narrowly based on their own convenience that no real moral issue arises. The whole libidinal situation of infancy has come to an end, though, naturally, the extent to which that is true varies in different cases. With parents whose own libidinal inhibitions are severe, the child may feel completely cast out of the Garden of Eden and faced with the angel with the flaming sword who forbids any return. The sexually exciting breast is replaced by the sword of moral retribution. When the child, whose deep emotional needs now seem to be disallowed, finds that the breast (and all breast equivalents) are forbidden, he secretly steals it back again by rediscovering it in his own body (as in thumb-sucking and masturbation) or in the body of another (as in childish sexual games and, later on, adult sexual relationships). He then feels terrible guilt. The moral level has been reached, albeit as yet only in the childish form. The guilt that attaches to sex arises out of the struggle to overcome infantile dependence by repression of the L.E. Pre-moral infantile anxiety and fear have become childish moral shame and guilt, with the earlier emotions persisting underneath. Thus an able, unmarried, business man in the forties had three times been overwhelmed with a sense of dread and doom, coupled with severe sexual guilt, over attempts to get engaged and married. He was in the habit of drawing phantasies and making up stories about them, and one day he drew a beautiful garden surrounded by a high wall guarded with fearsome steel spikes on the outside. In the shadows outside the wall a baby sat forlorn, holding out its arms towards the garden. His story was that the baby had once been in the garden and had been cast out, and now 'is not only not allowed to return but mustn't even remember it or think of it'. Marriage and a happy sexual relationship to him meant forcing a re-entry into the garden, and aroused the furies of a forbidding conscience which was largely based on the internalization of an exceptionally 'strong-minded', high-principled, righteously anti-libidinal mother.

Guilt arises from two sources—from the infant's anxiety over being destructive to his love-objects as a result of the intensity of his greed and hate, and from the fact that parents who have failed to enable the child to mature his libidinal needs beyond the 'infantile dependent' level feel they must force him to give them up, in order that he may grow up to be what they regard as a normally mature and independent adult. The child has to be emotionally weaned. The more rapidly, harshly and unwisely this is done, the more frustrated and angry the baby feels for the more unsatisfied he remains deep down; and the more aggressive feelings are roused, the more guilt the child feels over the persistence of libidinal desires in infantile form. These it may be forced to give up at the conscious level before it has had time to grow out of them by a true maturing. The result may be more or less complete libidinal repression, instead of a gradual development of libidinal needs into maturer forms. The problem is to wean the child emotionally and physically from infantile personal-cum-sexual needs and dependence without arousing too much aggression, and without setting up guilt and inhibitions which prevent his achieving the adult level of character and therefore of sexuality. This, it seems, is extremely difficult, perhaps impossible to do with total success. At any rate it is rarely achieved in fact without some residue of inner conflict situations. The danger is that libidinal inhibition is not confined simply to the narrowly sexual sphere of functioning; it inhibits general spontaneity and creativity throughout the whole personality.

To the six immature pre-moral patterns of relationship already considered we have now to add *four immature childhood moral patterns* : the small and essentially dependent child, who inwardly cannot give up his longings for a libidinal relationship to parents and who feels his libidinal needs in an angry and aggressive way, is faced with a powerful parent who is a judge and condemner of his 'naughty' impulses. He may no longer have and do *what he wants*, he must be content to have and do *what parents approve* (and other authorities as well). In proportion as he rebels and defiantly goes back to his earlier libidinal desires and frustration-rages concerning them, as when he masturbates, or plays childish sexual games, or seeks to gratify his growing sexual curiosity about adults, finally seeking adult sexual relationship, and in general wants to enjoy and feel secure in intimate love-bonds, he is made to feel guilty. The sexual element in all this represents unsatisfied infantile dependent needs for satisfying personal relationships, not 'instinctive sexuality' *per se*. One patient's mother set herself, during his school and adolescent days, to make him a serious-minded boy who did not 'frivol away' his time with girls but achieved brilliant exam results. Life was switched over from the emotional to the intellectual, from enjoyment of personal satisfactions to duty. The results of such a policy are seen in the extreme cases of the brilliant student who commits suicide on the eve of an exam, and is said to have been 'studying too hard'. The parents as *moral figures* are internalized and form the Ideal Object (I.O.) (super-ego *qua* ego-ideal) to help the Central Ego (C.E.) to reject and defend itself against those other aspects of parents who were internalized earlier as *libidinally exciting and rejecting figures*. So there is now set up in the inner world an endopsychic situation in which a childish ego is for ever guilty, fearing the criticism and disapproval of a parental judge either for its libidinal need or its aggression ; as in a patient's nightmare of his mother, twelve years after her death, appearing to him with a violently angry face shouting, 'What have you done ?' These two immature moral relations, condemnation of libidinal need and aggression, involve four different individual patterns.

This is not the adult level of freely developed moral evaluation and insight of a realistic order. It is a child's morality of fear based on the dread of the loss of parental love in the form of approval, and acquiescence in a relationship solely in terms of the parent's will. The aim now has to be no longer to 'enjoy' but to 'do the right thing', i.e. right in the other person's eyes, not in one's own, since the child's need dictates the aim of keeping the needed object at all costs. This internalized moral dependent object-relationship is, like the libidinal and aggressive dependent ones, *unequal* and *hostile*, since it is still a child-adult relation resting on frustration of deeply felt needs. It is also a *painful* relationship because it operates by means of guilt, and is frequently represented in dreams in terms of the criminal and the police, law-court scenes and the inflicting of punishment. Furthermore it is inherently *unstable*, generating urgent desires to escape from the inferior criticized position; thus it is also *reversible*, escape being achieved by the see-saw tipping of the balance the other way, turning the tables and criticizing other folk. Thus we find many people who practically always feel and behave towards others either as a guilty, worried child expecting to be blamed, or as a sharp-eyed, nagging parent looking for faults. The situation persists internally in the form of self-criticism, and is externalized either as a need for punishment at the hands of others or as vindictive moral ruthlessness towards them. In terms of this endopsychic situation people alternately play the roles of guilty inferiors with a bad conscience (of a quite unrealistic kind) or of morally superior critics of all and sundry.

This moral object-relation overlays the earlier pre-moral ones, and then takes the forms either of dependent or aggressive morality. Thus a person may be unable to act without the approval of others or else unable to abstain from attempts to control and direct others' lives; and again, in the aggressive sense, liable to masochistic punishing forms of suffering, including the compulsion to turn vocational work into a punishing way of life, or compulsive desires to inflict cruel punishment on others, a compulsion which accounts for much parental sadism towards children. All immature morality has a cruel streak in it, a compulsion to inflict and to accept suffering as punishment. The immature moral relationship exists in two recognizably different forms, that of the C.E. repressing the L.E. and E.O., and that of the C.E. repressing the Anti-L.E. and the R.O. In proportion as the C.E. is occupied chiefly with repression, it tends more and more to take on the characteristics of the Anti-L.E. Each of these forms can be 'lived out' as it were from either end, giving us four immature moral-relationship patterns, those of the person frightened of condemnation and those of the person finding a hostile satisfaction in the act of condemning, for either libidinal or aggressive activities. The 'Nonconformist Conscience' has all too often exhibited this kind of immaturity, and so also in even more marked form has the 'Hell-fire Preaching' of many evangelicals of a past generation. But this type is by no means confined to religion of an immature kind but is a general phenomenon. Much of the so-called sexual morality embodied in public opinion is kept alive by immature people whose frustrations are revealed in their prying curiosity about their neighbours' 'affaires', while their moral condemnations reveal all too clearly the workings of an aggressively Anti-L.E.

We may now tabulate the minimum irreducible types of object-relationship, which appear to be eight in number, giving rise to fourteen relationship-patterns. Six of these can be realized in two forms since they represent immature relations between persons who are not emotional equals, one being dependent on the other. These patterns are essentially properties of the internal psychic world, developing out of the infant's struggle to outgrow infantile dependence in terms of dealings, in Fairbairn's transitional period, with objects internalized in the earliest period. The fifth (ix) relationship-pattern is really the attempt to abolish emotional object-relations and replace them by mechanical ones. The eighth relationship-pattern, being a relationship between two fully mature and emotionally equal partners, is the same either way and admits of only one form. It is, moreover, not a relationship that belongs to the inner world, but one that is realized objectively in outer reality. It is the goal towards which the psyche is growing through all the earlier forms, and it implies a full capacity to live in creative and loving ways with one's fellows.

THE BASIC FORMS OF HUMAN RELATIONSHIP

1. ORIGINAL LIBIDINAL : *Infantile Symbiosis with Mother.* A satisfying and non-aggressively dependent relation of ego to object. Satisfaction experienced in oneness based on primary identification of ego with object. In the womb, a state of bliss, of direct enjoyment of the object in complete but unrealized dependence. Its attempted revival by secondary identification after birth, and regression in feeling and phantasy leads to claustrophobic anxieties of being stifled, swallowed. The original bliss partly recaptured by the baby at the satisfying breast. The relationship is stable when satisfying since there is no inner motive for change.

   i. The baby depending on the mature and satisfying mother.
   ii. The mature and satisfying mother carrying, or nursing, the baby. Regressive escapes from later disturbed positions back to (i) give rise to the pattern of the helpless child and the protective comforter.

The Schizoid Level. Pre-Civilized Disturbed Patterns

2. PRE-MORAL LIBIDINAL : *Aggressively Dependent.* The *Libidinal Ego* with natural needs stimulated by the unsatisfying *Exciting Object.* An unequal relation between a needy child and a needed parent, a reversible parent-child pattern involving frustration and instability.

iii. The infantile dependent person possessively longing for a mother-figure.

iv. The infantile dependent person possessively trying to be a mother-figure.

3. PRE-MORAL ANTI-LIBIDINAL : *Aggressively Rejective.* The *Libidinal Ego* as a needy, frightened, rejected child masochistically suffering under the angry, Rejective Object, the sadistic adult. An unequal relationship giving rise to a child-parent pattern involving great hostility and therefore unstable and reversible.

v. The infantile dependent person persecuted and rejected.

vi. The infantile dependent person persecuting and rejecting another.

4. PRE-MORAL MIXED : *Libidinal and Aggressive.* The *Anti-Libidinal Ego*, the child, placating the *Rejecting Object* by giving up needs and identifying with the parent's anti-libidinal attitudes. A frustrating relationship, unstable; and a reversible pattern.

vii. The weak fearfully admiring the ruthless strong.

viii. The pseudo-strong infantile dependent person demanding admiration from the submissive weak one.

There are only two ways out of the difficulties of the disturbed immature relationships of 2, 3 and 4; the real solution is that of growth to maturity, 8. A false solution is often attempted by the ego in the form of an escape, 5.

5. SCHIZOID WITHDRAWAL. The escape from too great pressure by abolishing emotional relationships altogether in favour of an introverted and withdrawn personality which is unable to show any feeling.

ix. The cold, detached person who acts mechanically with people.

The Depressed Level. The Struggle to Reach the Civilized Level

6. IMMATURE MORAL : *Dependent Morality.* Relationships based on the childish conscience founded on fear, the child seeking

security through approval, for the giving up of his libidinal
needs and aggressions.

    x. The infantile dependent person fearing disapproval of his
       libidinal (sexual) needs.
   xi. The infantile dependent person fearing disapproval of his
       anger.

7. IMMATURE MORAL : *Aggressive Morality.* The former relationships are unstable because of the hostility involved, and the
pattern can be reversed thus :

  xii. The infantile dependent person condemning others' needs.
 xiii. The infantile dependent person condemning others' angers.

The Mature Civilized Level

8. MATURE BOTH LIBIDINALLY AND MORALLY. The fully adult
relationships between emotional equals, characterized by
mutuality, spontaneity, co-operation, preservation of individuality and valuable differences, and by stability. The relationship
is irreversible and stable, having no motive for change. Its
morality is implicit, not imposed, a natural acceptance of obligations to other people.

 xiv. The relationship of mature dependence in equal partner-
      ship and friendship ; love, i.e. capacity to give to another a
      relationship in which his personality can flourish.

In the actual experience of human beings all these patterns jostle
one another at times almost inextricably in the ebb and flow of
emotional reactions. Conceptualization demands clear statement,
but this does not have to imply a false isolation of any of the
tendencies in practice. This is not intended to be a rigid theory of
'types'. It is, however, true that some one pattern can become the
most marked character trait of an individual, and its fixity may
be very difficult to undermine.

A brief hint at the sociological bearing of this analysis may be
given. The actual relationships of men and women in society are
characterized by the ultimate aim of striving to achieve xiv, the
mature adult capacity for equality and co-partnership in general,
with mutuality in private friendships and free unselfish love in
marriage. But this aim is perpetually obstructed and often defeated
by the fact that individuals live, not only in the outer social world
of the present day, where it would be possible, other things being
equal, to react in realistic and reasonable ways, but also in the
inner world of psychic reality which perpetuates childhood. Here
a large part of their emotional and impulsive resources are tied

up in the immature object-relation situations of i to xiii. They are compelled by infantile need systems to deal with their outer world in terms of their inner world, and their behaviour, needs and moods become unstable, unreliable, changeable, critical or guilty, hostile or subservient, dominating or demanding by turns. A major defensive technique adopted to avoid these painful situations is the attempt to stifle all feeling, break off all real human relationships and live as a merely efficient, impersonal, mechanized human robot, the schizoid type of personality. One might almost call this denial of relationship a negative type of relation.

Psycho-analytically orientated anthropologists have made pioneer studies correlating the patterns of child-rearing prevalent in a given society and the culture of that society. Prevailing patterns of child-rearing must result in similar internalized situations in the unconscious of the majority of individuals in a culture, and these will be externalized back into the culture again to perpetuate it from generation to generation. A vicious circle is set up of internal patterns on the one hand and social traditions and political trends on the other. Politics, as much as other spheres of life, is a happy hunting-ground for the 'acting out' of immature relationship-patterns, especially in disturbed times.

1. *Mature.* Democracy at least aims at achieving a social order in which people function as responsible, free and equal co-operators, though in a 1946 broadcast Herbert Read suggested that large-scale democracy was now wedded to centralization and control, and only anarchism and decentralization could secure the original democratic aims. How a large-scale society of mature people would organize their life we have yet to see.

2. *Moral.* Theocratic, state-paternalistic, puritanical and legal systems come broadly under this head, including modern totalitarianism in its role of controlling the entire life of, and even dictating opinion to, the individual citizens, by the identification of education and propaganda.

3. *Anti-Libidinal.* Military dictatorships and empires based on conquest or financial domination, and modern totalitarianism in its role of the police state with Gestapo or Ogpu, and its apparatus of concentration camps and persecution, and its relapse from civilized standards to cruelty and the denial of human rights to dissidents, come under this head.

4. *Dependent.* In a degenerate form, the welfare state of a 'panem et circenses' type, or any kind of state which undermines individual initiative and responsibility, is of this type. The 'Fear of Freedom' (*vide* E. Fromm) that leads nations to barter liberty for security under 'The Leader' comes into this category.

Ultimately social organization will reflect the dominant psychological trends in the majority of the individuals who make up the group. One major issue emerges from all this. The instability of the childish and immature types of relationship is due, not only to their inherently unsatisfying and painful nature, but also to the developmental urge to grow up and become self-reliant and normally independent. For a mature person the necessary element of dependence in any real relationship does not compromise the essential integrity and proper independence of the individual. For an immature person, whose dependent needs are so strong as to menace independence, dependent and independent needs are felt as incompatible goals and there is a perpetual oscillation between them. Life becomes an unremitting struggle to defend one's need for independence against one's need for personal relationships. This basic conflict underlies all personal and political phenomena, and emerges as the conflicting aims of security and freedom, and as the fight for liberty of class or nation *versus* the hunger for leadership and a 'Fuehrer'. With the increasing large-scale destructiveness of modern scientific weapons, the world's greatest danger lies in the rise to absolute power of types of men who combine top-rank intellectual ability with deeply disturbed and immature personalities wedded particularly to sado-masochistic motivational patterns. They have a fatal and profound attraction towards destructiveness and, like Hitler, can be equally prepared to conquer by ruthlessness, or to destroy themselves amidst a universal ruin.

Chapter XVIII

THEORY AND THERAPY

IT was stated in chapter I that the ultimate purpose of theoretical enquiry was to further the aims of psychotherapy. We seek to understand human nature so that we may solve the serious and dangerous problems of human maladjustment in personal relationships. The opinion is frequently voiced that in our time the failure to solve these problems might well lead to the extinction of this phase of civilization, if not of the human race : for at present all peaceful and constructive uses of scientific knowledge are overshadowed by its use to increase our capacity for mutual destruction. Can scientific knowledge about the human mind be saved from the fate of being put to destructive uses? Hate-ridden and destructively motivated dictators, and rulers with paranoid and psychopathic personality trends, could make use (and perhaps have already made use) of scientific knowledge of the weak spots in human personality to further their ends of power-politics. I have expressed the view elsewhere that 'psycho-analysis as a purely scientific technique of investigation . . . may discover facts about the way the human mind develops from infancy onwards, that could be used for the shaping of psychological conditioning techniques of diabolical efficiency. The mobilization of childhood guilt in political prisoners to "soften them up" before trial, is a case in point.' (1956b, p. 165.)

Nevertheless, our fears of the probable misuse of discoverable knowledge cannot now prevent the progress of scientific research any more in psychology than in nuclear physics. The only safeguard is to see the dangers clearly and sharpen our realization of the need to defend those freedoms which express respect for human personality as such, while we push on with the constructive uses of the knowledge we have. What, then, are the fundamental conclusions that emerge so far, as a result of this particular historical and comparative study of the course of development and the differing emphases in the field of psycho-analysis? I shall seek to present these conclusions in this chapter in a more general theoretical form, as a picture of the 'human situation', of which theory gives an abstract account to clarify the implications for psychotherapy.

Fairbairn has arrived at one general and fundamental conclusion, namely, that the root cause of all personality disturbance and neurosis is the unconscious persistence within the adult personality of too strong an element of infantile dependence. Psychopathology reduces in the end to the description of infantile dependence, its forms of persistence and ramifications in the personality, and the psychic defences set up against it. The human child, for whatsoever reason, does not always grow up to be psychically adult. That is what we seek to understand. Emotional resistances must have always obstructed the perception of this really very obvious fact, and prevented its statement as a simple, basic, general truth; for there is nothing that grown-ups feel to be so humiliating as the 'accusation' of childishness (and psycho-analytical interpretations are usually at first felt to be accusations). Adults fear the child in themselves and everything that keeps him alive inside, as a danger to the maintenance of their adult social and vocational roles, and as likely to expose them to unwelcome criticism or even scorn from those who are secretly as afraid as themselves. They deny the existence of the child in the unconscious.

It will be well, therefore, first to present this unpalatable truth, that we do not succeed very well in growing up, in a broad and impersonal way. It makes a great deal of difference to the direction of therapeutic efforts, whether psychoneurosis is regarded as due to hereditary or to developmental causes; but, beyond that, it also makes a great difference whether the cause of neurosis is sought in some particular factor such as the Oedipus complex or in a general factor such as a too-strong undercurrent of infantile dependent feeling expressing a basic immaturity of development in the personality as a whole. Is the Oedipus complex the cause of infantile dependence persisting into adult life, or is it simply one expression of that dependence? Freud began with the former view. To the present writer the clinical evidence that determined Fairbairn to the latter view is convincing. In the Oedipus complex and infantile sexuality, Freud discovered the clinically verifiable evidence of the infant still unconsciously emotionally alive inside the biological adult. How and why is this possible?

1. *Biological and Social Dependence of the Child*

We are on solid ground in saying that what makes neurosis possible to begin with is the prolonged biological dependence of the human offspring on the parents. In the lower forms of life, days, weeks or months suffice to make the young independent of those who begot them. The period of dependence lengthens as the forms of life grow more complex, but nowhere is there any real parallel to the case of the human child. Here biological dependence is profound for a very long time, so utterly helpless is the human infant to fend for himself. As time goes on, both in the life of the individual and in the historical development of cultures, the original biological and physical dependence is lengthened into educational, social and economic dependence. The increasing complexity of civilization makes this inevitable. Thus, whereas in primitive tribes adolescence occurs in the earlier teens, in our modern society it has been pushed forward into the late teens. In simple cultures a male can acquire the status of a man in the middle teens and a female may be a wife at fifteen years or earlier, and physical maturing comes early. In our modern Western culture a male may not be able to achieve adult status in his own right, socially and economically, by the age of twenty-five, and marriage for both males and females may well come nearer thirty than twenty.

Thus, even in primitive cultures the dependence of childhood remains an overriding factor for some fifteen years, and amongst ourselves it persists in the material circumstances of life for anything from twenty to thirty years, long after the natural desires for independence reach maximum conscious force. But we have also to reckon with the fact that, in addition to this fundamental *dependence* characterizing most of the first twenty years of life at least, the human young are also endowed with the human gifts of high intelligence and imaginative, creative powers far above all other forms of life. These confer on the developmental process an urge to activity and exploration, i.e. a premature drive to *independence* which makes it difficult to tolerate basic dependent needs. This setting for our early development predisposes human beings as such, and conspicuously in modern civilization, to experience acute conflicts of the 'dependence *versus* independence' order. For underneath all the external and visible ties and bonds, the primary emotional dependence of the child on the parent has had years in which to consolidate its hold on the basic structure of the personality. Even though the struggle to achieve freedom for independent action begins so early in childhood, the conditions of human existence make it an exceptionally difficult thing for the child to grow out of the infantile dependence of its earliest relationships to the mother and the father. Freud regarded that as the deepest conditioning factor in the development of religion, whereas he regarded science as the fruit of man's attempt to master his universe and make himself self-sufficient. Put that way it is easy to regard religion as infantile and science as adult, but the matter is not so simple. Dependence is, in fact, an ineradicable element in human nature, and the whole development of love and the affections arises out of our needs for one another. From this point of view religion is concerned with the basic fact of personal relationship and man's quest for a radical solution to the problems that arise out of his dependent nature. Without the acceptance of that measure of dependence that lies at the heart of all human needs for relationships, one becomes incapable of love, friendship, marriage or any truly human co-operative activity. On the other hand, science, by concentrating on impersonal investigation and by the quest for power which aims at self-sufficiency, may well cultivate mental attitudes unsympathetic to the basic emotional dependencies of life. We cannot simply equate religion with immaturity and science with maturity as Freud wished to do. The problem of dependence in human nature cannot be solved as easily as that.

The problem is not dependence as such, for that is a permanent feature of man's nature, but the persistence of dependent characteristics in too infantile a form. Naturally, religion, dealing as it does with the emotional needs of human beings as persons, will be more liable to adulteration by the importation of infantile dependence into its motivation than will science. Nevertheless, man has shown an age-old desire for the emotional security that would result from the knowledge that our life as 'persons' arises out of and remains rooted in a fundamentally 'personal' element in the structure of the universe. It is the task of philosopher and theologian to show whether that is realistic, but he would be a bold, foolish man who should insist that that is in itself a neurotic wish. It appears to the present writer that it would be easier to prove, on psycho-analytic grounds, that a sustained attitude of solitary defiance of an indifferent, impersonal, ultimate reality (*vide* Bertrand Russell) is neurotic. To show that man's infantile dependence has sought succour in religion seems to imply two things: first, that such infantile dependence is a universal human phenomenon to be found in all races, cultures and times, and, secondly, that the problem of human life is how to deal with this infantile dependence in such a way as to free the person for growth to a kind of dependence that is an essential part of maturity. Religion has not ignored this problem, even though it has had to struggle with it in the absence of scientific knowledge of human nature.

The discovery of psycho-analysis that grown-up people are still children at heart elaborates in factual detail a truth that has always been part of the religious view of life. In what sense and how far 'a child' is the question. For, allowing for the inherent difficulty of outgrowing dependence of a childlike order in view of our profound biological dependence on parents in early life, the fact is that the majority of human beings do not grow out of that even to the extent that would be possible. *Mature religion* would express man's fundamentally dependent nature, in a relationship of emotional rapport with and reverence for external reality as a whole, immediate and universal, symbolized in a meaningful philosophy of life representing that mature dependence which is part of the adult character) while *psychotherapy,* and also religion in so far as it has functioned all down the ages in a psychotherapeutic manner, are concerned with helping individuals to deal with their immature dependence of an infantile order. The usual course of events is that at the deepest mental levels this infantile dependence is not and cannot be, completely outgrown. It persists as an unconscious factor even in the maturest adult. Every human being feels to be in the depths of his nature a dependent being and spends a third of his life in bed asleep to prove it. For the rest he struggles to maintain a transitory independence for a short space of time in the world of adult responsibility and satisfaction. The political phenomenon of the rise of totalitarianism in our time, and what Erich Fromm called 'the fear of freedom', is evidence of how widespread this problem is.

2. *Pathological Dependence*

When we seek to understand this, psycho-analysis directs our attention unequivocally to certain facts. If, in addition to the prolonged natural dependence of the human child on parents, the child meets in the parental and family situation with additional difficulties, the task of growing up to emotional maturity may well prove insuperable. So absolute is the infant's need for reliable maternal support in the form of full satisfaction, not only of nutritional but even more of psychological, personal needs, that the best mother is bound to be a 'bad object' sometimes. Fairbairn writes :

It must be recognized, of course, that no individual born into this world is so fortunate as to enjoy a perfect object-relationship during the impressionable period of infantile dependence, or for that matter during the transition period which succeeds it. Consequently, no one ever becomes completely emancipated from the state of infantile dependence, or from some proportionate degree of oral fixation; and there is no one who has completely escaped the necessity of incorporating his early objects. It may consequently be inferred that there is present in everyone either an underlying schizoid or an underlying depressive tendency. (1952a, p. 56.)

If in large numbers of cases mothering is, to use Winnicott's phrase, 'good enough' to enable the child to get through life without specific breakdown, it is not good enough to produce a high level of mental health and maturity of personality throughout the community. Perhaps it would be surprising if it were, when we consider all the difficulties that the mother herself may have to contend with, ranging from those that spring from her own upbringing to those that arise from, maybe, a disturbing husband or social and economic insecurities. Varying degrees of neurotic instability, though short of definite illness, are the rule rather than the exception. Enormous numbers of children find their parents too unreliable and disturbing to be coped with successfully. The children do not obtain those 'vitamins of personality growth' that collectively make up mature parental love or 'cherishing'. As Fairbairn puts it, the parent does not succeed in convincing the child that he is loved as a real person in his own right. The parent does not have to be a grossly bad parent to fail the child in this respect. Dr. L. Housden mentions, in the Ministry of Health pamphlet, *Hostels for 'Difficult' Children,* that out of four hundred and eighty-six cases, a quarter came from what seemed to be good homes, and adds :

Recently I went into the cases of twenty-five boys who had all, except one, been convicted of stealing. Of these boys twenty-two came from homes where they lived with both parents and in eighteen cases they said their homes had been happy ones. . . . There are three urgent needs of all children and young people. The first is the feeling of being a valued member of the family; the second is the possession of their parents' affection and interest; and the third is happy occupation. 'Difficult' children do not come from homes where these three needs are supplied. (1945, pp. 8–10.)

All this is now generally accepted and we simply have to remind ourselves here that all types of difficulty in childhood—material, economic, psychological and personal, but basically those that enter into the relationships of the parents with the child—serve to intensify the child's consciousness of his own smallness, weakness, helplessness, lack of self-confidence and fear of active venturing. He becomes a prey to feelings of insecurity, inadequacy, timidity and guilt, and is unable to develop a sense of joyous confidence in

spontaneous activity as the years go by. Then, finding his feet in
the big world outside the home, becoming able to accept his
responsibilties in it and adjust to its standards becomes a frightening task. As the child passes from the pre-moral level of purely
infantile life to the moral level of more specifically co-operative
social adjustment, he finds that the overcoming of infantile dependence is more than he can achieve by normal methods. Fairbairn makes the important point that it is not the difficulties of the
infantile period alone that account for psychoneurosis; it is rather
the fact of being pushed back into them at deep emotional levels,
when later childhood life proves to be simply a continuation of
disturbances in the midst of which no stable and non-anxious
personality can be developed. Deteriorating relationships with
parents in the post-infancy years, involving not being understood,
valued, helped, respected for his own sake, set up in the child an
unconscious regression to, and revival of, infantile dependent
modes of feeling.

3. Active and Passive Aspects of Infantile Dependence

Infantile dependence, however, as the foundation of personality
disturbances in later life is not a simple thing. Nor is it the same
thing as, or a mere residue of, the natural biological dependence
of the infant, though it is related to it. It appears in two strikingly
different forms, *active* and *passive*. According to Fairbairn, the
two chief characteristics of infantile dependence are marked tendencies to *emotional identification* with, and, at the same time,
oral incorporation of, the love-object, the breast and the breast-
mother. Identification, in so far as it is a persistence of gradually
diminishing primary identification, the feeling of oneness with the
mother in the womb, is a naturally passive characteristic. Oral
incorporation, the infant's urge to take in from the breast, is an
active characteristic. If all goes well, the first fades out more and
more and the second develops into a dual capacity, not only to
take in but also to give out, in the satisfied baby and growing child.

As soon as frustration is met with, a very different state of
affairs arises. Deprivation imparts an aggressive quality to unsatisfied needs, and oral incorporation turns into the impulse to
sadistic devouring. We should qualify 'aggressive' more explicitly
as 'angrily aggressive' for there is a 'playful aggressiveness' or
'energetic assertiveness' which is natural and healthy. The infant
comes to feel both dangerous to his love-objects and persecuted by
them in retaliation. Thus *active infantile dependence* comes to be
experienced in the form of intense, compulsive, but destructive

and frightening needs towards love-objects which, if it breaks
through into adult behaviour, takes the form of ruthless possessiveness and exhausting demandingness, of the type seen in severe
hysteria. In unconscious phantasy emerging in dreams this oral
sadism gives rise to symbols of devouring wild animals and fills
the psyche with terror. One patient had hallucinations of leopards
leaping across the room with open bloody mouths.

This state of affairs leads to a sharp reversal. The oral sadistic
L.E. becomes afraid to exercise its infantile dependence in this
destructive way. The intense anxiety generated puts a stop to that,
and the sadism is drawn into the Anti-L.E. to be used for crushing
and sabotaging the active libidinal self with its needs. A *passive
infantile dependence* arises which is very different from the
original restful passivity implied in primary identification. Infantile dependence can now be exercised only in an enforcedly
passive form. The infant has become afraid to be active. He unconsciously devotes his anger, not to the expression of his frustrated
needs, but to their suppression, or at least to the inhibition of any
active expression of them. He can now be only passively dependent, helpless, inhibited, clinging, suffering, *the dependent
masochist* because of the terror he experiences over being in feeling and phantasy *the dependent sadist*. This type of dependence
is even more strikingly exhibited by the hysteric.

The serious emotional position has now arisen in which the
growing person can be libidinal only in passive ways, and can
be active only in aggressive ways. To cope with this problem in
adjusting to everyday living in the outer world a third position has
to be developed. While the L.E. is repressed in a passive masochistic state, and the Anti-L.E. is repressed in a sadistic state to
use its aggression against the emergence of libidinal needs, the
C.E. has to force a controlled activity on the basis of duty and
service in order to meet the demands of the outer world. In the
unconscious inner world the unremitting attack kept up by the
sadistic Anti-L.E. upon the masochistic L.E. gives rise to the personality tensions and physical and other symptoms that constantly
disturb the outer adjustment which the C.E. struggles to maintain. This is the basic hysteric and schizoid position which Fairbairn regards as the fundamental endopsychic situation and the
root of psychoneurosis. Genuine libidinal responsiveness to outer
reality is lost.

This complex pattern of a basic activity repressed because it is
in a sadistic state, and transformed into a masochistic passivity
which threatens to undermine energy and initiative, and which is
hidden by a tense, forced, active, social self on a conscious level,

reflects the threefold splitting of the original ego, and must be correlated with the respective appropriate internal objects to give the full inner structural organization. The pattern has to be worked through in reverse in most analyses, in the attempt to undo it and restore the pristine self to freedom for spontaneous healthy living.

The attack of the Anti-L.E. on the L.E. is illustrated in the following clinical material. A male patient, who carried heavy business responsibilities in everyday life to the accompaniment of considerable internal tension and conflict, dreamed that he had just had his glasses mended and then broke them again. In fact, these glasses were awaiting attention and he commented: 'My sight has gone off a bit, I think, but it's as if I don't intend to see to it.' I pointed out that in the dream, where he had done so, he had spoiled the result for himself. He replied by saying, as he often did: 'If I can possibly do myself in I always find a way to do it. In fact I don't kick myself around, or others, as much now as I used to. I put off going to the dentist because I feel he'll have all my teeth out. I didn't realize I feared that.' I suggested that he turned everyone into potential persecutors like that, roping them all into the conspiracy to 'do him in'. He answered: 'Yes. It's to keep me in my place. "We'll have all your teeth out, that'll teach you. Now try to bite your mother's nipples." It's to make me impotent so that I can't attack anybody any more, it's to get me fixed.' His oral sadistic ego was to be put out of action. Naturally he suffered from periods of fatigue, longed above all to go to bed and stay there, and yet resisted sleep as frightening passivity which he could not get out of in the morning. During the night he would have to get up and have a meal, a protest of his persecuted L.E.

As psycho-analytical therapy gradually leads to a diminution of the sadistic hostility of the Anti-L.E., and the patient comes slowly to be able to take up more of his analyst's permissive and friendly attitude to himself, the passive trends show signs of disappearing. But then anxiety comes to be felt about the release of the primarily active L.E., since at first the sadism that is released from the Anti-L.E. flows back into the L.E. where it originally belonged as an angry reaction to early deprivation. The patient quoted above said: 'There's no doubt that I'm coming alive, but I'm not liking the process, it's frightening.' A striking picture of this situation is supplied by the following dream of a male patient. 'I was in a house I lived in as a child and terrified of some unknown danger. I was going round locking all the doors and suddenly in the hall saw a large wicker-work cage with an enormous, furious leopard in it. It snarled at me and I felt it would gnaw through the cage in no time. Then you were with me and you said, "Let it out, it's not as dangerous as you think." Terrified, I let it out, and at once it became a very beautiful, strong, but friendly animal and was licking my hands.' Fear of loss of control as a result of the release of the originally deprived L.E. is one of the more obvious sources of resistance to analysis. This patient had for years dreamt of wild animals raging in cages while he feared they would get out.

This internal and unconscious situation is phantasied and felt and worked out over and over again at each developmental level after its oral origins. It can be discovered and analysed in anal, genital and Oedipal terms, and worked out by the patient in terms of object-relations in the present-day outer world. Thus, the patient who had the leopard dream opened his analysis with a run of homosexual dreams in which he was in the woman's position being raped or attacked by a sadistic male. In one of these dreams he lay on his back waiting while a man ran at him with a sword, but after a lengthy analysis of this material he suddenly produced one dream in which he was the sadistic male violently attacking a woman. Later on he had a most disturbing nightmare in which he was watching a male horse violently attacking a female horse and slashing it with a knife, while the female horse endured this torture passively and made no attempt to get away. This represented to him the primal scene between parents, and also his own sadistic phantasy of sexual assault on a mother-figure, and finally the constant attack going on in himself of his Anti-L.E. upon his L.E., out of which his painful conversion symptoms arose. But the analysis of this pattern on the genital level invariably opens up the same pattern on the primitive oral level.

So heavily involved is 'passivity' in this pathological situation that the view of Ferenczi and Balint that the primary relation of the infant to the mother is passive dependent love compels us to distinguish this masochistic passivity from the restful passivity of the primary identification of the infant with the mother in the womb. After birth the infant exercises very active needs towards the mother and is both 'taking' and 'receptive' but not merely passive. After birth, passivity is a term perhaps best reserved for the pathological state of inhibited sadistic activity. Ferenczi recognized earlier than any other analyst the importance of the primary mother-child relationship. Freud's theory and practice was notoriously paternalistic, Ferenczi's maternalistic. His concept of 'primary object love' prepared the way for the later work of Melanie Klein, Fairbairn, Balint, Winnicott, and all others who to-day recognize that object-relations start at the beginning in the infant's needs for the mother. Ferenczi held that this primary object-love for the mother was passive, and in that form underlay all later development.

Balint, in *Primary Love and Psycho-Analytic Technique* (1952) writes: 'Not only pregenital love, but also so-called post ambivalent genital love, originates in passive object-love' (p. 66). Zetzel observes that this implies a different technical approach to analytical therapy. She says: 'Balint believes that the true aim of analysis cannot be achieved unless the patient is able to revert to a stage of primary passive love in the transference situation. This he describes as "the new beginning".' (1955, p. 538.) The ante-natal infant is primarily passive and 'vegetative'. The post-natal infant is rather 'active receptive'; and there is a pathological 'passivity' resulting from the enforced suppression of sadistic libidinal needs. Balint, it seems, allows for a passive object-love between the intra-uterine passivity and post-natal active object-love. This perhaps does involve a new approach to therapy, though this is involved in any case in the recognition that object-relations begin with the mother-infant relation. That is the rationale of Ferenczi's 'mothering technique' in analysis which so disturbed Freud. It is the rationale of Winnicott's stress on 'therapeutic regression', and here also is the rationale of Fairbairn's object-relations point of view in both theory and therapy.

4. *The Characteristics of Pathological Dependence*

The extent to which infantile dependent characteristics are allowed to manifest themselves on the level of consciousness and behaviour varies greatly. In the Hysteric such traits are easily recognized, in the Obsessional severely controlled. They may be strong in the deep unconscious when they show least in real life, as in the case of the detached and impersonal schizoid character. In the depressed person they are mastered by the arousal of guilt. When analysis has the chance to go deep enough it is truly astonishing how powerful and frightening to the patient is the degree of primitive infantile rage, unsatisfied need and intense fear-ridden dependent longing that is revealed. This is the realm of deep psychopathology, against which a tremendous defensive battle is waged internally, in the effort to grow up sufficiently to cope ultimately with adult life in the outer world. This struggle is the level of what Fairbairn calls 'the moral defence'. We will illustrate concretely, first this deep-down *infantile dependence* itself, secondly the *defensive struggle* against it, and thirdly the persistent *ego-weakness* in an overall sense which is its reverse side.

(*a*) *Infantile Dependence*. Its two characteristics of identifica-

tion and oral incorporation are to be understood as essentially
ways of manifesting a needy dependence on another person of that
absolute kind peculiar to the 'total need' of a disturbed infant.
The infant cannot, in the nature of the case, achieve security for
himself. It must be provided for him and guaranteed to him by
another person on whom his dependence is meanwhile complete.
As a result of normal growth of body, intelligence and personality,
such complete dependence on another person steadily lessens. But
it is this early absolute dependence that the growing child is
driven back into in his deepest feelings, when in later childhood
he meets with difficulties in personal family relationships which
he cannot resolve. What he cannot do for himself, he cannot but
long to find someone else to do for him, and his basic emotional
life comes to be a compulsive and often frantically anxious quest
to find and keep adequate support from other people. But passivity
enforced by anxiety fastens an attitude of helplessness on him.
Such strong dependent needs are, in general, not well received by
other people who have enough to do to carry their own responsibilities. Hence, infantile dependent needs come mostly to be expressed in disguised ways outwardly while they flourish inside in
the repressed unconscious to find some expression in dreams and
symptoms.

An attitude of incorporative dependence is often shown in
ways that are superficially rationalized and justified. A father who
behaved as a domestic tyrant to his wife and two daughters, giving
them no independence and insisting on having them sitting round
the fire with him every evening, had persuaded himself that he
was acting on high principles of the proper valuation of the
sacredness of family life, which was to be defended against modern
disintegrating trends. In fact, he was utterly dependent on them
and afraid to be left alone and was seeking to swallow them up
into his own life as a guarantee of security to himself.

We can recognize a difference between identification, which
seems to imply a passive assimilated condition, and active incorporation of the object. In describing symptoms, however, it is
often a moot point which label is most appropriate. Melanie Klein
uses the term 'projective identification' for the imaginative putting
of a part of oneself into another person and assimilating it to that
person. We might speak of 'incorporative identification' to describe the attempt to assimilate others to oneself, and incorporate
them into one's own way of life and ideas. Identification seems
more a passive feeling of oneness with the object, while incorporation is more an active struggle to get possession of the person on
whom one feels dependent, but the two fuse together. One patient

becomes alternately anxious if she finds that she thinks differently from the friend with whom she lives, and angry if the friend disagrees with her. Either way, what she is wanting is that she and her friend shall be 'one' in all respects so that she can feel safe in complete union with and total dependence on a good mother-figure. Much intolerance of differences of opinion is a rationalization of infantile dependence. To those who must feel identified to feel secure, all difference means separation and the dread feeling of being alone and unable to support oneself.

Crude greediness and demandingness, the obvious expression of an incorporative dependence, are quickly recognized and angrily checked by other people and are usually held under repression or at least control. On the other hand, identificatory characteristics can be expressed in subtle ways and are easily rationalized. All forms of 'feeling one with' valued people lend themselves readily to idealization. Two people who cannot bear to be parted, who go everywhere together and couldn't exist without each other are 'great lovers' or have a 'David and Jonathan friendship', but do not usually recognize that they may be infantile dependents in an immature relationship. The man whose feeling of importance and self-valuation rests largely on his being well-dressed, or having an impressive car or house, or a big bank balance, or public office and recognition, may not at all see that his normal and natural objective enjoyment of these good things is less than his identificatory dependence on them, and that without them he may feel very unsure of himself. One patient reported that he kept a model railway engine called 'The Duchess of Montrose' on his mantelpiece. He believed that his mother had some distant connection with the Montrose family, and he always felt more alive when looking at this Montrose engine with its bright paint and shining steel. Similarly he felt better and more satisfied with life if his motor-bike was clean and bright, and depressed if it was dirty. He could counteract depression by going out as a well-dressed 'man about town'. He found his security not in the normal self-assurance of a well-developed personality, but in identificatory dependence on someone or something other than himself, representing in the last resort his mother.

Another patient reported that if she went to visit a friend who was ill, she had 'such a sympathetic nature' that she began to feel ill herself ; if she then visited a friend who was well, she felt better. One of her most troublesome symptoms was an inability to be left alone without a panicky feeling that she was going to faint or die. All her life she had been haunted by a fear of dying, ever since as a child she would say when her mother left her in bed, 'I won't

die, will I?' Her comment was : 'It has always seemed to me necessary that someone else besides me should be alive,' evidently to
guarantee her own existence by giving her someone to feel identified with. She had, in fact, been an unusually rejected and ignored
baby.

One can see some reason in identification with the living as
some guarantee of security, but one male patient went so far as to
identify himself with his dead father, so great was his fear of
losing him and being left to cope alone with his violent, near-
psychotic mother. His father was killed when the patient was a
young lad, and he showed no outward grief but he had secret
phantasies of climbing into the coffin to be with father. In adult
life, for years he suffered 'night attacks' when he would wake to
find his face and arms stiff and cold, and he would leap up in
terror thinking he was dying. In analysis, at first he automatically
went to the couch, folded a cushion in a peculiar way to prop his
head and lay quite still all through the session talking with his
hands folded on his chest. Ultimately it dawned on him that he
was identifying himself with his dead father as he had seen him
laid in the mortuary with his head propped on a brick.

Identification can be experienced as either protective or persecutory, when, in the medium of bad-object relationships in the
family, the child cannot develop a self-confident personality, he
slips back in his deep unconscious feelings to seeking security in
the original state of protective identification with another person,
at bottom the mother. This may go so far as to activate feelings
and phantasies of a return inside the womb, especially when oral
sadism is deeply inhibited.

(b) *The Struggle against Passive Dependence.* What Fairbairn
describes as using a maximum of aggression to subdue a maximum
of libidinal need, thus setting up the structural differentiation of
the Anti-L.E. as a sadistic persecutor of the now masochistic
L.E., creates the problem of internally forced passivity. This constitutes a serious problem in view of the need for vigour and
energy in the conduct of everyday life. Patients complain of being
assailed by deadly fatigue and longings to give up work and go to
bed, and of various manifestations of inhibited mental activity
such as inability to think or remember. The whole problem is
vividly portrayed in the following dream. The male dreamer was
sitting at his table in a downstairs room writing and doing his
business correspondence. He knew that in a bedroom upstairs there
was a pale, passive, invalid woman, and suddenly he became
aware that a mysterious bond existed between him and her which
acted as an irresistible pull drawing him away from his work, out

of the room and up to her bedroom. He knew that there it would lead to his being absorbed into her and losing his own identity and active self. He fought and struggled against the pull. He gripped the table and was forced away from it. He clung desperately to the mantelpiece, and at last broke the power of this thing over him, and woke palpitating and frightened. This dream reveals the fierce internal struggle that has to be waged against the danger of passivity. The following dream shows rather the way in which the C.E. repression of the needy infant undermines the self of everyday living, causing a longing to surrender to passivity. The dreamer, a woman in the forties with a husband and two children in their late teens, dreamed that she was overburdened and struggling to cope with the pressures of life; she had her family and six visitors to see to and was exhausted with cleaning, shopping, baking and so on, because all the time she had a hungry baby hidden under her apron that needed to be fed and she could not feed it. She too would repeatedly retire to bed in the early evening, feeling that she could not keep going any longer. But the danger of passivity trends undermining the C.E. is complex. There is the masochistic passivity of the inhibited oral sadistic drive; and the restful passivity of regression to an unconscious womb-state (protective secondary identification).

(c) *Ego-Weakness*. It is not realized by people in general what tremendous struggles 'neurotics' carry on inside themselves to keep going and cope with life, because it is not realized how formidable are the passivity trends that undermine them. Internal conflict, not being just a conflict of incompatible wishes and feelings, but arising in psychoneurosis out of a radical splitting of the wholeness of the ego, involves therefore an overall weakening of the psyche in every direction. Internal division means weakness in the face of the outer world. We recognize, in the hectic, frantic, anxiety-ridden over-activity of many people, the signs of a desperate struggle to prove equal to the demands of active living. This has to be carried on by the C.E. after it has been deprived of much of its natural supply of energy, as a result of the splitting off of the L.E. and Anti-L.E. All the energy inherent in those repressed structures is locked away in the unconscious and is productive of effects that hinder rather than help in coping with the outer world. The sense of strain consciously experienced is in part a reliving of the experience of strain in childhood in face of insoluble problems of bad-object relationships at a time when human nature needs support and not to be overburdened. But it is also a realistic experience of the present day in the battle to cope with life with such depleted resources.

This has an important bearing on psycho-analytical therapy. This kind of therapy is in fact an exceedingly realistic and 'adult' activity. It calls upon the C.E. for maximum co-operation in first uncovering and then facing steadily in consciousness the full force of internal conflicts. It does actually put upon the already hard-pressed C.E. an additional heavy demand to meet. It is little wonder that patients often express grave fears as to whether they can carry on with analysis and cope with their everyday responsibilities at the same time. It would not perhaps be possible at all were it not for the fact that, once rooted in the psychotherapeutic situation, the analyst becomes a powerful source of support. That is illustrated by the leopard dream, in which the patient dared not let the leopard out alone but could do it when he felt the therapist was with him. A similar implication was contained in a dream in which a patient had to confront a fearful witch in a cave and dared not do it until he had found Christ to go along with him. Yet another patient dreamed that she had to go down a dark stair-case into the bowels of the earth to face a woman hating a girl-child. She dared not go till she could hold my hand and go down with me. Ego-weakness means that patients require not only analysis but reassurance and positive support from the therapist if they are to be able to cope with psycho-analytical therapy and daily life at the same time. Our discussion has brought us to the problem of psycho-analytical therapeutic technique, and it seems that very far-reaching implications for this are involved in the new object-relations orientation. That is particularly forced on our attention by Winnicott's views about therapeutic regression.

5. *Theory and the Approach to Therapy*

We can here deal with only one aspect of this large problem which is immediately relevant to the subject of this book. We have traced the way in which theory has moved back behind the Oedipus situation to the mother-infant situation of the earliest stages of life, and how, along with that, theory has moved also away from its early basic emphasis on biological and instinctive factors towards the present emphasis on social and object-relation-ship factors. Both of these new orientations of theory are bound to have direct effects on psychotherapy. Elizabeth Zetzel entertains some anxiety on this point. She states that the capacity of the British Institute of Psycho-Analysis 'to contain within its existing framework controversial and possibly divergent views and their proponents', views which 'might well have led to overt schisms in the United States', is due to 'the fact that theoretical differences

have not on the whole involved serious changes of basic technique'
so far as therapeutic analysis is concerned. (1955, pp. 534–5.)
This state of affairs can hardly last indefinitely. The results of
psycho-analytic therapy are not so uniformly encouraging as to
lead to a complacent acceptance of an unchallenged *status quo* in
this matter. The problem of psychotherapy is a much greater and
more urgent problem than that of psychodynamic theory, the
elucidation of which is undertaken mainly in the hope that it will
lead to greater success in therapeutic endeavour.

The work of Ferenczi and Balint shows that the approach to
therapy does not remain unaffected by theory. In the case of
Melanie Klein a revolutionary therapeutic technique—the development of play-analysis for children—led to the most far-
reaching changes in theory and it would be strange if this did not
work the other way as well, especially at a time when the need for
more effective therapeutic methods is so widely felt. Fairbairn has
delayed writing specifically about psychotherapeutic problems,
not because he thought that 'Object-Relations Theory' had
nothing new to say on that head, but because he felt that it had
so much that was new to say that it required a great deal of
caution and time for testing to discover what were the sound implications in practice. The work of Winnicott provides an outstanding example of courageous grappling with the implications
for therapeutic analysis of the present theoretical position, namely
that the roots of personality disturbance are to be found in the
earliest mother-infant relationship. We shall therefore consider
the work of Winnicott here, and in this special context.

6. *D. W. Winnicott's Views on Therapeutic Regression*

Winnicott explicitly traces the origins of mental disturbance
back to the very beginnings of life in the mother-infant relationship. His work as a paediatrician-cum-psycho-analyst has enabled
him to make particularly important contributions to the development of this point of view. His studies of infantile emotional development cover problems such as integration, personalization,
realization, body sense. His article on *Primitive Emotional Development* (1958, ch. 12) makes it clear that these gave rise
to a turning-point in his thought. His work on transitional objects,
illusion and disillusionment (1958, chs. 17 and 18) is outstand-
ingly important, both for problems of early development and
for problems of cultural, especially artistic and religious, experience. Bearing on the theme of this book, he writes:

I assume a psychological basis for mental disorder. I assume that psychiatry can be studied in cases in which the brain tissue is good ... it is possible to establish a clinical link between infant development and the psychiatric states, and likewise between infant care and the proper care of the mentally sick ... in the emotional development of every infant complicated processes are involved, and lack of forward development or completeness of these processes predisposes to mental disorder or breakdown; the completion of these processes forms the basis of mental health. The mental health of the human being is laid down in infancy by the mother, who provides an environment in which complex but essential processes in the infant's self can become completed. (1958, pp. 158–60.)

This is a more definite emphasis on the importance of the environment and the actual mother as the first external object than we find in Melanie Klein. He states that :

The environment is so vitally important at this early stage that one is driven to the unexpected conclusion that schizophrenia is a sort of environmental deficiency disease. (1958, p. 162.)

It is in the emphasis on the mother-child relationship and the importance of the first year of life that present-day psychoanalysis has most clearly moved beyond Freud's paternalistic and Oedipal theory.

Winnicott, however, retains both emphases by holding to the Oedipus complex as the cause of psychoneurosis, while he regards the disturbed mother-infant relationship of the first year as the cause of psychosis; making a sharp distinction between them. He writes :

It is already an accepted view that neurosis has its origin in the early interpersonal relationships that arise when the child is beginning to take a place as a whole human being in the family ... the health of an individual in terms of socialization and of absence of neurosis is laid down by the parents when the child is at the toddler age ... disturbances which can be recognized and labelled as psychotic have their origins in distortions in emotional development arising before the child has clearly become a whole person capable of total relationships with whole persons. (1958, p. 220.)

Winnicott is primarily interested in the bearing of this distinction on psychotherapy. The distinction itself is orthodox. Abraham traced the psychoses back to the oral period and the psychoneuroses to the post-oral phases. Winnicott writes :

There is a vast difference between those patients who have had satisfactory early experiences which can be discovered in the transference, and those whose very early experiences have been so deficient and distorted that the analyst has to be the first in the patient's life to supply certain environmental essentials. (1958, p. 198.)

He is emphatic about this distinction.

A perfect environment at the start can at least theoretically be expected to enable an infant to make the initial emotional or mental development which predisposes to further emotional development and so to mental health throughout life. An unfavourable environment later is a different matter, being merely an additional adverse factor, and not to be listed as causal in respect to psychosis. (1958, p. 162.)

There are important differences between the views of Winnicott, Mrs. Klein and Fairbairn. Mrs. Klein carries the Oedipal situation back into the first year, while Winnicott regards it almost as a distinct and separate later stage, that of socialization in the family group by comparison with which the pre-Oedipal stage is hardly to be called one of 'object-relationship'. Melanie Klein and Fairbairn both regard object-relationship as going back to the beginning. In his criticisms of Fairbairn's views Winnicott apparently held the orthodox Freudian view of an original objectless stage. This is borne out by the following :

As soon as an object-relationship is possible it is immediately a matter of significance whether the object is outside or inside the child. I assume, however, that there is a stage prior to this at which there is no relationship at all. I would say that initially there is a condition which could be described at one and the same time as a stage of *absolute independence* and as of *absolute dependence*. There is no feeling of dependence, and therefore that dependence must be absolute. (1958, p. 163.)

The problem here is that with which we dealt in considering his criticisms of Fairbairn ; namely, that there is a relationship in fact between the mother and the infant, but consciousness of relationship grows gradually out of primary identification, and in the beginning the infant must fluctuate between the two states in confused ways. Winnicott's statement that at first 'there is no relationship at all' is the traditional Freudian view which present developments have challenged.

Closely connected with Winnicott's orthodoxy on this point is his conception of the psychic condition of the first-year infant so far as the ego is concerned. He accepts Ed. Glover's theory of 'ego-nuclei' which become organized together as a result of early integration processes into an ego. (1958, p. 225.) The primary state of the psyche he describes as one of 'unintegration'. He writes :

It may be assumed that at the start the personality is unintegrated, and that in regressive disintegration there is a primary state to which regression leads. We postulate a primary unintegration . . . the primary unintegrated state provides a basis for disintegration and delay or failure in respect of primary integration predisposes to disintegration as a repression. (1958, pp. 149–50.)

This view is much closer to Janet's theory of dissociation as the falling to pieces of a weak ego that has not the strength to hold itself together, than it is to Freud's theory of dynamic repression which requires a great expenditure of energy internally to produce a splitting of the psyche, a view which is the basis of Fairbairn's theory. Winnicott says :

In regard to the environment, bits of nursing technique, faces seen and sounds heard, and smells smelt, are only gradually pieced together into a being to be called mother. (1958, p. 150.)

The view more usually accepted by psychologists is that perception develops not by an addition of separate bits and pieces mosaic-wise, but by the enriching internal differentiation of an at first vaguely perceived whole. Gestalt psychology should be a corrective of Winnicott's atomistic view at this point. It supports Fairbairn's theory of a psyche which is an ego of pristine if primitive unity. This becomes differentiated by splitting processes in bad-object relationships. However, Winnicott can hardly carry object-relationships back to the beginning if his primary psyche is not yet an ego but only an unintegrated collection of 'ego-nuclei'. His own concept of a 'true self' requires more than his views as above stated can give.

A further difference between the views of Winnicott and of Mrs. Klein and Fairbairn is his sharp separation between the psychoses and psychoneuroses. He holds that difficulties in later childhood can precipitate a psychoneurosis when the infancy situation has been excellent, while psychosis is related to disturbance in the earliest oral period. Both Mrs. Klein and Fairbairn regard the psychoneuroses as defensive operations of the ego in its struggle against the problems of the earliest oral stage in which internal bad objects have been created. Furthermore, Fairbairn regards later difficulties as vital factors in precipitating regression to oral positions in the inner world, thus reviving the internal bad-object situations that lead to schizoid and depressive conditions. The difficulties of infancy, unless altogether too severe, may be overcome if later childhood is helpful; if not, they are reactivated to produce psychotic reactions calling for defences in later life. The interrelation of early and later phases seems to be much more subtly portrayed in the work of Mrs. Klein and Fairbairn than in that of Winnicott. He applies the 'internal bad-objects' theory to psychosis, but apparently not to psychoneurosis. This matter is important since Winnicott founds his views on psychotherapeutic method on his conception of this difference. He holds that classic psycho-analysis is the correct method for dealing with psychoneurosis as a problem of the socialized and Oedipal situation. By contrast he speaks of 'Management' as the appropriate method for dealing with regressed and psychotic patients whose problems are on the pre-Oedipal level where good mothering is the supreme desideratum. If psychosis and psychoneurosis are not as separate as he implies, but are much more subtly intertwined, then psychoanalysis and management cannot be so definitely set over against one another. We may preface the consideration of Winnicott's views on this crucial problem of 'theory and therapy' by studying his conceptions of the inner meaning of schizoid and depressive states in the infant. He regards the infant's need as so absolute at first as to require a 'perfect' environment in theory, and as near perfect as is attainable in practice. Only this can lay the foundations of mental health. This 'perfect' environment is provided by the mother who *actively adapts* to the infant's needs as they develop and are expressed. Her material intuition recognizes and provides what the baby wants as and when he wants it. This active adaptation is the opposite of the bad mothering which he describes as *impingement* on the infant, i.e. forcing the infant to become aware of the pressure of an external and interfering reality at times when he is not feeling needs and not reaching out actively to his needed object of his own accord. Active adaptation is response to the baby's own initiative in 'seeking', a time when he is capable of accepting and dealing with the movement of the mother towards himself. This allows his internal psychic development to go on undisturbed, according to his own inner nature and laws of growth. Impingement is an intrusion on the infant at times when he is not reaching out, and the result is that he withdraws from an unwanted impact. This 'disturbs the continuity of the going-on-being of the new individual'. (1958, p. 245.) He is forced to react prematurely to an outer reality which he begins to experience as a threat. Here are the origins of persecutory anxiety.

This definition of good mothering as active adaptation to the child's needs without impingement is, in principle, the same as Fairbairn's definition, framed to cover, not just the infancy period but the whole of childhood, namely loving the child for himself as a real person in his own right. Once a good start has been given, the mother's task becomes more complex. She has, slowly, to dis-illusion the infant as to the perfection of his environment by mixing the meeting of his needs with 'graduated failures of adaptation' which do not go beyond the child's capacity to cope with and understand. By means of 'mental activity or by understanding' the baby becomes able to cope with not too much frustration at once, and so to learn to tolerate reality. Winnicott thinks it likely that the better the infant's I.Q., the sooner he is able to do this, provided he is not overtaxed. On the other hand, overstrain pro-duces an over-reaction and can lead to hypertrophy of the intellect. The child grows up to live by thinking rather than feeling, and de-velops a 'false mental self'. It has to withdraw into itself to deal with its problems with the environment.

Certain kinds of failure on the part of the mother, especially erratic behaviour, produce over-activity of the mental functioning . . . there can develop an opposition between the mind and the psyche-soma, since in reaction to this abnormal environmental state the thinking of the individual begins to take over and organize the caring for the psyche-soma, whereas in health it is the function of the en-vironment to do this. . . . The gradual process whereby the individual becomes able to care for the self belongs to later stages in individual emotional development, stages that must be reached in due course, at the pace that is set by natural developmental forces. . . . As a more common result of the lesser degrees of tantalizing infant-care in the earliest stages we find *mental functioning becoming a thing in itself*, practically replacing the good mother and making her unnecessary. (1958, p. 246.)

This is the basis of many dreams that schizoid patients bring, in which they are depicting an inner situation where they are struggling to take care of their own infantile self which enters into the dream as a baby or very small child. This is the situation out of which *the schizoid reaction* develops.

Winnicott's view of the schizoid problem differs somewhat from that of Fairbairn, in a way that appears to be determined by his more orthodox Freudian underlying theory. He quotes Freud's paper on *Instincts and Their Vicissitudes* (1915) to the effect that we cannot say that instincts love and hate; only whole egos love and hate, and he comments:

Does not this mean that the personality must be integrated before an infant can be said to hate? However early integration may be achieved . . . there is a theoretical earlier stage in which whatever he does that hurts is not done in hate. I have used the word 'ruthless love' in describing this stage. Is this acceptable? As the infant becomes able to feel to be a whole person, so does the word hate develop meaning as a description of a certain group of his feelings. (1958, pp. 200–1.)

If there is an early stage of unintegration in which hate is not yet possible, then neither is love possible, and one would feel difficulties about the term 'ruthless love'. This difficulty does not arise with Fairbairn, for whom the pristine ego is a whole, however primitive, from the start, and he regards 'love' as appropriate to describe the infant's quest for the satisfaction of needs from the mother. He does not describe this early love as 'ruthless' in itself, a term influenced by the Freudian and Kleinian theory of active innate aggression. He rather regards libido as becoming 'ruthless' or aggressive in response to frustration or lack of satisfaction. Winnicott regards libidinal need as innately ruthless. We have to choose between Winnicott's naturally ruthless love and Fairbairn's love made ruthless by deprivation, a choice behind which lies once again the old problem of instinct theory. Winnicott writes :

It is not certain that all the damage that may be done to a finger or mouth (by thumb sucking) is part of hate. It seems that there is in it the element that something must suffer if the infant is to have pleasure : the object of primitive love suffers by being loved, apart from being hated. (1958, p. 155.)

He here accepts the distinction Fairbairn had already made in the view that the schizoid dilemma is that love seems destructive, while the depressive dilemma is that hate is destructive. But for Winnicott, this 'oral sadism' is natural and innate ; for Fairbairn it is a development from oral deprivation. Winnicott says explicitly :

[The] coincidence of love and hate to which I am referring is something which is distinct from the aggressive component complicating the primitive love impulse, and implies that in the history of the patient there was an environmental failure at the time of the first object-finding instinctual impulse. (1958, p. 196.)

He regards oral sadism as innate *qua* impulse, 'the aggressive component complicating the primitive love impulse', and as existing prior to the 'environmental failure at the time of the first object-finding instinctual impulse'. Winnicott and Fairbairn agree that primitive love can operate destructively but, as regards the causation of the schizoid reaction of withdrawal, Winnicott adds to the anxiety aroused by the prospect of making the love-object suffer, the further reaction of withdrawal from impingement. In that case schizoid introversion is both an effort to protect the love-object from the infant's destructive need and also to protect the infant from the unwanted impact of the disturbing external object.

Winnicott himself asks whether the term 'ruthless love' is acceptable. The meaning of words is to an enormous extent determined by the aura of associative meaning they have acquired in common usage, and the word 'ruthless' carries with it the feeling-sense of positive cruelty that would appear to ally it too closely with hate for Winnicott's purpose. It would be appropriate if one believed in a death instinct, or alternately if one holds that primitive love becomes destructive through too great lack of satisfaction, in which case primitive anger and rage impart an aggressive quality to the expression of needs, as Fairbairn holds. Out of this schizoid problem of libidinal needs operating destructively arises the internal situation which creates terrors of disintegration. Winnicott writes:

No one can be ruthless after the concern stage except in a dissociated state. But ruthless dissociation states are common in early childhood, and emerge in certain types of delinquency, and madness, and must be available in health. The normal child enjoys a ruthless relation to his mother, mostly showing in play, and he needs his mother because only she can be expected to tolerate his ruthless relation to her even in play, because this really hurts her and wears her out. Without this play with her he can only hide a ruthless self and give it life in a state of dissociation.

I can bring in here the great fear of disintegration as opposed to the simple acceptance of primary unintegration. Once the individual has reached the stage of concern he cannot be oblivious to the result of his impulses, or to the action of bits of self such as biting mouth, stabbing eyes, piercing yells, sucking throat, etc., etc. Disintegration means abandonment of the whole person-object to his impulses, uncontrolled because acting on their own; and further this conjures up the idea of similarly uncontrolled (because dissociated) impulses directed towards himself . . . it is usual, I think, to postulate a still more primitive object-relationship in which the object acts in a retaliatory way. (1958, pp. 154-5.)

The fear of disintegration, or 'going to bits', seems to be specific for psychotic terror and panic, and its explanation is fundamentally important. It is a more drastically undermining experi-

ence than the feeling of ego-weakness that results from the original
structural splitting of the oral ego referred to on pp. 394–5. The
fear of disintegration under retaliatory persecution is a L.E. experience. It constitutes a 'Disintegration Complex' of which the
later 'Castration Complex' is only one part. One patient of mine
who had had a paranoid schizophrenic breakdown lasting three
months was very liable to 'go to bits' in any situation in which the
outer world put extra pressure upon her. On one such occasion she
said that she felt like a jigsaw puzzle being taken to pieces and left
broken up, flung in the box. She further experienced the process
of psycho-analytical interpretation at first as like her mother
'forcing the bottle into her mouth' (i.e. impingement) and then, as
literally 'analysis', breaking her down into pieces. This became
very clear after a friend had observed that the analyst was good
at 'taking you to pieces but not so good at putting you together
again' (the old stock objection is invited by the term 'analysis' when
the patient fears disintegration). Is this psychotic terror a matter
of falling back into the earliest state of 'unintegration' under external pressure? It appears more likely that it arises as a result of
fears both of impingement and of retaliation by the object of the
oral sadistic libidinal ego with its biting and devouring needs. The
patient quoted felt terror when she learned that a great friend
was dying of cancer because she phantasied that she had bitten
him and that his cancer was one of her teeth left in his body. By
identification with him as bitten to pieces and through fear of his
retaliating on her as an internalized dangerous object, she felt that
she was 'going to pieces' and about to be destroyed. Another
patient who modelled a small child disembowelling a mother-figure
and then being frozen to the spot in horror at what he had done,
went on to paint a picture of a witch literally tearing the small
child bodily to pieces. The first patient once painted a picture in
which she herself lay suffering in the corner of a square framework
of sharp teeth all pointed at her, while swords and hammers were
aimed at her inside the framework. This is the basic schizophrenic
terror situation in the inner world. The clinical material suggests
that it is produced by dynamic splitting of a primary whole ego,
rather than a falling back into primitive 'unintegration'. One of
the things that this type of patient most urgently needs is that the
psychotherapist should protect his wholeness.

Winnicott regards the early phase of 'ruthless love' as leading
on to the next phase of the development of 'concern', with the
arising of the depressive problem. He distinguishes between the
achievement of 'the depressive position' in the Kleinian sense and

'depression' as an illness. Thus he says that 'depressive position' 'is a thoroughly bad name for a normal process, and the only excuse is that no one has been able to find a better. My own suggestion was that it should be called "*the Stage of Concern*".' (1958, p. 246). He regards the 'depressive position' in this sense as a development beyond and out of the earliest stage of 'ruthless love' to the achievement of a capacity for 'ruth' or 'concern' about the 'results of instinctual love' for the love-object. As to the earlier stage, he says : 'The infant does not feel ruthless, but looking back . . . the individual can say : I was ruthless then.' In that case 'ruthlessness' is not a quality of the infant's feeling, but expresses what an observer feels about him. It seems that this observer must be an orthodox Freudian who interprets what he sees in the light of the theory of innate, instinctive, aggressive drives. Whether, on a Kleinian basis, a normal 'stage of concern' can be distinguished from 'depressive anxiety' as an illness depends very much on whether specific aggression is a factor in the infant's primary love for the mother. One cannot help but feel that the Freudian and Kleinian theory of innate aggression influences Winnicott in his choice of the words 'ruthless love', since it leads him to regard the infant's primary, instinctive, energetic, self-assertiveness and libidinal activity as something of which the word 'aggression' should properly be used. In psycho-analytical thinking, strict usage as regards the meaning of words is necessary. The word 'aggression' has lost, by usage, its original significance of 'going towards' (Latin, *ad*, and *gradior*, I go or step) and has come to mean quite definitely 'hostile approach', offensiveness and attacking. Both Freud and Melanie Klein, whose views Winnicott holds in this particular, believe that the infant is aggressive by nature and attacks the breast and the mother, even when it is not frustrated or unsatisfied. Thus Winnicott *interprets* the infant's energetic prosecution of his instinctive needs as an *attack* on the mother in the full sense of aggression, and he equates 'aggression' and the 'excitement of instinct tension'. He writes :

The baby [must] experience 'excited' relationships and meet the consequences. . . . A new kind of need has arisen based on impulse and on instinct tension that seeks relief, and this involves a climax or orgasm. . . . Once the excitement has started and tension has arisen, risk has entered in . . . the mother [is] used, even attacked, at the instinctive climax. . . . There appears cannibalistic ruthless attack, which partly shows in the baby's physical behaviour, and which partly is a matter of the infant's own imaginative elaboration of the physical function. (1958, pp. 267–8.)

As a result, he states that an adequate feed can leave the baby not only satisfied but also feeling cheated.

Often distress follows this fobbing off, especially if physical satisfaction too quickly robs the infant of zest. The infant is then left with : (1) aggression undischarged—because not enough muscle erotism or primitive impulse, or motility, was used in the feeding process; and/or (2) a sense of 'flop', since a source of zest for life has gone suddenly. (1958, p. 268.)

If the infant's natural vitality and normal energetic self-expression is to be interpreted as actual 'aggression' and 'attack', then it is extremely difficult to distinguish between a normal, healthy stage of concern and pathological depression. It seems, in fact, necessary to distinguish between 'excitement' as normal and pleasurable energetic loving which is capable of leading on to a feeling of concern for the mother who is thus vigorously loved, and 'aggression' as the result of lack of satisfaction and frustration, which leads on to a morbid fear of destroying the love-object; from this arises the schizoid fear of destroying by love and later the depressive fear of destroying by hate. This could give the basis for the distinction Winnicott makes between healthy and morbid guilt.

What he describes is the gradual dawning on the infant of the fact that, in getting his needs met, he takes something out of the mother's body and from the mother as a person. In the absence of anger and aggression, a *concern* for the mother develops as a vital part of the process of true maturing, and it leads to the perception of the reality of both 'give and take' in a loving relationship. One does not exhaust one's love-object because it is possible to contribute as well as to get. Fairbairn regards the process of maturing as a progress from taking to giving. Inherent in this is the capacity for normal and healthy guilt-feeling over the hurting of the love-object. For this achievement, 'stage of concern' is certainly a much better term than 'depressive position'. Winnicott stresses the difference between this 'concern' and the morbid guilt of depression which arises out of true aggression and destructiveness. He regards the achievement of the 'depressive position' as characteristic of the second half of the first year, though he does not rule out its possibility at an earlier age. But he states that 'to reach the depressive position a baby must have become established as a whole person, and to be related to whole persons as a whole person'. (1958, p. 264.) Thus an earlier occurrence of the feeling of 'concern' would be ruled out really for Winnicott, since he regards the infant in the early stage as not a whole person but simply 'unintegrated'. That difficulty would not exist for Fairbairn, for whom the baby is a whole ego from the start. For Winnicott the 'stage of concern' is delayed by the fact that what he calls 'unit-status' has to be reached by growing out of primary unintegration first, with the help of a good environment. For Fairbairn, it would be delayed by the extent to which the pristine wholeness of the ego had become split by the influence of a bad environment.

Winnicott's approach to the problems of psychotherapy is determined by this theoretical position. He writes :

A feature of the depressive position is that it applies to an area of clinical psychiatry that is half-way between the places of origin of psychoneurosis and of psychosis respectively. The child (or adult) who has reached that capacity for interpersonal relationships which characterizes the toddler stage in health, and for whom ordinary analysis of the infinite variations of triangular human relationships is feasible, has passed *through and beyond* the depressive position. On the other hand, the child (or adult) who is chiefly concerned with the innate problems of personality integration and with the initiation of a relationship with environment is not yet at the depressive position in personal development. (1958, p. 262.)

Thus he regards the place of origin of psychoneurosis as 'the toddler in the family situation, working out an instinctual life in interpersonal relationships' and, for this, classical psycho-analysis is the requisite treatment. The place of origin of psychosis is 'the baby being held by the mother who adapts to ego-needs', and here the therapist is confronted by totally different problems for which classical psycho-analysis is not the answer, but rather a modification or adaptation of classical analysis enforced by the need of the psychotic patient to regress and the need of the analyst to manage this regression. Problems are dealt with which arise from the earliest period, a time when the infant's need was for a mother who could adapt to his needs, and this need is repeated on the analyst by means of regression. He is required to fulfil the role of the adaptive mother and so give the patient at last a chance to grow a real self. Winnicott writes :

Psycho-analysis which involves clinical regression is very much more difficult all along than that in which no special adaptive environmental provision has to be made. In other words it would be pleasant if we were to be able to take for analysis only those patients whose mothers at the very start and also in the first months had been able to provide good enough conditions. But this era of psychoanalysis is steadily drawing to a close. (1958, p. 291.)

The type of psychotherapy needed is thus determined by the extent to which the patient experienced good enough mothering, in the first year of life. Winnicott's theoretical formulation is that good enough mothering has enabled the infant to achieve an ego and to become a whole person. When the infant has not had such mothering, he cannot get beyond the original stage of unintegration and his basic need is still for the type of mothering that can give him a real start in personality development. Winnicott's work undercuts the view of Zetzel that, among British analysts, new theoretical developments have not led to new techniques and approaches in therapy. He speaks of 'the influence on analytical practice of the new understanding of infant care which has, in turn, derived from analytical theory'. (1958, p. 295.) He feels compelled to reserve the term 'psycho-analysis' for the treatment of psychoneurotic patients in whom one can assume an ego and a whole person, while he speaks rather of 'management' in reference to the treatment of psychotic patients who have not achieved an integrated ego and are not whole persons.

Winnicott here makes an extremely sharp division. He writes :

With regard to the more schizoid people, and the whole mental hospital population of persons who have never reached a true self-life or self-expression, the depressive position is not the thing that matters; . . . by contrast, for the whole manic-depressive group that comprises the majority of so-called normal people the subject of the depressive position in normal development is one that cannot be left aside; it is and it remains *the problem of life.* . . . The child, healthy in having reached the depressive position, can get on with the problem of the triangle of interpersonal relationships, the classical Oedipus complex. (1958, p. 277.)

The depressive problem is 'the great divide' for psychotherapy. Before the depressive position is reached, human beings are not whole persons and have not got an ego, so that true psycho-analysis is not possible. Afterwards, they are whole persons and have an ego, so that classical psycho-analysis is the correct treatment for problems of the depressive position, of clinical depression, and above all for problems of interpersonal relationships and the Oedipal triangle. He writes :

As we look back now we may say that cases were well chosen as suitable for analysis if in the very early personal history of the patient there *had been good enough infant care.* This good enough adaptation to need at the beginning had enabled the individual's ego to come into being, with the result that the *earlier stages* of the establishment of the ego *could be taken for granted* by the analyst. (1958, p. 295.)

By contrast, with psychotic cases,

the ego of the patient cannot be assumed as an established entity, and there can be no transference neurosis for which, surely, there must be an ego, and indeed an intact ego, an ego that is able to maintain defences against anxiety that arises out of instinct the responsibility for which is accepted. (1958, p. 296.)

Winnicott puts the matter still more explicitly in his paper on *Regression*.

I divide cases into the following three categories. *First* there are those patients who operate as whole persons and whose difficulties are in the realm of interpersonal relationships. The technique for the treatment of these patients belongs to psycho-analysis as it developed in the hands of Freud at the beginning of the century. Then *secondly* there come the patients in whom the wholeness of the personality only just begins to be something that can be taken for granted; in fact one can say that analysis has to do with the first events that belong to and inherently and immediately follow not only the achievement of wholeness but also the coming together of love and hate and the dawning recognition of dependence. This is the analysis of the stage of concern, or of what has come to be known as the 'depressive position'. These patients require the analysis of mood. The technique of this work is not different from that needed by patients in the first category. . . .

In the *third* grouping I place all those patients whose analyses must deal with the early stages of emotional development before and up to the establishment of the personality as an entity, before the achievement of space-time unity status. The personal structure is not yet securely founded. In regard to this third grouping, the accent is more surely on management, and sometimes over long periods with these patients ordinary analytic work has to be in abeyance, management being the whole thing. (1958, pp. 278–9.)

To clinch matters Winnicott adds further the fact that

When work of the special kind I have referred to (i.e. management) is completed it leads naturally on to ordinary analytic work, the analysis of the depressive position and of the neurotic defences of a patient with an ego, an intact ego, an ego that is able to experience id-impulses and to take the consequences. (1958, p. 299.)

(Compare also 1958, chapter 12.) What does Winnicott mean by the 'management' of regression? By regression he does not mean the usual and familiar concepts of going back to a trauma or to a fixation point simply; it is something more subtle and constructive than that. It is a return in search of the lost core of the real self. He distinguishes between a 'true' and a 'false' self, in the sense that when, owing to inadequate mothering and disturbing 'impingement' in infancy, the child is not able to become a whole person and achieve a real ego, its 'true self' is hidden away, 'frozen', and kept out of touch with the impinging outer world until some time when it is hoped that a chance may once more arise of bringing it out under more favourable circumstances. Winnicott regards the existence of this hidden and secret hope as decisive for the prospects of therapy. The analyst has to reach and help this hidden self with its secret hope. In order to find this starting-point for proper development, the patient is compelled to make a 'therapeutic regression' as far back as it is necessary to go. In one case Winnicott describes, this regression went back as far as a recapitulation of the birth process. The patient had had an orthodox analysis but found her problems still fundamentally unsolved. He writes : 'In the course of the two years of analysis with me the patient has repeatedly regressed to an early stage which was certainly prenatal. The birth process has had to be relived, and eventually I recognized how an unconscious need to relive the birth process underlay what had previously been an hysterical falling off the couch.' (1958, p. 249.)

Faced with this return to infancy, the analyst and the setting he arranges for the treatment must function symbolically as the mother who adapts 'perfectly' to the needs of the infant. This imposes far more strain on the analyst than does ordinary analysis, and only later, if enough progress is made, does the patient come to realize, like the growing child with the mother, how much he has demanded and needed of the parent-figure.

Acting out has to be tolerated in this sort of work, and with the acting out in the analytic hour the analyst will find it necessary to play a part, although usually in token form. . . . The actual acting out in the analysis is only the beginning, however, and there must always follow a putting into words of the new bit of understanding. (1958, p. 289.)

One of the most striking aspects of Winnicott's work is the way it is dominated by the conviction that the psychotherapeutic process is really aimed at enabling the patient to achieve true 'personhood', and one cannot but feel that this type of thinking far transcends the early Freudian emphasis on 'gratification of instinct'. Winnicott writes :

A belief in human nature and the developmental process exists in the analyst if work is to be done at all, and this is quickly sensed by the patient. (1958, p. 292.)

The 'true self' has been hidden practically for a lifetime behind a 'false self' constructed on the basis of compliance to the demands and expectations of the outer world. The real dynamic potential of the patient does not operate in this 'false self'.

While the individual's operational centre is in the false self there is a sense of futility, and in practice we find the change to the feeling that life is worth while coming at the moment of shift of the operational centre from the false to the true self . . . that which proceeds from the true self feels real. . . . (1958, p. 292.)

In favourable cases there follows at last : A new sense of self in the patient and a sense of the progress that means true growth. (1958, pp. 289–90.)

If this is followed right through the depressive position in terms of ordinary psycho-analysis, then

We see, more positively, a release of instinct, and a development towards richness in the personality, and an increase in potency or in general potential for social contribution. (1958, p. 271.)

This approach to the problems of psychotherapy is outstanding for its courage and freshness. It takes full account of the way modern psycho-analytical theory and practice have had to delve ever deeper into the earliest and pre-Oedipal stages of infant development, resulting in the establishment of the mother as the true basis of personality growth. It was inevitable that sooner or later this should powerfully affect treatment techniques, especially in the case of the most ill and regressed cases. Psycho-analysis is being driven to become, as Winnicott puts it, 'a study of environmental adaptation relative to patients' regressions'. (1958, p. 291.) As obviously high personal cost in taking strains, Winnicott has pioneered in largely unexplored territory and his work must have far-reaching consequences. This book is about theory and is not the place in which to explore further the practical aspects of his findings. They appear to be in strict line of development from the present-day theoretical trends. His views have so much in common with those of Fairbairn in principle that it seems to be only Winnicott's more Freudian basis that keeps these two thinkers from a closer rapprochement. His overall conception of the aim of psychotherapy coincides with Fairbairn's view of a growth from infantile dependence to mature dependence. Difficulties concerning Winnicott's views arise mainly over the fact that his Freudian foundations do not really support his own superstructure. These difficulties centre particularly around his ego-theory and his concept of the 'true self'. This is a valuable concept, though the term 'true' is too tinged with evaluatory meanings and is not sufficiently scientifically descriptive. Fairbairn would prefer the term 'the natural self', one aspect of which is the L.E., the primary needs, potentialities and vitalities. There is, however, no room in Freudian theory for any such 'true' or 'natural' self. There is a manifest incompatibility when Winnicott first tells us that prior to the 'depressive position' stage there is no whole person and the infant has not yet achieved an ego, being still in an unintegrated stage; and then goes on to say that his 'true self' can be frozen and hidden, as it were in cold storage, awaiting the time when it will be given another opportunity to emerge and grow. His theory of the distinction between the 'true' and 'false' selves calls, not for a theory of original 'unintegration' of ego-nuclei, but for Fairbairn's theory of an originally unitary ego which is the real basic self, and which becomes split under bad environmental pressures. Winnicott's 'true self' is the L.E. and his 'false self' on the basis of compliance is the C.E. denying internal reality and merely adapting to external reality. If the ego has not come into being in the earliest stage, if it is not original, how can it be hidden away and protected from further damaging impingement?

A further difficulty is related to this, namely Winnicott's use of the term 'an intact ego' to describe one of the prerequisites for ordinary analysis. If Fairbairn's structural analysis is correct, there cannot be any such thing as an intact ego. Winnicott can only mean that the superficial Freudian ego must be strong enough, in the sense of having adequate 'defence mechanisms', to prevent 'acting out' and 'regression' and psychotic instability, the problems that underlie his conceptions of 'management' in the treatment of the most ill cases. But it is misleading to speak of patients who are suitable for ordinary analysis as having an intact ego and being whole persons. If they were, they would not be in need of treatment. This theoretical position obscures the intricate continuities that exist between the deepest layers of the personality and the later developed ones. After all, the patient of Winnicott who needed to regress even to the birth stage, at first presented herself as suitable for orthodox analysis, and presumably was supposed to have an intact ego and appeared to be a whole person. Winnicott's terminology hides the facts that are made so plain in the work of Melanie Klein and Fairbairn, that the psychoneuroses are defences against deep anxieties of psychotic type, and they cannot be dealt with in terms simply of interpersonal relationships of the present day on the triangular Oedipal pattern. The tendency for analyses of the psychoneuroses to grow longer and longer is due to the fact that a more penetrating ego-theory involves analysts in uncovering ever deeper levels of inner reality that give rise to and maintain neurosis. The roots of psychoneurosis are now found in the internal bad-object situations brought into being in the first year, and Oedipal problems are but later and disguised forms of these. Thus it would seem that the sharp line of demarcation Winnicott draws between management for the psychotic and psycho-analysis for the psychoneurotic breaks down.

The position that seems to be emerging is that at all stages psychotherapy has to be an appropriate mixture of mothering (management) and analysis (giving insight). The deeper the level on which treatment has to operate, the greater the patient's need for the mothering he failed to obtain. Yet, as Winnicott says, whatever is acted out must be expressed ultimately in words if there is to be a real gain in insight such as will enable the patient to benefit by what is happening to him in the object-relationship with the analyst. As progress is made, it is certainly true that the patient can more and more 'take' analysis, and treatment becomes increasingly something more than a co-operation in terms of infantile dependence, something that grows into a partnership of two increasingly equal adults as the child-patient grows up to the parent-analyst's level. Analysis has by then long ceased to be felt in terms of a psychotic terror of being torn to pieces and can be accepted as the helpful and friendly insight of one with whom the patient is developing a steadily more realistic relationship.

7. *Fairbairn's Views on Object-Relations Theory and Psychotherapy*

Fairbairn has latterly turned his attention to the problems of psychotherapy. When he was working out his revision of theory, he had indicated that object-relations theory must have a bearing on therapeutic technique. He wrote :

It is significant that, where psycho-analysis is concerned, it is now generally recognized that therapeutic results are closely related to the phenomenon of transference, i.e. to the establishment of an object-relationship of a special kind with the analyst on the part of the patient. On the other hand, it is an accepted article of the psycho-analytical technique that the analyst should be unusually self-effacing. As we know, there are very good reasons for the adoption of such an attitude on his part; but it inevitably has the effect of rendering the object-relationship between patient and the analyst somewhat one-sided from the patient's point of view and thus contributing to the resistance. . . . When the self-effacing attitude of the analyst is combined with a mode of interpretation based upon a psychology of impulse, a considerable strain is imposed upon the patient's capacity for establishing satisfactory object-relationships (a capacity which must be regarded as already compromised in virtue of the fact that the patient is a patient at all). (1952a, p. 87.)

He further, at that time, arrived at the conclusion that it is only when the patient feels sure that the analyst is a real good object for him that he becomes able to give up his libidinal cathexis of his internal bad objects. In 1955 he wrote :

What the patient seeks above all is salvation from his past, from bondage to his (internal) bad objects, from the burden of guilt, and from spiritual death. . . . I am convinced that it is the patient's relationship to the analyst that mediates the 'curing' or 'saving' effect of psychotherapy. Where long-term psycho-analytical treatment is concerned, what *mediates* the 'curing' or 'saving' process more specifically is the development of the patient's relationship to the analyst, through a phase in which earlier pathogenic relationships are repeated under the influence of transference into a new kind of relationship which is at once satisfying and adapted to the circumstances of outer reality. (1955, p. 156.)

In his papers in 1952, 1954 and 1956, his interests were more clinical and technical than theoretical, and in 1957 he stated his views in a way that calls for careful but definite experiment in therapeutic technique. But in his latest paper, on treatment, he says :

the practical implications of my views have seemed so far-reaching that they could only be put to the test gradually and with the greatest circumspection if premature or rash psychotherapeutic conclusions were to be avoided. (1958, p. 374.)

He writes :

The relationship existing between patient and analyst is more important than details of technique; and it would seem to follow that the role of the analyst is not merely to fulfil the dual functions of (1) a screen upon which the patient projects his phantasies, and (2) a colourless instrument of interpretative technique, but that his personality and his motives make a significant contribution to the therapeutic process. (1957a, p. 59.)

He points out that the play technique used with children involves a considerable measure of active participation on the part of the analyst, and also a considerable degree of activity during sessions on the part of the patient. He comments that the use of the couch imposes

a taboo upon any form of activity except verbal expression; and, since inhibitions upon activity constitute such an important factor in the genesis of symptoms and inner difficulties, it becomes a question whether the artificial reinforcement of such inhibitions by the conditions of the analytical session does not in many cases constitute a serious emotional trauma for the patient, increase his resistance and perhaps even favour negative therapeutic reactions . . . it would seem reasonable to pose the question how far, if at all, the psychoanalytical treatment of adults should aspire to the condition of child analysis. (1957a, pp. 59–60.)

In 'Observations in Defence of the Object-Relations Theory of the Personality' (1955, pp. 154–6) he does not regard psychotherapy as primarily a scientific activity, for science aims only at explanation of morbid, or of any processes. Indeed, for science a process is not 'morbid', a term which implies a value-judgment, but merely a process to be explained like any other process. Psychotherapy is a practical activity based on human values and making use of scientific explanatory knowledge to further its ends. This involves that Fairbairn does not regard 'interpretation' as *the* therapeutic factor *per se*. Since in terms of object-relations theory it is bad-object relations with parents and others in the formative years that laid the foundations of illness, it must be a possible good-object relationship between the patient and analyst as persons that confers on the analytical situation the value of a re-growing period, and operates as the therapeutic factor capable of eliminating the legacy of the past. Because the analyst is capable of being a reliable *real object* (and Winnicott has made it plain how necessary and exacting a business that is), the patient can work through unrealistic transference relations with the analyst, and becomes capable of recognizing and accepting the reality of the analyst as a person, and of growing in a real, appropriate, personal relationship. We are here on the same ground as Winnicott when he says that in some cases 'the analyst has to be the first in the patient's life to supply certain environmental essentials'. (1958, p. 198.) It would seem, however, that Winnicott limits this real object-relationship between patient and analyst to regressed cases requiring 'management' and does not regard it as applying to cases requiring 'psycho-analysis'. Fairbairn would not admit such a distinction to be realistic, and regards the real personal relationship between patient and analyst as the only thing that makes it possible for transference relationships to be worked through, and therefore as the truly therapeutic factor. He writes :

From a therapeutic standpoint, interpretation is not enough; and it would appear to follow that the relationship existing between the patient and the analyst in the psycho-analytical situation serves purposes additional to that of providing a setting for the interpretation of transference phenomena. In terms of the object-relation theory of the personality, the disabilities from which the patient suffers represent the effects of unsatisfactory and unsatisfying object-relationships experienced in early life and perpetuated in an exaggerated form in inner reality; and, if this view is correct, the actual relationship existing between the patient and the analyst as persons must be regarded as in itself constituting a therapeutic factor of prime importance. The existence of such a personal relationship in outer reality not only serves the function of providing a means of correcting the distorted relationships which prevail in inner reality and influence the reactions of the patient to outer objects, but provides the patient with the opportunity denied to him in childhood, to undergo a process of emotional development in the setting of an actual relationship with a reliable and beneficent parental figure. (1958, p. 377, col. 2.)

The fact is that as ego-analysis goes deeper and leads analysis into ever more detailed investigations into the very foundations of personality, Winnicott's phases of 'management' and 'analysis' merge into the one total process of personality liberation and regrowth. This process is compelled to be a more active one on the part of both patient and analyst than the original classic technique allowed for. One of my patients who at the start was a very severely ill hysteric, and for whom a very long treatment led ultimately to an increasingly satisfactory therapeutic result, went through three fairly clearly marked stages. In the first, orthodox analysis accomplished the abandonment of her physical symptoms and restored her to the best physical health she had ever known, at the price of her becoming completely aware of the extent of her deep unhappiness. In the second stage, she took the lead in acting out her fear, hate and need, and I had to help and support and encourage as seemed best. She would say, 'It's no good talking. Words don't mean anything to me. I must do something, you must do something.' In this stage she literally resorted to a child's play-therapy, bringing her own 'play materials', and it was fascinating to watch her 'games' progressing through age levels until, as it were, she became adolescent and began to face the task of becoming an adult. That led to the third period of tackling tasks in real life in a quite new and more active way until she achieved an independence of her parents and a capacity for steady self-reliance and personal and social relationships that she had never before possessed.

In the 1958 paper Fairbairn dealt at length with some implications of the recognition of the personal relationship of patient and analyst in reality as the therapeutic factor. The standardization of a rigid technique is inappropriate to the highly personal needs of the patient, and is likely to be more of a defence of the analyst against the patient than a realistic adaptation to the situation of each fresh patient as a unique 'individual'. From this point of view the 'rigidity' of the 'classical psycho-analytical technique, as standardized by Freud more than half a century ago', is too impersonal to meet the full demands of psychotherapy.

Fairbairn mentions that Gitelson regards a psycho-analytical cure as involving four factors—insight, recall of infantile memories, catharsis and the relationship with the analyst—and he adds :

In my own opinion, the really decisive factor is the relationship of the patient to the analyst, and it is upon this relationship that the other factors mentioned by Gitelson depend not only for their effectiveness, but for their very existence, since in the absence of a therapeutic relationship with the analyst they simply do not occur . . . what I understand by 'the relationship between the patient and the analyst' is not just the relationship involved in the transference, but the total relationship existing between the patient and the analyst as persons. (1958, p. 379.)

The paper ends with a clinical study of the psychotherapeutic problem which raises the basic issue of why therapeutic change is so hard to promote.

8. *The Final Problem*
(a) *The Hard Core of Resistance to Psychotherapeutic Change*

The present time is a fresh period of psychotherapeutic experimentation. Such periods occur repeatedly. The use of hypnosis, the development of Freud's psycho-analysis, Ferenczi's more active and personal technique, Mrs. Klein's play-therapy, are cases in point. To-day the relationship of patient and therapist has become the focal point. Psycho-analysis of the psychoneuroses has led steadily down into the realm of psychotherapeutic intervention in schizophrenia, where it seems to be agreed by all workers that the personal factor in the therapeutic relationship overrides everything else. This must inevitably lead to a reflection back into treatment at every stage of what has been learned on these deepest psychic levels. We have seen that the upshot of recent theoretical and clinical trends is to bring to the front : (1) Ego-psychology and (2) Object-relationship as the ultimate therapeutic factor. They are two aspects of one whole, since we now know that the foundations of all sound ego-development are laid down in the primary infant-mother relationship, and the elaboration of ego-identity comes about through all the later personal relationships that succeed that first one. Accurate knowledge of the earliest stages of ego-development is of the utmost importance for psychotherapy ; since psychotherapy now appears to be a process by which the patient can belatedly develop, in the therapeutic relationship with the analyst, sufficient basic ego-strength for the purposes of living an adult life. The patient needs to accomplish that growth with the therapist which he was unable to make initially with his parents.

In non-technical language, the purpose of psychotherapy may be simply stated as that of helping the patient to grow till he feels strong enough in himself to be capable of living without unrealistic fears of internal origin and their attendant hates, guilts, defences and conflicts. Looking at the matter from the point of view of psychopathology rather than psychotherapy, we are arriving at the view that the root cause of all pathological developments in the personality in later life is a fundamental ego-weakness, established as a persisting structural phenomenon in the earliest stages. Adler's somewhat superficial theory of the 'Inferiority Complex' and the 'Will to Power' as an over-compensation for felt inferiority, now dissolves back into the deepest unconscious depths when looked at from the point of view of the searching ego-analysis started by Freud's structural theory.

The one thing most characteristic of all patients, whether they show it openly or hide it behind defences, over-compensations and resistances, is that they do not feel strong enough as personalities to cope adequately with adult living. This is now revealed to be, in the last analysis, not just a matter of anxiety and the struggle for power in a competitive social setting as Adler, and also Karen Horney, saw it. It is something that goes back and back, deeper and deeper, till at last we reach the earliest period where we find failure to achieve the first steps in sound ego-development right at the start. Moreover, as Winnicott states, this failure in early ego-development arises out of the failure of the environment to provide the child with what it needs for healthy emotional growth, so that he calls psychosis, in the last resort, 'an environmental deficiency disease'. The problem differs in degree but not in kind as between different individuals, and clearly is not to be confined to schizophrenia, but rather regarded as the tap-root of all troubles according to its degree of severity. Winnicott's theory of the true and false selves and the need for therapeutic regression to discover and free the true self for sound development, Fairbairn's view that the root cause of psychoneurosis lies deeper than the Oedipus complex and is to be found in the persistence of Infantile Dependence, and Balint's view that the patient must be able to go back to what he regards as primary, passive, dependent love to make a new start in growing, all point in different ways to the fact that basic structural ego-weakness is the starting-point of all later psychopathological processes.

The technique of psycho-analysis thus becomes an endeavour, not to release repressed impulses and recover repressed memories, nor even to break up repressed complexes, all of which are intermediate matters which are incidental to the ultimate aim, namely, to help the patient to tolerate the conscious re-experiencing of his profoundly repressed and fundamentally weak infantile ego, which he has spent his life trying to disown in his struggle to feel adult. When he can tolerate its return to consciousness, he secures at last an opportunity to start growing again towards maturity in this all-important, dynamically fundamental part of his personality which represents his primary nature. What makes this possible is that he now finds he has a relationship with his analyst which is more reliable and mature than that which he originally had with his parents, one in which he comes to feel accepted as himself a real person.

All the thorny problems of psycho-analytic therapy arise out of this. The extent of the patient's dependence on the therapist conflicts with his need for independence, and drives him to attempt to force a false independence instead of waiting to develop a true self-reliance. This situation sets up an automatic resistance from the start and gives rise to most of the transient panics and crises in the therapeutic setting, and also to what some analysts seem to regard solely as the patient's attempts to exploit and manipulate the therapist; though even manipulative behaviour must be motivated by the fact that the patient's deep, terrifying, inner weakness makes him feel he could only be safe if he could have the analyst wholly in his own power and possession. The tremendous difficulties both we and our patients are up against in promoting real changes at this deepest level in the personality need to be illuminated by greater knowledge of this early period. Also the question, raised by some, as to whether it is a good thing to take the patient back so far, needs a factual answer. Clearly it is a major psychological operation. Whether the view is held, theoretically, that basic ego-weakness goes back to Winnicott's primary unintegrated state or to the splitting of Fairbairn's pristine, whole, unitary ego by involvement in bad-object relationships in the earliest months, it is in this region that the ultimate knowledge for psychotherapy must be found. Only the sufficiently strong ego is capable of undisturbed personal relationships and of further growth and enrichment in them. To arrive at that condition is what we mean by a psychotherapeutic 'cure'.

'We may, therefore, state the problem of the psychodynamic hard core of resistance to psychotherapy in this form : when once the infantile ego has become disturbed and arrested in its development in the earliest stages, so that it comes to feel its weakness and to exist in a state of fear, what is it that keeps it thereafter fixed so stubbornly in that position of basic ego-weakness? What is it that leads to the perpetuation of a weak, undeveloped, fearful, and therefore "infantile dependent" ego (in Fairbairn's sense)? It remains buried in the deep unconscious and makes no progress to maturity, in spite of the strenuous efforts of the "self of everyday life" (Fairbairn's Central Ego) to grow and function as an adult. Why is this endopsychic situation so hard to change? And in what form does it persist so statically?' (Guntrip, 1960, p. 170.) Fairbairn has recently described this problem in terms which are a challenge to psychotherapy because they illuminate the seriousness of this recalitrance to change. I can outline only briefly his statement of the problem and indicate the direction in which it seems to me that the answer is to be found.

In his paper 'On the Nature and Aims of Psycho-Analytical Treatment' (1958, pp. 380–5) he puts forward three related concepts which taken together make plain the unyielding fixity and strength of the hard core of psychoneurosis. He regards the aims of psycho-analytical treatment also as three :

(i) 'The chief aim of psycho-analytical treatment is to promote a maximum "synthesis" of the structures into which the original ego has been split', i.e. to promote the development of a whole strong ego out of the Libidinal Ego, Anti-Libidinal Ego and Central Ego.

(ii) 'To achieve . . . a maximum reduction of persisting infantile dependence', i.e. a maturing of the Libidinal Ego, and

(iii) 'a maximum reduction of that hatred of the libidinal object which . . . is ultimately responsible for the original splitting of the ego', i.e. a diminution of the Anti-Libidinal Ego. He observes that 'the resistance on the part of the patient to the achievement of these aims is, of course, colossal'. Thus, one of Freud's earliest discoveries—the fact of the patient's resistance to psychotherapy—still remains the major practical problem to be solved.

The nature of resistance Fairbairn describes in three related concepts:

(iv) 'A defensive aim, which I have now come to regard as the greatest of all sources of resistance—viz. the maintenance of the patient's internal world as a closed system.'

(v) This internal world, this 'closed system of internal reality', he further describes as 'a static internal situation' which is made up of 'self-contained situations in inner reality, which persist unchanged indefinitely, and which are precluded from change by their very nature so long as they remain self-contained'.

(vi) Fairbairn then brings into relation with this concept of the patient's internal psychic reality as a closed, static, self-contained system, his re-interpretation of Freud's death instinct, namely as 'an obstinate tendency on the part of the patient to keep his aggression localized within the confines of the closed system of his inner world'. In illustration of this tendency, which has long been recognized under the form of 'turning aggression back against the self', he cites the following impressive statement of a patient: 'It is vital to my internal economy not to waste hate on you. I feel I need the hate for myself. I need the hate to run myself on. . . . I want my hate to keep me short-circuited. Instead of running myself on outside people and things, my sex-object is myself. . . . I hate you for trying to stop me doing this. I need to hate you to get energy for my inner persecution. . . . That is my life—a drawn-out ecstasy of slowly killing myself. . . . I hoard my anger to use for inner purposes. . . . My aim is to sail as near the wind as I can to killing myself. . . . My ordinary life is an interference with my neurosis. . . . I feel my unconscious life is my true life. . . . There is a bit of me that keeps me alive; but my true purpose is directed to killing myself and frustration. . . . I must accept that I frustrate myself. I expect that originally I was frustrated from outside; but now I impose frustration on myself; and that is to be my satisfaction. . . . It is a terrible perversion.'

This remarkable statement shows us what we are up against. The patient's inner life is a 'closed system' so that outer and ordinary life is a mere interference with it, and so is the analyst's endeavour to rescue him from this plight. While this closed system is a dynamic high-tension system in itself, its pattern nevertheless is 'static' from the outside point of view, 'a drawn-out ecstasy of slowly killing myself' which must not succeed and come to an end but must keep going, only 'sailing as near the wind' as possible in a state of keeping oneself alive in a condition of perpetual self-destroying frustration. This inner 'closed system' with its static internal situation of persisting self-destruction is run on the dynamic of self-hate or inturned aggression. A dream of a patient of my own illustrates concretely and symbolically this conception of the hard core of neurosis as a psychic deadlock in which the patient is shut up in his unconscious in a situation of unremitting self-persecution, while his inability to break out arises from his motives for staying in. This male patient dreamed : 'I was in a concentration camp and I thought, "Why don't I escape?" Then I thought, "I know my way about in here. If it's bad, it's probably worse outside and I'm used to this and know how to make the best of it." So I decided to stay in there.' Here is the closed system, the static internal situation, and the using up of the hate and aggression inwardly in persecution of the self. This is the inner state of affairs which somehow the therapist has to find out how to break up, if the patient is to be released.

At this point the importance of psycho-analysis is evident, for there is little hope of releasing a patient from this concentration camp in his unconscious unless we can discover and expose to him his motives for staying there and help him to recognize that he is really aiming, in spite of appearances, at self-preservation, but by the wrong methods. This dream and the statement of Fairbairn's patient give us two clues as to the motivation which supports this extraordinary internal state of affairs. The motivation seems to be twofold : fear and libidinal attachment. My patient stayed in his concentration camp because he feared that it would be worse outside. It is a schizoid withdrawal from outer reality. This is confirmed by another dream of a male patient which came at the end of a long series of dreams of escape from prison which always ended in recapture. This unceasing rhythm of escape and re-imprisonment was his static internal situation and the reason was frankly stated in a big dream as follows : 'I was in prison in an old ancestral castle (i.e. home, the family set-up). A young man my own age came in and gave me a file to file through the window bars and escape. I said, "I don't need that. The doors are not locked." He said, "Why don't you escape then?" I said, "Look out of that window. See how dangerous it is out there. How would I get on if I found myself out there all alone?" At that moment I discovered my mother was standing behind me as my jailoress.' His mother was the parent with whom he had experienced the greatest difficulties and he elects to stay behind in her power inside himself because any alternative seems far more dangerous, and he feels too weak and afraid to face it.

Furthermore, Fairbairn's patient finds herself committed to an internal perverse system of self-hate and self-destruction about which she says, 'My aim is to sail as near the wind as I can to killing myself.' In fact, she added, 'My aim is to carry out my mother's and father's wishes.' She clearly regards these as identical statements. In some way her self-hate is at first an expenditure on herself of her hate of her parents as her 'original frustrators', but in the second place it is also a repetition on herself of what she feels to have been their own aims towards her. She has come to identify herself with the rejective and destructive attitudes towards herself of her original bad objects. This is a libidinal attachment which issues in self-destructive behaviour, yet which cannot be given up because it rests on a deep and paralysing fear that any alternative would be worse. We have here taken up a fourth view of Fairbairn, put forward earlier—namely, that the ultimate source of resistance is the libidinal cathexis of the internal bad object. This completes the description of this utterly resistant hard core of psychoneurosis. Analysis has to establish each separate patient's individual version of this dilemma, and help him to experience it consciously in his own personal terms. The using up of aggression in internal self-persecution rests on a libidinal attachment to an internalized bad object, and this has taken up into itself both the infant's hate of his parents because they are unsatisfying and therefore (to him) destructive, and also what the infant feels to be the parents' hate of himself. This is due to the fact of the infant's identifying himself with his anti-libidinal bad object. The energy of his hate of the bad parent now animates his identification with that bad parent and is changed into self-hate. Yet this self-hate is the disguised form of a libidinal attachment to a (bad) love-object. It constitutes the sadistic element in what Freud called the 'super-ego', and is what Fairbairn calls the 'Anti-Libidinal Ego', which functions as an 'internal saboteur'. Thus what in descriptive terms is the closed system of a static internal situation in which aggression is permanently internalized against the self, is now seen to be in structural terms what Fairbairn calls the Anti-L.E.'s persecution of the infantile L.E. The advantage of Fairbairn's terminology over Freud's on this issue is that it yields a more exact analysis. The L.E. is the infantile dependent self, which is kept in a condition of persisting ego-weakness by the unremitting hate and attack to which it is subjected by another part of the personality which remains in a state of identification with parents as internalized bad objects. This is why it has so often been held that psychotherapy must issue in a modification of the cruelty of the Freudian 'super-ego' to use the older term.

This, however, is just what is so difficult to achieve. The patient by himself seems powerless to change his own internal set-up. He cannot be got to accept himself and leave himself in peace to live naturally and develop his own individuality. On the contrary, he feels convinced that the only way he can keep going at all is by driving himself. Here is the citadel of the resistance. Why does the patient stick so stubbornly to his identification with his internalized bad object when it exposes him to depressive and persecutory anxiety? In recognizing the full implications of the motivation which sustains this inner situation, we come to the heart of the problem of psychotherapy. The self-destructive identification which results in the formation of the Anti-L.E. is maintained, as we have seen, by a double motivation, both fear and libidinal attachment. Fear is an ego-motive, libidinal attachment is an object-relations motive, and we have now arrived at the stage where stress must be put decisively on the ego-motive. 'The nature of the problem involved seems to me to be this : the primary drive in every human being is to become a "person", to achieve a solid ego-formation, to develop a personality, in order to live. This, however, can only be done in the medium of personal object-relationships. If these are good, the infant undergoes a natural and unselfconscious good ego-development. If these are bad, ego-development is seriously compromised from the start ; and there are no fears worse or deeper than those which arise out of having to cope with life when one feels that one just is not a real person, that one's ego is basically weak, perhaps that one has hardly got an ego at all. These are the ultimate fears in our patients.' (Guntrip, 1960, p. 165.) Not that the infant can conceptualize all this, but he can feel it, and the situation being desperate, desperate remedies are blindly resorted to. He feels so terrified, because he has no adequate ego of his own when faced with a bad-object environment, hates his own weakness and seeks to identify himself with the powerful figures around him, who are, of course, his rejective bad objects. It is as if he concludes that it is his very weakness and dependence that they hate and that he must hate too. In order to possess himself of an ego strong enough to live by he rejects himself and substitutes by identification the personality of his persecutors. This manoeuvre is clearly shown in the following dream of a female patient. 'I was eating my favourite meal and saving the nicest bit to the last when mother came in and snatched it out of my hand saying, "Don't be a baby." ' But the mother who is intolerant of the baby, and prevents the satisfaction of the patient's libidinal needs and the nourishment of her personality, has now become a part of the patient herself, and by identification with this internalized mother she develops an Anti-L.E., and turns into a self-destructive denier and persecutor of her own L.E., suffering from Anorexia. A different but parallel manifestation which is peculiarly instructive is to be found in a patient who used to hit herself. Needless to say, her mother used to beat her. Her greatest conscious dread was of showing any kind of weakness. The extent to which she rejected the weak and frightened child in herself in favour of a blind and unrecognized identification with her beating mother appears when, on one occasion, she began beating herself in session. I remarked, 'You must be terrified being beaten like that.' She stopped and stared at me in silence and then said, 'I'm not being beaten. I'm the one who's doing the beating.' She could not give up that position for sheer fear that if she did she would have nothing to fall back on but the weak, terrified little girl who was the victim. The patient cannot let himself be robbed of his identification with his internal bad object and allow his Anti-L.E. to dissolve away, for he feels he will have nothing left but the need to come face to face again with his basic and terrifying ego-weakness. He has found a false solution to the problem of ego-weakness which, once accepted, he cannot give up because it perpetuates and actually worsens the very weakness it was supposed to cure.

We may now summarize the problem of the hard core of resistance to psychotherapy. This resistance operates at two levels which, in Fairbairn's terminology, are the C.E. level and the L.E.-cum-Anti-L.E. level. *Central Ego resistance* is usually dominant in the earlier stages of analysis. From a very early age the anxieties of the infant are often hidden under a premature hypertrophy or over-development of the C.E., the ego of everyday life. This sets into a rigid pattern as an anxiety-driven adaptation to outer reality and a defence against anxiety-outbreaks from the inner world and the emergence of the infantile L.E. It develops into a pseudo-adult personality, Winnicott's 'false self' and Fairbairn's 'false independence'; Erikson's researches into ego-identity in adolescence concern the weakness or strength of the C.E. (1959).

If the resistance of this rigid C.E. to the uncovering of infantile experience is overcome, we then come upon a deeper resistance, that of the static closed sado-masochistic system of internal bad objects and the Anti-L.E. persecuting the weak, infantile dependent L.E. This represents the original infant finding himself in an unsatisfying, unsupportive and hostile parental environment and being forced to become aware of how little, helpless and unable to defend himself he is. He becomes terrified and takes flight for safety into an identification with his bad objects who seem so powerful. Thus the infant, having no adequate good-object relationship and no adequate ego—for the two go together—is driven to substitute an identification with bad parents inside himself for both ego and object. Once that is done he is caught in an internal situation from which he cannot escape, and in which while he feels to be 'the one doing the hitting' and therefore in an illusory way strong, he still remains in fact 'the one being hit' and therefore weak. He cannot give up this position, for it would feel like the terror of collapse into nothingness without object or ego.

No wonder psychotherapy comes up against stubborn resistance, but this is the problem to which we have to find the answer. How can the patient be helped, in the psychotherapeutic relationship, to risk experiencing and to go on enduring the fears that will break out as he ceases to identify with his internal bad objects?

8. *The Final Problem*
(b) *The Re-orientation of Psychodynamic Theory*

(i) *A New Orientation*

In surveying the position we have now reached, it does not seem possible to rest satisfied at this point. Firstly, the nature of the underlying ego-weakness (p. 394) with which the patient will be faced if he gives up his libidinal cathexis of internal bad objects calls for further investigation. This should be the crux of the entire problem. It seems probable that it is the lack of understanding of this matter that accounts for the second ground of dissatisfaction, namely, that the hard core of anti-libidinal resistance to psychotherapy still remains excessively unyielding. The sado-masochistic 'closed system' of internal bad-object relations, including the persecution of the L.E. by the Anti-L.E., is certainly the hard core of the *active* neurosis. This 'static internal situation', run on hate and self-hate, produces all the positive painful symptoms and distresses, physical and mental; the active suffering. Yet, in my experience, the uncovering of the motives for its creation and maintenance mentioned in the last section does not by any means lead to its dissolution; at best, only to its moderation. Why is it so hard to give up?

There seems to be a vital link in the chain of understanding that is still missing. Fairbairn's patient (quoted on p. 421) said: 'There is a little bit of me that keeps me alive.' What and where is that little bit? It cannot be part of the internal bad-objects world; that is dedicated to 'sailing as near the wind as I can to killing

myself'. Also this anti-libidinal activity must have a positive function that calls for deeper understanding. This was made clear by
a patient whose hate was being alternately turned outwards and
inwards, and when turned inwards was labelled by her 'M.C.'
(My Conscience). I pointed out how self-destructive this was, and
that it seemed to be a wrong method of aiming at a right result.
She replied with all the tension of great fear : 'You don't understand that it is the only way I can keep going at all. Without it I'd
collapse entirely.' What does 'collapse entirely' mean, in psychodynamic terms; and 'collapse' into what state ; and what is the
relationship of that fear to the other patient's 'little bit of me that
keeps me alive' ? We are back at the problem of the ultimate nature
of ego-weakness. There is something further to be explored if we
are to solve the problem of the intractable resistance to psychotherapy of the hard core of the *active* neurosis. That phrase suggests the opposite idea of the *passive* neurosis which is encountered
in exhaustion phenomena and deeply regressed states.

This leads us to the third ground for dissatisfaction, which is
theoretical rather than practical. All the varied psychopathological phenomena we are acquainted with appear to have been
gathered together and conceptualized in such a way that they can
be fitted into a reasonably consistent pattern, developmentally and
structurally, all with one exception. The phenomena of 'regression' have not yet been given any really intelligible place in the
general scheme. Regression seems generally to be regarded as a
nuisance clinically, a menace that ought to be cut short. Regression is, however, a stubborn fact of great importance, and the
practical difficulties it creates are not, in science, a valid excuse for
ignoring it. Yet it remains the Cinderella of theory, awkward and
neglected. Winnicott stands out for the courage with which he has
grasped this nettle and been prepared to be stung by it in an
attempt to understand it and give it its proper place in the therapeutic scheme. In his concept of 'therapeutic regression' he has
brought together the problems, practical and theoretical, which
appear to be still unsolved. I have come to feel that the problem
can be solved if linked to Fairbairn's contention that the schizoid
position is the fundamental one for psychopathology, and if it is
approached from the point of view of his ego-psychology. This
re-orientation of theory implies that the basic drive behind all
psychopathological conditions is the need to become and remain
'a person in one's own right', or, in the narrower sense, *the
struggle to preserve an 'ego'*.

Psychodynamic theory has progressed by successive re-orienta-
tions. It was first re-orientated from neuropsychiatry, in the

earlier work of Freud, by the concept of the need to satisfy and control discrete instinct-entities rooted in biological drives. In Freud's later work, particularly as developed by Melanie Klein, theory was re-orientated again on the basis of *object-relationships with special emphasis on the object* regarded as internal. In further developing this 'internal object-relations theory', Fairbairn, it is now clear, worked out a further re-orientation, *an object-relations theory with emphasis shifted to the ego*. As Ernest Jones says :

Instead of starting, as Freud did, from stimulation of the nervous system proceeding from excitation of various erotogenous zones, and internal tension arising from gonadic activity, *Dr. Fairbairn starts at the centre of the personality, the ego,* and depicts its strivings and difficulties in its endeavour to reach an object where it may find support. . . . *All this constitutes a fresh approach in psycho-analysis.* [Present writer's italics.] (Fairbairn, 1952, p.v.)

The final consequences of this have perhaps yet to be made fully explicit.

Freud himself began this re-orientation when the phrase 'Analysis of the Ego' occurred in the title of his 1921 monograph, and when he placed the term 'ego' before 'id' in the title of *The Ego and the Id* in 1923. How new that point of view was is clear from Anna Freud's comment : 'Whenever research was deflected from the id to the ego—it was felt that here was the beginning of apostasy.' (1936, p. 3.) In 1933 Freud wrote of 'the therapeutic effects of psycho-analysis' that 'their object is to strengthen the ego'. (1933, p. 106.) This makes the ego the true centre of both the practical and the theoretical concerns.

Nevertheless, before the psychology of the ego could be fully developed, the psychology of the object and of object-relations had to be thoroughly explored. The work of Melanie Klein had to be done, and 'internal object-relations theory' created. The fundamental fact that has emerged from this is that the importance of object-relations lies in the fact that there can be no ego-development without them. Actually, in a vacuum the ego cannot maintain itself at all. So true is this that the infant clings to bad objects if he has no sufficiently good ones, rather than have no objects. That is as true of internal bad objects as of the original external bad objects. We have seen how that is responsible for much of the difficulty of analysing and dissolving away the Anti-L.E. The patient clings to this and to the internal bad objects on which it is formed by identification in order to keep his ego in being, and then suffers the persecutory and depressive anxieties with resulting defences and secondary conflicts which constitute neurotic illness.

When psychopathology is looked at from the point of view of internal bad objects, it seems evident that these disturbing structures are the cause of psychoneurosis. When, however, we look at the problem from the point of view of the ego, the entire world of internal bad objects appears rather in the light of a desperately operated defence against the last and worst psychic danger, the loss of the ego. That this is the root problem, emerges from Fairbairn's view that the schizoid rather than the depressive position is the fundamental one. The schizoid reaction of withdrawal from objects because they are experienced as intolerable, generates the final schizoid danger, that of the loss of the ego. Derealization of the outer world and depersonalization of the ego go together. When object-relations are broken off, the ego is emptied, and if the process were not arrested, increasing apathy, psychic collapse and death would eventuate.

I have, therefore, now come to regard the entire range of psychopathological phenomena which we have been studying as masking, by various defensive tactics and strategies, the basic problem of the patient's struggle to retain a viable ego after he has once begun to experience the object-world as bad to him. From this emerge new ways of looking at many familiar facts. In attempting here to adumbrate the way in which this re-orientation works out, I have been influenced, apart from clinical evidence which must always have first place, by three contributions.

(a) *Fairbairn's* view of the schizoid process as determining his analysis of endopsychic structure in terms of ego-splitting in bad-object relationships, leading to the conclusion that unconscious infantile dependence is the cause of psychoneurosis.

(b) *Winnicott's* view of the necessity for 'therapeutic regression' in search of the lost (i.e. split-off) 'true self', involving maybe even a working-through of a rebirth process in treatment, while the 'false self' conforming to social demands carries on with a 'caretaker function'; and

(c) *Balint's* view that radical psychotherapy involves the patient in going back to where he can make 'a new beginning' in a condition of 'passive object-love' for the therapist. Out of these points of view I believe there now emerges a radical reconstruction of psychodynamic theory as a whole.

(ii) *Schizoid Withdrawal from the Object-World*

The foundations must be laid in the adequate analysis of the early *schizoid withdrawal from bad-object relations.* This is best looked on as the primary regression, a move backwards rather than forwards. It is a process which clinical evidence seen in the light of Winnicott's views leads me to believe takes place in two stages. When the infant finds himself in a relationship to outer reality which imposes on him greater strains than he is capable of bearing, he mentally withdraws from the outer world into his inner psychic life. The reasons for this must be complex and can be looked at from the side both of the ego's need for the object and the ego's need to preserve itself. Fairbairn's view is based on the ego's need for the object. Faced with lack of satisfaction of primary libidinal needs, the infant's needs become so over-intensified as to feel dangerous to love-objects. As with the patient who said : 'I can't make moderate demands so I don't make any at all', the schizoid withdrawal from object-relations is motivated by the fear that one's love is destructive. Winnicott looks at the matter from the point of view of the ego's need to preserve its own existence. He regards good mothering as consisting of *adjustment* to the infant without *impingement*. The mother must supply the baby's needs at the time when he feels them, but not force attentions on him when he does not want them. If she does the latter, she *impinges* on the baby's sensitive psyche, puts pressure on him, and he shrinks away into himself. Fairbairn has also recently stressed in private conversation that the baby's troubles arise not only over his own needs for parents, but also over the pressure of the parent's needs and problems on the child.

The first move towards the creation of the schizoid position has been made. The infant has withdrawn from the outer world into himself. If at that stage the breaking-off of object-relations were complete, it would be followed by a collapse of the ego so that the child could hardly be kept alive. He must therefore detach a part of himself to remain still in touch with the reality from which he retreats. What Fairbairn calls the Central Ego, Winnicott the False Self and Freud the outer 'reality-ego' is left with depleted energies, like a forward screen of front-line troops 'in touch with the enemy' and struggling to hold its position by whatever manoeuvres seem useful. The emotional heart of the personality has drawn back inside out of reach of being hurt. A patient once told me of her sister's little boy being a very shy and 'shut in' child, and how she had a vivid memory of him as a baby being left screaming and she was not allowed to pick him up. Then quite suddenly he stopped dead and was silent. In a recent radio play a little girl was made to say : 'It doesn't matter what you do to me now, you can't hurt me any more.' A split in the psyche has occurred. A libidinal self has drawn back leaving a de-emotionalized self to maintain somewhat mechanical touch with the outer world.

If, however, the withdrawn ego remained without objects it would become depersonalized and no doubt undermine the Outer-Reality Ego as well. To ward off this danger a world of internal objects has to be set up and an inner world created. These will, of course, be psychic duplicates and developments of the original external objects, and now apparently a desperate situation arises. The enemy has, so to speak, infiltrated behind the front lines. It seems that here a stand must be made and no further 'withdrawal according to plan' is possible. Certainly here a stand is made and the withdrawn ego struggles to solve its problems in object-relationships by elaborating an inner world of psychic reality. Here, as Fairbairn says, the ego tries to master its bad objects (in their duplicate psychic version) since it could not master them in outer reality, but only to find itself tied to a fifth column of persecutors secretly attacking it inside the inner world where safety had been sought in retreat. The world of internal bad objects is set up.

The first split, between a C.E. in touch with the outer world and a L.E. inside seeking ways of coping with its now-internal objects, leads to a splitting of the internal object into an exciting libidinal object which arouses needs and a rejective anti-libidinal object which denies them. This leads to a further split of the ego into a starved masochistic L.E. for ever failing to obtain satisfaction from its E.O., and a sadistic Anti-L.E. that sides with the R.O. and persecutes the L.E., in a struggle to achieve independence by the suppression of weakness and needs. Here is the elaboration of the internal bad-object world as a closed system inside which the inner self becomes a prisoner. A patient says : 'I don't know that I want to come to terms with this blasted world of daily life. It's better to keep my own fairy-story going. Better not see people or things as they really are. Retire into your fairy-story of wicked witches and bad dragons. Why the hell should I go into the outer world? Why should I have any further dealings with my impossible father? Why go out and meet strange people I probably won't like? Better go to a theatre or read a book. But my troubled dream world is my real fairy-story world.'

This Kleinian world of internal bad objects is where we find our patients imprisoned. It is Fairbairn's sado-masochistic closed system run on hate, and we are up against the intensest resistance in trying to help the patient to get out of it, even though in it he suffers all the risks of psychotic and psychoneurotic illness, persecutory terrors, crushing depressive guilt, phobias, hysteric pains, obsessional compulsions and ever-present chronic anxiety. Yet he holds on to it, because, in fact, he dare not give it up. *The entire world of internal bad objects is a colossal defence against loss of the ego by depersonalization.* The one issue that is much worse than the choice between good and bad objects is the choice between any sort of objects and no objects at all. Persecution is preferred to depersonalization. The phenomenon of internalization of bad objects has hitherto been regarded as arising out of the need to master the object. We have now to see it as arising even more fundamentally out of the need to preserve an ego.

I have become convinced that in order to realize the full import of this we must take one further step in structural analysis. I suggested that in this internal bad-object world a stand has to be made because no further retreat is possible. In fact, there is abundant clinical evidence in the phenomena of regression that that is not true, ultimately. The L.E., masochistically suffering persecution in the internal bad-object situation, repeats the manoeuvre originally made by the whole ego facing a bad outer world. It splits itself into two parts. It leaves one part in the internal front-line position in touch with the enemy, *an Oral needy L.E.* suffering from internal bad objects and the Anti-L.E. ; while the other part beats a further and final retreat, *a Regressed L.E.* that has cut off all clear object-relationships. Where does this Regressed L.E. go? It withdraws back into its original safe 'base camp', the warm, protected place from which it first emerged. It withdraws, if not back into an actual womb, then deep into the unconscious into an even more secret and hidden 'closed system' of an illusory though psychically real reproduction of the intra-uterine state. This is the source of the 'return to the womb' phantasies with which analysts have always been familiar, the importance of which Freud stressed in connection with his criticism of Rank's views.

I suggest that Fairbairn's basing of the whole of psychopathology on the schizoid position involves one further extension of his endopsychic structural scheme, namely, the splitting of the L.E. under internal persecution into an Oral sado-masochistic L.E. which remains tied to the internal bad-object world, and a Regressed L.E. which retires deep into the innermost recesses of the psyche and which can remain out of reach for a lifetime. This is Winnicott's 'true self', not, however, 'frozen' or 'put in cold storage' till it can obtain a second chance to be reborn. It is in very warm storage and, though itself hidden, it exercises a powerful backward pull on all the rest of the personality in proportion as pressure, fear and anxiety are experienced in real life. It is the true source of all passive and regressive phenomena, exhaustion and fatigue, compulsive sleep, agoraphobic anxieties and the claustrophobias which are a reaction from them, phantasies of a return to the womb and retirement and escapist phantasies and longings in real life. Unremitting struggle to keep going and keep in touch with the object-world is carried on in the rest of the personality. This usually leads to an intense drive to over-activity in real life, and/or all forms of sexual compulsion, genital and perverse and aggressive trends (for these are all object-relations activities). When relations with real objects weaken or diminish, then recourse is had to the inner world of internalized objects, in daytime phantasy and night-time dreaming. This world of internal bad objects, from which the Regressed L.E. has withdrawn in fear, is also the world of object-relations to which the masochistic Oral L.E. must cling if schizoid ego-loss is to be warded off, since a full return to external object-relations is precluded by the initial schizoid split of the 'first stage withdrawal'. The internal-objects world is itself a schizoid phenomenon and only inside it can depression develop. This way of looking at things involves a reassessment of the purpose of all the phenomena of internal-object relations.

(iii) *The Regressed Ego*

I have thus come to regard the phenomena of regression as implying and deriving from a specific, structurally persisting Regressed L.E. This appears to me to be equally implied in Winnicott's view about the 'true self' and 'therapeutic regression'. The term 'true self' is inexact and open to some objections, since the Regressed L.E. is a partial ego produced by splitting processes, and is in an over-strained and frightened state. But the term does indicate the fact that, whereas all the other parts of the psyche tend to the rigidities characteristic of defensive structures, the Regressed L.E. retains the primary capacity for spontaneous and vigorous growth once it is freed from fears. There lies the ultimate hope of psychotherapy. This last and deepest structural differentiation makes certain dreams intelligible. One of my earliest patients, long before any views of mine could have influenced him, dreamed, 'I was in bed. You knocked on the door and invited me to come out. I said, "I can't. The door's locked." You replied, "I know, but it's locked on your side."' The dream was reported at the second interview before I had had time to say anything, and could only represent his own unconscious awareness of a profound determination to lock himself into his withdrawn state. After six sessions he abruptly broke off analysis. The dream quoted on page 422 of the son imprisoned with his mother as jailoress, actually seems to effect a compromise between the sado-masochistic 'closed system' involving being in the power of the bad mother, and the *safe inside* 'closed system' of the Regressed Ego.

One of the important pieces of evidence for the existence of a Regressed Ego is the tendency in real life, in both great and small ways, to seek *safe inside* positions. Marked introverts, the so-called 'strong silent man' and shy retiring people, seek mentally *safe inside* positions. The tremendous determination born of fear that goes into the regressive drive is seen in the following : a male patient lay in bed all one day feeling exhausted and covering himself with the bedclothes, and wishing to be left entirely alone. That night he dreamed of a baby sitting on the edge of a vagina wondering whether to come out or go back inside, and he stated that he would half-wake in the night with a compelling urge to sexual intercourse; but he had no sense of his wife's personality behind the vagina, only of a need to get as deep in as he could. An unmarried patient had a sexual phantasy of pressing into an impersonal vagina with the feeling of its opening out into a wonderful unknown world beyond. The great force and purposiveness which determines regression also works to maintain it. A markedly schizoid woman patient dreamed of watching a baby being born, and said : 'They couldn't get the baby out. Its head came but then it stuck. They even tied ropes on to its head and passed them through the window and fastened them to horses which pulled, but it made no difference. The baby could not be got out.' Two schizoid wives who had babies while under treatment, both reported that the birth was very prolonged and difficult and they had been told that at one point they had drawn the baby back inside. Evidently they identified their baby with their own Regressed Ego. Winnicott stresses the secret hope of one day finding conditions in which the hidden 'true self' can be reborn. It is evident that it cannot be forced to a premature rebirth, a most important fact for psychotherapy.

When, in the course of treatment, a patient is beginning to feel in the depths of his psyche, in his Regressed Ego, that he might re-emerge to a fuller life, he goes through a period of growing amidst alternating hopes and fears. As Fairbairn puts it, he is like a timid mouse peeping out of his hole and rushing back again. If too much of the personality is drawn into the Regressed Ego, then the self of everyday life is progressively denuded of energy, capacity for interest and feeling, and becomes aloof, detached and apathetic. Thus there are two sides of the schizoid phenomenon : the visible side—the devitalized conscious self tending towards depersonalization—and the invisible side—a retreat of the vital heart of the psyche to a secret 'safe inside' position which is felt and phantasied as a return to the womb. The cause of psychopathological developments would thus seem to be, not sexual or aggressive instincts, but 'fear and flight' from a bad-object world that the infant is too undeveloped to cope with. Flight precipitated by fear is certainly an innate potential reaction, an 'instinctive tendency', and can be accepted as the truth in Freud's comment on Rank (quoted in full, p. 318):

In my own language : some instinct must be associated with the birth trauma which aims at restoring the previous existence. . . . Rank shows how men alter the outer world in the service of this instinct, whereas neurotics save themselves the trouble by taking the short-cut of phantasying a return to the womb.

But it now turns out that the 'neurotic' is the person who has been driven without option to make this drastic regression in infancy to save his very existence, and spends the rest of his life struggling against it.

(iv) *The Fear of Good-Object Relations*

Once the psyche has been reduced to this condition, of more accessible parts of itself clinging to object-relationships, external and internal, while a very secret part of itself has withdrawn, probably permanently to a 'safe inside' good 'relationship', a new and grave problem arises in the shape of overwhelming fears of all other kinds of good-object relations. The 'safe inside the womb' position represents security and comfort. It is not, however, a world of object-relations with specific, differentiated objects. The place of the good object is taken by the good environment, and there is a deep, obscure but quite definite experience of feeling 'good and comfortable inside something'. This must be the most elementary object-relations experience, corresponding to Fairbairn's view that identification is the primitive form of object-relationship. The patient who said it was better to live in his bad fairy-story world than in his outer world, also said, 'I can at times have five to ten minutes in bed when I'm not in my troubled dream world nor facing getting up into the real world, but I feel *in a state of real peace*.' A number of patients have described this to me as sinking into a deep, absolutely passive, heavy doze, and feeling the body merged into the bed, and only the barest flicker of consciousness as an awareness of utterly untroubled comfort. If any even simpler form of the same experience becomes a reality before birth, and regression is a return to a vaguely remembered lost happiness (as Freud implied), this would invalidate and dispose of all theories of a primitive unintegrated state of the ego. The Regressed Ego is a very purposive whole in its own right.

From the point of view of the rest of the personality, however, this state represents complete detachment from outer reality and loss of both contact and personality. It is feared as an undermining of the active ego both in consciousness and in the world of internal object-relations. The profounder the regression of the withdrawn L.E., the more the C.E. or outer-reality ego is liable to feel claustrophobic in any 'safe inside' situation. An intense fear of good-object relationships develops, for to the deepest self they can be felt only as the satisfaction of the longing to give up separate existence and be 'safe inside'. Identifications show the same phenomenon from another viewpoint. Fairbairn speaks of :

> The tendency of those with schizoid characteristics to treat libidinal objects as means of satisfying their own requirements rather than as persons possessing inherent value; and this is a tendency which springs from the persistence of an early oral orientation towards the breast as a partial object. . . . This type of regressive process may perhaps best be described as *Depersonalization of the Object*. (1952, pp. 13–14.)

This is true of the Oral sadistic L.E. which regards good objects as exciting breasts to be captured by force and devoured. But it is a truth that goes even deeper. The Regressed L.E. depersonalizes the object more radically into a womb, a place to be safe in, which all the more leads to fears of depersonalization of the ego as well, or perhaps rather of the smothering or stifling of the ego, from the conscious point of view. So the schizoid person in one part of his personality dreads the good-object relationships that he feels so much need for in another part of himself, because he feels that if yielded to they will reduce him to the most primitive emotional level of existence in which he will feel he has lost himself entirely as a distinct ego. In consciousness this emerges as a fear of being suffocated, stifled, robbed of freedom and independence. The dream of a patient who fled from a good friendship and dreamed of being swallowed by a monstrous mouth is a case in point.

(v) *The Defensive Value of Bad-Object Relationships and their Dangers*

The full tragedy of the schizoid person is that his Regressed L.E. is in flight from all bad objects, and causes his C.E. to take flight from good objects. He is in danger of finding himself in a no-man's-land without objects and of losing his ego. In the outer world this danger is usually countered by some form of alternation between being in and out of object-relations, or of compromise or 'brinkmanship', i.e. neither in nor out but on the fence, on the edge of things, uncommitted, a precarious position.

In the inner world and sometimes in the outer world as well, a more drastic defence is operated, the frank choice of bad-object relations in preference to none at all. They keep the ego in being. Freud's paper 'A Neurosis of Demoniacal Possession in the 17th Century' (1923, pp. 436–72), describing Haitzmann's pact with the Devil whom he wanted to have as 'a father unto him' after his actual father had died, is a striking instance. Here, I believe, we find the rationale of the whole Kleinian world of internal bad objects. While the Regressed L.E. retreats altogether to await a favourable chance of rebirth, the Oral L.E. with all its later anal, genital and other phases and aspects holds fast to the position of a baby born into a bad world, a child growing in a hostile environment. This is *the troubled dream world lying midway between the Regressed Ego 'in the womb' and the C.E. dealing with outer reality*. Most of what psychopathology has discovered has, of necessity, been about this region of psychic life. Here are to be found the psychodynamics of the schizophrenic and depressive psychoses, and the psychoneurotic defences of paranoid attitudes, obsessions, hysterias and phobias. These are all examples of internal bad-object relationships.

When it is felt that good-object relations stifle and swallow and smother the separate and independent ego, then bad-object relations seem more valuable for safeguarding the separate identity of the ego. A bad relationship always involves two separate persons, one persecuting the other in some way, and whether you are the aggressor or even the victim, you are definitely there, an individual over against another individual, having some kind of sadistic or masochistic experience. A male patient once said : 'My wife was in a rage with me last night, but I'd rather have her like that than indifferent to me, not noticing me. That makes me feel I'm hardly there at all.' Another patient remarked : 'If I were a real person to you, you'd get angry with me.' She meant that she would feel more real if I were angry with her, and when patients are needing to ward off a drift to depersonalization they not seldom try to get up a quarrel with the therapist. The reason why it is so hard to cure patients of illnesses expressing internal bad-object relations is that they have always felt that these were the only means of safeguarding the integrity of their ego. In the long run they are a defence against the danger of schizoid states and ego-loss. A hysteric patient who had suffered body pains for years, representing the dramatization of internal bad-object relations, lost them under analysis, and her first reaction was : 'I feel frightened, queer, unreal, without my pains. There's nothing there to feel related to.' Another patient said : 'If I haven't things to worry about, I feel funny. I don't know myself.'

At this point I would suggest that there are four ultimate psychic dangers : (a) *Schizoid Depersonalization* and loss of the ego; (b) *Schizophrenic Disintegration* of the ego, the terror of the feeling of going to bits, or being torn to pieces; (c) *Claustrophobic Suffocation*, the dread of absorption into another's personality, and (d) *Depressive paralysis*, the crushing of the ego under a crippling load of guilt. I would further suggest that while the schizoid state is the ultimate danger, representing a total loss of objects and ego, (b) and (d)—schizophrenic terror and depressive paralysis—arise as a result of using bad-object relationships too persistently as a defence against an incipient schizoid state, while (c)—claustrophobic suffocation—is the danger attendant on regression. In Freud's paper Haitzmann's pact with the Devil led to psychosis.

The purely *persecutory* bad object engendering Mrs. Klein's persecutory anxiety is usually phantasied and felt as physically violent. One patient 'painted out' a terror state in a picture of a witch tearing an infant to pieces. The castration complex is a reduced version of this. Another patient, after a harrowing experience of an official inspection at work, said : 'I feel like a jigsaw puzzle taken to pieces and flung in the box.' Both of these patients had persisting masochistic phantasies of persecution, beating, etc., and so long as this proceeded no further, these internal bad-object situations enabled them to hold on to their ego. The second of these patients would dream of being swallowed up by her good mother, but fought her father openly as a child to preserve the independence of her personality. But bad-object relations are a dangerous means of safeguarding the personality, for they may get out of hand. Then on a primitive unconscious level the threat of schizophrenic disintegration ensues.

On a more developed level, bad-object relations more generally take the form of *accusatory* relations. It is not 'the object is bad to me' but 'I am bad and deserve to be attacked'. This leads to pathological guilt and depression, and this also can go too far till it leads to depressive paralysis or suicide. But short of this dangerous extreme, depression is also best understood as arising out of the operation of accusatory bad-object relationships as a defence against schizoid withdrawal. Thus a patient who had a severe fright, being taken to court on a false charge, developed a deeply depressed state of mind, feeling wicked, bad, guilty, not fit to carry on his work, and dreamed of a man pointing a finger at him and saying, 'You are to blame.' His depression showed little sign of moderating under the usual analytical approaches, till one day I said : 'I suspect that this depression is not your real trouble. It hides the fact that you've had a terrible shock and fright, feel unsafe all round and are struggling with a strong urge to run away from life altogether. Having yourself blamed and accused in this way keeps you in touch and face to face with your situation.' This brought an immediate rush of evidence, of things he had not mentioned before, showing a marked schizoid withdrawal, including 'feeling queer and unlike other people', and 'everything seems at times far away', retiring to bed at seven o'clock ('though I'm not usually a beddy person') and finally the intense phantasy already quoted of penetrating deep into a vagina into a mysterious and wonderful world beyond. His depression arose out of a desperate attempt to use accusatory bad-object relations to drag himself back into his object-world again.

It may be remarked that schizophrenic terror arises out of bad-object relations with objects that are *entirely bad*. When escape to objects who are regarded as *entirely good* is felt to be just as destructive to the ego, in a stifling way, then a compromise is sought. Depressive paralysis by guilt arises out of carrying on the needed bad-object relations with a good object who will not retaliate and tear you to pieces. Then guilt arises out of hurting a good object, the problem of ambivalence, of loving and hating at the same time. I have had a number of patients say such things as 'I'd rather hate you than love you' and 'Hating feels safer than loving'.

We may now summarize the position in which we find our patients, one which is more marked and recognizable in proportion as they are seriously ill. The menaced ego is like a hare hunted by hounds; whichever way it turns it runs into a different danger. If the total self, weakened by a basic Regressed Ego, takes refuge in good objects it feels claustrophobically suffocated; if it chooses bad objects, it risks schizophrenic disintegration; if it compromises by an ambivalent relationship with an object which is seen as both good and bad, it heads for guilt and depressive paralysis, and if in despair it takes flight from all object-relationships it runs into loss of itself by depersonalization, by feeling emptied and reduced to nothing by having nothing with which to maintain any living experience. In fact, the only hope lies in seeing through and overcoming the fears of loss of independence in good-object relations and the chance of this is what the psychotherapist offers.

(vi) *The Child Burdened with Caring for Himself*

An important aspect of the whole schizoid problem is that it involved a struggle on the child's part to do for himself what his environment was failing to do. Winnicott notes this when he writes:

Certain kinds of failures on the part of the mother, especially erratic behaviour, produce over-activity of the mental functioning. . . . In reaction to this abnormal environmental state, the thinking of the individual begins to take over and organize the caring for the psyche-soma, whereas in health it is the function of the environment to do this. (1958, p. 246.)

With adequate environmental support the infant's ego-maintenance and development should not be a burden to himself. It goes on naturally. But once the schizoid retreat in fear from an environment experienced as intolerable has taken place, the child must then find some way of providing for himself. This is the main cause of the apparent self-sufficiency and independence of some schizoid people. One patient remembers thinking at the age of nine: 'I can manage by myself. I don't need to trouble mother and I don't need anyone to play with.' This self-sufficiency is, however, precariously maintained over the top of great repressed strain and anxiety.

A patient who was off work and alone in her flat for some days, suddenly thought, 'I haven't seen or spoken to anyone for three days', and began to feel very disturbed. Then she said: 'I revived my masochistic phantasies of being beaten (which had disappeared for some time) and of arguing with the person beating me. I had to have someone to talk to.' Here is a clear example of the creation and maintenance of a world of internal bad objects as a means of maintaining the ego. The patient has to bear the burden of creating an environment to live in, and then living in it, in order to keep her ego in being. The entire world of internal objects arises out of the child's struggle to solve his own problems alone and without help. From this point of view also the Anti-L.E. can be seen to be the child's tense struggle to carry the burden of his own upbringing unhelped by his environment, to force himself to 'keep going' at all costs; and he can do it only by trying to crush out his fears and needs and master his Regressed Ego. He does not know that ultimately this over-driving of himself is the very thing that will break him down. The whole task is beyond the child's powers and contributes to the deep loneliness, isolation, fear and increasing underlying exhaustion to be found in the schizoid person. It involves not only having to create one's own internal-object world, but also having to become an object to oneself. Many patients' dreams reveal a situation in which the C.E. is having to care for the infantile L.E. Normal self-reliance in a mature person is almost automatic. This secret inner burden of responsibility for self, beginning at far too early an age when the child still needs the closest parental care, is gravely undermining. At best it can lead only to rigidity in the C.E. One patient all her life had had to live by making lists of duties and doing everything in turn, even compiling a book of games to be played in turn as a child. She had lost the capacity for spontaneous decision. This was because she could support the burden of self-management only by creating these lists to have something to depend on.

(vii) *Psychotherapy*

This rapid survey, of necessity supported at this stage by all too little evidence, will, however, give some idea of what the results may be of re-orientating psychodynamic theory on the basis of ego-psychology and the fundamental nature of the schizoid position. This recasting of theory is put forward tentatively as a pointer to the direction that recent developments seem to indicate. A host of details need close consideration, and even when regression is satisfactorily accounted for in theory, it still remains a most difficult practical problem demanding a vast amount of clinical research.

The question of 'therapeutic regression' runs up against the practical problem of the danger that regression can undermine a patient's capacity to carry on his life in the external world. Some patients have begun to break down in 'illnesses' that are masked regressions before they come to us. All psychogenic illness can be seen as concealing this problem, some symptoms representing relapse into passivity while others represent the tensions of the struggle against that. We need to find out whether the regressive trends are a freely available resort to a retreat and withdrawal reaction in the face of extra severe environmental stress, or the break-through of a consolidated reaction that belongs to a deeply disowned part of the personality of very early origin. Either way our hope is that the patient will be able to find sufficient support in the therapist to enable him to deal with his internal problem. But is there not a danger that a regressed part of the personality, unearthed for the first time in and by the treatment, may have disastrous repercussions on the patient's adult life and responsibilities? The answer would be simpler if we could rely on its being always true that if the patient can regress constructively inside and under the control of the treatment situation, he will be saved from the need to regress in the outer world. That is certainly true of some patients, and when it is true it gives the maximum chance of a conclusive ending to treatment in a healthy regrowth of personality. In the natural order of things, sound foundations of strong ego-development are laid down at the very beginning while the infant is in a state of dependent love on and for the mother. In no other kind of situation can they be laid. If they are not laid at the start, then psychotherapy has to find out how the required situation can be reproduced later on without risking the breakdown of as much of an adult personality as the patient has been able to build up. For, to start the Regressed Ego growing again, the patient may need to go back as far as the original passive dependence of the womb-state for a time. If it is not possible, then psycho-analytical and all other forms of psychotherapy will have to rest content with the limitation of being able to secure only varying degrees of strengthening of the ego of everyday life, and not a radical reconstruction of the personality. But, as contrasted with all other forms of psychotherapy, psycho-analysis has always set out to achieve just this latter and so much more difficult result; and the work of Winnicott shows that in some cases such a result is possible. Two or three patients of my own, whose analyses have contributed much to my present point of view, encourage me in a cautious hope that it is possible, and that where such a goal can be reached it will only be along the psycho-analytical pathway : and that, furthermore, the nature of psycho-analysis is such that we may hope that when the analysis and treatment of regression is better understood its dangers will be reduced. On the other hand, when the forces of our culture have for his lifetime driven the patient to believe that 'salvation' for him lies in strength, independence, a somewhat aggressive self-reliance, opposition to interference, contempt for fear, and resentment at dependent ties, it is extremely humiliating to have to face the need for what Balint calls a 'new beginning' of personality growth from the starting-place of a passive dependence on a therapist. Patients will need to be very sure of the quality and motives of their therapist, and many will perhaps prefer still to retain their denial of their Regressed Ego and maintain their rigid and hardened defensive ego if they can. And always we must halt with humility before one final question, are we expecting more of 'this particular patient' than he is capable of, even with our support; for the treatment of the Regressed Ego must expose the patient to the full range of his internal terrors.

A different kind of difficulty would arise if, when a patient genuinely needs to regress in treatment, this is not recognized, interpreted and utilized. Probably only in a treatment situation can a necessary regression be converted into a regrowing and rebirth process, and one hopes that this will obviate the need for more than a minimum of regression in real life as the patient goes along. Not enough is known about this to make certain judgments as yet. In any case, the patient under analysis is always faced with the danger of 'acting out' in real life what ought to be brought into the analysis. It appears to me that long analyses may well end inconclusively because the Regressed Ego is not reached. Moreover, if regression is either ignored or regarded with disfavour, then the analysis of the intermediate defensive positions of internal bad-object relationships may well turn out to be an interminable process, a possibility that Freud envisaged. Psycho-analysis could operate unwittingly in a subtle way to maintain the traumatic endopsychic situation of the child forced back on himself and having to bring himself up in the end, and yet being unable to achieve anything better than keeping himself going in an internal world of bad-object relations, since no one will give his Regressed Ego a chance to regrow. Analytical exposure of infantile trends may then well feel to the patient like an implied attempt to force him to grow up. It may be that real progress is made on the C.E. level, and yet this may prove to be less stable than one had hoped. One of the cases that forced me to rethink things was that cited on pages 416–17 of the severe hysteric who got rid of all her physical symptoms, and then regressed to the oral stage and made a phase-by-phase return, working her way back to a much more mature and stable capacity to lead her own life. I must, however, now add a further note to that. Just when I felt treatment might be nearing its end, she acquired a male friend and when it seemed likely that he would propose marriage to her she suddenly cracked badly and panicked, even though she had been wanting this very development. Then there emerged unmistakably the deepest repressed factor, her Regressed Ego, in full force as a fear that 'if you get too close to anyone you get swallowed up, you go inside'. This Regressed Ego, at a deeper level than the Oral Ego, demanded help and attention before stability could be slowly and more stably restored. Only then did I recognize the opportunities she had presented much earlier of making this very analysis.

I would suggest that radical analytical psychotherapy involves three things :

(a) Support for the struggling C.E. of everyday life, as it tries with depleted resources to deal with the outer world and resist the strain of the inner one at the same time ;

(b) Analysis of the intermediate internal bad-objects world, not as an end in itself, but directed to the uncovering of the deepest repression, the Regressed L.E. In this, the defence of internalized good objects must also be taken into account; and

(c) The provision of what one can only call a safe symbolic womb for the Regressed Ego in which the patient can, on his deepest feeling levels, feel understood, accepted, given the right to be there and grow to a rebirth in his own time without pressure from the therapist who in fact helps him ultimately to ease off self-pressure from his own Anti-L.E. and C.E.; for all pressures only arouse more fear and put things back. Slowly the Regressed Ego will emerge with renewed vigour to revitalize the rest of the personality. This is the aspect of psychotherapy that appears to me to involve what Winnicott calls problems of management. How to provide the required situation needed for the regrowth of the Regressed Ego is the difficult problem the therapist faces. Fortunately patients are already well accustomed to symbolic substitutes which have great emotional value for them, even when it is only drawing the curtains and locking the door and drawing the armchair up to the fire and dozing in warmth and comfort. But in psychotherapy it must represent the person of the therapist, and rest securely on the patient's assurance that the therapist really does understand and accept his need. Without that, nothing avails. With it, I have found some patients can find an important symbolic significance in the use of the therapist's couch, repudiating it when they are fighting against their dependent needs, going back to it as they can accept them, sitting on it in a half-and-half position when the conflict is in the balance. It is in this connection that Balint's view is relevant, that the patient must go back to where he can make a 'new beginning' from a position of 'primary passive love' of the therapist. At this stage the patient is losing his fears of being swallowed up in a good object, and can really begin to use his relationship of trust in his therapist to make a genuine development towards inner strength and maturity.

BIBLIOGRAPHY

ALEXANDER, F. (1925), 'A Metapsychological Description of the Process of Cure', *Int. J. Psycho-Anal.*, vol. 6, pt. 1, pp. 13–34.
(1949), *Fundamentals of Psychoanalysis* (London, Allen and Unwin. New York, Norton).
(1952), *Our Age of Unreason* (New York, Lippincott).
ALLPORT, G. W. (1949), *Personality: A Psychological Interpretation* (London, Constable. New York, Holt, Rinehart and Winston, Inc.).
BALINT, M. (1952), *Primary Love and Psychoanalytic Technique* (London, Hogarth. New York, Liveright).
(1956), 'Pleasure, Object and Libido', *Brit. J. Med. Psychol.*, vol. 29, pt. 2, pp. 162–7.
(1957), 'Criticism of Fairbairn's Generalization about Object-Relations', *Brit. J. Phil. Sc.*, vol. 7, no. 28, p. 323.
BIBRING, E. (1947), 'The So-called English School of Psycho-Analysis', *Psychoanal. Quarterly*, vol. 16 (New York).
BONAPARTE, M. (1951), In *Psychoanalysis and Culture*, ed. Wilbur and Muensterberger (New York, Int. Universities Press).
BRIERLEY, M. (1951), *Trends in Psychoanalysis* (London, Hogarth).
BUBER, M. (1937), *I and Thou* (Edinburgh, T. & T. Clark. New York, Scribner).
COHEN, J. (1946), *Human Nature, War and Society* (London, Watts).
COLBY, K. M. (1955), *Energy and Structure in Psychoanalysis* (New York, Ronald Press).
DICKS, H. V. (1950), 'In Search of Our Proper Ethic', *Brit. J. Med. Psychol.*, vol. 23, pts. 1 and 2, pp. 1–14.
DREVER, J. (1917), *Instinct in Man* (Cambridge Univ. Press).
ERIKSON, E. (1959), 'Identity and the Life Cycle', *Psychological Issues*, vol. 1, no. 1, monograph 1 (New York, International Universities Press).
FAIRBAIRN, W. R. D. (1938a), 'Prolegomena to a Psychology of Art', *Brit. J. Psychol.*, General Section, vol. 28, pt. 3.
(1938b), 'The Ultimate Basis of Aesthetic Experience', *Brit. J. Psychol.*, General Section, vol. 29, pt. 2.
(1952a), *Psychoanalytic Studies of the Personality* (London, Tavistock Publications. New York, Basic Books).

(1952b), 'Theoretical and Experimental Aspects of Psycho-Analysis', *Brit. J. Med. Psychol.*, vol. 25, pts. 2 and 3, pp. 122–7.

(1954), 'Observations on the Nature of Hysterical States', *Brit. J. Med. Psychol.*, vol. 27, pt. 3, pp. 105–25.

(1955), 'Observations in Defence of the Object-Relations Theory of the Personality', *Brit. J. Med. Psychol.*, vol. 28, pts. 2 and 3, pp. 144–56.

(1956a), 'A Critical Evaluation of Certain Psychoanalytical Concepts', *Brit. J. Phil. Sc.*, vol. 7, no. 25, pp. 49–60.

(1956b), 'Considerations Arising Out of the Schreber Case', *Brit. J. Med. Psychol.*, vol. 29, pt. 2, pp. 113–27.

(1957a), 'Freud, The Psychoanalytical Method and Mental Health', *Brit. J. Med. Psychol.*, vol. 30, pt. 2, pp. 53–62.

(1957b), *Brit. J. Phil. Sc.*, vol. 7, no. 28, pp. 333–8.

(1958), 'On the Nature and Aims of Psycho-analytical Treatment', *Int. J. Psycho-Anal.*, vol. 29, pt. 5, pp. 374–85.

FENICHEL, O. (1945), *The Psycho-Analytic Theory of Neurosis* (London, Kegan Paul. New York, Norton).

(1954), *Collected Papers. First Series* (London, Kegan Paul. New York, Norton).

FOULKES, S. H. (1957), *J. for Phil. of Science,* vol. 7, no. 28, pp. 324–9.

FREEMAN, T. (1955), Review of 'Clinical Psychiatry' by Mayer-Gross, Slater and Roth, in *Brit. J. Med. Psychol.*, vol. 28, pts. 2 and 3, pp. 194–6.

FREUD, A. (1936), *The Ego and the Mechanisms of Defence* (London, Hogarth. New York, International Universities Press).

FREUD, S. (1908), 'Civilized' Sexual Morality and Modern Nervousness, *Collected Papers* (1924), vol. 2, p. 76 (London, Hogarth).

(1914a), 'On the History of the Psychoanalytic Movement', *Collected Papers* (1924), vol. 1, p. 287 (London, Hogarth).

(1914b), 'On Narcissism : An Introduction', *Collected Papers* (1925), vol. 4, p. 30 (London, Hogarth).

(1915), 'Instincts and their Vicissitudes', *Collected Papers* (1925), vol. 4, p. 60 (London, Hogarth).

(1917), 'Mourning and Melancholia', *Collected Papers* (1925), vol. 4, p. 152 (London, Hogarth).

(1920), *Beyond the Pleasure Principle*, Standard Ed. (London, Hogarth. New York, Basic Books).

(1921), *Group Psychology and the Analysis of the Ego*, Standard Ed. (London, Hogarth. New York, Basic Books).

(1922), 'Psycho-Analysis', *Collected Papers* (1950), vol. 5, p. 107 (London, Hogarth).

(1923), *The Ego and the Id* (London, Hogarth. New York, Norton).

(1926), *Inhibitions, Symptoms and Anxiety* (London, Hogarth). U.S.A. title, *Problems of Anxiety* (New York, Norton).

(1927), *The Future of an Illusion*, Standard Ed. (London, Hogarth. New York, Basic Books).

(1930), *Civilization and Its Discontents* (London, Hogarth. New York, Norton).

(1933), *New Introductory Lectures* (London, Hogarth. New York, Norton).

(1937), 'Analysis, Terminable and Interminable', *Collected Papers*, vol. 5, p. 316 (London, Hogarth).

(1938), *Outline of Psycho-Analysis* (London, Hogarth).

(1954), *The Origins of Psycho-Analysis* (Letters to Fliess (London, Hogarth. New York, Basic Books).

FROMM, E. (1942), *The Fear of Freedom* (London, Kegan Paul). U.S.A. title, *Escape from Freedom* (New York, Holt, Rinehart and Winston, Inc.).

GINSBERG, M. (1934), *Sociology* (Oxford, Oxford University Press).

(1947), *Reason and Unreason in Society* (London, Heinemann. New York, Macmillan Co.).

GLOVER, E. (1945), 'An Examination of the Klein System of Child Psychology', *The Psychoanalytic Study of the Child*, vol. 1 (London, Hogarth. New York, International Universities Press).

GUNTRIP, H. (1949), *Psychology for Ministers and Social Workers* (London, Independent Press).

(1952), 'A Study of Fairbairn's Theory of Schizoid Reactions', *Brit. J. Med. Psychol.*, vol. 25, pts. 2 and 3, pp. 86–103.

(1953), 'The Therapeutic Factor in Psychotherapy', *Brit. J. Med. Psychol.*, vol. 26, pt. 2, pp. 115–32.

(1956a), 'Recent Developments in Psychoanalytical Theory', *Brit. J. Med. Psychol.*, vol. 29, pt. 2, pp. 82–99.

(1956b), 'Centenary Reflections on the Work of Freud', *Leeds University Medical Journal*, vol. 5, no. 3.

(1957), *Mental Pain and the Cure of Souls* (London, Independent Press). U.S.A. title, *Psychotherapy and Religion* (New York, Harper).

(1960), 'Ego-Weakness and the Hard Core of the Problem of Psychotherapy', *Brit. J. Med. Psychol.*, vol. 33, pt. 3, pp. 163–84.

HARTMANN, KRIS AND LOEWENSTEIN. (1946), 'Comments on the Formation of Psychic Structure', *The Psychoanalytic Study of the*

Child, vol. 2 (London, Hogarth. New York, International Universities Press).

HORNEY, K. (1937), *The Neurotic Personality of Our Time* (London, Kegan Paul. New York, Norton).

(1939), *New Ways in Psycho-Analysis* (London, Kegan Paul. New York, Norton).

(1951), *Neurosis and Human Growth* (London, Kegan Paul. New York, Norton).

HOUSDEN, L. (1945), *Hostels for 'Difficult' Children* (Worcester, Littlebury).

HUTTEN, E. H. (1956), 'On Explanation in Psychology and Physics', *Brit. J. Phil. Science*, vol. 7, no. 25, pp. 73–85.

JONES, E. (1954, 1955, 1957), *Sigmund Freud: Life and Work*, vols. 1, 2, 3 (London, Hogarth).

KLEIN, M. (1932), *The Psycho-Analysis of Children* (London, Hogarth. New York, Grove Press).

(1948), *Contributions to Psycho-Analysis* (London, Hogarth).

, et al. (1952), *Developments in Psycho-Analysis* (London, Hogarth).

, et al. (1955), *New Directions in Psycho-Analysis* (London, Tavistock Publications).

(1957), *Envy and Gratitude* (London, Tavistock Publications. New York, Basic Books).

KRIS, E. (1952), *Psychoanalytic Explorations in Art* (New York, International Universities Press).

LA BARRE, W. (1951), In *Psychoanalysis and Culture*, ed. Wilbur and Muensterberger (New York, International Universities Press).

LORAND, S. (Ed.). (1948), *Psycho-Analysis Today* (London, Allen and Unwin. New York, International Universities Press).

MACIVER, R. M. (1937), *Society: A Textbook* (London, Macmillan. New York, Holt, Rinehart and Winston, Inc.).

MACMURRAY, J. (1933), *Interpreting the Universe* (London, Faber. New York, Humanities Press).

(1935), *Reason and Emotion* (London, Faber. New York, Humanities Press).

(1939), *The Boundaries of Science* (London, Faber. New York, Humanities Press).

MARKILLIE, R. E. D. (1956), Review of Fairbairn, *Brit. J. Med. Psychol.*, vol. 29, pt. 2, pp. 169–71.

MAYER-GROSS, SLATER AND ROTH. (1954), *Clinical Psychiatry* (London, Cassell. U.S.A., Williams and Wilkins, 1st edn.).

MULLAHY, P. (1949), *Oedipus Myth and Complex* (New York, Nelson. London, Allen and Unwin).

O'CONNOR, W. A. (1948), *Psychiatry: A Short Treatise* (Bristol, Jn. Wright).

PEAR, T. H. (1948), 'Perspectives in Modern Psychology', *Brit. J. Psychol.*, vol. 38.

PETERS, R. S. (1956), 'Freud's Theory', *Brit. J. Phil. Sc.*, vol. 7, no. 25, pp. 4–12.

PILLSBURY, W. B. (1929), *History of Psychology* (London, Allen and Unwin. New York, Norton).

REICH, W. (1935), *Character Analysis* (London, Vision Press).

SCIENTIFIC WORKERS, ASSOCIATION OF. (1948), *The Social Sciences: A Case for Their Greater Use* (London, 15, Half Moon St., W.1).

SULLIVAN, H. S. (1955a), *Conceptions of Modern Psychiatry* (London, Tavistock Publications. New York, Norton).

(1955b), *The Interpersonal Theory of Psychiatry* (London, Tavistock Publications. New York, Norton).

SZASZ, T. S. (1956), 'Is the Concept of Entropy Relevant to Psychology and Psychiatry', *Psychiatry: Journal for the Study of Interpersonal Processes*, vol. 19, no. 2.

(1957), 'On the Theory of Psycho-Analytic Treatment', *Int. J. Psycho-Anal.*, vol. 38, pts. 3 and 4, pp. 166–82.

THOMPSON, C. (1952), *Psychoanalysis: Evolution and Development* (London, Allen and Unwin. New York, Nelson).

THOULESS, R. H. (1935), *General and Social Psychology* (London, University Tutorial Press).

TINBERGEN, N. (1951), *A Study of Instinct* (Oxford, Clarendon Press).

WALKER, N. (1955), 'How Does Psycho-Analysis Work?' (London, *The Listener*, Oct. 6, p. 544. U.S.A., *Psychoanalysis* (1957), vol. 5, no. 3).

(1956), 'Freud and Homeostasis', *Brit. J. Phil. Science*, vol. 7, no. 25, pp. 61–72.

WINNICOTT, D. W., AND KAHN, M. (1953), Review in *Int. J. Psycho-Anal.*, vol. 34, pt. 4, pp. 329–33.

WINNICOTT, D. W. (1958), *Collected Papers: Through Paediatrics to Psycho-Analysis* (London, Tavistock Publications. New York, Basic Books).

WISDOM, J. O. (1956), Review in *Brit. J. Phil. Science*, vol. 7, no. 25, pp. 105–9.

WITHERS, R. F. J. (1956), Review in *Brit. J. Phil. Science*, vol. 7, no. 25, pp. 110–13.

ZETZEL, E. (1955), 'Recent British Approaches to Problems of Early Mental Development', *J. Amer. Psycho-Analytic Association*, vol. 3, no. 3.

INDEX